WRESTLING UNTIL DAY-BREAK

Searching for Meaning in the Thinking on the Holocaust

ELIEZER SCHWEID

UNIVERSITY
PRESS OF
AMERICA

Lanham • New York • London

THE JERUSALEM CENTER
FOR PUBLIC AFFAIRS

University Press of America®, Inc.
4720 Boston Way
Lanham, Maryland 20706

3 Henrietta Street
London WC2E 8LU England

Co-published by arrangement with
The Jerusalem Center for Public Affairs

Managing Editor: Mark Ami-El
Typesetting: Custom Graphics and Publishing, Ltd., Jerusalem

Library of Congress Cataloging-in-Publication Data

Schweid, Eliezer.
Wrestling until day-break : searching for meaning in the thinking on
the Holocaust / Eliezer Schweid.
p.   cm.   –   (Milken library of Jewish public affairs)
1. Holocaust (Jewish theology)   2. Holocaust, Jewish (1939-1945) –
Moral and ethical aspects.   I. Title.   II. Series.
BM645.H6S393   1994   296.3'11–dc20   93-39954   CIP

ISBN 0-8191-9358-5 (cloth : alk. paper)
ISBN 0-8191-9359-3 (pbk. : alk. paper)

"And Jacob was left alone; and there wrestled a man with him until day-break"

(Genesis 32:25)

THE MILKEN LIBRARY OF
JEWISH PUBLIC AFFAIRS

Made possible by a gift from the
Foundations of the Milken Families

For the memory of
My father-in-law
The sacred Jacob Fuchs,
Who was murdered
In the Town of Z'borow
On the 9th of Tamuz 5703
One of the Six Million.

CONTENTS

FOREWORD

Daniel J. Elazar

Eliezer Schweid, one of Israel's leading philosophers of Zionism, here turns his attention to one of the great philosophic stumbling blocks of our times — the Holocaust. He has done so by reviewing and analyzing the different responses of various Jewish thinkers to this immeasurable tragedy. Schweid discusses the efforts of those who were caught in the Holocaust to respond to the problems of faith and ethics it posed, placing the various respondents in the context of Jewish tradition as well as more general philosophical-theological concerns, raising questions of the justification of religion in the crisis of the Holocaust, and the Holocaust as a challenge to Jewish religious thought in our age.

Professor Schweid takes a hard look at the thinkers of our times who passed through those gates of hell to emerge on the other side struggling with life and faith. His analysis concerns itself with the impact of the Holocaust, not only on abstract principles of religion and faith, but on the religion, faith and life of a particular nation, who Leo Baeck, a very distinguished German Jewish rabbinic leader and a survivor who is the subject of Schweid's first chapter, came to refer to as "this people Israel." So, too, his concern with the "existential and moral dilemma" of armed resistance in the ghetto focuses on the realistic thought of Shimshon Drenger (Chapter 4) and the Zionist theodicy of Rabbi Issachar Shlomo Teichthal (Chapter 5).

In Part Two, the author focuses on problems of faith and ethics after the Holocaust. Professor Schweid represents the new breed of Israelis who confront these issues not as abstract spiritual ones — individual questions of faith and belief — but also as the concerns of the community, the nation, that perforce must be embodied not only in the actions of individuals, but in the way the nation and its communities chart their course and draw spiritual sustenance. His is a world where actions have consequences for the many and not merely for the one; where choices are rendered even more difficult by the inseparable link between the individual and the community. In this volume, Professor Schweid not only brings to our attention several world-recognized thinkers, but those who spoke either out of necessity or choice to a more limited audience but whose concern with faith and ethics was not in any respect limited because of that. The Jerusalem Center for Public Affairs is proud to present this work to the English-reading public as part of its efforts to encourage serious and critical discussion of the great questions of our time.

ACKNOWLEDGMENTS

This book was written during a sabbatical at the Oxford Centre for Hebrew Studies. I am thankful to the Frank Green Foundation which granted me the needed accommodations for work of this kind, and to Prof. David Patterson, President of the Centre, for his generous help. My research on the subject had been initiated at the suggestion of Dr. Jerry Hochbaum, secretary of the Memorial Foundation for Jewish Culture in New York. A grant from the Foundation enabled both a part of my research and a part of its translation into English. For the completion of the translation and for the publication of the English version I am indebted to the Jerusalem Center for Public Affairs and especially to its President, Professor Daniel J. Elazar, and its Director-General, Mr. Zvi R. Marom. Many thanks are due also to Mr. Amnon Hadary who has done an excellent job of rendering this book into clear and faithful English.

The writing of a book on problems raised by the Holocaust is a deep, devastating, emotional and intellectual trial. I would not have stood it without the love, care, and good advice of my wife Sabina. Indeed, her insights, based on her own direct experiences, guided me in many moments of frustration and pain.

Eliezer Schweid

INTRODUCTION

This book is divided into two parts. The first consists of five essays dealing with a number of important Jewish thinkers who wrestled with problems of faith and ethics raised by the Holocaust, in its evolvement under the Nazi yoke. The second part consists of three essays which examine some of the same problems from a post-Holocaust perspective, a generation later.

The thinkers whose thoughts were discussed in the first part of the book are: Rabbi Leo Baeck, the central communal leader of German Jewry during the Nazi period; Dr. Victor Frankl, a world-renowned psychiatrist and religious philosopher whose experience as a Jewish prisoner in a Nazi concentration camp was fundamental to the development of his existentialistic world view; a group of Jewish intellectuals, most of them leaders of the underground or of ideological movements in East European ghettos; Rabbi Issachar Shlomo Teichthal, a prominent talmudic scholar and a member of the radical fundamentalistic Jewish community in Budapest; and Shimshon Drenger, one of the leaders of the "Akiva" underground in Cracow. (The last two essays deal with two positions which were described very briefly in the third essay, but were considered worthy of a fuller analytical account.)

The problems discussed in the second part of the book are: 1) Could religion (in its Christian as well as in its Jewish version) justify its role in the period of the Holocaust? 2) Can modern Jewish religious thought justify belief and faith in God after the Holocaust? 3) What is the role of the memory of the Holocaust in the shaping of Jewish identity in the post-World War II period?

The first part, which is the largest and most detailed section of the book, is to be considered its main contribution to the philosophical confrontation with problems raised by the Holocaust. Its aim is to lay an experientially insightful ground on which one can grasp the spiritual and ethical questions as they were actually raised, in their concrete existential context. This is, it seems, a sine qua non condition for a serious philosophical discussion of such problems, which are central for religious and moral orientation in our age, yet esoteric from the point of view of the absolutely extreme human experiences behind them. Thus the aim of the second part is not a new comprehensive philosophical confrontation, but only a suggestion of some new beginnings, based on insights which were gained in the first formative part.

One may raise the question — in what ways and in what measures are the thinkers discussed in the first part of the book to be considered representative of their time? In what ways are they historically significant? What is common to them, and what divides them? It therefore seems that some comparative remarks are due in the format of an introduction to the particular discussion in the separate essays.

As said, the first part of the book deals with thoughtful responses of certain individuals who were active, each in his own way, in Jewish communal life under the Nazi yoke. Early on, each of them became aware of the unprecedented character and the enormity of the trial their people would soon face, unprecedented even in the context of a long Jewish history replete with memories of destruction and murder. Most of them regarded themselves as responsible leaders in their communities. As such they grasped the crucial need to recognize, without illusion, the situation which prevailed while retaining hope and faith as the *sine qua non* for existence and survival. The Jews would have to face reality without fear, unsparingly define and analyze events, and be ready for the worst that could be imagined. They would have to find within themselves the grounds for faith and hope, the existence of an inner strength with which they could confront reality. This strength is the drive to live, the will to exist, the decision to overcome and be victorious. As leaders they articulated the understanding that the courage to see and perceive is a manifestation of moral freedom and human dignity which can and should be maintained even against the radical evil of Nazism. Those who persist in the exercise of moral freedom and self-respect as human beings and as Jews will find meaning and purpose in life. Those who are able to find meaning and purpose will prevail and be victorious, either in life or in death.

These teachings were aimed at a four-fold goal: to define, as clearly as possible, the nature of the abnormal life-situations created by the Nazi regime; to interpret the characteristics of the trial; to identify the main ethical and spiritual problems to be confronted as immediate necessities of life; and then to show, both in words and deeds, a possible way to withstand the trial. In fact, all these teachers justified the necessity of their deeds with their words, and testified to the truth of their words by their deeds. Their lives and teachings were as one.

This is the source of our interest in these teachings as people living in the post-World War, post-Holocaust age. Time has not obscured the harrowing memory of the cruel events that took place. On the contrary, recent study justifies a growing sense of terror because these events, though unprecedented and unnatural, do not appear as aberrations. Nor are they devoid of context in the history of Western civilization. There is ample reason to fear that precisely in its modernist phase Western civilization possesses a syndrome of attitudes and inclinations which could eventually develop into similar abnormalities. In similar — though altered — conditions, holocausts may recur.

If it is correct to diagnose the appearance and rise of Nazism as a "pathology" of Western civilization, then the passage of time should make it possible to examine the phenomenon in perspective. The aetiology of the pathology can be studied together with the fissures in our social, political and cultural system, through which this kind of pathology may penetrate and affect society. An immunization process has not yet been formulated. Therefore we should be committed to an orderly process of historical, political, social, anthropological and psychological Holocaust studies in the broadest possible context. Historical research of the Holocaust has now reached a stage where it can be integrated into the general study of Jewish and European history, especially in the modern era, providing an overall comprehension of the significance of this cataclysmic event, and from which we can draw necessary insight and wisdom. It is this striving for a comprehensive understanding and a search for certain consequences that explains the growing interest in discussions of the problems raised by the Holocaust in the philosophical arena.

In fact, in the last decade there has been a significant growth, at least in volume, of philosophical literature on the Holocaust. Problems of religion and humanism — theological, ethical, political — and the existential situations raised by modernity are etched against the specific background of the Holocaust. Not many intellectuals, let alone less-qualified philosophers, dared to put the ethical, spiritual and existential problems raised by the Holocaust to a systematic, philosophical discussion. This was especially true of the period between the end of World War II and the beginning of the 1970s. Contrary to the impressive development of scientific research — especially in historiography, political and juridical sciences, sociol-

ogy and psychology — and to prolific activity in belletristic literature on the Holocaust, the effect of a difficult-to-overcome internal
obstacle can be detected in the field of philosophy. To a lesser
degree, this is true also for theology. On the historiographical plane,
the Holocaust has been described as an absolute abnormality, sur-
passing the enormity of formerly known events of such order. It
appeared to be beyond any comparison. Indeed, an enormous
emotional intensity was mobilized to reject any comparison. It
derived mainly from deep personal involvement and a need to
struggle against attempts, mainly by German scholars and thinkers,
to reduce or minimize the significance of the event. Thus, there was
almost a taboo, among Jewish scholars, against any comparison of
the Holocaust to other historical events. At the same time the
Holocaust was described as a formative event that testifies to a
demonic element in the nature of humanity. The impulse to philosophize was therefore impeded by itself. How can one submit an
incomparable historical event to a philosophical discussion? Yet
equally, how can one avoid a philosophical discussion of such a
"formative" event?

Be that as it may, one may claim that this inner debate around the
problem of its feasibility was in effect the beginning of the philosophical discussion itself (or the beginning which preceded discussion
because, as we know, for the sake of gaining a "sure" starting point
philosophers are inclined to question the legitimacy of their own
method of discussion when confronted by a radically new problem). In
fact, this intellectual enterprise now proceeds with full impetus, the
indication of an urgently felt need. For along with the earlier realization that broad scientific comprehension required a philosophical
grounding, a more pressing situation now demands a philosophical
base which will enable the educational system to transmit the memory
of the Holocaust and its significance to successive generations.

The educational task with regard to the Holocaust faced many
emotional and intellectual difficulties from the beginning. These are
today further complicated because education must be conducted not
only for a student generation born after the event, but also by teachers
and educators who were themselves born after the events. Unless we
develop a more perfectly articulated comprehension of its meaning, its
relevance, and its message, effective teaching of the Holocaust may
become completely impossible. Education requires a process of philosophical retrospection as a necessary condition for competent continua-

tion. Here again we face the impact of former difficulties in the form of a distinction in the historical perspective of the discussion itself. Recent philosophical discussion was preceded by a phase of doubt and debate over the legitimacy of such discussion. The philosophers engaged in this topic in our generation tend to a "natural" conviction that they lack any former ground for the resolution of their task and thus they have to rely almost entirely on their own work. They take it as obvious that systematic philosophical analysis began only in the last decade, thus they have no former "tradition" on which they may rely. During the Holocaust itself, they argue, it was almost a physical impossibility to be immersed in cool, objective, detached philosophical observation, which would have required tranquility of mind, existential distance, and historical perspective. After the Holocaust, the formerly described feeling arose as an impediment causing such complete silence that it seemed that they had to take only the achievements of historiographic research as their sure starting point.

This would appear to be a reasonable contention, and against the background described above, one not devoid of a factual base. Yet after a close examination it appears sufficiently inaccurate to cause distortion. It fails to appreciate the contribution of a number of important and thoughtful personalities. Precisely during the Holocaust itself, they confronted the Holocaust as a direct personal experience, so that almost as an existential condition of life, an insightful spiritual response was demanded of them.

We must begin then with a factual correction and an evaluation. In the first place, it is necessary to recognize that historiographical, sociological, political, psychological and anthropological research could not avoid important philosophical insights, and that the creative literary response to the Holocaust in poetry and prose is in fact brimming over with such insights. Though not all these insights are framed methodologically as disciplined philosophical discussions, their importance should not be discounted. Philosophers need to immerse themselves in these creative works and let themselves be led by such literature into existential realms where symbolically grasped insights precede conceptualization. Secondly, in spite of the recoil and doubt alluded to above, there were some daring philosophers who did relate qua philosophers to the Holocaust. They related to the Holocaust indirectly and by implication as they dealt with basic problems of the post-World War II period, the post-modernist era. The third critical note is the most important. While it is almost trivial to state that under the Nazi yoke there were not even elementary conditions for philosophical reflection on the evolving unprecedented events, an actual review of the literature (underground periodicals, diaries, letters, archive documents, and even complete books) created in the Eastern European ghettos, in the conquered countries of Western Europe, as well as in Germany, point to the existence of a body of reflective literature whose contribution may be originative and formative. Of course, even the few complete books that were written on the Holocaust from within the evolving events could not be systematically philosophical. In the most coherent achievements (as, for example, the first part of Leo Baeck's *Dieses Volk*), previously developed philosophical ground could be relied upon. However, what these books contain is more important for philosophical comprehension than even a systematic methodology and conceptual precision. It may be claimed that uniquely only they could contain the directness of empathetic insight into human experience, behavior and inner response under extremely abnormal situations. It must be emphasized that, contrary to our *ex post facto* prejudice, only a few rare individuals achieved such insights and felt an absolute need to express themselves, their feeling of necessity being itself an overpowering insight which sprang forth as a religious revelation from an unfathomed depth. Why the emphasis? Because it explains the intellectual honesty, the intensity and the special kind of precision which is unique to a literature written in such conditions. In spite of their hardships — or precisely because of their hardships — these thinkers could achieve a clarity unrivaled by others who, though possessing a tranquil mind and historical perspective, lacked the ability to touch that extraordinary reality from within so as to be able to ask the right questions, or did not experience the hidden spiritual power out of which one can adequately answer such questions.

A detailed examination of the reflective literature created during the war and the Holocaust reveals a complicated process. In the first years of Hitler's rise to power and even after the war broke out, one senses an internal barrier. While it was almost impossible to grasp the extraordinary dimensions of the events through recourse to formerly acceptable tools — philosophy and ideology — political leaders had nothing else to rely upon in their enforced confrontation with the enormity of the events. They could not deny the fact that the extent of murderous atrocities, destruction, and acts of dehumanization exceeded any previously conceived philosophical or ideological "prognosis." Yet they desperately depended on their old ideologies in order to establish an orientation. From this point of view, anti-Marxist pessimistic thinkers such as those who relied on A.D. Gordon or on Jabotinsky were no better off than those who chose to rely on Borochov and Tabenkin, or on Lenin and Trotsky. Leaders could not but admit that, at least on the face of it, something had escaped their historical calculations which had been arrived at on the basis of "scientific" or philosophical analysis. But in order to interpret and reorient themselves, to grasp motivations and aims, to understand policies and decipher their implications, and especially in order to foresee coming events and prepare an adequate response, they could not but push the evolving events back into the categories of a "scientifically" recognizable reality. Therefore, they were mainly engaged in the strange but humanly understandable process of readjusting reality to former ideological views.

Thus, during the years of Hitler's rise to power and in the first years of the war, a recognizable phenomenon can be observed among movements: a reaffirmation and realignment of ideological dogma. This classic dialectic disdains any detachment of events from their historical context. It cannot entertain deviations from the "laws of history." Yes, we face here the often preached demand for "deeper thinking" as a way of resistance to the Nazis, but ironically the intention was to suggest the "discovery" that in spite of superficial observation, historical truth remains unchanged. Which means that "our" ideology is still a reliable guide. It gives us adequate tools with which to orient ourselves and, what is most important, its truth protects our faith, our hope, our belief that what we are doing will not only save our persecuted people, but will also ensure us final and lasting victory. Yes, we must keep our hope and trust, for in such conditions hope is an absolute condition of life.

But sooner or later it became almost impossible, at least for young intellectuals whose attainment of intellectual maturity was contemporary to that period, to adjust to this dogmatic demand. The established ideologies could hold true for them regarding ethical, social or spiritual values and ideals. Yet they could not but reject the entire historical, social, political and anthropological construction which proved itself inadequate to reality. Nonetheless, it must be emphasized that these thinkers, without exception, remained firmly faithful to the convictions of their movements with regard to values and ideals, believing them to be a source of trust, human dignity, moral freedom, and spiritual integrity.

They had only to reevaluate the historical process and the motivations behind it. The dichotomy of their stance worsened as it became evident that the first practical ideological responses to the Holocaust based on former ideological understanding were mistaken, tragically so. Having understood the fatal mistake, they had to recognize that it was late, almost too late, to make corrections. This feeling intensified as the Nazi regime began the systematic implementation of the "Final Solution." No one could have expected this solution even after the atrocities which began with Hitler's rise to power and accelerated from month to month. In particular, no one could have foreseen the implications of a decision to apply this "solution" through a practical systematic process of mass murder. It was beyond any ideological prognosis because it was beyond what normal human beings could imagine as humanly possible, in practice, on the evidence of former experiences. This bears emphasis: it was not the abstract idea of a total genocide that was unbelievable — even before the beginning of the "Final Solution" there were Jewish leaders who clearly surmised that Hitler aimed at total destruction of the Jewish communities under his power. What was unbelievable was the readiness to use those utterly cruel techniques, the satanic strategies of dehumanization, and the efficient systematic methods which were needed for the execution. Especially inconceivable were the methods by which a complete spiritual breakdown of the victims was achieved, depriving them of moral choice and inducing utter powerlessness and beyond. They were forced to participate in their own spiritual dehumanization and physical annihilation. The inner core of personal being was encroached upon so as to transform their humanity and force it to become a function of that Absolute Evil that attacked them.

At the moment that this meaning of the "Final Solution" was recognized and fully realized, a completely new understanding of human reality was demanded as an urgent spiritual need. It was not only an understanding of the historical process — its "laws," possibilities and aims — which needed a radical reinterpretation, it was mainly a basic understanding of the existential situation of man and of Jew. It was the realization that confronting Radical Evil means, in practice, that one had to reinterpret one's understanding of personal and collective (social and national) moral responsibility as man and Jew. It exposes one directly and daily to terrible moral dilemmas such as how to survive while retaining human dignity and how to resist dehumanization while avoiding the direct or indirect guilt of aggravating the suffering and the death of other victims. This then was the moment in which the meaning of "Radical Evil" was understood. As against the perverted humanity of satanic Nazism, this was also the moment in which one could discover an unfathomed spiritual courage with which one could face even such onslaughts upon one's humanity.

During the first years after the end of the war some Holocaust survivors attempted to sum up their experiences and pass their new insights on as a signal message. They had a sense of mission: to speak in the name of the millions who had been murdered and to teach the lessons learned in the ghettos, the concentration camps, and the death camps to those who had watched from a distance and were unable, or perhaps even unwilling, to understand. But after a while most gave up the mission. It appears that they turned to an inner silence, or else transmitted their insights through story and poetic imagery. The main intellectual effort then turned, so it seems, in the direction of bearing testimony, of documentation and historiographical research.

What motivated the change? The growth of a creative literature on the Holocaust may reflect some deep-rooted cause for it. A seemingly insurmountable difficulty was recognized and dealt with at length in belletristic writing, a most personal means of communication. Writers and poets who wrote during the Holocaust (Y. Katzenelson, A. Suzkower, Y. Spiegel and others) were unaware of difficulty as long as they recorded their experiences while under the Nazi yoke. Using the direct, simple language of daily life, they pointed to a shared reality relying on their readers' understanding. But with the end of the war, the writers and poets began to realize that the new public whom they wanted to reach, those who had not shared their experiences, were perhaps incapable of understanding the meaning of the words, lacking, as they did, insights into situations of such existential "absurdity." The Holocaust had severed these Jews from the sphere of direct human communication. They were now confronted with the tragic fact that if the World of the Holocaust had indeed been a separate "Planet," it remained so for them even after their release from the ghettos and the camps.

There were poets and novelists who succeeded in transcending this overwhelming problem by the use of sophisticated means of expression, extending the linguistic communicative potential beyond its "usual" capacity. The compulsion was too great to be resisted, and the unresisted became the possible. Even if earlier evidence assumed that it was an impassable barrier, ingenious poets, being endowed with a rare talent for creating "sub-languages," overcame the obstacle. In fact, we have now an impressively wide range of creative literature on the Holocaust replete with existentialist philosophical insights. But what proved to be possible in the area of artistic expression continued to be an insurmountable barrier for the philosopher, committed as he is to a direct, precise, fully articulated conceptual language.

The philosopher is constrained from using such devices as irony, concealing through hints or hinting through concealment, or creating insightful moments of silence or multi-dimensional symbols. To philosophize means to state objectively the objective dimension — even of a subjective experience, to use clearly defined, one-dimensional concepts based on a certain common ground of human understanding. A philosophy must be conceptual, analytical and critical, otherwise it falsifies its method and is diverted from its aim. The feeling which prevailed was that the philosophical attempt must fail, that it might be too painful for the philosopher and for his readers should "cold," objective, analytical tools be introduced into this realm of tangled feelings of suffering, mourning and guilt.

Such were the immense difficulties that blocked the flow of philosophical reflection almost as it was begun, and led to the preferred mode of giving testimony and engaging in historiographical research. However, even in these two areas a powerful sense of restraint was present; one could not entirely escape presenting certain existential and moral dilemmas and proposing certain judgments. Questions were raised, and there were attempts at answers, but it was an unwilling response which repeatedly stressed the illegitimacy of judging human behavior in such situations while standing in the distance, on the outside. This was especially true for research done on topics such as the behavior of the Jews in the ghettos and the camps, problems faced by Jewish organizations and Jewish leadership, etc. In the historiographical arena, one cannot refrain from such questions, nor can one refrain from an attempt at answers. Some answers were indeed presented, though reluctantly, reluctance being the essential message of the answers. It must be admitted that the philosopher should be the one best equipped to deal with such questions. It is he who should be approached with questions about "lessons" and "conclusions." But can even he do it? Should he? Ought not the historiographer do it instead?

If this was the process through which thoughtful reflection on the Holocaust passed at the end of the war, and if it is true that philosophical reflection is required as a definite necessity, the first conclusion must be that we should turn back to the cognitive literature which was written under the Nazi regime, during the Holocaust. This literature appears to be the only source from which a philosopher, endowed with existential and historical perspective, may draw his basic insights, his first definitions of personal and collective human situations, his first and formative questions. From this literature he may also grasp new religious and humanist insights, which gained ground vis-a-vis a situation of "absurdity" and proved themselves sufficiently sound to serve as a starting point in the search for solutions. Indeed, "turn back" means: study, widen the context, empathize, analyze, define — and then proceed to more and new insights, meanings and conclusions.

*   *   *

Earlier we noted the common denominator which exists between the intellectuals and thinkers whose ideas are the subject of this study. There are, as well, many essential differences between them. In some aspects of their personal experiences and cultural backgrounds, Viktor Frankl and Leo Baeck were very close to each other, particularly in the method in which they focused their world outlook around a modern existentialist understanding of the religious experience. Still, the dissimilarities which existed in their backgrounds and in their interests, experiences and ways of thinking cannot be overlooked: between the psychiatrist whose role was to confront the scientific and philosophical schools in his universalist professional realm, and the rabbi who was an eminent expert in Jewish religious texts as well as in the sources of Christianity and classical, medieval and modern religious philosophy. There was more than a "functional" difference in the way each applied his wisdom to the various arenas of human experience.

Victor Frankl chose to confront the problems of single individuals caught in the existential pitfalls and trials of our age. He was a part of the Jewish people and its singular destiny, with a deep attachment to certain dimensions of traditional Jewish religious teachings. Yet in applying his wisdom to the private and personal dimension of human existence, he related to human beings beyond the diversities which exist between nations, cultures and religions. In contradistinction, Leo Baeck took on the responsibility of a leader in his Jewish community. He related to individuals, but as parts of their community, and though he was committed to a universal religious and ethical vision, it was his people's singular understanding of the universal which enlisted his commitment. It was the problem of his people's singularity of historical fate and their religious message that captivated his attention and stood in the center of his philosophical and theological enterprise.

There is, however, a complementary relationship between the existentialist theologies of Leo Baeck and Victor Frankl, while there is an overt antagonism between both of them and the group of Jewish thinkers whose views are discussed in the third and fifth essays of the first part of the book. The basic experience of this group of intellectuals was secularistic, not religious. Indeed, they were all humanists. They were deeply rooted in Jewish historical memories and in Jewish traditional values, especially in the national arena, but their basic conception was secularistic. Thus, the gulf between them and Teichthal's fundamentalistic views was extremely deep. Of course, humanism could serve as a common ground between Baeck's and Frankl's humanist-Jewish religiosity and the Zionist Socialism of Abba Kovner, Emmanuel Ringelblum, Eliezer Geller, Mordechai Tennenbaum-Tamaroff and Shimshon Drenger. Still, there is an essential disparity between "this-worldly" humanist sets of values and faith in a transcendental personal God, and such disparity must result in a significant difference in interpreting the reality of the Holocaust, its challenges and problems, and in the direction to be taken in the search for meaning, aim, purpose and hope.

In Leo Baeck's theologically bound understanding of reality, the Holocaust is grasped as a recurring episode in Jewish history. Even in his post-war writings, when he was fully aware of its extraordinary scope, Baeck referred to the Holocaust as one more destruction in the long, long chain of destructions that mark the history of the Jewish people; the people whose mission was and is to sanctify the name of God through the teaching of His word to all humanity. When necessary, the mission led to martyrdom. The trial of the Holocaust might be the most severe; still it should be accepted and confronted in the same spirit of faith in God, fully trusting in the mystery of His redeeming grace. Many would die, yet the people will live forever and will testify to the "Deeds of the Lord." It would appear that for the sake of justifying his basically traditional understanding, Leo Baeck had to develop new theological insights as answers to the unprecedented historical situation. Yet what is really astonishing in his thinking is his capacity to relate to the Holocaust, even in the midst of the trial, from the wide perspective of a messianic, holistic understanding of Jewish history as falling within the history of all humanity.

Victor Frankl developed an analogical position in the realm of the single individual. For Frankl, the extraordinary event represented a general human condition which recurs in infinite variations, wickedness being a constant element in human nature. In other words, it seems that Frankl did not consider that his experiences in concentration camps presented a challenge to his previously developed "philosophy of man." He did not feel that any essential correction was required. What was demanded was only a more detailed, more profound understanding of certain elements within this existential-humanist philosophy, particularly the human aptitude for wickedness which influenced Frankel's attitude — it became more pessimistic. Conversely, a test of the absoluteness of human moral freedom was also called for; and from this point of view Frankl's attitude became much more optimistic through his Holocaust experience. Indeed, this achievement of a more profound understanding of human nature, for good and for bad, was instrumental in evolving his original existentialist psychotherapy. Nonetheless, it is clear that his innovation was conceived as a development of existing philosophical and scientific traditions, and not as a revolution or a new beginning.

Things appear manifestly different with the group of Zionist-Socialist thinkers in the Eastern European ghettos and especially with Drenger. They were united in the clear insight that what was the extraordinary aspect of their experience was not only a "quantitative" matter, but that what was happening to them was indicative of the existence of a demonic-pathological source of evil. Their experience also attested to a hitherto unsuspected resource of moral sublimity within humanity. Both these phenomena challenged human self-understanding. The secular humanists too came to the conclusion that man is able to resist and thrust against the cruel-crafty attack on his moral freedom. But realizing the full meaning of the perfidious attack, they came to a different conclusion: firstly, that the individual must identify with his people, and act for the sake of his people in order to stand against the vicious attack (this nationalistic point clearly does not appear in Frankl's account of the situation), and secondly, they became much more conscious than were Frankl and Baeck not only of the superhuman difficulty of such a trial, but also of the superhuman price one is forced to pay even when one's resistance to this sort of demonic evil succeeds. They discovered something that took them far beyond both the traditional religious and the modernist humanist philosophy of man.

In conclusion, let us refer again to the essays included in the second part of the book. As said before, they are not comprehensive nor conclusive. They serve only as suggestions for a new beginning which reflect the insights gained through an analytical discussion of confrontations during the Holocaust and through a critical discussion of several main post-Holocaust responses.

PART I: PROBLEMS OF FAITH AND ETHICS VIEWED DURING THE HOLOCAUST

Chapter 1

FROM *THE ESSENCE OF JUDAISM* TO *THIS PEOPLE ISRAEL*: LEO BAECK'S THEOLOGICAL CONFRONTATION WITH THE PERIOD OF NAZISM AND THE HOLOCAUST

Leo Baeck (1873–1956) was recognized as a preeminent Jewish theologian in Germany even before World War I. From the standpoint of age, he belongs to the generation that follows Hermann Cohen; in terms of his general philosophical background, Baeck was Hermann Cohen's disciple, perhaps his closest one.[1] However, in terms of the history of Jewish theology in the twentieth century, he belonged to Hermann Cohen's generation since the first edition of Baeck's best-known work, *The Essence of Judaism*, was published before Cohen conceived of his work, *Religion of Reason*. (The final, complete edition of *The Essence of Judaism* came out shortly after the first edition of *Religion of Reason*).[2] This would mean that these two classic works of Jewish theology were written contemporaneously, drawing from the same Jewish and philosophical-cultural milieu, and on the same historical German-Jewish background. This was the period between the beginning of the century and the end of World War I, the same period in which the thoughts of two other eminent disciples and disputants of Cohen, Martin Buber and Franz Rosenzweig, were framed and challenged.

Baeck is then one of the "founding fathers" of modern Jewish philosophical theology in this century. Though it had absorbed much from the so-called "Science of Judaism" of the nineteenth century, this theology was subsequently revised in order to "return" from an assimilationist universalism to an integral, more particularist, more complete Jewish essence which was directly grounded in the historical continuity of traditional sources.[3] From a certain perspective, it might well be claimed that Baeck was the most well-integrated and consequential representative of this trend. The scion of a distinguished rabbinic dynasty, he was raised in a traditional home and

3

from childhood was educated to be a rabbi. But on his way to fulfilling a rabbinic destiny, he diverted from the orthodoxy of his father. Baeck went first to the Conservative Jewish Theological Seminary in Breslau, then to the Liberal Higher Institute for Jewish Studies in Berlin where he was ordained as a "reform" rabbi.[4] As he moved into the general field of European and German research, philosophy and humanist culture, he also strove to bring the reform movement back to a fuller Jewish authenticity, both in its relationship to Jewish peoplehood (which included the national sense) and its view of faith and religious lifestyle. Baeck's theological thinking clearly and forcefully considered the movement for "return" a necessary corrective in understanding the Jewish situation in Germany. The success of the struggle for enlightenment and emancipation, which he thought positive and fully justified in itself, had produced unwarranted effects of assimilationism and alienation.[5]

All this is fairly well known and has been evaluated by many students of Baeck's teachings. Though he is not Cohen's equal, Baeck has neither been overlooked nor neglected; both Buber and Rosenzweig devoted significant attention to his work. Baeck's book *The Essence of Judaism* was very well received and elicited much response, even in its first, shorter form. He had a brilliant career as a leading rabbi in Germany, and then as the recognized spiritual leader of German Jewry. As such he was extraordinarily respected and appreciated. Moreover, though *The Essence of Judaism* may not be considered equal to *Religion of Reason, The Star of Redemption,* or *I and Thou,* from the point of view of philosophical ingenuity and originality, it is a much more readable book, open to popular understanding. It became the "representative" work which one could offer an intelligent, erudite reader interested in acquiring a deeper understanding of Judaism as a total idea. From an educational aspect, Baeck's book was far more influential than others and more widely published. Indeed, during its first publication it became a "classic."[6]

This popularity was even more pronounced following the Holocaust. After Baeck's liberation from Theresienstadt Concentration Camp, despite his age and the suffering he had undergone, he remained active for another ten years. During this decade his work continued to hold a central position and commanded intense interest. Nor did that attention fade after his death. On the contrary, the scholarly and the theological efforts devoted to it became even more intensive. The most important research, study and reassessment of

4

Baeck's teachings were written after his death by scholars and spiritual leaders of the Reform and Conservative movements, and by a number of Christian theologians interested in the Jewish-Christian dialogue.[7] The reasons for this growing interest are clear. Baeck's stance as the recognized leader of German Jewry after Hitler's rise to power and his suffering as a great Jew who sanctified the Holy Name in a Nazi concentration camp, crowned him with an authority, both religious and national, which transcended the limits of his own movement. Baeck became a Jewish "ecumenical" leader, rising above the division of movements. As such he gained international and inter-religious fame, and his theology appealed to some of the most important Christian theologians of his age.[8] Blessed with energy and spiritual vitality up to the last moment, Baeck was able to maintain his position as a leader in writing, teaching, and symposia, as well as in public affairs. He was responsive to his admirers, thus enhancing the interest in his personality and work.

However, reviews and researches of Baeck's teaching tend to concentrate on his first book, *The Essence of Judaism*, along with the two collections of papers and essays which were published later,[9] while his last works, which summarize his thoughts in the period of the Holocaust and the years after his liberation, were relatively neglected or considered marginal. This disregard seems all the more unexpected because, in its holistic systematic approach, the *Dieses Volk Israel*[10] is equal to *The Essence of Judaism* and in terms of sheer volume it is no smaller than Baeck's early, ambitious *magnum opus*. Nonetheless, the claim is made again and again that Baeck's systematic, original and innovative contribution is found in the final edition of his first work, and that the later writings are additions, completions, interpretations or even very interesting specific developments of his first essential thesis. Thus, the man whose strength as a spiritual leader of his community during the Holocaust has brought him both sympathy and interest, is presented as a representative of a modern classicism which antedates the Holocaust. Consequently, Baeck's writings are scarcely consulted in discussions about theological problems raised by the Holocaust,[11] though these dilemmas become increasingly central to the Jewish theological debates of our age.

Clearly the possibility that this is a result of their carelessness can be ruled out. On the contrary, if the interest in Baeck after the Holocaust centers on his pre-Holocaust work, one should assume

5

that it stems from Baeck's own teaching. Further, it may echo Baeck's own preferences. Evidently Baeck remained attached to his first teaching and considered it as his classical work. While he did feel the need to write a new great work during the Holocaust, it was not because he had discovered something which necessitated a change in his philosophical system. On the contrary, confronting the Holocaust, he felt the need to reaffirm his former stance. Secondly, astonishing though it may seem, Theresienstadt does not stand at the center of the book he wrote in the period during and after his stay there.

Far more than that, Theresienstadt — or the event which it symbolizes — does not directly occupy any place in the book which was written inside its walls. Reminders of the time and place of the work are found in only two instances; the first in the short introduction to the first part, in which the author tells the reader where and under what conditions the book was written. The book, he states, should be read as a testimony of its time, but he does not elucidate whether it is meant as a testimony of Theresienstadt itself and what happened there or whether it is a testimony about the way the Jews stood their test. There is no way to decide. The second reference appears in a short paragraph in the last chapter of the second part. That short section is subtitled, "The Nazi Terror." The paragraph is less than a page in length and is immediately followed by a paragraph on the establishment of the State of Israel. The book then returns to a discussion of the national and universal tasks and missions of Judaism.[12] It is crucially important to realize how resolutely Baeck refrained from placing Theresienstadt in the center of his theological discussion. The entire paragraph reads:

> But soon other voices sounded forth out of the world of Europe, striving to submerge all else, voices that served untruthfulness, that praised crime and jeered at righteousness. States disregarded their duties of faithfulness toward their citizens. Houses of prayer, in which faith, righteousness, and justice had been proclaimed, were burned to the ground; congregations, in which reverence for God, humility, philanthropy and a feeling for the total society had been nurtured, were dismembered; hundreds of thousands, children of this people, human lives containing a soul, were destroyed. And those that committed this knew what they committed. And the powers which practiced every crime

created the readiness for new crimes. They stretched forth their hands — in the name of peace — to powers in whose midst right and righteous dwelt. The peace was profaned; and profaned peace brings an even worse destiny than a breach of peace. War always follows it, a worse war than that caused by a broken peace. The second world war thus developed, and when it came to an end, the victor undertook the task of expiating the profaned peace through a labor of pure peace. In a sense they wanted to reconsecrate humanity. The United Nations was to be the foundation for that task, so that a sanctuary of hope might be built. Will this come to be? Is this a commencement of a humane epoch, an epoch at the beginning of which the affliction of this people stood as a sacrifice for many? Those who come later will hear the answer.[13]

Our attention is captured not so much by the section's brevity or by its position in the chapter. It is captured first by the context: mention of Theresienstadt comes as a *caesura* in the middle of a description of the progress of humanity as a whole (the Jewish people being a central force within that humanity) toward the fulfillment of the messianic ideal. Then the parameters in which Baeck deals with the event, and the components which he includes in it, call for a critical examination: he appears to have focused his narrative on the way in which the Nazis initiated their war against the Allies, and on what happened to German Jewry alone, omitting the murder of the six million and the death factories invented to achieve the Final Solution! Reading it one feels compelled to ask: can Baeck really have realized, through his direct experience in the Holocaust, the full significance of what was done to the Jewish people, and to European humanity? How could he ignore the enormity of the calamity? How could he pass so smoothly and so quickly from the ethical collapse of Europe during World War II and the Holocaust to a renewal of all the good old hopes through the institution of the United Nations? How could he pass so quickly from the catastrophic destruction of most of European Jewry to the interpretation of sacrifice for the sake of the redemption of all humanity? These painful questions will be discussed subsequently at some length. It is clear, however, that Baeck related to the Holocaust as a passing episode in the history of the Jewish people as well as in the history of humanity. Moreover, in his view it was an episode which ought

7

not characterize the entire historical context in which it "happened to
happen!"

How accurate is this representation of Baeck's stance? It can be
verified, in the first place, by careful examination of other statements made by Baeck after his liberation from Theresienstadt.

The following illustration is oral, comprising the conclusion of
a lecture Baeck was invited to give in 1946. The occasion was the
renewal of "The Arthur Davis Memorial Lectures" series, initiated
by the Jewish Historical Society of England. The circumstances are
telling. The annual lecture series was originally established when
the Society was founded. In 1931 the series was suspended, to be
reinstated only after the war. In his introductory remarks, the Chairman, Dr. R.N. Salamon, emphasized the significance of renewing a
tradition which had been broken on the eve of the recent tragic events
in Jewish and European history. Baeck had been chosen deliberately
and was presented to the audience as the heroic representative of the
Jewish people which had endured the Holocaust. Baeck could not
have missed the assumption of the sponsors: plainly, he was expected to say something about the historical significance of the
tragic events just ended.

The title he chose was "Changes in Jewish Outlook." His main
thesis was that the Jewish people, as every other people, has been
permanently influenced by the cultures which surrounded it. Given
this axiom, the Jewish people nonetheless always maintained its
freedom to choose which of the various surrounding cultures would
be at the center of influence, and what it would accept or reject from
the culture it had selected. In this way the Jewish people protected
the essential uniqueness of its original religious culture. Baeck
chronicled this thesis with a broad, general review of Jewish history
vis-a-vis other cultures, from the meeting of Judaism with Babylonian
and Egyptian cultures to the era of Emancipation and Enlightenment.
Only towards the conclusion of his lecture did he feel he must
respond to his public's expectation, namely, to say something about
the salience of his view of Jewish history in the light of recent events
which he had himself experienced.

"These are our times," said Baeck, referring to the period which
begins with the Enlightenment and Emancipation. For here, as well
as in his *This People Israel*, and in a series of lectures and articles
covering the last period of his life, he counts the Holocaust as a short
episode that he incorporates within a long inclusive epoch which

began and took its basic direction from the positive, hopeful events of the Enlightenment and Emancipation.

> These are [then], our times, and history cannot yet pass judgement regarding them. But one thing may yet be said in conclusion. It has become apparent that there are recurrent forces at work in our history, though their forms may change. And these forces are ever influenced by the world around us.
>
> The laws of gravity and attraction operate in history as well. Jewish history, therefore, can be grasped only in context with forces active in the world; it can be understood only in apposition to world history. But in all this mutual interplay of forces, in this polarity of isolation and vision, in which this people in the course of time has never lost itself nor lost its horizon, a higher power seems to speak. That power led and guided us in the past. We thus feel assured that it will yet lead and guide us. These sober expositions, which are intended to point to a way of history, may be concluded with a word of poetry. For according to Aristotle, poetry "is more philosophical yet and more incisive than historical research" — with a word from the song which Moses and the children of Israel sang unto the Lord: "Thou in thy mercy hast led forth the people which thou hast redeemed." Despite trials and tribulations, torment and torture, it is this that this history recounts more than does any other history. It is nevertheless the last and everlasting word of each epoch. This despite all the tragedy, in the changing course of time and outlook, in the eternal poetry of our history.[14]

When this passage is read detached from its full context, it seems to be poetically over-generalized and lacking in either historical or philosophical precision. But it contains precise and well-calculated elements of theological and philosophical thinking. Baeck did substantiate his poetic vision, both historically and philosophically. Yet it is quite clear, even without such validation, that he considered the Holocaust a passing episode, and that he would not permit his personal experiences in the Holocaust to darken his vision of the vast expanse of Jewish history. This means that the scholars who studied Baeck's teaching may be justified in their judgement that Baeck did not substantially change anything from what he had said in his first *magnum opus*. Therefore, it is his classic work which remains to be examined if one is to understand his singular contribution to modern Jewish theology.

Nonetheless, the implication of this critique borders on the trivial. If a book was written partly while the author was in a concentration camp and partly after liberation from that camp, if it was published so as to bear witness to the time of its composition, yet refrains from any reference to the existence of a concentration camp and relates to the Holocaust as a passing episode, then these very facts must mean that the book, which is comprised of what it intentionally omits as well as what it relates, is an intended and thoughtfully calculated response to the Holocaust. Moreover, if during the Holocaust Baeck felt the need to begin a new systematic work and after the Holocaust he felt the need to complete and publish it, then clearly he thought that he had something new to say, something that had not been previously articulated, either in his first *magnum opus* or in his other two books. At the very least, he wanted to say something in a different mode, something demanded by the hour. True, in *This People Israel* and in his many other works written before and after Hitler's rise to power, Baeck did not recant on his former ideas. Instead, he reaffirmed the credo he had stated in his first book. Does that mean that he had nothing significantly new to add? Is it not obvious that the need to restate a certain truth in response to a most challenging event, points to an effort to go beyond what has already been said? Should we not examine the restatement in order to see whether it contains new dimensions which incorporate the writer's response to the events, though he describes them as episodic? Is he not, at least, trying to justify his strange diminutive description which cannot be accepted as "self-evident"? In order to concretize the common paradox which is met here, should *This People Israel* not be classed as Baeck's apologia for *The Essence of Judaism* in the wake of the Holocaust? Or rather, should not the effort in Baeck's later theological thinking to "lay aside" the Holocaust be regarded precisely as an intensive and focused confrontation with the central challenge of the Holocaust?

These are, of course, rhetorical questions. Leo Baeck saw himself first and foremost as a rabbi, and from the time of his ordination he interpreted the task of a rabbi in terms of spiritual leadership which was related to the historical present. This self-perception was augmented when, at the beginning of the Nazi regime, he was appointed as rabbi of the entire German-Jewish community. Even in

Theresienstadt he saw himself as a rabbi of a congregation. He felt that his primary task as a rabbi required that he respond to the great spiritual anguish of his community.

Even as a scholar of academic stature, he never dealt in historical topics or in historiosophical problems in the abstract. When he probed the depths of Jewish historic memory, as he frequently did, his aim was to draw a lesson which would be significant for the tangible present.

In order to ascertain Baeck's essential spiritual response to the Nazi regime and the Holocaust, one must delve beyond what is said in his first book, and beyond the work he wrote after Hitler's rise to power. But prior even to that, it is necessary to reexamine the way in which he functioned as a spiritual leader and the message he addressed to the Jewish community during those years.

Naturally, from the beginning of his leadership in the German-Jewish community, Baeck's educational policy was based on his entire world outlook. In this he resembles many Jewish spiritual leaders who found that in order to respond with solid, reliable answers to the difficult questions raised by the Holocaust they must first reaffirm their former orientating views. For Baeck the orientating view was the understanding of Jewish history in terms of *Kiddush Ha-Shem*, which he formed through the influence on him of Hermann Cohen's *Philosophy of Judaism*. Baeck's disciple and student, A. Friedlander, in his excellent monograph on his teacher, points to two formative ideas to be found in the first edition of *The Essence of Judaism*. Both refer to the centrality within Judaism of the commandment of *Kiddush Ha-Shem*, the readiness to sacrifice one's life if need be for the sanctification of the Holy Name. In both ideas the influence of Cohen's ethical religious outlook is felt strongly. Let us recall that Cohen did not base his rejection of Zionism and his dedication to Judaism's universal mission to humanity on the naive optimism of the nineteenth century, but on a sense of moral duty — to be ready to suffer for the sake of a redeeming truth.[15] The two ideas are very important and deserve being fully cited.

> Human suffering is a religious resource only in so far as it becomes an assumption of an obligation. We are not merely to *suffer* pains passively — it would turn them into the saddest misfortunes if we just knew to bear suffering — but we must actively *carry* them, we must meet their tests with all of our strength. We should not deny

pain and persecution by sinking ourselves in God and explaining all suffering as deceptive appearances; we must affirm suffering with secure certainty, by turning it into an ethical imperative. Do your duty, and the worst will have to become good for you; all the masters and teachers of Israel are agreed upon this. The question of theodicy is answered — or eliminated — for them since life is viewed as an integrated whole. It is not a gift granted us, but a task to be fulfilled; and therefore life is worthwhile.[16]

And further on:

Martyrdom is the truest sanctification of the Holy Name, the clearest testimony to God, the most certain proof of God's existence. It is the final word, the ultimate consequence of moral responsibility. Where there is the unconditional duty to testify to God through faith in Him and obedience to His imperatives, the boundary of our existence is not the boundary of the duty. Our life is little and poor against the exaltedness and fullness of the task. The finest life means nothing compared to the moral demand. And thus we must be ready to sacrifice our life to the good. The ethical will finds its sole goal in its agreeing with God. And to agree with God, man must be able to surrender his will for life.[17]

Baeck returned here, indeed, to the traditional stance of *Kiddush Ha-Shem*, but he reinterpreted the position in ethical terms, in the spirit of ethical monotheism as understood by Hermann Cohen. On this basis he could shape his first reaction, as the spiritual leader of the Jewish congregation in Germany, foreseeing a time of trial when the believers would be constrained to fulfill their ultimate duty. As early as 1925 he wrote in a letter which was later published and became well-known:

It is true that the elements which constitute our essence are dual. We incorporate them in our soul, and therefore every one of us may discover them unaided, if he is a thinking person. Kant has already stated that every man is a citizen of two kingdoms, and this is true even in more dimensions and in a more far-reaching meaning than he himself intended to say. Along with these elements everyone receives dual tasks, and with them certain contradictions. Every martyrdom is derived from this fact. Human beings belong to the kingdom of the state and to the kingdom of God. Which law should they prefer when a contradiction appears? In the same way we should understand the conflict in the consciences of decent pacifists between their national and their international duties, and the same is the conflict in the hearts of decent Social Democrats between their national and international duties!

Whenever an inner contradiction of such dimensions appears the moment must arrive when one will have to opt between the earthly and the eternal. *"Lech Lecha m'Arzekha"* (Get thee out of thy country). And to opt means to be prepared for the sanctification of the Holy Name through the recognition of the primacy of religion and its commandments over every other thing. This was what the Jews of Spain did when they faced the choice between God and their home. They could keep their home only if they would have been ready to abandon their religion, and for the sake of their religion they gave up their home. The Jews of Palestine stood before the same kind of choice when they were defeated and persecuted in their own land. They departed from their land in order to remain faithful to the God of Israel. And the act of the sanctification of the Holy Name became greater, the greater and stronger God's commandment became engraved in their souls.

The spiritual and ethical misfortune of Germany is that too many of its leaders deny the existence of the two kingdoms, making of Germanism a religion. Instead of the belief in God they believe — and the Lutheran priests are those who lead it — in Germanism. This is nationalism in its most precise meaning, when one recognizes only the nation and not the world of God. (And by the way, the spiritual dullness of some of the *"Central-vereinllers"* is manifest in their will to make Germanism into a kind of substitute religion.) Wherever the world of God is denied there the sanctification of the Holy Name of God in public is also denied, because these two bear witness to the same Truth. We, the Jews, are rooted more deeply than the other nations in the spiritual world, in religion, as we are God's people. Therefore we experience this conflict in a deeper and more frequent manner, indeed not only frequent, but actually constant manner. This is the tragic motif in our history. A tragedy not in its small bourgeois meaning, but in the sublime meaning, that tragedy through which history

13

becomes spiritual and great. Indeed the last few years have lead us back in a most intensive way to this uniqueness of our destiny. We have re-experienced the depth of our roots in the kingdom of God.[18]

The importance of this letter to our discussion is not only its delineation of the continuity in Baeck's thought between a passage published as early as 1905, and another which dealt with the commandment to sanctify the Holy Name. Nor is it only a matter of what it was that Baeck would say when the dangers which he had foreseen materialized. Its importance is as well in the typical historical analogy which the letter contains. The analogy throws a clear light on the manner in which Baeck tended, *ab initio*, to interpret a current historical moment, not as an episode, but as a constant phenomenon in the history of the Jewish people. It is perhaps in this context that one should understand the famous statement which Baeck made eight years later, in 1933, at the first meeting of the Committee of German Jewry which he was called upon to head, namely that "The end of the history of the Jewish people in Germany has arrived."[19] Did he intend to say that German Jewry was facing the same fate as the Jews of Spain at the threshold of the great Expulsion, or the same fate as the Jews of Palestine after the failure of Bar-Kochba's revolt? Did he intend to say that the Jews of Germany would have to choose between their religion and their fatherland, or between obedience to the law of the State and obedience to the ethical commandment of God?

His words in a letter to Heinz Warshauer in the same year affirm that, indeed, this was the way Baeck understood the historical situation. "Hitler and his like cannot turn back history. We Jews will suffer. Some of us may die. But we will survive. We Jews have old eyes."[20] The clearest expression of Baeck's state of mind is found in the prayer which he composed and which was to be said in all the synagogues of Germany on the eve of the Day of Atonement, 1935.

In this hour every man in Israel stands erect before his Lord, the God of justice and mercy, to open his heart in prayer. Before God we will question our ways and search our deeds, the acts we have done and those we have left undone. We will publicly confess the sins we have committed and beg the Lord to pardon and forgive. Acknowledging our trespasses, individual and communal, let us despise the slanders and calumnies directed against us and our faith. Let us declare them lies, too mean and senseless for our reckoning. "God is our refuge." Let us trust Him, our source of dignity and pride. Thank the Lord and praise Him for our destiny, for the honor and persistence with which we have endured and survived persecution. Our history is the history of the grandeur of the human soul and the dignity of human life. In this day of sorrow and pain, surrounded by infamy and shame, we will turn our eyes to the days of old. From generation to generation God redeemed our fathers, and he will redeem us and our children in the days to come. We bow our heads before God and remain upright and erect before man. We know our way and we see the road to our goal. At this hour the house of Israel stands before its God. Our prayer is the prayer of all Jews; our faith is the faith of all Jews living on the earth. When we look into the faces of one another, we know who we are; and when we raise our eyes heavenward, we know eternity is within us. For the Guardian of Israel neither slumbers nor sleeps. Mourning and desolation overflow our hearts. Devoutly and with awe let us look into the innermost of our souls, and let that which cannot be spoken sink into the silence of meditation."[21]

Baeck's understanding of his task as a rabbi and a spiritual leader was that he was to make the people of his community strong through belief in the truth of God and in their destiny as a people. Thus strengthened, they would be able to withstand the hardships which lay before them as a religious test in which they must sanctify the Holy Name. There is no contradiction in Baeck's not identifying the evolving events as an historical "episode," but on the contrary, describing them as a constant motif which characterizes Jewish history. In *This People Israel*, he does not deny the constant, tragic motif in Jewish history, even perceiving the "Nazi Terror" in the light of former historical destructions. For Baeck, the episodic character of such events was as constant as their reappearance. It is not scarcity that makes such occurrences into episodes, but their nature and status as passing events which are never permitted to decide either the general direction of history, its aim or its meaning. Baeck's understanding of history was that such events are episodic because they vanish as they appear, with no possibility of deflecting the course of history from its divinely-oriented direction. God's truth will stand forever. That is to say, that frequent, and even constantly recurring events are episodic in their essence, as they are accidents with relation to the eternal truth of God which is revealed in history.

The real difficulty to be faced as one reads Baeck's reaction to the evolving Holocaust does not inhere in the "contradiction" between the episodic or constant nature of such events, but in his obstinate grasp of the Holocaust as the "regular" reappearance of a constant pattern, as a "one more of the same kind" event. It is in the meaning that he attaches to the historic pattern itself. Does Baeck's view of the sanctification of the Holy Name, as a decision of choice between faithfulness to the law of the State and faithfulness to the law of God, truly represent the classic understanding of this encounter throughout Jewish history? Is it not the case that such an understanding is typical of specifically modern, post-emancipationist, historical circumstances, perhaps even to the modern situation peculiar to Germany and German Jewry? This is, in itself, a very difficult question, but a second question is still more difficult. At that tragic, historic moment, did the Jewish people, in Germany as elsewhere in Europe, really have an alternative between obedience to the law of the State and faithfulness to the moral law of God? Did Baeck understand in 1925, in 1933, in 1935, or when the mass extermination began, or when he became a prisoner in a concentration camp, or at last, when he sat in London and wrote the second part of *This People Israel*, when all the facts relating to the nature and the proportions of the Holocaust were before him, did Baeck understand that this time there was no alternative, that this was a struggle for physical survival against the threat of systematic total annihilation? Was it not hairsplitting to ask at this juncture whether it could or could not be interpreted as a situation which demands the sanctification of the Holy Name? This time the Jewish people did not have an alternative, either obedience or faithfulness; the motive behind this threat was not the Jew's faith as such, or his world view and way of life, but the mere fact of his being born a Jew? Did Baeck ever admit this plain fact in his religious thinking? The answers are revealed when these questions are posed against the background of Baeck's entire spiritual theological response to the Holocaust. This must include the few overt statements that Baeck made, as well as the many indirect and implied statements found in his rich literary output during the years he was the spiritual leader of German Jewry. Here are the assumptions and ideas with which he attempted, both factually and by implication, to justify the relationship of his formerly-shaped religious system to the evolving events.

It is obvious that Baeck felt that his was not a self-evident method of interpretation. Indeed, it might appear quite problematic to some Jews and very unconvincing to others, mainly the radical Zionists who criticized him strongly despite the growing favor with which Baeck regarded Zionism.[22] Consequently, his position called for justification. Obviously, if this claim is correct, it means that in spite of Baeck's loyalty to his philosophical theology as expanded in *The Essence of Judaism*, it was, for him, practically impossible to refrain from developing his position, let alone making adaptations, even significant changes, in it. This would be so even if his main aim was to underscore his original concept of Judaism, thereby demonstrating his own position as a Jewish leader. It was precisely to that end that he had to embark on a reevaluation through restating his thesis.

But in order to detect and define the full meaning of the developments and changes, it is necessary to reexamine Baeck's position from its underpinnings within the broadest context of Jewish thought.

Students of Baeck's teachings are generally attentive to the variety of Baeck's sources: as a disciple of Hermann Cohen and Dilthey, as the partially imitative antagonist of Harnack, and as Buber and Rosenzweig's partner for dialogue and controversy. Baeck's teaching is also much discussed in the perspective of his ambivalent relationship with a number of new Protestant theologians in Germany. But it is also necessary to see Baeck in another context; a context which has been neglected for the most part: the struggling movements at work within the Jewish people in the pre-Holocaust period, during the Holocaust, and immediately after it. Their confrontation with the problems of the future of the people certainly had an impact on Baeck's view of the essence of Judaism.

Baeck's religious philosophy is more formally rooted in the established religious movements of European Jewry than are the teachings of his two colleagues, Buber and Rosenzweig. Educated first at the Breslau Seminar and then in the Higher Institute in Berlin, from his ordination he served as a congregational rabbi, propounding his theology and developing his educational and political activities within the established framework of Liberal Judaism. Fully conscious of its historical background, he tried to develop the thinking of his movement, not less than his own, in a full and faithful continuation of the scientific-historical and philosophical-theological foundations which had been laid down in the nineteenth century. Throughout his long life he was fully committed to his movement, identifying himself with its main religious ideology, though he was always an original, independent thinker who was determined to be a leader rather than be led by others. Of course this meant a choice must be made and a resolute determination effected on a number of issues: the polarized controversy concerning the identity and image of the Jewish people, and its integration in the modern national state, in general society, and in European secular culture. Baeck was active in a movement which defined Judaism as a pure religion in spiritual terms of ethical monotheism, and in political and social terms of a denomination. Originally the movement was basically antagonistic to any form of separate national framework for the Jewish people. It was an approach that emphasized the positive value of the Jewish dispersion among the nations. The movement saw in the integration of the Jews into their various countries, societies and cultures not only a perfect solution for the "problem of the Jews," but also an ideal fulfillment of the universalist "mission" of the chosen people to advance the truth of pure ethical monotheism throughout humanity.

It was on these assumptions that the Liberal movement based its claim that Judaism is intrinsically identified with idealistic humanism. The movement believed that Judaism is a dynamic and progressive historical entity, that it has constantly undergone change and adapted itself to progressive historical development. Consequently, in the modern period too, Judaism is again required to prove its dynamic and progressive character through radical reforms in *halakhic* norms, in ritual, and even in some religious concepts. All of this was to be achieved by using the tools of rationalist philosophy and the humanist sciences (mainly history, which then encompassed the political, sociological and anthropological sciences). In this way Judaism would again become synonymous with the best and highest achievements of universal human culture.

It should be emphasized that during the period that the young Leo Baeck was being educated for the rabbinate and began functioning as an ordained rabbi of a congregation, his movement was totally committed to its earliest idealistic and universalistic ideology. The fact that the young and ambitious rabbinic candidate had opted for this movement rather than follow the traditional way in which he had been educated by his father, or the "positivist-historical" approach in which he had been schooled at the Breslau Seminar, means that, after due study and serious deliberation, he decided to adopt precisely this religious ideology and to identify with it. Thus, he laid the foundations for his own theology and interpretation of a Jewish way of life, and indeed these choices marked his philosophy of religion, his religious lifestyle and his role as a Jewish leader. Let it be stressed that during his entire lifetime, Baeck remained a fully convinced Liberal rabbi.

But at the same time and in the same measure, we should emphasize the fact that Baeck brought with him a uniquely rich cargo of Jewish traditional education, together with a peculiar sensitivity to far-reaching change that can be the hallmark of scions of a new generation. Changes were occurring both within the Jewish community and on the outside, in German society. It was Baeck's particular sensitivity that made him aware of the need to rethink and readapt the policies of his movement in light of these changes.[23] In his personality, style of public activity, and in his teaching, Baeck embodied the same deep reorientation which characterized the thinking of the later Hermann Cohen and the young Buber and Rosenzweig, in fact, a whole generation that had to face the dramatically changing conditions of the Jewish people in Germany and Europe in general.

From Baeck's point of view the new situation presented him with four challenging dangers:

1) *Assimilation*, which had already crossed the boundary of full integration within the society and culture of the country, almost totally eradicating the uniqueness of Jewish spiritual identity. At best this resulted in a shallow, marginal remnant of culture and at worst in a boring vacuum. Coming to the movement which had been most affected by this process, Baeck could not remain unconcerned. Early in his career he recognized that as a Jewish educator he would have to confront the problem of assimilation as one of his central tasks.[24]

2) *Anti-Jewish tendencies* in society and culture in Europe in general, but particularly in Germany. Emancipation as a political-juridical process, and on the level of the educational-professional process, had been practically achieved, but social rejection of the Jews was growing steadily. It took the form of a virulent anti-Semitism among the masses, and of anti-Jewish prejudices in both the Christian and the nationalist elites.[25]

3) *The emergence of political Zionism and of a Jewish Socialist movement*, as new alternatives to movements which had been established during the nineteenth century, against the background of

profound social change in the situation of the Jewish people, especially in the East European Jewish community. Massive emigration
meant, in fact, a process of eradication of older Jewish centers in
Europe, and the planting of new centers, especially in America and
Palestine. Challenged by these developments, the previously established institutions had to react both to the new movements and to the
conditions which had enhanced their growth. One of the most
important results of this reformulation of the Jewish agenda within
the movements was a shift in the axis of the great debate from the
level of a spiritual-cultural controversy on the "essence of Judaism,"
to the existential national-political, social-economic and cultural-
social levels dealing with problems of Jewish survival and with ways
of reorganization with which to confront the problematics of a "post-
Emancipation" period.[26]

4) *The growing polarization* within the Jewish people which
developed out of antagonistic approaches to such existential dilemmas. The fact that the existential polarization developed into an
existential crisis needs emphasis, because in itself it was a fearful
threat to Jewish survival. How could the Jewish people manage to
protect its basic unity in the face of such bitter antagonism between
the various conflicting streams?

These new challenges and threats which emerged between the last
two decades of the nineteenth century and the beginning of World War
II did not quash the historical optimism rooted in the doctrine of
development and progress. On the contrary, in some quarters this
optimism was reborn through the emergence of a variety of twentieth
century messianic movements, in both secular and religious Zionism
and in Marxist and neo-utopian Socialism. As for the Liberal Jews, it
seems that a movement of this kind cannot give up its optimism without
giving up its *raison d'etre*. Historical optimism has been identified
with its essence. This is more than exemplified in the case of Leo
Baeck; optimism was the most characteristic expression of his attachment to the nineteenth century tradition of idealistic philosophy and
scientific historicism. But how could even those men most stubbornly
committed to hope and faith in the course of progress deny the social
and political tragedies of European history on the eve of the great
"world revolution" and World War? As Jews how could they deny the
concrete results of "progress" from the Jewish point of view: the
pogroms, the persecutions, the political efforts of burgeoning anti-
Semitic movements to force the Jews back to their previous deprived

status. In spite of the great hopes, or perhaps within the dialectical nature of such messianic hopes which arise in times of deep suffering, there hovered a dark cloud of fear even before the eyes of those who were full of the vision of a messianic future. A horrendous destruction, the dimensions of which had never been experienced in Jewish history, loomed on the horizon. Admittedly, no one could have foreseen the Holocaust. Yet there were Zionist thinkers who prophesied near catastrophe, greater in the number of victims and in the crushing results to the material and spiritual foundations of Jewish national existence than any similar event in the past.[27] There could be no doubt that the difference between being prepared or not being prepared for a catastrophe could be crucial; first, because of the need to recognize and realize what was actually happening to the Jewish people, and then, of course, so as to determine a proper response. This became increasingly important after World War I, especially at the outset of the Holocaust with Hitler's rise to power and the start of racist jurisdiction and riots against Jews, and finally, as World War II broke out.

How did Baeck formulate his response to the historic challenges? It must be conceded that although his *modus operandi* was characterized by a striving to harmonize paradoxes, which is essentially optimistic, this did not prevent a clear and sober identification of impending danger. On the contrary, up to a certain point it was precisely that optimistic faith which could serve as a source of courage to see and define danger, even to draw radical conclusions. With no illusions, Baeck saw the shallowness, lack of knowledge and marginality in things Jewish which typified the majority of the "emancipated" and "enlightened" Jewish masses in Germany. In his general evaluation of the historical perspective, Baeck was a believer and an optimist. The recognition, therefore, of sad facts did not cause him to despair or to regret the positive acceptance of Emancipation, so essential for the Jewish liberal world view. Notwithstanding the critical opinions of either Orthodox Jews or Zionists about Liberal Judaism, Baeck rejected the claim that assimilationism was the inevitable result of full emancipation. It was, as he saw it, the natural consequence of a first stage, which could not be achieved without a radical attack against the super segregationist mentality of Orthodoxy as well as the elimination of overly particularistic aspects of Jewish life. Once the aims of the first stage were achieved, this one-sided radicalism could and should be tamed. Emancipation could be maintained as a balanced process so that integration into general culture would not end in the disappearance of the Jewish people, or the collapse of its unique and particularistic character. Rather, the combination of great achievements in the fields of general culture along with a sense of dissatisfaction in the Jewish sphere would motivate a movement of reorientation towards re-assembling, re-absorbing and re-creating. The result of this would be a new balance, a new harmony between Judaism and general European culture.[28]

Baeck predicted this development on the basis of an historical study of earlier periods in which Judaism confronted great influential cultures, but his main evidence seems to have been drawn from the contemporary period. A group of brilliant young Jewish intellectuals, men like Rosenzweig, Buber, Brod, Scholem, and others who were steeped in modern Western civilization, brought the insights of that culture to bear on Jewish sources. Their marvelous creativity and the strong positive response which they evoked in the hearts of many young Jews who were stirred to a new interest in Judaism were, for Baeck, the beginning of fulfillment, more than proof that his hope was not an illusion. He was certain that this was only the beginning of a vast movement which would balance the bias of the first stage of Emancipation. Nor was he content to rely on spontaneity alone. He called for an organized program to be initiated and institutionalized for the enhancement and growth of the educational process. Baeck's contribution to this initiative was to shape a theory of Jewish religious education which would be suitable to the needs of the new era,[29] and to persevere in his role as rabbi and as an educator of rabbis.[30] He devoted his attention to the development and maintenance of a broad network of Jewish educational institutions in Germany which subsequently culminated in the impressive educational activity which he and his colleagues initiated after Hitler's rise to power.[31] Teaching and communal religious activities were in the forefront of these interests. As the leader of German Jewry, Baeck's policy emphasized two lines of action: to increase the emigration of young Jews from Germany, and to make Jews proud of their Jewishness by strengthening their feelings of belonging and identification with their heritage. He was proud of his achievements because — as against the persecution, slander and insults — he saw genuine signs of a recovery of Jewish self-respect, Jewish knowledge and Jewish commitment.

For Baeck, the recovery was not merely a temporary reaction to a contemptible anti-Semitic attack; it was the coherent continuation of an historical process which was motivated by a positive internal power — the love of Judaism for its sublime values, the love of the Jewish people for its sacred destiny. The anti-Semitic attack had accelerated the process, but that in itself was the indication of an inherent Jewish quality. These were the assumptions on which Baeck based his proposed educational theory. The goal was to provide the knowledge necessary for a Jewish individual to develop within himself feelings and qualities which would enable him to be fulfilled in his personal, familial and communal Jewish life, while fully participating in an open, modern society with its rich and attractive culture.[32] Baeck's reaction to anti-Jewish attitudes in German society was also marked by a combination of optimism and radicalism. As a scholar and a rabbi he addressed himself first and foremost to Christian theological anti-Jewish prejudices. Vulgar, racist anti-Semitism he considered too base to deserve a direct ideological refutation; this kind of vulgarity was the result of a growing nationalist prejudice developed as a form of substitute religion. He despised its dullness and narrow-mindedness. In the letter cited from 1925, it is already obvious that Baeck did not underrate the evolving danger. Even then he predicted an approaching hour of trial in which an act of martyrdom might be demanded from the Jews. Yet his basic optimism underlay his readiness to sanctify the Holy Name in the struggle. His optimism is clearly expressed in two themes which are reflected in his religious liberalism. First, Baeck saw Judaism as one of the trenchant, leading forces of European and German humanism in the fight against its enemies; therefore, he did not feel that the Jewish community had been cut off or separated from the positive elements of German society. In his view, Jews were the true representatives of the best in German society and culture, and they were not alone in their struggle.

This conviction never left him, not even during the darkest periods of oppressive Nazi rule. Even before the Nazi rise to power, Baeck was aware of the dangers which inhere in the tendency of the modern centralized state to rule over and overwhelm society. He saw this as a kind of idolatry of the state, dangerous not only for Judaism, but for religion as such, and — what seemed to be quite the same in Baeck's understanding of religion — to the ethical foundations of society.[33] This was the "rationale" of his struggle against nationalism in general — the source of Nazism and racist anti-Jewishness. Second, in spite of his awareness of the great danger, he considered it a passing sickness, the result of a pathological historical situation. He did not

23

allow such deviations from the general line of humanity's positive progress to darken his optimistic religious vision. The positive forces of society, even in Germany, always remain stronger and in the end overcome danger. In the darkest days of "Nazi terror" this firm conviction never left him. The term "Nazi terror," in itself, defines a situation in which a minority temporarily succeeds in conquering the positive majority by using instruments of tyranny. Even during those dark days, Baeck did not consider Nazism as an expression of something deeply rooted in German society; his struggle and the struggle of the Jewish community were the true expression of German society. Nothing captures this better than his proud answer to a Nazi official's question: How would Baeck explain the fact that hatred against Jews is so widespread? "When I leave your office," said Baeck, "the German citizens that I meet on my way will respond to me, as they usually do, with the greatest respect and sympathy. I do not think that your leader," he added, referring of course to Hitler, "can expect such a reception when he walks alone in the street."[34]

Nazi anti-Semitism ruled the hour, but for Baeck it did not represent the majority of German society. It is important to emphasize again what may now seem to be an almost incredible point of view for a Jewish leader of Baeck's stature under Nazi conditions: Baeck remained convinced that Emancipation had been crowned with success; this included the readiness of the German majority to accept the Jews as an integral part of society.[35] Precisely because of this optimistic evaluation, he believed that the sanctification of the Holy Name was, in that hour, the only adequate response to anti-Semitism. The Jew's response would be his testimony of truth, the redeeming truth for him as for all of humanity, in a public arena which encompasses all peoples.

It would appear that because he reacted to anti-Semitism in a general, humanist context, Baeck attached great importance to confronting the new Christian theology of his time. He was preoccupied with its renewal of anti-Jewish prejudices. He was alarmed by the fact it was just those progressive theologians who were trying to regain for Christianity its leading spiritual status in modern European culture that were trapped by such prejudices. This could, he felt, increase anti-Jewishness in German society. But Baeck was even more afraid of the effect of such intellectual-spiritual anti-Judaism on assimilated Jewish youth who knew almost nothing about Judaism from its own sources. They could therefore be further alienated from Judaism as they saw its unsympathetic reflection in the influential works of a theologian like Harnack. This was Baeck's main consideration, prompting a radical response which not only attempted to expose prejudices and clarify misconceptions, but engaged in a direct criticism of Christianity itself in order to reveal the source of its prejudice against Judaism. Nonetheless, Baeck's interest in a true dialogue with progressive Christianity should not be underrated. He believed that a frank exchange would be facilitated by a full and free articulation of views.[36]

It is well accepted that Baeck's entrance into the Jewish theological debate of his time was directly connected with a polemic response to modern Christian theology. His first book *The Essence of Judaism* evolved from a critical response to the way in which Judaism has been portrayed in Harnack's *The Essence of Christianity*.[37] Subsequently, this topic became a central component in Baeck's "repertoire," and he took it up again and again in a cycle of topics for scientific research as well as for direct polemic. Following World War II, Baeck was among the most important of the Jewish respondents engaged in the Christian-Jewish dialogue which opened against the background of the Holocaust.[38] This theme in Baeck's work has been thoroughly studied and clarified,[39] but some attention to its method and aim is useful here.

From the start Baeck opted for a strategy of criticism and not of defense, and, as noted, he was critical not only of Christian prejudices against Judaism, but of the source of such distortions within Christianity itself. He expounded a full critical evaluation of Christianity, on Jewish grounds, indicating the essential differences between the two religions, and trying to show that Judaism is closer to religious truth. But students of Baeck's work point to the fact that, in spite of his criticism, Baeck was influenced by Harnack's work. *The Essence of Judaism* was consciously developed as a Jewish analogy to the criticized Christian work, and the derivative name of the book openly admits to it.[40] Though the work is first and foremost an apologia-polemic, that does not exhaust its motivation. There was also a positive internal Jewish motivation which reflected more than Baeck's concern with Harnack's possible influence on assimilated Jewish intellectuals. More important than rejecting a false, alienating picture of Judaism, Baeck wanted the opportunity to offer a comprehensive picture of Judaism. Its style was meant to be attractive and compelling to an intelligent Jew, educated as a modern humanist. Baeck wanted

25

to achieve for his community just what Harnack wanted to achieve for his own. This complementary need of the other, for the sake of self-knowledge and self-identification, was the source of Harnack's impact on Baeck's thinking. More than he wanted to refute Harnack, Baeck wanted to compete with him. What had begun as a controversy continued as a dialogue based on a common denominator.

This is the secret behind the long process in the development and growth of Baeck's classical work, from edition to edition, to consummation in a final product several times larger than the original. Readers of the final edition will realize that the polemical impulse has been reduced to a minimum, while the thrust of positive educational motivation has come to the forefront. *The Essence of Judaism* has grown into a comprehensive portrayal of Judaism as a faith with a full set of values, a world outlook and a way of life for the individual and the community. The portrayal is such that it would appeal to the empathetic discernment of a modern, intelligent man of humanist background. Although this meant that the book reached a mainly liberal Jewish audience, it does not mean that Baeck had lost interest in the Jewish-Christian polemic. On the contrary, for him, as well as for his teacher Cohen and his colleagues Rosenzweig and Buber, there was a compelling connection between a return to authentic Jewish religiosity and a re-evaluation of Christianity, struggling as it was to regain its place in European culture. These two competing sisters were wrestling with each other in the same European womb. Neither could dismiss the other. Baeck repeatedly went back to the subject, advancing each time beyond what he had written in his first book. What catches the eye in the later phases of his polemic is that he developed a separate scholarly framework for the study of Christianity in its relation to Judaism, and that his criticism became even more radical as it became more intimate and subtle.

From this point of view, there is a significant difference between Baeck and Rosenzweig. In his highly acclaimed study, "Romantic Religion,"[41] Baeck returned to Hermann Cohen's position, but on a much broader basis of historical research. Using his own phenomenological method, Baeck strived to achieve an empathetic criticism. He tried to grasp the inner spiritual experience of the Christian believer in order to articulate it in terms of its own structure, according to its own logic. In doing so he never forgot his own classical Jewish conviction, which was expressed in a definition through negation. Through his empathetic understanding of the other,

26

he reassessed his empathetic understanding of himself as a Jew. A dialectical progression is at work here. It is clear that the more he understood himself through the other, the more he became critical of the other. Consequently, the more assured he became of his criticism of the other, through the employment of himself as a mirror, the more assured he became of his better understanding of the other, better indeed than the other could understand himself. In the final phase of this subtle process it must dawn upon the reader, even if he is a Christian, that Judaism, identified as the "classical religion," is, according to Baeck, much superior to Christianity from the ethical, anthropological, political and social points of view.

> The classical religion pushes again and again, always, towards the transcendental aim, in which all will be united, and it draws the commandment from God. These are two sides of the same coin, because every future we really have is the future of the commandment, the future of fulfillment and duration. In this the Romantic religion and the Classic religion differ from each other in the clearest way.[42]

The last sentence is also the critical conclusion: Christianity as a Romantic religion is the opposite of Judaism from the point of view of the commitment to the "future of the commandment," which means the commitment to fulfill the ethical commandments in our earthly existence. With the aid of a phantasmic poetry and imagination, which is characteristic of the Romantic mentality, Christianity, according to Baeck, is devoted to a miraculous past which it has raised to the level of eternity. It thus inspires its believers with an elevating aesthetic experience, instead of committing them to the ethical commandment which they should try to fulfill here and now. Attractive as this may seem, it is merely a kind of individualistic-egoistic self-fulfillment.

Baeck's striving for empathetic understanding through self-exposition of the other was, however, an honest effort to achieve a dialogue beyond polemics. How? Through the hope that the two debating opponents would achieve self-understanding not only in each other's reflection but also by finding something of themselves in the other. For this purpose, Baeck recognized in Christianity an authentic, and even vital, development of Jewish religiosity. He attached a great deal of importance not only to the fact that Christianity was born out of Judaism, but to a second fact which he observed and studied, that Judaism had been continued, authentically, within Christianity.

> It is possible to discuss the history of Jewish ideas in two realms. These ideas lived and developed, flourished and faded, became sometimes fertile and sometimes barren, within Judaism itself, and in the same manner they were also present outside the Jewish realm, in the great world of ideas. In this world too the Jewish ideas were vital, like ferment, they were influential in a quite significant measure. For even in this world these ideas created and defined changing periods. In this sense there exists beside the Jewish history a general history of Judaism.[43]

This is an opening passage of "Judaism in the Church," an article published immediately after the previously discussed article in Baeck's studies, obviously as its complement. In fact, this was only the beginning of a fruitful project which Baeck developed to uncover the extent of Jewish influence within Christianity. Baeck's exposition highlighted the permanent struggle inside the Christian churches between the Paulinean elements, which alienated Christianity from its Jewish sources, and the remaining elements of Jesus's original ideas, which were, according to Baeck, typical Pharisaic ideas. Believable or not, Baeck was able to uncover even in Paul's writings evidence of an on-going struggle between the Pharisaic foundation which Paul was unable to uproot from his Jewish soul, and the "Romantic" revolution which Paul had initiated.[44]

In the process of such studies Baeck seemed to take upon himself a "mission" — in the evangelical sense — to rediscover, for the sake of a consciously alienated Christianity, Christian sources in Judaism and its continuous attachment to Jewish history. Was this to bring Christianity back to its authentic origins? Perhaps it was to bridge the gap between Judaism and Christianity? Or perhaps it was to find a way by which Judaism would be able to fulfill its universalist mission in humanity through Christianity, yet without being separated from its own particularist national sphere? Baeck preached his historical lessons in the framework of a dialogue rooted in a growing reciprocal interest on both sides, each out of its own interests. He was not challenged to declare his goal, nor did he seem anxious to offer an explanation. He may have assumed that the interchange of ideas would achieve a certain good. But alongside all these possibilities one can observe an obvious aim common to both Judaism and Christianity; in that historic hour it was this aim that was most important for Baeck as a Jew in the alienated German milieu. One need take notice of only the first example which Baeck offered to substantiate his thesis on the influence of Judaism in the general world of ideas with regard to the modern "social movement."

According to Baeck there are two sources for this movement: the first was Plato's political philosophy, the second was the Bible, especially the prophetic ideal of social justice. The first source led in the direction of the centrality of the state and the dictatorship of the so-called "General Will." The second source pointed to the idea which "does not emanate from the state, but from individual human beings, from the idea of solidarity, from the love of your neighbor."[45] It appears that Baeck's first example of a Jewish ethical influence in Christianity indicates a task which Judaism and Christianity have in common — the struggle against the growing danger of the idolatrous pagan state.

Baeck indeed returned to Hermann Cohen's critical stance toward Christianity, a stance originally characteristic of the founding fathers of Liberal Judaism.[46] At the same time, he strived to reassess the idea of a uniquely Jewish universal mission, without giving up the national dimensions of Jewish particularity in the differentiated historical cycle of the Jewish people.[47] This way he could admit the important particularistic mission of Christianity for the nations that came under its influence. On the other hand and as a complement, he sought commonly held ethical-religious interests in the struggle for political and social justice in Europe against the towering dangers of totalitarianism. From his point of view, this could solve the problem of relationships between Judaism and Christianity.

In dealing with Baeck's response to the third challenge, it is necessary to distinguish between his marginal, measured response to Marxist Socialism within the Jewish sphere and his highly value-laden, pivotal response to Zionism. Baeck's negative attitude toward Marxism has already been noted. Obviously he could not see a solution to the existential problems of the Jewish people in its materialistic philosophy, certainly not in its radical rejection of religion nor in its German nationalist-like expansion into a kind of substitute religion. The only form of socialism which he could adopt was of the idealistic "utopian" kind, such as Moses Hess's,[48] or

Hermann Cohen's and Martin Buber's, which were consciously attuned to the biblical ideal of social justice. This positive response to socialism, derived from Jewish sources, was integrated into his somewhat complicated relationship to Zionism.

As a young rabbi, Baeck deviated from the anti-Zionist stance of his liberal movement. Though he did not identify himself as a Zionist, he was far from relating to Zionism as a "heresy" against the spiritual essence of Judaism, or against its universalist mission. On the contrary, he considered Zionism a legitimate Jewish view which should be endured even within the framework of the Liberal movement.[49] He assumed that a true liberalism should be capable of this minimum of tolerance. His own quality of tolerance was much warmer, rooted in an emotional predisposition which favored the traditional, folk-emotional dimension in Judaism and its strong emotional attachment to the Land of Israel. This was an attitude he had known in his home, and the Seminary in Breslau could only be affirmative about such traditional attitudes. But gradually Baeck's ideological and practical relationship grew more positive, stronger and more open. Various elements played a role in this process — love of the Land of Israel, sympathy toward "spiritual Zionism," and a favorable attitude toward the socialist-idealist stream of Zionism. But Baeck appears to have gone much further in reconsidering the practical arguments of political Zionism, that the Jewish people needed a political, territorial home. After Hitler's rise to power, this notion turned into a firm conviction. In a short oration at the grave of Trude Herzl, who died in Theresienstadt, Baeck said, "If we had listened to the words of the father of this unfortunate woman, we would not all be here today."[50] Baeck participated in Zionist activity and had close connections with Zionist world leadership even before Hitler's rise to power. After the war he expressed the warmest self-identification with the State of Israel. While it may be claimed that he was *also* a Zionist, it would be a gross exaggeration to say that Zionism defined his Jewish world view. Baeck remained faithful to Jewish religious liberalism, but his version of religious liberalism was wide enough and sufficiently pluralistic to encompass the spiritual components of cultural and social Zionism, of Judaism as a complete culture,[51] and political Zionism as a practical necessity. The various trends which struggled one against the other and which seemed to their radical exponents as mutually exclusive, could find their partial resolution in Baeck's holistic Jewish world view.

This touches on his response to the fourth challenge — the dangerous dichotomies which appeared within the Jewish people. If in his approach to the European environment, Baeck was searching for an operative definition which would maintain a balance between the particularist, separate existence of the Jewish people and its full integration into society, then in his attitude toward trends within the Jewish people, Baeck searched for the most open, the broadest and most flexible definition. He sought a definition which could tolerate the spectrum of positive approaches to Jewish life and the diversity of opinions which had been created in the ancient as well as the recent past. It may be said that this was simply a wise, pragmatic policy on the part of a Jewish "ecumenical" leader who took upon himself the responsibility of unifying his people in one of its darkest hours. But in Baeck's case, the fact that it was he who was called to the task is an indication of his acknowledged stance and position. Had he not been known as a great unifier who might be acceptable to a profusion of antagonistic parties within German Jewry, he would not have been approached. For Baeck it was more than merely a wise political post or a practical necessity. It was the outcome of a firmly based holistic Jewish philosophy which was rooted in Jewish religious liberalism and which embodied pragmatic and ideological elements from all of the positive Jewish movements, without relinquishing a selective critical approach or surrendering the integrity and consistency of a harmonious world view.

This is a good starting point for understanding Baeck, the Jewish theologian, in the period following the publication of the first edition of his book, *The Essence of Judaism.* His scholarly studies show most convincingly that he was influenced by Hermann Cohen's conceptual work and Dilthey's methodology. But has it nothing to do with his initial inclinations? In his lecture on "Changes in Jewish Outlook,"[52] Baeck argued that the choice of influences from surrounding cultures was not a matter of chance or fate. There is some existential truth to the idea that such choice is influenced by a previously held inner conviction of the recipient, who is choosing, consciously or not, only what suits him. Accordingly, it would not seem to be distorting biographical evidence to claim that Baeck actively chose those teachers who responded positively to his expectations, and supplied him with the necessary tools and content for his own aims. Dilthey's modern methodology seemed to be ideally adapted to the *traditional interpretative* task which Baeck took upon himself: to develop an interpretative reaffirmation of religious truth which would be drawn from all the traditional sources which had been accepted by the Jewish people as authoritative and binding throughout the generations.

This was indeed the approach of those great Jewish thinkers whose creative works have been included in the continuous chain of Jewish sources. The classical status accorded to Baeck's book almost as it first appeared, like the classical status of Krochmal's *The Guide for the Perplexed of our Time,* or Cohen's *Religion of Reason from the Sources of Judaism,* was achieved not because of methodological innovation as such, but for the successful attempt to renew an old tradition. An evaluative sentence is in order here: Baeck both wished to and succeeded in remaining faithful to Jewish traditional sources far more than did his modern predecessors. Both Krochmal and Cohen were consciously making selections from the historical compound of the whole of traditional sources, so as to create a much narrower "representation," which exactly suited their *a priori* philosophical expectations. Baeck really referred to the totality as it was transmitted by Jewish history, a totality which he first tried to comprehend by using his scientific philological and phenomenological tools; only afterward did he attempt to integrate a compound pluralist message through his own modern philosophical interpretation. In fact, for purposes of this holistic aim, he could not have found a better methodology than that suggested by Dilthey.

Of course, Baeck had his own preestablished assumptions, but these were quite in tune with the assumptions which unified the historical Jewish religious tradition as such. He assumed that Judaism had been established by Divine revelation which was incorporated in the teachings and the commandments of Torah. He assumed that this Torah unified the people of Israel as a nation and guided the history of the nation at all levels and in all realms, individual and collective. The continuous response of the people to the commands of God created a continuous chain of sources which is contained in the concept of the Oral Torah. This is a process which is renewed from generation to generation through the instrumentality of great teachers, prophets, priests and sages. This is the source of the unified diversity and the ever-changing stability which characterizes the teachings of Judaism throughout the generations. As the revelation of the will of God, the teachings of Judaism are intended as an eternal word of truth and justice for all humanity, and therefore their fulfillment serves a universal destiny. However, from the aspect of its particular relatedness to the Jewish people, the Torah must be considered as idiosyncratic, the singular characteristic expression of the life of the Jewish people. Therefore the Torah protects the separate, particular existence of the Jewish people as well as its positive openness to humanity. By cultivating the fullness of its particular religious culture, the Jewish people is fulfilling its universal destiny. It does so first in its own milieu, within the containing borders of a separate existence. But in tandem with this, through its particular achievements as an ideal model, the Jewish people also influences its surroundings.

These basic assumptions present Judaism as a continuous dynamic process motivated by an internal force which is generated from a complex set of tensions: the tension between the transcendental absolute Divine command and the willed response of a living people; the tension between a universal destiny and a commitment to a certain particularistic historical entity; the tension between changing needs in different times and different places, and the commitment to eternal truth. These tensions generate an infinite diversity which is multiplied and renewed from generation to generation. They are manifested in many contradictions and dichotomies in the historic life of the people. But as the source of this diversity is a pre-established unity, all of the partial movements in Israel carry with them the urgent expectation of a transcendental unity which is symbolized by the messianic vision. Here again there is a significant difference between Baeck, and between Krochmal and Cohen. Baeck's closeness to the traditional approach is also manifested in his understanding that the unity of the Jewish ideal is not achieved through an abstract dialectical synthesis. Such a synthesis would not be historical since it could only be achieved through the elimination of all contradictions and through the "elevation" of the human mind to a "pure" abstract level of intellectuality. Baeck, in fact, did not even try to nullify the contradictions or to "solve" them. They persist, though they are always changing, and they are unified because they meet in the historical reality of a people committed both to life under actual historical conditions and on various levels of social existence, and to the ideal vision of unity. Thus, according to Baeck, one may present different and even contradictory opinions, ideals and values which are inherent in the spiritual creativity of the people, as different "attributes" of the same "substance," each attribute being justified in its own realm and for its own function. Therefore the real historic tension in which these attributes clash, restraining each other and putting each other into a proper balance, is actually the on-going process of unification in which there is a striving for harmony, but not for abstract unity, as a final outcome. And, from time to time, this is indeed achieved in the best intellectual achievements of Jewish thought.

These reformulated traditional assumptions served as an infra-structure in Baeck's ambitious attempt to achieve a comprehensive unity and continuity with which to overcome the external dangers and the internal fractures which rent the Jewish people as they stood at the fateful and historic crossroads in the beginning of the twenti-eth century.

How did this conception of Judaism fit into the general Jewish map of philosophical or ideological positions which had been formu-lated in the first half of the twentieth century? At least at the beginning of the period, within the context of his own movement, Baeck appeared to have a singular, even extraordinary stance.[53] He clearly deviated from his movement's established ideology toward Zionism, as well as toward other Jewish religious movements. However, in the broader arena of Jewish ideologies and philoso-phies, he does not appear to stand alone but has a place within a recognizable group of singular personalities who are not dogmati-cally identified with the ideologies of their various parties or move-ments because they bear responsibility to the whole Jewish people.

It is a very significant phenomenon because in almost all the major movements we can discover influential individuals who diverged from the bias of an established dogma toward a more flexible "middle" stance. Such a stance may have related more positively toward rival movements, or even in the direction of a tolerant holistic approach seeking a "center" around which it would be possible to unify the people. Perhaps with the exception of the Marxist left,[54] this may be described as a general tendency. In Orthodoxy, one may point to Dr. N. Birnbaum, Rabbi N. Nobel, and, from a certain perspective, even to Dr. I. Breuer. In religious Zionism, names that come to the fore are Rabbi I.J. Reines, Rabbi A.I. Kook and Rabbi Ch. Hirschensohn; in the "spiritual" stream of Zionism there are such personalities as Ahad Haam, Ch.N. Bialik and A.D. Gordon. The Conservative movement, from its establishment, opted for a respectable place in the middle; this was also true regarding its response to Zionism.

34

From The Essence of Judaism *to* This People Israel

Looking at the map of established Jewish movements in the diaspora and in Palestine we can discern a clear tendency toward the radical polarization of movements. However, as against this tendency we can clearly discern an unorganized reaction of some responsible and very influential individual leaders who were moving in the opposite direction, striving to guard against the collapse of the unifying center. These great individual thinkers who consciously transcended the boundaries of their respective movements were deeply committed to the unity of the Jewish people. At the same time it was typical of most of them that they were unwilling to achieve their goals through pragmatic, political compromise. On the contrary, they considered themselves radical thinkers striving for a consequential, integral philosophy which would be broad enough to embrace in its holistic system the composite, diversified totality of Jewish world views. If Baeck's views were to be compared to those of any of the aforementioned thinkers, there is no doubt that significant and substantial differences would be apparent between them. Each of these intellectuals drew from different sources; they used different methods; each had his personal philosophy. It is highly unlikely that they were directly influenced by each other. In some cases, it cannot even be assumed that they really knew much about each other or carefully read each other's writings. Taking Baeck as an example, one cannot detect in his work the influence of any of the intellectuals noted above, with the single exception of Rabbi N. Nobel.[55] There is no sign in Rabbi Kook's writings to indicate that he may have read any of Baeck's books. The same can be said about the reading of Rabbi Kook's works by Rabbi Baeck. This, paradoxically, is in itself an indication of the fundamental similarity and closeness between them; each of them having developed from his own individual background, together reflect the typical results of creative tension in Jewish public life.

What, then, are the elements which make up the common denominator between these remarkable individuals? We can summarize it in the following propositions:

1) A conscious attempt to present Judaism as a broad, comprehensive, dynamic totality which unifies within itself a rich and compound diversity, a fullness which may be expressed in many ways on various levels. This diversity is considered as an expression of a basic dynamic unity; real contrasts and contradictions are not hidden, nor is there an attempt to blur them. On the contrary, each of these thinkers endeavors to overcome dichotomies by means of a full

assessment of the truth contained in each ideal, philosophy or ideology as clearly expressed by significant Jewish thinkers. There are deep conflicts, but this does not disturb the acceptance of contrasts as parts of a unified whole which is expected to be achieved through a higher, more comprehensive truth. This truth, once revealed, will define the exact, positive place for each opinion in the construction of a whole structure.

2) An assumption that the unity and fullness of Jewish ideas and values is a compound which is grounded in a living, creative subject. This compound is composed of the Jewish individual and the Jewish people, their modes of behavior, lifestyles, emotions, characteristic ways of thinking, and historic fate. In its origin, Judaism is a concrete, living unity, not an abstract idea.

3) An assumption that the compound, which is full of tensions and contradictions, is unified within the Jewish people, by the force of an "organic" identity in which two elements complement and restrain each other: religious faith and national consciousness. These elements are considered to be two aspects, or attributes, of the selfsame living entity. As with body and soul, they cannot be separated from each other since neither can be reduced into the other. The destruction of the soul is the destruction of the body and vice versa, yet each needs its own resources and conditions. Which is to say that these "unifying" intellectual leaders are either religious thinkers who are fully conscious and appreciative of their national affinity, or national thinkers who are deeply attached to the Jewish religious inheritance, at least as an original cultural resource. There is an awareness that complete detachment from either of these elements means that the code which enables a dialogue with the other parties would be lost. Furthermore, though the leaders understand national identity in organic, spiritual terms and not in political terms, this must not mean that they reject a political framework. Most of them recognized its importance but perceived it as a necessary tool or external expression rather than an originating force.

This approach tends to formulate its teachings in a variation which may be defined under the title of "National Theology."[56] The definition is created by the writer of this essay as a scholarly category; it does not emanate from within the conceptualized systems themselves. Although none of the intellectuals mentioned above identified himself in this category, the term does not refer to marginal or eccentric thinkers. On the contrary, the reference is actually to a central phenomenon, rooted in the constitutive ancient sources. Included among its first exponents in the modern era are some of the most influential Jewish philosophers of the nineteenth century, such as Rabbi Nahman Krochmal, his son Abraham Krochmal and other leaders of East European Jewish Enlightenment, who considered themselves disciples of Spinoza. Coming from another direction, there were thinkers quite close to the Conservative movement, such as Moses Hess and his East European disciple, Perez Smolenskin. A detailed analysis of this stream would be too far removed from the focus of this study, but it is necessary to examine the essential components which justify the term.

The term "National Theology" includes a variety of theological teachings whose direct interest is centered not in the Divine as a transcendental entity, not even in the fundamental categories of creation, revelation, etc., which determine the relationship between God, world and humanity, but concentrate on the Jewish people, its attributes, historical destiny and creativity. They not only consider the Jews the chosen people, but also the outstanding, unique incorporation of Divine revelation within humanity. Let us emphasize that this body of theologies does not regard Judaism as a transcendental "idea" or an abstract conceptual system, but as a concrete historical entity: a people whose inherent "organic" qualities express themselves in its unique mode of faith and religion, and, to emphasize again, whose originating national qualities are adjudged to be earlier and more important than temporal, changing ideational expressions.

Such an understanding of Judaism suggests an option with which to explain the contradictions and divisions in the differing conceptions of Judaism. It accepts diversity and even dichotomy as legitimate manifestations of one and the same generative spiritual quality which was revealed from period to period in different conditions, in various realms or in the unique individualized setting of each personality or group. Indeed, once this "secret" of unity behind apparently extreme dichotomies is discovered, a hope of recovery is gained — first by a thorough historical understanding of the specific cause of each development in Jewish life, then by the employment of the internal unifying code in a process of educational dialogue. Through this kind of therapeutic thinking, all the fractures in Jewish life and thinking can be healed.

Can Baeck's teachings be placed under this title? If reference is restricted to the name of his first *magnum opus, The Essence of*

Judaism, the probable answer is "No." But a careful, empathetic reading even of that book will confirm that the name, adapted as a polemical device from the criticized book *The Essence of Christianity,* is not an accurate indication of its contents. One of the main differentiations between the "essence" of Judaism and the "essence" of Christianity, as Baeck interprets them, is that Judaism has no Church and no dogma.[57] It is not a creed in the Christian sense because it belongs to a living people and it flows through the fullness of their creative life, personalities, families and congregations. In his first book, Baeck had already described Judaism as a manifestation of the life of a whole people devoted to God. In his studies and theological papers which followed publication of *The Essence of Judaism,* Baeck continued to develop this conception until its culmination in his second *magnum opus,* which bears the similar yet distinct name, *This People Israel,* a fact which cannot be incidental.

Let us now observe the fact that the thinking process which began with *The Essence* and concluded with *This People* occurred precisely at the time when Baeck was struggling as a Jewish leader in the evolving Holocaust. This is an indication of the claim that emotional and ideational reactions to the fate of his people were being silently incorporated into Baeck's developing thinking process. But in order to substantiate this assumption, it is important to detect and analyze the changes in Baeck's thinking and the focus of his spiritual interest during the period.

Indeed, it is not an easy task. We assume that Baeck's writings on scholarly topics and spiritual issues of the day reflected the impact of events and changing existential conditions. But, factually, he wrote without referring directly to what was occurring in the background. In part it may have been the necessary result of political conditions: Baeck could not, of course, express himself freely. But it might also be explained by his subjective feeling that he was only developing his former views. Be that as it may, the consequence is that we must detect the changes through comparisons both to his former views and to the analogous development in the views of similar spiritual leaders during the evolving events. In order to gain the needed perspective we will start with the second comparison.

As we stated in the introductory essay, it was only "human, too human" that the first personal reactions to the shocking events were rooted in long established world outlooks, philosophies or ideologies based on past experiences. Not surprisingly, this was even truer

38

of the first organizational reactions. Yet, even as observers from a distant perspective and after the event, it is hard to imagine such extraordinary responses. It seems somehow to contradict our expectations that events which evidently exploded every former prediction could, nonetheless, evoke such hard dogmatic reactions. As it appears now, the reactions reflected a stubborn refusal to recognize any deviation from previous ideological predictions, expectations or historical explanations. Reading such ideological reactions with empathy, one may discern within them a shade of self-defense: the events are indeed amazing in their unbelievable cruelty. They seem to be lacking any rational explanation. However, if we examine them carefully, if we refrain from being too disturbed by emotion, we should arrive at the reassuring understanding that this is what we should have been expecting. Our scientifically-based ideology did not let us down, so we may trust in our hope that after this calamity is over, the expected historical redemption will come. Indeed such dogmatic reaffirmations rightly provoke the suspicion that they only masked an anguished frustration and growing doubts. Nevertheless it would be an exaggeration to describe such reactions as simply conscious or unconscious attempts to hide from an "unacceptable" reality. Among those who reacted in this way were many who were courageous in facing up to what they saw, at least to some degree. And in certain cases the reaffirmation of a formerly held ideological position served as a source of courage to look directly into the eye of the approaching catastrophe. The real motivation was different, and it was openly expressed. If one really understands the necessity to face such threatening events and remains strong enough to fight for survival, one will need to draw much sustenance from the future. Without hope, the individual will quickly be broken. People who respond out of a healthy will to live, look beyond the greatest threat for hope, and the greater the observed threat, the greater is the hope required. But in order to get a loan of hope from the storehouse of the future, one needs guarantees from the past. A reliable hope must be based on a certain historical continuation, on a certain knowledge of the necessary, the possible and the probable in history. In other words, one must bridge the sudden gap between the past and the future if one wants to cross with any hope of survival. For this, a reassuring ideology is like air to the lungs. The stability of the individual's outlook, his ideology or philosophy becomes the ground for his hope, for his personal continuity, even for the protection of his self-identity and his sense of belonging. If, in the moment of crisis, he gives up the particular sustaining truth by which he lived yesterday, he will lose not only his orientation and hope, but also the basis for his personal identity. This would signify a total personal collapse.

This manner of thinking may be stated as characteristic of the thoughtful reactions which were documented in Jewish underground periodicals from 1939 onward, especially in Poland. Every party or movement — the Communists, the Bundists, the Left Poalei Zion, Hashomer Hatzair, Dror, Gordonia, Akiva and the Revisionists — had its own cherished ideology, and each defended it in the same measure of nervous dogmatism. The same may be said of the reactions reflected in the papers from Ringelblum Archive[58] and in various documents published during the first years after the Holocaust.

The personal diaries which chronicle the moods and spontaneous reactions of private people are naturally more flexible and less devout in their dogmatism, yet even there, a certain tendency in this direction is to be found. One wished to explain away Fascism and Nazism, the outbreak of the war, and the fate of the Jews under Nazi conquest as the unavoidable fulfillment of former scientific predictions based on firm laws of history. One needs the trust that these are the days of the "final battle" in the war between Capitalism and Labor. The reactionary powers are enlisting all of their resources to save their doomed regimes. Their cruel ferocity is a clear sign of their desperation. It is their last attempt to hold power. Which means that they are doomed. Humanity, and the Jewish people as part of it, will still have much to suffer, but the dawn of a new day is not too far off. In some papers we can even find a self-righteous polemic motif. The cruel events seemed to supply the opportunity to close accounts with "reformists" and other deviators from Orthodox Marxism, Marxist-Leninism or Marxist-Trotskyism, or Borochovism. It proved that those who believed that there was an evolutionary way to save humanity from the tragic but unavoidable atrocities of revolution were all wrong. Which means precisely that the classical radical theories were perfectly true. And as this part of the theory has proved to be correct, so the other predicted developments will shortly come true. After the war, we will witness the fulfillment of the Communist [or the Socialist] [or the Zionist-Socialist] vision. We must overcome this passing moment of hardship and prepare ourselves by self-education, study and ideological profound thought, and by doing whatever is possible for survival, for the sake of the constructive task which will soon be demanded of us to be fulfilled when the war is over.

In Gordonia, the war and the fate of the Jewish people in the war was considered to be an assessment of Gordon's insights on the fate of modern humanity and its shortcomings, and on the nature of exile. In the Akiva movement, events evoked the need to draw spiritual sustenance from the historic Jewish national memory and from the spiritual legacy of the nation. Bialik's poetry and Bialik's views on the nature of Jewish national education were studied as sources of consolation and faith in the eternity of the Jewish people. The main theme in their movement's reaction is that we must learn from our fathers and forefathers how they drew strength and hope from the darkest catastrophes, because this indicates a source of inner power which must prevail, as it has always prevailed. We should know that this is not the first time that we face extraordinary hatred against us. We know that we are strong enough to overcome it, as we have always done. The messianic hope, which expresses the power of our will to live, is the secret of our eternity. Let us live by it.

In the Revisionist movement, events seemed to affirm the worst predictions of their great leader, Z. Jabotinsky, who loudly rang the bells of alarm and preached his version of Zionism as an immediate solution against the catastrophe that was so close upon the people. His words came true, therefore, we may rely on his prediction that after the war historical conditions will be ripe for the establishment of a Jewish state.

Religious responses — fundamentalist, Orthodox and Zionist-Orthodox — can be followed from the small quantity of direct documentation that is available[59] and from the abundant collection of testimonies, memories and tales which have recently been published.[60] The picture appears to be a similar one. The extreme fundamentalist trend interpreted the events as clear signs of Divine wrath, a punishment for the sins of atheism, assimilationism, Zionism, Reform, etc. Religious ideology was thus affirmed in overflowing measure, with Divine punishment pouring forth not on the sinners alone. On the other hand, Zionist Orthodoxy could affirm the opposite ideological stance: the Jewish people failed to realize in time God's demand to quit Exile through a national initiative. Perhaps that is why God is hiding His countenance from His people, and lets the enemy pour out his beastly enmity. In fact most Orthodox thinkers

41

considered the events a result of the "natural," eternal hatred of the idolatrous peoples against Israel, the chosen people, while God was absenting himself. It meant that the hour for the sanctification of the Holy Name had recurred, the same old story. At the same time, events were interpreted as the last catastrophic stage of the messianic process: as events have exceeded any remembered persecution, it must be the End, the birth pains of the Messiah, the war of Gog and Magog. This means that after the war we are sure to be redeemed, and this time — forever. Indeed, there are many testimonies which affirm a wide, popular mood of messianic expectation, especially in Hassidic and other fundamentalist circles.[61]

It is obvious that all these "apocalyptic" understandings of the event were based on a refusal to grasp the full bitter truth that the Nazis aimed at complete annihilation. Only toward the end could the Nazi intention to exterminate the Jewish people, to the last Jew, no longer be hidden by deceit from the Nazi side, and illusion from the Jewish side. Clearly the extraordinary dimensions of the Holocaust were not only quantitative but indicated a phenomenon of a different category, not comparable to former catastrophes in Jewish history. Only then did there occur in the thinking of some individuals, mostly from the younger generation, an ideological revolution. To be exact, even they did not fully reject the ideologies in which they had been educated and with which they were spiritually identified. These were their religion, their source of faith and hope. They remained devoted to the values and visions, but they felt strongly that they would not be able to save their faith without a profound change in the analysis of the historic process as it was being acted out and without a new, competent understanding of the practical conclusions needed to come to grips with reality. It was a revolution within existing ideological frameworks in an effort to reshape them as guiding truths which would be valid for the contemporary historical experience.[62]

In reviewing Baeck's first direct reaction to the Nazi rise to power and the initial anti-Jewish activities, it appears clear that he behaved according to the same pattern. First and foremost, he felt the need to reaffirm his religious and ethical Jewish convictions so as to make sure that nothing the Nazis did could put his faith in question. His convictions were, for him, a source of enduring hope with which the persecuted Jewish community could withstand its present trial. To the extent that the sober realism of his historical understanding allowed him to, he assessed the situation. The better he was able to analyze and evaluate reality by using his pre-established intellectual models, the better he could reaffirm his hopes in spite of the worst occurrences. And vice versa, on the basis of his hopeful historical outlook, he could allow himself a sober, realistic understanding of the situation, at least within a certain limit.

This relationship between hope and realism which derived from the satisfactory use of previously forged intellectual tools, characterized Baeck's reaction to evolving events until the end of the war, and after it. It did not change even in Theresienstadt. He projected the same level of realism grounded in hope, and hope grounded in realism, which he could afford without completely breaking down the grounds for hope. Furthermore, even the content of his reactions seems to belong to one of the previously described ideological patterns.

Reference has been made to the development of a certain type of "National Theology" in religious and Jewish cultural thought at the beginning of the twentieth century. As with other ideologies and world views, this one too was devoutly reaffirmed in the struggle to cope with the growing threat. Especially in the work of poets and artists responding to the Holocaust on an existential-emotional level, beyond ideology or theology, this was the extant approach. Poets, who were able to respond creatively to the Holocaust, used a variety of national theological metaphors and symbols. This was true for those like Y. Kazenelson and A. Suzkower, who were the victims of Nazi rule, as it was for those who watched empathetically from afar, like Uri Zvi Greenberg, A. Shlonsky and J. Fichman. There were also a number of distinguished thinkers who opted for this kind of poetic-existentialism. Especially interesting is the change that took place in the thinking of some Zionist writers and publicists. Some had formerly been radical exponents of the "negation of the exile" theory, complete with its bitter criticism of the Jewish people and its "pretended" image as a chosen people. Against the frightening light of burning townlets in Eastern Europe, such thinkers as I. Demiel (Schweiger), A. Kariv, D. Sadan and E. Steinmann paused in remorse. Suddenly they had rediscovered the traditional vision of grandeur of the eternal chosen victim, crucified at every historic crossroad. A similar process can be seen in Central and East European Jewish thinkers. There is a heart-felt "return," after 1933, reflected in the teachings of such prominent personalities as N. Birnbaum,[63] and of H. Zeitlin, who was murdered in Treblinka.[64] An ideological reaction in the periodical of the Akiva movement was inspired by Bialik's poetry; indeed the similarity to Baeck's religious response seems to be instructive here.

But the closest analogy is to be found in the highly articulated response of the Hebrew-Yiddish writer, Zelig Kalmanowitz from Vilna: as the analogy seems to be extremely instructive, we think it suitable to bring his words in full:

A year ago certain intellectual groups in the Ghetto were much concerned with the problem of what is a Jew? or who is a Jew? This problem disturbed everyone tremendously. Formerly only a few were interested in such questions. Everyone felt that he was a Jew, some more, some less, and there were those who did not feel anything at all, and if there were some who suffered from their Jewishness, they managed to find their therapy in their own private way; generally they preferred to be engaged in other, more practical topics, rather than deal in such "abstract" matters. But now these people have been persecuted, expelled and pushed forcefully into the narrow quarters of the Ghetto. People who spoke different languages, were educated in different cultures, possessed different interests and beliefs, different hopes and wishes — sometimes even in opposition to one another — found themselves assembled under the same rubric: Jews [they would hasten as if to be punished].

Which means that they had sinned, and that their sin is that they are Jewish. Indeed many of them did not know what to say concerning their "sin." They did not know what it meant "to be a Jew." We must be honest and say, all these thoughts and soul-searching efforts were invalid. There was no way to find a clear, unrefutable answer to the question "Who is a Jew?" in our time. This is because only recently, in our generations, in the last 150 years, has the term Jew become so ambiguous. Formerly the term Jew was a clear, well-defined concept. A Jew was a person who observed his Jewishness (the commandments of his religion) and belonged to the Jewish collective. Now many people are recognized as Jews, by themselves and by others, who are of various types, including people for whom the Jewish religion is completely unimportant, who know nothing about it.

Yet even in such instances, I have received an answer to the question "Who is a Jew?" from one of the children of the Ghetto. Out of the mouths of babes and sucklings these issues are reaffirmed. One teacher of religion in the Ghetto school told me a tale from his own experience. In his class are children for whom Jews are complete strangers. Neither in their homes nor in their schools nor in the street did these children ever hear anything about the Jewish past, about Judaism (the Jewish religion). Now in the Ghetto many of these children are listening with interest to tales from the ancient and holy history, and from the Pentateuch. One of these children, who had been educated in a Polish school and spoke Polish in his home, began to study the tales of the Pentateuch. When they read about the story of Jacob and Esau in the weekly portion of "Toldot," this child suddenly opened his mouth and said, "Teacher, we are the descendants of Jacob, while *they* (those who are persecuting us) are the descendants of Esau, isn't that so? Good. I want to belong to Jacob and not to Esau."

I thought about the story of this child and came to the conclusion that I can use it as the basis for a method to determine who is a Jew. The human imagination is free, no wall can block it. A man in the Ghetto imagines that he is offered an alternative. He will be permitted to take off his depressed and beaten Jewish "self" and take on the "self" of the Ghetto's ruler. I pose the question: What would he choose? How would he behave? If he is willing to change, and willingly take on the image of the ruler, then we may assume that he is not a Jew. On the other hand, if he chooses out of his own free will to remain a Jew, then he is a Jew. And if I may continue my thoughts, the Jewish child has instinctively chosen to be a Jew. He feels himself naturally at home among Jews. I am thinking of a grown man; if he freely chooses to be a Jew, will he share the same instinctive feeling as a sufficient reason, or will he need intellectual considerations? I answer this question in the affirmative.

Be that as it may, to be a Jew always means to be on an elevated level. The hardships and the sufferings which are heaped on the Jews have reason and meaning. These harassments are not for nothing; therefore they cannot demean the Jew. The Jew is part of a three-fold unity: Israel, the Torah and the Holy Blessed One; that is, the Jewish people, the ethical law, and the Creator of the world. This triple unity exists. It is active in history. It is a reality which has withstood countless tests, and has been proved convincingly. Our fathers were devoted to this unity and lived by its strength. And even today, the Jew who cannot clasp this triple unity is to be pitied; he is wandering in a world of emptiness, he is suffering and cannot find meaning in his suffering. He can of course detach himself from the people, that is, he can wish for a change of his "self." But the Jew whose hold on this unity is strong — for him you need not feel pity. He lives on the firm ground of a standing covenant.

Of course, history is now storming; there is a war against the Jew, but this war is not against only one part of the triple unity, it is against all of it: against the Torah, and against the Holy Blessed One, against the ethical law and against the Creator of the world. Can anyone doubt who is the stronger? It may happen that in a war, a troop is defeated, beaten or falls into captivity. The Jews of the Ghetto must feel themselves as such captives. But they must also remember that the army has not been defeated, and it cannot be defeated. The Passover of Egypt is a symbol of an ancient victory of the holy three-fold. Let us pray that we will survive and together reach the Passover of the future.[65]

The last part of this long quotation is an accurate summary of that understanding of Judaism which Baeck tried to disseminate in his community during the Holocaust. He had the same conviction, one troop may be defeated, may even be exterminated, but there is no doubt whose will be the final victory in the war. Baeck felt, as Kalmanowitz did, that the war was essentially a war against everything which is represented by Judaism in human history. This was the ultimate message with which he tried to strengthen his persecuted community and which he took with him when he left Theresienstadt: Israel remains faithful to its destiny, it willingly chooses its original "self." The Holocaust did not deprive Israel of its freedom to choose its own meaning and aim, and as Israel has chosen its way and stood the test of Nazi terror, there is no doubt that it has won the war. But this lengthy entry from Kalmanowitz's diary is cited here because the "preliminary" considerations, which Baeck would probably have rejected, are instructive; the more so because Kalmanowitz overtly pointed to something in recent Jewish history which Baeck preferred to leave silent and untouched. What has been presented here is the reaffirmation of a former position; the complex background to this should not be forgotten. On the one hand, there was a very deep process of deterioration, alienation, and estrangement — even the evidence of Kalmanowitz's argument is accepted[66] — an unmitigated moral degeneration which spread into the very tissue of the Jewish people, so that it was only in spite of themselves that a great multitude of Jews were driven to recognize their Jewishness and to choose a moral attitude toward being Jewish. On the other hand, there was oppression, spite, insults, and the threat of complete annihilation. The question must be raised, on such a background and under such conditions, is a free moral choice to re-enter the covenant between the people and God, according to the Torah, really possible? Can one accept as convincing the traditional self-image of the Jewish people as a chosen, elevated people? Would it not be more natural and understandable to opt for denial and flight, even to try to join the camp of the despised strong enemy, those who rule the Ghetto? Were there not clear signs that the majority of the Jews "in spite of their will" behaved in a way that bears a completely different testimony regarding the nature and fate of the Jewish people today? Answers to these questions were far from simple, especially in the case of the "negation of exile" theories in Zionist and Socialist ideologies. A positive decision was in fact an act of faith which demanded great emotional and intellectual effort so that the vision of an idealized past and future might stand against the external and internal distortions of the present.

Kalmanowitz's observations, and here he differs from Baeck, expose with stark clarity the complex background and show the anguished, scrupulous process by which, after much hesitation, he reached his final conclusions. From his frank account, something can be learned as well about Baeck's situation. It may indicate that what seems to be merely a dogmatic reaffirmation of a former position may in actuality necessitate a profound creative process which could not be achieved without pain and effort. Baeck, like Kalmanowitz, did not reach that threshold of ideological change which is psychologically possible only for young people.[67] He remained where his previously shaped world view had posited him at the beginning of the era. But in order to reaffirm his stance in the face of a void which he wanted to realistically grasp, he, too, had to break new ground. He had to discover something previously unfathomed; to visualize his people not as they appeared to him in the present, but as he experienced them on an inner spiritual level, or on the level of "meta-history."

The intellectual and emotional act required was in itself an act of self-transcendence, of idealization of the people, and of oneself with the people. It could be claimed that through this very act, one might directly experience a redemptive value. Whoever succeeds in an act of

47

self-transcendence has already discovered a way to liberate himself from siege, while yet physically in it. Baeck saw himself above his enemies. He could despise them. He freed himself from the physical, demeaning fear. This psychological achievement may explain the motivation of persons like Zeitlin, Kalmanowitz and Baeck in their respective leadership roles. But strong motivation is not enough. To make headway against extraordinary hardships, evidence and convincing arguments are needed for those not as inwardly strong. This is especially true when one takes upon himself, as Baeck did, the responsibility for a broad educational enterprise intended for the entire Jewish public. Baeck, one learns from his impressive prayer on the eve of the Day of Atonement 1935, understood the power of a proud and lofty exclamation, at the right hour, in which the honored traditional code is carefully used and invested with fresh experiential meaning. But he knew that this alone would achieve nothing, that he must supply historical knowledge, deeply convincing philosophy, and profound spiritual experiences. He strived to achieve this partially through his prolific writing — the scholarly studies, thoughtful articles, and especially his second major work, *This People Israel*.

One must assume then that the reaffirmation of his early positions, which were put forward in these writings, included his creative effort to convince, to prove, to justify, and to bridge the gaps between the present, past and future. Though he did not declare it openly, what was added was not only by way of appealing to the reader, but was concerned as well with the quality and range of the material itself.

The first topic which should be discussed in this context is the historical evidence of the meaning attached to the Jewish people, its fate and destiny. This is a question related to the philosophy of history from one side, and to the theology of Divine providence from the other. The extraordinary hardships raised emotional and intellectual difficulties on these two levels of discussion. Baeck continued to rely on positions he had taken early on, without putting them in question for the sake of reaffirmation. From a superficial reading, one does not sense that he was making efforts to overcome new difficulties. Still, it was at just that hour of crashing events that he found it important to delve into the study of older pages in Jewish history and Jewish sources. It would seem that indeed this was Baeck's way to relate, on a deeper level, to the stormy events of the time.

As previously stated, Baeck's historical and theological views were identical with those of his great teacher Hermann Cohen.[68] The history of humanity, and the history of the Jewish people within humanity, have been described as a slow but endless process of enduring achievement. The final vision is never achieved, but is gradually fulfilled by the advancement of moral relations between man and man, between man and society, between man and the world. God is the transcendental unity in the ideals of Truth (from the aspect of Cognition), and Good (from the aspect of Will). As such, God is the source of the ethical commandment that guides humanity in its path. As such, He is also the source of our faith in the persistent advance toward Redemption.

In this neo-Kantian system, the human being is considered a spiritual being capable of overcoming natural, elemental drives, who is, of course, free to choose and accept full responsibility for his deeds. This conception rejects any assumption of natural determinism in history. Nor is there any preordained structure of development in history. Humanity, as a collective social entity, decides its fate and prescribes the limits of progress. Which means that humanity can also choose moral degeneration and retreat, and sharing as it does in the world of nature, it faces both necessity and accidentalness. Being free, man may prefer moral servitude to his elemental drives, which is why history cannot delineate a direct and steady process of moral advance. There are retreats in history; there are grave failures. There are sins in the life of the collective as well as in the life of the individual. It may even be stated, according to Cohen, that it is impossible to avoid sin. Cohen's optimism is saved, however, by the assumption that the human being is essentially moral, and therefore his freedom prevails even when he sins. No sin is fated, not only because in every case there is a choice, but also because man, even after he has sinned, can correct it by Repentance (*T'shuva*).[69]

Cohen's optimism shows itself, moreover, in his trust that in spite of unavoidable sins and failures, the general outline of human history must express what is essential in humanity. From this point of view, progress is indeed taken for granted. It is guaranteed by God and by the idea of humanity, which is "co-related" to the transcendental idea of God. The sinner repents and God forgives. Man regains his moral freedom and corrects his ways. The same is true for peoples in their historical development. Ontologically, this means that sin, failure and retreat, though unavoidable, are expressions of accidentalness in history, while progress represents the essential, and the essential must finally prevail.

The belief in historical progress is based, then, on the assumption that Reason is the essence of humanity, and Reason, as against Nature, is inherently teleological; it is dutifully bound, or "co-related," to its transcendental ideal of Truth and Good. Humanity, and each human individual, knows the absolute command of Reason, and accepts through self-reason its own absolute moral responsibility before God. This is, one may say, an internal "covenant" of love between God and humanity, and it cannot be abolished. Thus God guarantees the fulfillment of the moral ideal in human history, through the moral force of the covenant of Reason between Himself and humanity, and not by some powerful compelling intervention from "above," as simple believers would understand it.[70]

Baeck reformulated these ideas in his own way. Some of the differences between Baeck and Cohen will be examined subsequently, but the main stream of Baeck's thinking remained the same as Cohen's: "If we would try to summarize in a short way the whole problem of Judaism from its inception in Egypt to our own days...," Baeck writes in one of his important theological treatises after the Holocaust, "we could say that the great problem of Judaism and of the Jewish religion from that time onward is the entrance of that which Is (*Des Siendes*), the infinite, the Eternal, into the finite, the limited, the transient, the human world; the entrance of the world of unity which comprises all and penetrates all...into the world in which we are situated...and now comes the crucial addition: This entrance achieved its completion in the form of the commandment."[71]

God is present in our world as the source of an eternal commandment which binds humanity, and as the source of the spirit of holiness which accepts the absolute commandment in this world of finality, limitation and transience. Baeck stated his reliance on Hermann Cohen more clearly in a short passage written after the Holocaust, in which he hinted briefly about his solution to the problem of theodicy: "It seems to me that the most fitting words have been said by Hermann Cohen in the relevant paragraphs of his 'Ethik' and 'Religion der Vernunnft.' What is most typical of Judaism and what marks the difference between Judaism and Protestantism are 'God's attributes' which are His ways, the ways through which man is commanded to walk. As He is merciful and full of pity, so you should be merciful and full of pity.[72] From here we start our solution to the problem of theodicy."[73]

The message, it seems, is plain: the idea of "providence" should not be understood as an outward intervention, through miracles, of God in history in order to enforce the progress toward the goal which has been appointed by God. The responsibility for morality in history is wholly human. It is man's decision either to respond to the Divine command and walk in the ways of God, or to refuse to go in these ways. God enters history as the creator of humanity in His image, as the source of the "Spirit of Holiness" which guides humanity — the recognition of truth and the moral will. God is present as a morally obligative ideal in which humanity may achieve the fulfillment of its destiny. When man walks in the ways of God, He is present in history. When man refuses, God "hides His Countenance." This is obviously the full theological context of Baeck's previously cited words on the commandment to sanctify the Holy Name: When human beings are ready to sacrifice their life for the sake of faithfulness to the command of going in God's ways, they reveal God's presence in the world of man. They become His witnesses. One may even say that they represent God in their deeds, which reflect His "ways" or "attributes," and are true to their destiny as having been created in His image.

This is the only way in which Divine providence should be understood. Yet one cannot avoid a question about the source of Baeck's absolute trust, his invincible optimism which burst out of the book he wrote while in Theresienstadt like the song of the choir in Beethoven's Ninth Symphony. An optimism that the will of God will be done in spite of human wickedness, even if wickedness seems to be so awful and so powerful, even when wickedness almost succeeds in annihilating any witness to the presence of God within the world of degenerated humanity. Though we can empathize with Hermann Cohen's trust in history, putting ourselves in his place to try and grasp how he experienced the balance of achievement and failure in European history, it would seem quite different with Baeck. Had he not sufficient reasons to doubt those assumptions which were still acceptable for Hermann Cohen? Could he not see that his Jewish community had sufficient reasons to despair about the historical significance of their martyrdom? True, precisely for these reasons he and his community needed, more than ever, the support of faith (indeed, the visionary chords in Baeck's theological choir greatly outdid those of Hermann Cohen), but did he not feel the need for a new, more convincing, more consoling historical justification for this overflow of messianic optimism?

The answer must be sought first in Baeck's approach to the study and teaching of history. Comparing his scholarly enterprise with that of his teacher, it is immediately apparent that Baeck devoted much more attention to philological-historical research. In fact, Baeck contributed proportionally as much to scientific historical research as he contributed to philosophy and theology.[74] Beside his two great systematic works (written in broad outlines from the top of the highest historical mountain with daring generalizations, based on a selection of some few details and much inspired idealizations), Baeck devoted himself to the minutest philological researches, using rigorous scientific methods and concentrating on narrowly defined topics. There is no doubt that even this scholarly research was written from a particular theological-philosophical point of view, and within the framework of Baeck's educational, rabbinic vocation. These were not studies for the sake of "pure science," rather they were focused on those historical topics which could be applied to contemporary theological, philosophical or historical problems. This was done either in the context of understanding *The Essence of Judaism* (research in ancient Jewish history and in the sources of Jewish thought in the Middle Ages) or in the context of a polemic dialogue with Christianity (studies in ancient Christianity and its sources, especially the Paulinian theology) or in the context of understanding the fate of the Jewish people in the modern era, from Emancipation onward. Baeck did not try to conceal the link between his detailed historical research and his broad historical-theological generalizations. On the contrary, he tended to be overt in showing the connection between these two areas of his interest.

The difference between Cohen and Baeck, from this point of view, should not be overlooked. Cohen was, of course, aware of developments in the field of historical-philological research in Judaic Studies and referred to them, but the main body of his work (there are really only a few exceptions and even they prove the *a priori* philosophical bias of their writer) was devoted to "pure" philosophy. He did not deny the tension which this one-sided attitude created between him and the philologists of his time, especially in biblical criticism, and he offered his reservations in the form of a philosophical criticism on the accepted historical-philological method.

Baeck paved his own road in research as well as in philosophy and theology. He did philological research and complied carefully and rigorously with the accepted norms of the philological profession which demands an empirical, inductive approach to history and empirical evidence for every historical generalization.[75] Clearly he strove for reliability. Baeck was very sensitive to the criticism of professional historians regarding the overgeneralized views of *a priori* idealistic philosophers (like Cohen) on history. He was aware that professional historians are considered more reliable, and that such historians do not attach much importance either to "historiosophical" generalizations, or to philosophical criticisms against the rules of philology since these criticisms were biased and attempted to legitimize certain preestablished historical concepts as against "unreasonable" facts. The philologists had already won the battle in the field of education in Hermann Cohen's day. Baeck had to draw the obvious conclusion. In his detailed rigorous philological studies, he wanted to bring facts that had been checked in evidence of his generalizations. The generalizations were daring in their totality, visionary and poetic in nature, but the references are grounded in empirical data. This is true for all the areas of Baeck's theological interest, including his messianic interpretation of history, especially in the modern era. In this context it is important to attend to the fact that precisely after he finished his work on *The Essence of Judaism*, the quantity of his philological-historical research grew in a recognizable measure. When he decided to start a second systematic and generalized work, it was after a long period of studious dedication to scholarly research and to specific, well-defined, theological, historical, ethical, and educational topics.

Factually, all these variations in form and method happened precisely during the period of the Nazi rise to power, and when, as the leader of German Jewry, Baeck had to confront the tasks of education. Was it only a coincidence? In the period that followed the composition of *This People*, Baeck's work was also marked by exact philological research. It is apparent that he felt the need to balance his systematic, generalized writings so as to show that his generalizations were sound, reliable, well-grounded in historical facts: "In these studies," states Baeck in his introduction to a collection of studies first published in 1938, "we shall try some special methods in the hope of opening new ways. The singular detail must find its place in the whole, and the whole must be grasped from the singular detail. Philology, which is devoted to the minutest detail, takes here its recognizable share, and this may serve as a correction and a justification. In former treatises I took upon myself the task of presenting *The Essence of Judaism,* and the *Ways in Judaism,* but the authority to speak about the whole can be based only on precision and rigor in relation to details, even the minutest ones."[76]

Typical of the period which followed *The Essence of Judaism* was Baeck's awareness of the regularity of destructions and catastrophes in Jewish history and the incentive of martyrdom. The idealistic school of Jewish theology in the nineteenth century applied its glaring optimism even to the interpretation of catastrophes in Jewish history: the people suffered and knew pain at a given time, but in the broad historical perspective these events were interpreted as positive. The Jewish people had been elevated to a higher spiritual level and the fulfillment of their universalist mission had been enhanced. Thus, the destruction of the Second Temple eliminated the "primitive" concept of serving God by sacrifices and replaced it with a concept of service and ritual which was raised to an ethical and purely emotional, intellectual realm. At the same time, the destruction of the kingdom, the detachment from the Land, and the dispersion among the nations made it possible for the Jewish people to carry on and spread its ethical monotheistic message among the nations. What had been experienced as a terrible tragedy at the time it occurred, became a source of blessing from an ethico-religious point of view. This understanding of Jewish history, typified especially by liberal Jewish theologians, has also been accepted by some Jewish theologians in the twentieth century. Hermann Cohen adhered to this interpretation of exile and dispersion, and even Rosenzweig repeated it in his own original version.

Baeck did not embrace this idealistic concept. In that negation, he came closer to Zionism. Indeed, in spite of his share of nineteenth century optimism, Baeck related to the destructions and catastrophes held in the collective memory of the Jewish people as they were traditionally remembered from generation to generation. He did not attach a "blessing" to catastrophe as such. Of course, those who sanctified the Holy Name were spiritually elevated; they fulfilled their task in history in that moment. It does not seem, however, that Baeck saw in such occasions a necessary means of influencing humanity.

As a historian, Baeck pointed to other channels of influence which he considered to be much more positive and creative. These are the peaceful processes of give and take between cultures that are in contact with each other which enable learning, adoption and imitation of whatever contributes to perfection and elevation. A catastrophe destroys such positive influences; it cannot contribute any good in itself. Therefore, Baeck related positively to Emancipation but not to the reactionary attempt to annul its achievements.

Nonetheless, Baeck did become increasingly aware of the regularity of catastrophes and destructions in the historical cycle of nations in general and in Jewish history in particular. Observing Baeck's place in the history of Jewish historiosophy in the modern era, the claim can be made that Baeck moved from Cohen's conception of history to that of Krochmal: a recurring cycle which may be described in the terms of the life cycle: birth, maturity, old age and death. Krochmal did not claim a miraculous transcendence from the law of the organic cycle for the Jewish people. As every other people, the Jewish people is also moving in the life cycle from birth to death; indeed, it has been born and died several times. The destruction of the First Temple and the first exile were a deadly blow. The death event recurred in the destruction of the Second Temple and the defeat of the Bar-Kochba revolt. The Jewish people died again in a chain of catastrophes from the expulsion from Spain to the massacres of Chmelnitzky. But what is "supernatural" about this people is that it could die so many times, and be reborn to live again the whole cycle of national life. The secret of Jewish persistence in history, in the face of the demise of so many nations, greater and stronger than this people, is the secret of its renewal.[77]

Baeck adopted this "model" of organic life cycle in history. It should be noted that he did not adopt the Hegelian dialectical element which Krochmal used in order to interpret every death at the end of an organic life cycle as a precondition to a higher level of spiritual achievement in a new cycle, thus interpreting the death of the nation as a positive precondition of progress. According to Baeck, the renewed life cycle grows out of the same "seed" which carries within itself the original genetic code. Of course, every birth is singular and unique. Of course, the special conditions of the place and time of rebirth have historical impact and shape Jewish history in a variety of diversified variations, and of course there must be a dimension of progress which is the result of the aggregated achievements from generation to generation, and from one life cycle to the other.

Baeck did emphasize, as would any liberal thinker of his age, the dynamic and the developmental character of history. Growth, development and adaptation to different surroundings result in an ever-changing Judaism, yet he did not accept the dialectical model of development. Each life cycle fulfills itself in its turn. It carries its own inherent life, creative value, and in the end the death is painful and mournful. Yet, thereafter we witness, as in the natural organic realm, the wonder of the renewed birth, a wonder which Baeck tends to describe in a manner which is reminiscent of Rabbi Judah Halevi's description of the emergence of the Jewish people, in his book *Kuzari*; that is, not as a gradual development, but as a fully developed entity which appears out of its own resources, as at Sinai, a new, complete creation.[78]

This conception of Jewish history raises two very difficult questions: Firstly, what are the causes of death in the life of a nation, and how can we integrate the regularity of national deaths in an optimistic, redemptive theology? Secondly, how should we account for the regularity of Jewish rebirth after its destructions? Factually, it must be stated that these questions did engage Baeck in the period following the final edition of *The Essence*. Baeck did not develop a complete theory of "deterioration and destruction" in the life of nations similar to that of Krochmal. The use of the metaphor of the organic life cycle hints at the assumption that the death of a nation is due to processes of decay, similar to those of old age in the individual body. However, in Baeck's discussion of catastrophes in Jewish history, no clear reference to such an explanation is found. Baeck refers to specific historical events (mainly wars against stronger powers), religious persecution by wicked conquerors, inner conflicts, social injustice, etc. Are all these to be considered symptoms of old age? At times, possibly, though not always and not necessarily. Generally, it may be stated that human nature, individually and collectively, is open to all the weaknesses or tragic accidents of life. This is the final, the limited, the transient in human nature. At times death may occur through deterioration of age, and at times through inner or external calamities.

We are confronted here, of course, with the old theological problem: how to account for evil, wickedness, suffering and death as unavoidable components in a world created by God, and for a good end. Though Baeck did not adopt the dialectical model of explanation, nevertheless his optimism equaled that of Krochmal, Geiger or Cohen. He only "receded" the basis of his optimism to the existential level.

His fundamental assumption was that Being is stronger than whatever contradicts it, that the principle of creativity overcomes processes of deterioration, that life and existence precede. The beginning is a fullness of Being which comprises within itself all the processes of life — even death as one of its necessary elements. For Baeck this assumption was a fundamental existential insight on which he based his conception of Judaism. He thus offered an originative distinction (typical of many Jewish theologians in the twentieth century) between Judaism as the product of an existentially positive attitude to life, and Buddhism as the product of an opposite insight.[79]

The Buddhist conception was rejected by Baeck as mistaken and misleading: it evaluates life from the point of view of death, and makes death the aim of life. This contradicts the most obvious self-approved intuition of life. The correct way then is to evaluate death on the basis of the precedence of life. Death is one of life's processes. Once this is grasped the positive meaning can be fathomed, because the absolute force of infinite reproduction and renewal, which is life's essence, is manifested only through the instrumentality of death. Death demolishes existing individuals; catastrophe may destroy a particular individual culture. This is painful. But no death and no catastrophe can reach the fundamental principle of Being or damage the infinite, absolute potentiality of Being. This is the source from which everything flows and to which all return in order to give way to a new creation. From this point of view, death and destruction represent the essentially temporal, transient, and final modes through which the eternal essence of life is revealed, remaining forever new. There is no death of life. Death is an event in life, the other necessary side of renewal.

In order to understand Baeck's message correctly it must be reemphasized that Baeck's position was a far cry from the classical philosophical understanding of death as "absence," or as "mere negation" in contrast to life which is existence and completion. No, illness, pain and death are in themselves concrete processes of life. They are real, and one cannot be redeemed from their sufferings through an intellectual denial of their reality. But they are transient, final and secondary, and as negative processes they destroy themselves in the body which they consume. The same argument is valid on the ethical level. Evil impulses and moral wickedness are described by Baeck in terms of pathology and spiritual deterioration. They are rooted in the processes of deterioration, sickness and death in nature,

57

and they use these self-same processes for all sorts of distorted satisfactions. They are then essentially identified with deterioration itself. They are destructive, so they destroy themselves even when they attack their victims. When you observe evil and wickedness, even when they are in their full power, you can see evidence of their self-destructive character; they cannot but deteriorate and collapse into the abyss which they themselves create. It is therefore certain that in the end of a relatively short, transient process of destruction, the destructive powers will themselves be destroyed. Then we will face again the emergence of the positive, creative principle of life. In its fullness it will be manifested as a new creation. Is this the meaning of redemption that is experienced after every great destruction: a powerful affirmation of the victory of life, singing "a new song?"[80]

Baeck proposed this view as a fundamental insight, as a firm belief. What are its credentials? What is the source of its evidence? A religious man would answer his absolute trust in God, "Who renews daily in His permanent goodness the works of creation," as the source of his belief in the permanence of the principle of life. God as the Creator reveals His absolute power and His everlasting grace in this miracle of life's renewal. If we believe in God we believe in the cogency of our instinct for life and its insights. It surely indicates an absolute source of power beyond. So vice versa: if we believe in our instinct for life and its insights, we experience the permanent presence of God. It is a closed cycle. Still there are moments in which we feel the need to affirm our insight of life's renewal through the evidence of God's presence. What then are the direct sources of this belief? How can we renew our faith in God when we are shocked by wickedness and death? It is typical of Baeck that he refrained from formulating the question in this way, but he was very much engaged in the problem.

It would appear that it is precisely around this existential problem, namely, the reassessment of faith against the sufferings of traumatic events, that one can observe in Baeck's writings (after *The Essence of Judaism*) his major deviation from Hermann Cohen. Indeed, although this deviation may be described as parallel to Rosenzweig's existentialist deviation from Cohen, Baeck paved his own unique way. It seems likely that his role as a religious leader contributed to the difference. Instead of Cohen's idealistic concept of "Co-Relation" between God and Man, grounded in pure Reason, Rosenzweig wrote of emotional love and an existential covenant of marriage. He arrived at this approach through a complicated, new method of philosophical thinking, admittedly much more difficult to understand than Cohen's philosophy, which in itself was far from popular. In contrast, Baeck stretched his philosophical discussion to the utmost in order to go beyond its limits, entering into the realm of the unknown, indeed to mysticism. But craving the limits of earthly life, he described it as a direct, emotional experience which is available to every human being. For mysticism, according to Baeck, is the direct spiritual experience which religion gives rise to through the intermediacy of its special art and poetry. Religion awakens dormant childhood experiences. Through study, prayer and the cycle of festivals and religious lifestyle, it articulates, educates and shows how to live and express the mystical experience, which for Baeck is a *ground experience* for every human being.[81]

It is through this direct experience in which man senses the presence of a hidden, transcendental God that belief can be reaffirmed. For it is a pure experience of presence, not an intellectual reflection, that can be really reassuring.

The topic of Baeck's relation to mysticism in general, and especially to Jewish mysticism, attracted much scholarly debate. In the first edition of *The Essence*, Baeck retained the "traditional" liberal restraint towards mysticism. He did not include Jewish mysticism in his holistic, synthesized conception of Judaism. Like the majority of idealistic theologians who were devoted to Reason as the source of "ethical monotheism," Baeck considered Kabbalist literature a product of outward influences, to be absorbed only marginally. In subsequent editions of *The Essence*, this attitude was revised. It was the beginning of a process in which Jewish mysticism was brought forward from its alien, marginal position to a central place of honor. To be precise, Baeck did not legitimize mysticism as such. He related to Jewish mysticism only, to which he then gave his own interpretation, stating clearly that every religion has its own sphere of mysticism.[82] Still, it was a remarkable change in a teaching which otherwise did not show much aptitude for change.

What was the cause of this "unique" change? Several explanations are possible and all of them may be true, each in its own right. Firstly, it can probably be assumed that this was the result of a more consequential development in Baeck's originative methodology. As a philosopher committed to the fullness of historical sources of Jewish religion, and as a philologist committed to objective empirical criteria in the definition of these sources, he really had no other choice. As a scholar who carefully followed developments in the scientific study of Judaism, Baeck could not permit himself to conceal historical facts, not even to the degree that a nineteenth century historian like Graetz could. According to the criteria of his own methodology, Baeck had to first interpret the meaning of Jewish mysticism, and then find its place in the complex system of tensions and paradoxes. Moreover, Baeck could not ignore the changes that were taking place in Christian and Jewish philosophy, especially in the first decades of the twentieth century, with regard to the mythological element in religion.

The liberal, idealistic theology of Reason considered mythology a typical pagan phenomenon, so it described Judaism as a "de-mythologized," rational type of religion whose greatness was the result of a complete spiritual, redemptive revolution. Obviously this approach necessitated the rejection of Kabbalism with its strong mythological attitude, which must have appeared as a corrupting pagan influence. However, in the beginning of the twentieth century, both scientific research and religious philosophy proved the superficiality of this *a priori* attitude. There are many kinds of mythology, and there is no religion without a mythological foundation. Thus, since its inception, Judaism has had its own mythology.

But when this statement, which Baeck could not deny, is pointed out, attention must also be given to the motivation behind the turn in the science and philosophy of religion; namely, that there was a growing need to better understand the language of religion, and the special code which is appropriate to its unique message. This need was the sign of a new interest in religion, indeed, the kind of interest that an idealistic type of "Theology in the Limits of Pure Reason Alone"[83] could no longer satisfy. Baeck's references to Jewish mysticism in his writing following the last edition of *The Essence* show indications of a growing awareness of this fact, that is, the articulation of a religious need which cannot be satisfied by reason alone.

It cannot be sheer coincidence that in Baeck's collection of articles and studies published in 1938, much attention is given to both problems of religious education and lifestyle, and to Jewish mysticism. In his paper on "The Development of an Ethical Personality,"[84] Baeck emphasizes the importance of mysticism in religious education, precisely after the crisis of adolescence, for a balanced maturity. In this period, says Baeck, man tends to concentrate on material, earthly interests and responsibilities, so that there is a danger of becoming completely "dried-up." Therefore, there is a critical need to balance this narrowing, one-dimensional attitude through a purposeful elevation to the "cosmic," spiritual sphere. In the same manner, Baeck reflects on the mystical qualities of Shabbat.[85] Shabbat is meant to elevate man from the level of the mundane, practical life to the level of the spiritual, the cosmic, the infinite. Baeck identified religion with the content which he attributed to mysticism: "This elevation to the cosmic sphere, while at the same time strengthening the ethical element, this expansion of the field of human activity further to infinity — these are the remarkable qualities of Jewish mysticism throughout all its periods."[86]

However, Baeck does not retract the definition of Judaism as "ethical monotheism." In this he remains faithful to Cohen and to the liberal tradition. Because of this, he needs to emphasize the ethical component as a qualifying element in Jewish mysticism. But even from the ethical point of view, mysticism as a religious phenomenon "continues" the ethically significant activity of man to a higher level, one which is far beyond the mundane, the social or the political, which is after all the proper practical realm of ethics. Jewish mysticism attaches cosmic significance to the fulfillment of Divine commandments. When such fulfillment is informed by Intent and Devotion, the effect is on the cosmic, and not merely on the social realm. A devoted fulfillment of divine commandments unifies the "worlds" and ties them to their source in the Beyond.

Baeck goes much further in his reassessment of mysticism in the opening chapter of his second great work, the book which was written in Theresienstadt. Here Baeck methodically established mysticism in a place of honor, as the foundation of religion or as its first moment of revelation. Indeed, this religious concept is reemphasized in the final pages of the second part of the book, so as to plant the end in the beginning, and the beginning in the end.[87] Baeck starts with the statement that from the very beginning "this people Israel" believed that its history as a people began with the eternal beginning of the whole cosmos, namely, that the people are rooted in infinity. Heaven and Earth were created by the Word of God, and the same Word of God created the people. This is, of course, mythology, not history, and Baeck does not confuse the one with the other, yet what is most important for him is that this national self-awareness defined the people as indissolubly bound to God. Moreover, it guided the Jewish people throughout history.

To repeat, this is not a historical or a rational insight, but Baeck fully approves of it. He uses the method which he used in *The Essence*, namely, the method of creating balanced and intercomplementary paradoxes. In this way mysticism is described not in contradiction to Reason and Rationality, but as its paradoxical complement. The historical-rational and the mythological-mystical are to be accepted as two dimensions of the same truth, the truth as it is observed outwardly by our senses, and the truth as it is grasped from within, through our feelings.

Men who reflect are at times more capable of entering the one sphere, at times more capable of penetrating the other. The same division is found in the talents of peoples. It is the characteristic genius through which the Jewish people defined its uniqueness that it constantly refined its knowledge; it attempted and succeeded in understanding both spheres. It understood them not only in terms of their own specific actuality, but also, above all, in terms of the relationships existing between them. The Jewish spirit has always sought to grasp the oneness of all reality...it comes from one God, is created by Him....The natural and the spiritual, the external and the internal cannot be separated from one another if they are to become known....The rational and the irrational do not contradict one another here. They are related. They cannot be understood without each other. The irrational is the root of the rational, the predicate of its existence and its validity, and the rational is the root of the irrational; and the rational is the expression of the irrational, a form in which the irrational reveals itself....This people Israel came to have a particular understanding of this view of reality through its history, and was persuaded by it. Its history is something clear to this people, a clear way, a clear task, a clear commandment; but it rises out of the world of the mystery, out of the supernal unity, out of the foundation of everything that is.[88]

Based on such passages, it would probably not be an exaggeration to say that Baeck's growing interest in mysticism, precisely in these years, stemmed from his feeling that it was essential to satisfy a growing religious need to overcome the widening gap between faith and reality. Since philosophy itself was powerless to bridge such a gap, tools which reached beyond philosophy were required. With the help of mysticism, Baeck tried to justify a super-rational faith — openly admitting that it was irrational — in the eternity of life, in the eternity of Israel, in the absolute victory which is promised by God to those who choose the historic path of the Jewish people, the path of morality and faith. Such a faith would sustain the people in spite of all that was happening, above and beyond all that would happen.

This statement sounds more persuasive if examined carefully in the light of Baeck's pedagogical methodology for religious education. As he applied this methodology in his own writing, Baeck tried again and again to "translate" his religious insight and shape it into a convincing message for his persecuted community.

In this way the role of art in general, and poetry in particular, gained importance in Baeck's religious thinking. In the paragraph cited from his lecture on "Changes in the Jewish Outlook," Baeck uses a well-known aphorism taken from Aristotle's "The Poetics" in which he writes, "Poetry is closer to philosophy than history." Relying on this maxim Baeck ended his lecture with a verse from the "Song of the Sea" as a closing message drawn from Jewish history. Reading Baeck's papers and articles, it is clear that he loved to cite the Aristotelian aphorism on poetry, and often did so, as he frequently felt the need to justify his use of poetry in scientific or philosophical essays.

Art in general, and poetry as the particular art of words, became then central in his thinking as well as in his public communication. Indeed, as Baeck quoted "Poetry is closer to philosophy than history," the words were an understatement. Actually, he wanted to say that poetry is closer to the ultimate truth — the religious truth — than philosophy; that in fact, this is the only language in which one can express the super-rational truth of mysticism. As noted, Baeck did not consider the tension between the mystical-irrational and the philosophical-rational as a contradiction; he could philosophically account for the preference of poetry to philosophy in the realm of religion.

Previously noted was Baeck's differentiation between the two spheres which are alternately open to "men who reflect." Introduced to such a statement in the opening chapter of a book, the reader may rightly interpret it as the author's personal statement, as "a man who reflects," with regard to his own book. So, which mode of reflection did Baeck chose to write this particular book? The message in the quotation from Baeck will be lost if the inference is that it was written solely in one mode. There is a philosophical element in *This People*.

Yet comparing the two books, *This People* and *The Essence*, the conclusion is that though these books are in many ways twins which resemble each other in method and content, yet each one possesses a certain unique character of its own. Each emits a clear, unique message and each is open mainly to one of the two spheres of experience, as well as to one of the two modes of writing. There is a poetic element in *The Essence*, but it is dominated by the philosophical-phenomenological element; there is a philosophical element in *This People* but it is dominated by the mystical-poetical element. The book was written in a poetic language, and should be read as an historical epic which rises at its height to pure lyricism. Obviously, it reflects Baeck's mood at the time of writing, but it reflects as well Baeck's wish to communicate a message which speaks to the hour and will find acceptance and empathy. His people needed religious consolation, a word of faith and hope. Baeck wanted to respond to the need and, therefore, he chose the only language which he considered appropriate — the language of poetry, or prophecy.

As a Jewish theologian, Baeck was aware of an inherent problem concerning the effective use of artistic language, especially on the background of his continuous polemical dialogue with Christianity. In the previously cited paper "Romantic Religion," Baeck wrote,

> It is Art's right to express for the sake of expression. For Art expression is an end in itself, and as such it is not bound to any other criterion, as something which is whole and complete in itself. Art, as Schopenhauer has taught us, is "everywhere in its aim." But for life, therefore, and in the same measure, for religion, this contains a danger, the danger of romanticism, for which an impression of experience consummates its meaning. This is dangerous because in this manner the commitment to the contents of life and the commandments of life, the commitment to the real and to the duties which are defined by reality, are evaporated. Instead of all these, Art can evoke a religious mood which is sensitive to itself, and therefore tends to grasp itself as complete in itself: Faith for the sake of Faith.[89]

Aware of the danger of art, Baeck nonetheless recognized its centrality to religious education, and its general role in religious communication.

This way one thing stands out as essential: the artistic element in the human personality. The activating effect which comes from the surrounding fullness contributed the objective, calm aspect of the collective artistic creation, while the influence which the educated person experiences now contributes the subjective motivating aspect, which is the task of the artist. Religiosity and educational activity are combined in this activity, because every education is an artistic act: an attempt to create the form which is designated for a human soul, given in its individual uniqueness, to build and to shape it. And in the same measure, every religiosity is artistic, because it is a permanent search and effort to shape and fulfill the life which we have received. Religiosity is education intended inwardly, to the self, while education is religiosity which is intended outwardly, to our fellow-man. Here we must beware of a confusing error concerning education and religion together, the error which is grounded in the conception of art as aestheticism, namely, when we put something which has been intended to accompany and decorate life instead of the inner content which endows life with its ultimate meaning. Only through the proper relation to art will we be able to avoid such substitutive relation. With regard to Judaism this observation is especially relevant, not only because Judaism forbids, for the sake of pure spirituality, every visual representation of the Deity, but first and foremost because art may deny the teleological, categorical element which is commanding and obligating in religion. Therefore, only that kind of artistic creation which is able to awaken the religious feeling and the religious longing (indeed, in a way, every authentic art can have this effect) will suit our purpose, because such artistic creation will pose in its center the symbol, the sign which points to the infinite. It is indeed very important to beware of the danger of the experience of the artistic expression as such, and this relates also to biblical poetry. We should aim instead at the self-revelation of the human personality in art.[90]

Baeck refers to two errors which endanger religious education. Besides the danger of romanticism, which he detected in Christianity, he refers to the danger of a "substitutive" approach to art. What did he have in mind? Where did he detect this kind of danger? It would

65

appear that his reference here is to the approach of a certain kind of idealistic philosophy of religion which reduced religious feeling to an aesthetic experience of the sublime. In this way it achieved a total reduction of religiosity to the level of social ethics, on one side, and to the level of aesthetics and artistic experience, on the other. Critics of Liberal Judaism were the first to expose this kind of falsification in the name of authentic religiosity, because nineteenth century Liberal idealistic theology had adopted this religious reductionism, accepting the aesthetic experience as a full substitute for religious ritual.

Baeck, then, was not only aware of criticism against his own movement, he accepted it and tried to correct the error. He sought a proper way to use art as a tool for religious education, while avoiding the danger of reductionism. Now it must be stressed that Baeck warns his readers of the dangers of art in religious communication precisely because he could not give up its use. On the contrary, he looked for a kind of art which would communicate an authentic religious experience beyond itself. For Baeck, this kind of suitable art is authentic art, art which is not concentrated in itself as expression for the sake of expression, but concentrates in the living, human personality, in order to communicate the message of eternal truth, which only art can do. Indeed, on this level, art, according to Baeck, is identified with religious education, and religious education is defined as art.

Baeck's notions on religious education as art and on the place of art in religious education are better understood in the context of his theory of imagination as a medium, both of art and religious experience. This must be related to his conception of prophecy, and the affinity between it and poetry. The first topic is broadly discussed in his articles on religious education, but the most coherent summary is to be found in one of his last treatises. This is in the context of a discourse on "genius" as a fundamental creative power and on prophecy as "religious genius." Baeck starts his discussion with a definition of a period in the history of a people; he then draws his analogy between the history of a people and the complete life cycle of an individual — childhood, adolescence, maturity and old age. He emphasizes the continuous relationship between these periods of life, not only because they are connected to each other, but also because they contain each other. Childhood must not disappear in the subsequent periods of life. It can and should be contained in them. This statement is very important to Baeck with regard to religious education because he understands religiosity to be rooted in the natural, fundamental, spiritual qualities of the child. He refers to creative imagination, which he believes to be the source both of childhood ground experience and of genius. A genius is one who was able to retain the original, creative imagination of childhood in all its freshness, as a grown, matured person. Baeck states that the creative imagination of childhood is also the source of childhood's natural religiosity; its most profound expression, an expression which Baeck actually identifies with both creative imagination and religiosity, is poetry.

Poetry is, therefore, to be considered as the fundamental inner source, the origin of all the sources of human creativity: "And the child has been endowed with the quality of poetry, the creative fantasy. It relies solely on itself: Imagination enables to comprise everything....The more one has been successful in retaining more of this poetic gift along his periods of life, the greater is his share in genius....When we speak of naivete we think mainly of childhood. But there is also a mature naivete — the superior artistic perfection is also a kind of naivete."[91]

Therefore, the main task of religious education, according to this passage, is to maintain the natural, fundamental, poetic quality of the child and his naivete, to draw these qualities into the life of the adult, mature person, and to develop them to the highest grade of perfection. The poetic quality is religiosity in its actual expression. So it would not seem to be an error to also identify it with mysticism, as Baeck interpreted it. This is the sort of mysticism which Baeck suggested in his article on the development of an ethical personality, especially for that period in which man tends to narrow his interests to his material, mundane tasks. Apparently the tool, full of content, which is needed for this educational task, is the highest type of poetry.

It will, therefore, not be a surprise to discover that Baeck indeed identified the highest type of poetry with prophecy. Who are the prophets? In the following passage of the same treatise, Baeck states, the prophets are "people who, as profound poets and profound thinkers, were endowed with the capacity to get knowledge from a higher sphere — or using another metaphor, from the depth of all that is thinkable and felt."[92] On the basis of these assumptions Baeck goes on and summarizes his discussion of the founding period of Judaism: "Sinai, Moses and the prophets, these are the main foundations of the first period of this history. Poetry has comprised all and shaped anew everything in an infinite creative power. But in the heart of this poetry lay these firm facts: Sinai, Moses, the prophet, and God, He Who Is. Now, where poetry speaks, there the words of Aristotle are newly approved again and again: Poetry is more profound and philosophical than history. Poetry invents the ultimate expression whenever we strive to express that which is beyond expression, when the word should cleave to the highest sphere."[93]

This short passage is most interesting from our point of view because it combines the two different methods by which Baeck strived to give definitive credibility to Jewish belief and faith. On one side, the strict scientific method which reflects earthly reality: concrete historical facts which Baeck carefully studied and rigorously detailed, using the best tools of philology and historiography.[94] On the other side, the mystical method which uses poetry to express the highest religious experience, as the experience of absolute truth. By combining these two methods, Baeck believed that he could endow the Jewish religious message with complete reliability. The first is based on the concrete historical level where religious truth is revealed on earth; the second is on the level of mystical experience, which one must cleave to in order to grasp ultimate meaning and ultimate validity. The meeting between the two methods and levels is complemented in Baeck's discussion of the place of genius in history.

As stated earlier, Baeck adopted a cyclical conception of history. He applied it, generally, to the history of every people, but Israel he conceives as unique in its capacity of renewal. After every full cycle which ends with death or destruction, Judaism is reborn and renewed from the same generic code. What is the "secret" of this wonderful renewal? Baeck's explanation is based on his theory of genius which is a development of his understanding of mysticism: according to him the Jewish genius, as a creative power, is revealed in the renewal of Jewish history. A critic might retort that this is not an explanation, but the substitution of one mystery by another. Every great national culture is a product of a certain kind of genius. In Israel it is the religious genius. This kind of genius is endowed with two unique qualities; it is not consummated in one life cycle but reappears again and again in its full freshness and full originality in every new life cycle, and in its specific essence it is the direct revelation of the infinite source itself: the Divine mystery. "The prophets," continues

Baeck in the article previously cited, "are men in whom the religious genius is alive....The genius is not continuing and he is not guided. On the contrary: he creates a break, because he establishes a new principle, he reveals a new, formerly unknown, point of view....With genius, a superior power penetrates our world, something from the sphere of the unknown is revealed in man."[95]

Based on this passage, perhaps it would not be an exaggeration to say that Baeck identified religious genius with the presence of Divine mystery, as a superior creative power in man, but — to be precise — not by his own intrinsic power, but by a power which flows into him from above. Is it an exaggeration to state that this fact is the source of the capacity to express what is beyond human expression? It seems that the capacity for expression emanates from the expressed truth itself, pointing to a meeting beyond humanity; which is to say that in the prophetic vision we experience the event of Divine revelation itself, but again, not as a truth which has been incorporated in words, but as a symbolized truth, a truth which remains transcendent even when hinted at. One must also be aware of the implication that the prophetic poetic speech is endowed with the power of inspiration. It is inspired, and it is also inspiring. It is convincing in its truth because it carries with it the capacity to reawaken in the listener the same power which he once experienced as a child. If prophecy is a revelation of the infinite mystery in man, it is capable of evoking the same revelation in the souls of those who are ready to hear.

As noted earlier, Baeck was persuaded that the religious genius of Israel, which had been manifest in Moses and in the prophets, was not consummated in a single period. It has been revealed again and again, in each period of Jewish history, each time in a different form, a different style, and in different historical-cultural contexts.[96] There is no reason to assume that the modern period will not repeat the pattern. Religious genius, as an indirect revelation of Divine power which is beyond man, and in man himself, is still active in our age. One may even claim that such a revelation is demanded for the sake of adaptation to the context of our age. The truth of the prophets, the sages, the poets, and the thinkers which enlightened the path of our fathers in former periods must reappear. The people who walk in the darkness of recent historical events need a telling light, for without a new world vision which can both motivate and have the conviction of an original religious event, these people will be in despair and under threat of death.

In light of Baeck's discussion of religious truth in history, his behavior as a religious leader, and the content and form of *This People*, the claim may well be made that it was precisely this task that Baeck took upon himself. It was toward this goal that he wrote his book during the darkness of the Nazi regime and the concentration camp. To fulfill this task he chose the language of poetry and vision with which to speak in the book. It is a language which dresses the scientifically verifiable facts of history in elevating images that refer to the sphere of mystery, and which tries to arrive at a knowledge of the future from the sphere of that which is still unknown. Such a claim is not a mere probability. It is the plain, overt message of the book, in content and in style: a concise historical narrative which emerges from an ancient past and cleaves passionately toward a supreme messianic vision. A prophetic book with which Baeck related to prophecy, its message is "Comfort ye, comfort ye My people." It is in this way that Baeck's second methodological book should be understood as his theological response to the Holocaust. He did not turn away from the Holocaust when he consciously avoided a discussion of its historical, anthropological and theological implications. On the contrary, he sought to overcome these problems with the strength of a new prophetic vision, which he obviously experienced in the Holocaust. His task, as he understood it, was not to "solve" deep theological problems. His task was to articulate an immediate, positive message which would be above and beyond the disaster and the tragedy, which would console, strengthen, give hope, and be as great as was the suffering and the mourning. If, as Baeck's introduction indicates, the book was written as a testimony, then the testimony was not of the catastrophe itself, but of the fact that in the depth of the destruction, faith did not die, and when the power of wickedness was broken, faith was rekindled with a vigorous light.

As one may expect, this prophetic response to the Holocaust evoked — and is still evoking — extremely contradictory responses: from exulted admiration to bitter distrust. Obviously, one may raise difficult questions about the convincing force of Baeck's consoling message. Even in the face of his admitted mystical experiences which overpower, at least subjectively, any rational doubt, can Baeck's words of consolation outweigh the evidence of the Holocaust when we examine all its dimensions in their full size and scope?

Is it not necessary to keep one's eyes at least half shut to the present in order to be able to visualize such pure light of faith and hope pouring out from the future?

However skeptical one may be, one cannot deny the subjective authenticity of Baeck's testimony from Theresienstadt. Obviously his unrelenting faith and hope endowed him with the strength to stand his trial both as an individual and as a leader of his community. From this point of view, Baeck's testimony from Theresienstadt fully exposes the paradox which was manifested time and again during the Holocaust (one may say, another paradox to add to the long list of paradoxes which built up Judaism according to Baeck's *Essence*). Those very experiences that seemed to destroy any grounds for belief and faith in God could also reveal in some believing people unfathomable inner resources of belief and faith. Eventually these resources made possible not only personal survival, but also active spiritual and moral resistance, and therefore a justified sense of victory over absolute evil and death.

Notes

1. Leo Baeck was recognized by Cohen as his closest disciple. See I) Alexander Altmann, "Theology in Twentieth Century German Jewry," *Leo Baeck Institute Year Book 1* (London, 1956), pp. 193-216. II) Hans Liebeschuetz, "Between Past and Future: Leo Baeck's Historical Position," *Leo Baeck Institute Year Book 11* (London, 1966), pp. 3-27.

2. The first edition of *The Essence of Judaism* was published in Berlin, in 1905, as a title in the series underwritten by The Society for the Advancement of the Science of Judaism. The second edition was published in Frankfurt am Main in 1923; the fourth and final edition in the same place in 1926. Hermann Cohen's *Religion of Reason from the Sources of Judaism* was first published in Berlin in 1918.

3. The principal Jewish thinkers in Germany in that period (Cohen, Buber, Rosenzweig, Baeck, Brod, etc.) expressed, in their way of life as well as in their writing, a distinct "returning." See my forthcoming book, *Prolegomena to Jewish Thought in the 20th Century*, ch. 7, "A Theology of Return." See also the papers referred to in note no. 1.

4. Basic biographical data: born in Lissa on May 23, 1873. His father, Rabbi Samuel Baeck (the Chief Rabbi of the District of Posen) was also his first teacher. From May 1891, he studied at the Conservative Jewish Theological Seminary in Breslau. In 1894 he went to Berlin to attend the Liberal Hochschule for Judaic Studies, at the same time studying philosophy at the University of Berlin. His first appointment as a Liberal rabbi was to a congregation in Oppeln in 1897; in 1907 he was invited to serve as the rabbi of Duesseldorf. In 1912 he was appointed a lecturer at the Hochschule and a rabbi in Berlin. In World War I, he volunteered to serve as a chaplain in the German army. In 1924 he was elected president of B'nai B'rith in Germany. He was a member of the executive of the Central Verein of German Jewry, active in the Jewish Agency, and president of Keren Hayesod in Germany. In 1933 he was elected president of the Central Committee of German Jewry; thus, he became the recognized leader of German Jewry under the Nazi regime. In 1942 he was arrested and deported to Theresienstadt. He was liberated in May 1945 and went to London where he led a very active life devoted to study, teaching and public affairs. Leo Baeck died on November 2, 1956.

5. See Baeck's article, "Theologie und Geschichte," in his book, *Aus Drei Jahrtausenden* (Tubingen, 1958), p. 41.

6. The wide dissemination and influence of the book are apparent from the numerous editions and translations which were published as well as responses in journals and periodicals. Also indicative of the book's importance was its inclusion in bibliographies as an exhaustive introduction to Judaism at an advanced educational level. In the first half of the twentieth century many books were published on this topic in a number of European languages and in Hebrew, but Baeck's treatise was recognized as one of the best.

7. Some of the most important studies and articles on Baeck and his work are: I) Albert H. Friedlander, *Leo Baeck, Teacher of Theresienstadt* (London, 1973). II) Leonard Baker, *Days of Sorrow and Pain — Leo Baeck and the Berlin Jews* (New York, 1978). III) Reinhold Mayer, *Christentum und Judentum in der Schau Leo Baeck's* (Stutgart, 1961). IV) M. Wittenberg, *Juedische Existenz nach Leo Baeck* (Neuendetteslau, 1955). V) Eva Y. Reichman, ed., *Worte des Gedankens Fuer Leo Baeck* (Heidelberg, 1959). VI) Hans Liebeschuetz, "Judaism and the History of Religion in Leo Baeck's Work," *Leo Baeck Institute Year Book 2* (London, 1957), pp. 8-20. VII) Franz Rosenzweig, *Apologetisches Denken, Bemerkungen zu Brod und Baeck* (Berlin: Kleinere Schriften, 1923), pp. 31-42.

8. For reactions of Christian theologians to Baeck's views, see Mayer's and Wittenberg's treatises (note no. III-IV) and some articles included in Reichman's book, (*ibid.*, no. V).

9. A full bibliography of Baeck's writing is included in Friedlander's book (see note no. 7, I). The following is a list of his books in the order of their publication: I) *Das Wesen des Judentums* (Berlin, 1905 –Frankfurt am Main, 1926). II) *Wege im Judentum* (Berlin: Aufsaetze und Reden, 1933). III) *Aus Drei Jahrtausenden* (Berlin: Wissenschaftliche Untersuchungen und Abhandlungen, Zur Geschichte des Juedischen Glaubens, 1938); *Nachdruck des Werkes* (Tubingen, 1958). IV) *Dieses Volk. Juedische Existenz* (Frankfurt am Main, 1955); *Ein Zweiter Teil* (1957). The English translation by Albert H. Friedlander (New York, 1965) contains the two parts in one volume. (Quotations used in this work are from this translation). V) *Epochen der Juedischen Geschichte* (Stutgart, Berlin, Koeln, Mainz, 1974).

10. See note no. 9, IV.

11. This view is shared by philosophers and theologians who deal with the Holocaust as their central subject. The serious philosophical confrontation, they say, began two decades later, and this claim is generally accepted. It is clear at least that "Twenty years after..." there has been a new beginning, motivated by needs recognized only then. Yet some philosophical and — even more — theological responses found in the literature written during the Holocaust and in the early years after it should not be overlooked. Be that as it may, Baeck's writings are not considered a source for the later discussions of philosophers and theologians on the Holocaust. Even Friedlander's monograph, though it introduces Baeck as the "Teacher of Theresienstadt," focuses on Baeck's philosophy of Judaism in *The Essence* and in the dialogue with Christianity. Indeed he assigns a whole chapter to "The Later Teaching of Leo Baeck," but even there the response to the Holocaust itself is not dealt with as a separate, distinct topic.

12. The following headings of segments before and after the short passage on the Holocaust may be useful in clarifying the context within which Baeck integrated this paragraph into the second part of *This People Israel*. "The Great New Hope: Herzl and Zionism," p. 379; "America's Promise," p. 381; "Developments in Eastern Europe," p. 383; "Arthur James Balfour and Zionism," p. 384; "The Nazi Terror," p. 385; "The State of Israel," p. 386; "The Cold War Between East and

West," p. 387; "The Righteous and His Faith," p. 389; "The Tension of Jewish History," p. 392; "The Encounter with God," p. 395; "Jewish Existence," p. 396; "The Great Readiness for God," p. 397; "Man and the Mystery," p. 398. "The Task," p. 400-403. There are two distinct motifs in this construction: a general progress towards the fulfillment of the messianic hope in humanity, in spite of two dangerous retreats (The Nazi Terror and the Cold War), and the closing of the circle of theological discussion which begins and ends in the Mystery, the Divine Revelation, and Israel's task for the sake of humanity.

13. *This People Israel, ibid.*, pp. 385-386.

14. Rabbi Leo Baeck, "Changes in Jewish Outlook" (London, 1947). The Arthur Davis Memorial Lectures. The Jewish Historical Society of England. (English in the original), pp. 41-42.

15. There is a well-known episode told by Rosenzweig in his essay on "Hermann Cohen's Jewish Writings." In response to the arguments of some Jewish students at a Zionist meeting, Cohen once retorted, "These youngsters really want to be happy!" This complaint should be understood on the background of Kantian "anti-Daimonistic" ethics which Cohen accepted very seriously and without much sense of humor, but it does reflect Cohen's conviction in his last years that much suffering was still in store for the Jews of Europe, especially in Germany. Cohen's refusal to give up his enthusiasm for the Jewish "mission" for the sake of humanity, as an argument against Zionism, was not due to a naive confidence in the redemptive meaning of Emancipation, but to his attachment to the command that one be ready to sanctify the Holy Name. This is a distinct motif in his bitter controversy with Buber about the legitimacy of Zionism.

16. Leo Baeck, *Das Wesen des Judentums* (Berlin, 1905), p. 75.

17. *Ibid.*, p. 80.

18. Caesar Seligmann, "Brief von Dr. Leo Baeck an Rabbiner," (Frankfurt a.M. Von 2 September 1925), in *Worte des Gedankens, op. cit.*, pp. 245-246.

19. See Max Gruenewald, "The Beginning of the 'Reichsvertretung'," *Leo Baeck Institute Year Book 1*, pp. 57-67. Also: A. Friedlander, *op. cit.*, pp. 41-42.

20. Leonard Baker, *Days of Sorrow and Pain, op. cit.*, p. 203.

21. Erich H. Boehm, ed., *We Survived* (New Haven, 1949). English translation by Leo Baeck.

22. From an early approach to Zionism which could be described as tolerant, Baeck developed a stance which may be defined as pro-Zionist. In note no. 4, reference was made to his activity in the Jewish Agency in Germany, etc. The Nazi rise to power surely strengthened his conviction that the Jewish people needed a homeland and a state of their own. In *This People*, Part Two, a clearly pro-Zionist and pro-State of Israel statement appears, as can be discerned from the sequence of headings cited in note no. 12.

23. The young Rabbi Baeck was one of two opponents of the decision taken by the Association of German Reform Rabbis to join the declaration of the "Protest Rabbiner" against the program of the first Zionist Congress in Basel (1898). Afterward Baeck publically expressed his solidarity with Rabbi Emil Cohen of Berlin when his congregation decided to dismiss him because of his Zionist activity. See Friedlander's book, *op. cit.*, p. 26.

24. See Baeck's article "Orthodox oder Ceremonioes?," *Juedische Chronik*, vol. 3 (1896). The article was written before Baeck's appointment to his first rabbinic position. Although he fully identifies himself with the dynamic Liberal understanding of Judaism, he takes a deviating position on the problem of dogma in Judaism and on the Liberal relationship to ritualistic commandments. In doing so, he clearly declares his bias toward strengthening the Jewish identity of emancipated German Jews through more serious study and through the renewed fullness of a *halakhic* lifestyle. The article may be read as a programmatic declaration of his aims as the rabbi of the congregation.

25. The threat of anti-Semitism which penetrated the German intellectual elite (very forcefully exposed by the controversy around Treitchke's anti-Semitic manifesto) was indeed alarming, but Baeck, as a theologian, chose for himself the fight against Christian anti-Jewish prejudices. The publication of A. Harnack's *Das Wesen des Christentums* (Leipzig, 1900) gave him the opportunity.

26. This topic is discussed at length in the first chapter of my forthcoming book, *Prolegomena to Jewish Thought in the 20th Century* (Hebrew).

27. The founder of Poalei Zion, Ber Borochov, foresaw a great tragedy and in his first Zionist articles stated that "Zionism is short of time." The same position of "catastrophic Zionism" was adopted by such

distinguished leaders, poets and teachers as Zeev Jabotinsky, Uri Zvi Greenberg and Hillel Zeitlin. Dr. Nathan Birnbaum also sensed a forthcoming catastrophe at the end of World War I.

28. See the article referred to in note no. 5.

29. The following are Baeck's papers on Jewish religious education: I) "Religion und Erziehung," *Wege im Judenthum, op. cit.*, pp. 159-174. II) "Philosophie und Religionsunterricht," *ibid.*, pp. 178-184. III) "Die Entwicklung zur sittlichen Persoenlichkeit," *Aus Drei Jahrtausenden, op. cit.*, pp. 348-360. IV) "Die Religioese Erziehung," *ibid.*, pp. 361-382.

30. As stated in note no. 4, Baeck was appointed to lecture in the Hochshule for Judaic Studies in Berlin. His particular subject was Homiletics, and he understood his task in the broad sense of training young rabbis to properly fulfill their roles as teachers and educators of future congregations. He devoted himself very seriously to his charge, personally attending to each rabbinic candidate; evidence of this is found in the numerous testimonies of his students. (See the book edited by Reichmann, *op. cit.*). After his liberation from Theresienstadt, he again devoted himself to this task at Hebrew Union College in Cincinnati.

31. Education programs to strengthen Jewish identity and Jewish pride were in the center of Baeck's activity during that period. Concerning the major educational project which Baeck led, see Ernst Simon, "Jewish Adult Education in Nazi Germany as a Spiritual Resistance," *Leo Baeck Institute Year Book* (London, 1956), pp. 68-104.

32. In "Die Entwicklung..." (*op. cit.*, note no. 29, III) Baeck proposed a detailed pedagogical approach to religious education, the aim of which was to enable each individual Jew to be sufficiently independent to maintain a Jewish world view and lifestyle in a modern society. Baeck characterized modern society as an open society in which it was not possible to retain the same supportive fullness of Jewish community life as was true of traditional society. The individual could not rely on the Jewish community to educate his children as Jews without his direct, active participation, which Baeck saw as the main challenge for modern Jewish religious education.

33. See "Staat, Famili, Recht und Religion," *Wege im Judentum, op. cit.*, pp. 224-228; "Wahlfahrt, Recht und Religion," *ibid.*, pp. 236-249.

34. This testimony is cited in Baker's book, *op. cit.*

35. See the article referred to in note no. 5. Eva Reichmann, who presents herself as very close to Baeck's position, stated in her book, *Hostages of Civilization* (London, 1950), that in actuality even under the Nazi regime the emancipation of German Jews was proved fully successful. According to her analysis, the majority of German society willingly received Jews and was open to full integration. Nazi anti-Semitism, according to her experience, was enforced by the totalitarian regime against the will of the majority in Germany. This conclusion, she thought, was vital and must be disseminated as a source of consolation and trust for the Jews, the majority of whom must remain in the diaspora, even after the Holocaust and the establishment of the State. Was it also Baeck's opinion after his liberation from Theresienstadt?

36. In spite of Baeck's critical attitude towards Christianity, in his *Romantic Religion*, Friedlander rightly argues that Baeck saw a form of a truthful dialogue in the overt criticism; this on the background of a common European culture and the recognition of Christianity as a channel of Jewish religious and ethical influence upon humanity. (In Calvinism especially, Baeck saw evidence of an authentic Jewish influence in Christianity.) Of course Baeck did not expect any merger between the two separate religions, nor the possibility that in a dialogue one religion would effect a major change in the other. It would seem that for Baeck overt criticism was a precondition for establishing an honest and respectful relationship. Dialogue, then, meant that each religion should be fully open to the other, including its opinion of the other's position, insofar as this opinion resulted from its basic world view. Christianity had included its criticism of Judaism as part of its very teaching, so in a dialogue the Jewish partner must respond to this criticism and correct its prejudices; this was not possible without being critical of those elements of Christianity from which the prejudices took their origin. Baeck was of course ready to listen to a sincere response. If the purpose of a dialogue is knowledge of yourself through knowledge of the other, this was the only possible way. Baeck continued in this direction after his liberation from Theresienstadt.

37. Baeck's controversy with Harnack started with a polemical article which preceded Harnack's *Vorlesungen ueber das Wesen des Christenthums*, Monatschrift fuer die Geschichte und Wissenschaft des Judentums (September 1901), pp. 97-120.

38. After the war, Baeck's participation in Jewish-Christian dialogues was very intensive. Among other activities, he led a series of lectures

in which he presented Judaism to a learned Christian public. See his book *Epochen* (note no. 9).

39. The most solid attempt at summarizing Baeck's approach to Christianity in its full context and evaluating it from a Christian point of view is Mayer's book (note no. 7).

40. The similarity between Baeck's and Harnack's books is evident in the goal to introduce Judaism as a totality and make clear its relevance to a modern educated Jewish public, and the method employed which is historical-topological. Compare Friedlander's book, *op. cit.*, ch. 4.

41. Leo Baeck, "Romantische Religion," *Aus Drei Jahrtausenden, op. cit.*, pp. 52-120.

42. *Ibid.*, p. 120.

43. *Judentum in der Kirche, op. cit.*, p. 121.

44. For a full review and detailed analysis of Baeck's studies on Paulus, see Reinhold's book, *op. cit.*, pp. 58-64.

45. *Judentum in der Kirche, op. cit.*, p. 122.

46. The controversy with Christianity played a central role in the theology of the founders of Liberal Judaism. The principle way to reveal the uniqueness of Judaism in the context of a one dimensional universalism was in its distinction from the flaws of Christianity. This is precisely why such assimilationist theologians as A. Geiger were hyper-critical of Christianity — especially Catholicism — expecting, and even demanding, a process of "purification" from the "remnants of paganism" in Christianity, a return to the original Jewish creed.

47. Baeck developed his understanding of Judaism as both universalist in its mission and particularist in its attachment to the Jewish people in two important papers included in his book, *Wege im Judentum, op. cit.*: 1) "Volksreligion und Weltreligion" and 2) "Weltreligionen," pp. 195-215. This two-dimensional characterization of Judaism was a concept he greatly emphasized. It was crucial for him to show that there is no contradiction between loyalty to a universal mission and loyalty to a particular people. On the contrary, the only way to authentically fulfill a universal mission is to create the ideal model in reality, which means in a particular people. Thus, particularity itself becomes universally significant.

48. Baeck's positive evaluation of Moses Hess is beautifully expressed in a series of lectures given in Germany, in 1956, on the understanding of the modern period in Jewish history. According to these lectures, during this period there were four authentic representatives of specific positive achievements in the history of German Jewry: Mendelssohn, Hess, Rathenau and Rosenzweig. See Friedlander's book, p. 258.

49. See note no. 23.

50. See Baker's book, *op. cit.*, p. 304.

51. Baeck's essential affinity with Zionism is expressed not only in his positive relationship to the idea of rebuilding the Land of Israel as the Jewish national home, but also in the conception of Judaism as a complete national culture. See especially two articles included in his *Wege*: 1) "Kulturzusamenhaenge" and 2) "Lebensgrund und Lebensgehalt," pp. 117-151.

52. See note no. 14.

53. In the beginning of his career, Baeck was a distinct nonconformist within his movement. It should be emphasized that he quickly achieved a place as one of the movement's leading personalities, and his ideas were elaborated on and gradually accepted. When Baeck's opinions are compared to those of the young generation of scholars and rabbis in the movement, he does not seem to be an exception, rather a typical representative.

54. This being stated, the fact that a particular move toward a more central position was possible, even in the Marxist-Zionist movement, should not go unrecognized; a respectful relationship to the Jewish religion was conceivable. Ber Borochov himself was quite positive in his approach to religion as an expression of a popular Jewish mentality and culture. Later, such an approach became even more dominant in the thinking of distinguished leaders of Poalei Zion like I. Ben-Zvi and S. Shazar.

55. See Baeck's article on Rabbi N. Nobel in *Wege, op. cit.*, pp. 336-357.

56. On the meaning and origin of the term "National Theology," see my paper, "National Theology in Zionism" (Hebrew), *Bar-Ilan University Year Book*, vols. 22-23 (Ramat Gan, 1988), pp. 391-409.

57. Baeck's opinion that Judaism has no dogmas in the precise meaning in which this term has been defined in Christian theology is an obvious

deviation from the typical Reform stance in the nineteenth century. Thus, on the one hand, Baeck took a more traditional view similar to that of Rabbi S.R. Hirsch, while on the other hand his position was close to that of Cultural Zionism. As noted, Baeck stated his opinion on dogma in one of his first articles (note no. 24), but he returned to the subject with a more detailed exposition in a later paper, "Hat das Ueberlieferte Judentum Dogmen?" which was included in his book *Aus Drei Jahrtausenden, op. cit.*, pp. 12-27.

58. All the material which was saved from Jewish underground periodicals in Warsaw was published in three volumes, *Itonut Hamachteret Hayehudit B'Warsha*, ed. J. Kermish (Jerusalem: Yad Vashem, 1980). E. Ringelblum's papers were published in two volumes, *Ktovim Fun Ghetto Verlag* (Tel Aviv: Y.L. Perez, 1985). Also, the Akiva movement's underground periodical in Cracow, *Hehalutz Halohem*, ed. Rina Klinow (Beit Lohamei Hagetaot, 1984).

59. Sources of Orthodox religious response: 1) Rabbi S. Huberband, *Kiddush Hashem*, eds. N. Blumenthal and J. Kermish (Jerusalem: Yad Vashem, 1958). 2) H. Zeidman, *Ghetto Warsaw Diary* (Tel Aviv, 1946). 3) Issachar Shlomo Teichthal, *Em Habanim S'mechah*, 2nd ed. (New York, 1959). 4) Klonimos Kelmish Shapiro, *Esh Hakodesh* (Jerusalem, 1960).

60. Working with memories, J. Ibeshutz initiated an expanded publication project on the behavior and deeds of religious Jews in the Holocaust. He published such anthologies as *Bikdusha Ubigevurah* (Kiryat Ata, 1978), and *Haisha Bashoa* (Jerusalem, 1982). *Zachor* (Bene Berak), a periodical devoted to collections of documents, has appeared since 1982.

61. There are many testimonies of phantasmic messianic moods in Poland during the Holocaust, especially in Hassidic circles. See, for example, Zeidman's *Diary, op. cit.*, pp. 231-232, 295-297. Also Rabbi Huberband's paper on religious life during the war, *op. cit.*

62. This ideological "rebirth" is dramatically expressed in Reizl Kortchak's book, *Lehavoth Baefer* (Merhavia, 1946), pp. 53-56. See also A. Kovner, *Al Hagesher Hazar* (Merhavia, 1981), ch. 1. The same feeling of revolution emanates in the articles of S. Drenger in *Hehalutz Halohem, op. cit.*, and in Tenenbaum-Tamaroff's *Dapim Min Had'lekah* (Jerusalem: Yad Vashem, 1984).

63. The similarity between Birnbaum and Baeck is quite distinctive in Birnbaum's *Um die Ewigkeit* (Berlin, 1920).

64. H. Zeitlin, *Last Writings* (Hebrew) (Jerusalem: Mossad Harav Kook, 1979).

65. Zelig Kalmanowitz, *Ghetto Vilna Diary*, ed. Sh. Luria (Tel Aviv, 1977), pp. 103-105.

66. Another citation from Kalmanowitz's diary:
     Who mourns the destruction of East European Jewry? The destruc-
     tion is an accomplished fact....And it was accomplished even
     without the war, because it was carried out on a large scale. No one
     seriously tried to stop it. On the contrary, those who were willing
     to deceive themselves and the world into thinking that they were
     building a dam only caused more damage. The full proof of the
     matter is clearly evident in the East. Everything was drowning.
     Cultural life was tasteless....Individuals would have remained
     healthy and well but they would have been lost to their people.
     Eastern Jewry is disappearing. The final result would not have been
     any different from what is now happening to us (*ibid.*, pp. 95-96).

67. The opinion of the *Heint* journalist, Aharon Einhorn, on the internal
     destruction of Jewish life in the Warsaw Ghetto, as cited by
     Ringelblum:
     The ghetto was once the incorporation of Jewish good manners. In
     the ghetto, Judaism flourished, religiously and culturally. In the
     ghetto, a rich culture was created. But the Warsaw Ghetto is a
     sorrowful page in the history of our people. Assimilation was never
     so widespread as it is now. In Kremelichka one never heard as much
     Polish speech as one can hear now....Illiteracy flourishes on a large
     scale; demoralization never before reached to such large cir-
     cles....The Jewish population has not stood the test. It has been left
     to its own devices, and it functions so badly that anything worse is
     impossible; it is much worse than what someone would have done
     against us....There were many participants in the discussion, and
     there were some (like Sagan) who argued that we should withhold
     judgement. This is not a ghetto in the old sense. It is a concentration
     camp, a concentration of many people who are complete strangers
     to each other, people who would not and cannot live together, and
     in terrible conditions (E. Ringelblum, *op. cit.*, vol. 2, pp. 694-696).

68. Cohen's conception of Jewish history is revealed, chapter by chapter,
     in his book *Religion of Reason from the Sources of Judaism*. See my
     study, "Hermann Cohen as an Interpreter of the Bible" (Hebrew)
     Daat, no. 10 (Winter 1983), pp. 91-101.

69. The ideas of repentance, atonement and purification are a main theme in Cohen's religious teaching. According to him, man is able to protect his freedom of will not because he is really able to completely avoid sin, but because even when he sins he can repent before God. Without this religiously granted possibility of repentance, the sins would have become man's fate, and he would have lost his "Holy Spirit." See my study, "The Foundations of Hermann Cohen's Religious Philosophy" (Hebrew), *Studies in Jewish Thought*, no. 2 (Jerusalem, 1983), pp. 255-306.

70. On God as Redeemer, see *Religion of Reason, op. cit.*, ch. 13.

71. *Epochen der Juedischen Gesschchte, op. cit.*, pp. 117-118.

72. Hebrew in the original.

73. A Letter to Dr. Jaser, *Leo Baeck Institute Year Book*, no. 10 (London, 1965), p. 236.

74. Baeck's two systematic works are, of course, more philosophic-poetic than scientific, but in the two volumes of his collected writings, most of the papers are scientific research. The same is true of his booklet, *Epochen*, and there are still some uncollected scientific studies in various periodicals.

75. From the aspect of accepting philological discipline, the difference between Baeck and his teacher, Hermann Cohen, necessarily developed into a methodical-philosophical difference. Baeck had to move from Cohen's idealistic neo-Kantianism to Dilthey's empirical-phenomenology. Compare to Friedlander, *op. cit.*, pp.19-22.

76. *Aus Drei Jahrtausenden*, Vorwort, *op. cit.*, p. 10.

77. Rabbi Nachmal Krochmal, *The Guide for the Perplexed of our Time*, ch. 7.

78. In the context of a direct controversy with the views of Hegel, Marx, Spengler and Toynbee about Judaism as an historic "fossil," Baeck introduced the idea that Judaism was manifestly a complete, revolutionary innovation, and that it had been renewed in the same way several times. See *Epochen, op. cit.*, p. 27.

79. See "Wohlfahrt, Recht und Religion," *Wege, op. cit.*, pp. 236-249.

80. See "Tod und Wiedergeburt," *ibid.*, pp. 195-218.

81. Compare to Friedlander's discussion on the differences between Baeck and Rosenzweig, *op. cit.*, pp. 141-150.

82. See "Ursprung der Juedischen Mystic" in *Aus Drei Jahrtausenden, op. cit.*, pp. 244-255.

83. Kant's book, *Religion Within the Limits of Pure Reason Alone*, had a dominant impact on the philosophy of the Reform movement in its first period. Religion was thus reduced to ethics and aesthetics. It was Hermann Cohen who first redefined a separate realm for religion, but even in Cohen's conception of the religion of reason there persists a necessary "co-relation" between religion and ethics.

84. See note no. 29, the third in the list of articles.

85. "Bedeutung der Juedischen Mystik fuer Unsere Zeit," in *Wege, op. cit.*, pp. 96-103.

86. See the article in note no. 82, p. 249.

87. The last two chapters in *This People Israel* are "Man and the Mystery" and "The Task." This is characteristic of Baeck's conception of Jewish mysticism, leading from the experience of the cosmic mystery of infinity to the commandments, from the transcendent to the fulfillment of man's earthly duties. Thus Baeck finished his book in the same philosophical stance from which he had started.

88. *This People Israel, op. cit.*, p. 7.

89. *Aus Drei Jahrtausenden, op. cit.*, pp. 57-58.

90. *Ibid.*, pp. 372-373.

91. *Epochen, op. cit.*, pp. 17-18.

92. *Ibid.*, p. 54.

93. *Ibid.*, p. 55.

94. *Epochen* was composed as a series of lectures of a scientific-philological nature. Of course the broad guiding concept was historiosophical. Baeck discussed in detail the first revelation of historiosophical Judaism (the exodus from Egypt, Mount Sinai and the desert, the possession of the land). In the context of these historical

events, he carefully pursued the sources of prophecy and its main ideas. Baeck managed to study only two periods in Jewish history, namely, the exodus and the possession of the land, but this served as the empirical ground for a wide conceptualization of Judaism and Jewish history in their entirety. One can read the *Epochen* as parallel and complement to *This People Israel*. The same history and the same philosophical contents are discussed in a philosophic-poetic mode and in a philological-historiographic mode.

95. *Epochen, ibid.*, p. 95.

96. See "Vollendung und Spannung," in *Wege, op. cit.*, pp. 9-32. Compare to Friedlander's profound discussion of this chapter in Baeck's philosophy, *op. cit.*, pp. 184-204.

Chapter 2

THE RENEWAL OF MUSSAR
LITERATURE IN THE
ETHICO-THEOLOGICAL TEACHING
OF VIKTOR FRANKL

Viktor Frankl is a psychiatrist in the professional meaning of the term. He presents himself as such even in those of his books which are, for the most part, philosophical and theological.[1] Though the theoretical and practical differences between himself and Freud are of an essential nature, Frankl does not hesitate to describe himself as Freud's disciple.[2] In the context of professional research, Frankl writes on psychology and psychotherapy as strict sciences which are provable or refutable by empirical standards. Nonetheless, his foremost students and critics have noted that his teaching has not only an original philosophical-theological dimension, but also an ethical-theological dimension which is closely related to certain classic religious traditions.[3] Christian students discovered his affinity to Christian morality, while Jewish students observed his obvious rootedness in classical Jewish sources.

Admittedly, one should suspect popular attempts to claim for Judaism the cultural achievements of great individuals who are of Jewish origin but whose works are sustained by and belong directly to general Western culture. To some degree, a claim can be substantiated that the Jewish origin of people like Karl Marx, Henri Bergson, Sigmund Freud or Albert Einstein has had an impact on their creative contributions to Western civilization. Yet it is overwhelmingly clear that they belong wholly and integratively to that civilization and attempts to define their work as part of a specifically Jewish heritage are a new kind of Jewish apologetics which contributes nothing of significance either to the understanding of their thought or to the understanding of Judaism in our era.

With the danger of apologetics in mind and proceeding with due caution, one may point to Victor Frankl's teaching as a very interesting exception. In many ways his work is similar to previously mentioned examples, yet the material is sufficiently different relative to Jewish sources to be significant within the context of Jewish tradition. It is an exception which may be defined as a "border-case" and is indicative of a process which characterizes an important part of modern Jewish thinking in the second half of our century. It is a "border-case" firstly because Frankl himself, though he would not present his "logotherapy" in terms of a particularist Jewish tradition, does not conceal his Jewish origin or his Jewish religious conviction; and secondly, because of the Jewish context of his teaching in terms of both his personal experience in the Holocaust and his references to Jewish sources.

Here is a teaching which claims universal validity but consciously and directly draws from Jewish experience and wisdom. It may even be said that the original dimensions which make Frankl's psychology and existentialism unique in modern thought are taken almost entirely from the stores of Jewish wisdom. In his most popular book, *Man's Search for Meaning*,[4] Frankl documented the connection between the development of logotherapy and his experiences as a survivor of German concentration camps. Indeed, he arrived at the camp with the complete manuscript of his first book which described his scientific achievements before the Holocaust.[5] He tells about a failed attempt to save that manuscript, and then about his efforts to restore it while still under arrest. Did he complete this task in the concentration camp? The answer is not known, but in the second part of *Man's Search for Meaning*, he states that his first published book (in German, 1955), *The Doctor and the Soul: From Psychotherapy to Logotherapy*, is practically the restored first lost book. It is obvious then that the foundation for Frankl's original teaching of logotherapy was laid down before the Holocaust. Nonetheless, Frankl attached enough symbolic meaning to the story of the lost and restored book to reassure his readers of the crucial importance of his experiences in the concentration camp to the development of his teaching after the war. Defining his autobiographical narrative as *An Introduction to Logotherapy*, Frankl clearly states that the success of his survival and the ability to creatively overcome his trials (even making of them a part of his positive achievements) was due to his decision to relate to his own and his friends' experiences, as well as to the behavior of his Nazi persecutors, as material for research, and to the camp as a scientific laboratory. He would try to discover — even in the depth of these extraordinary human sufferings — a healing message, a transcending truth, a source of redemptive hope, for himself, for his friends, for humanity. He offers proof of this claim just before the conclusion of the autobiographical narrative when he relates how he actually helped friends overcome their psychological crisis on the threshold of liberation by transmitting his own acquired wisdom as a prisoner. This was to save them from deadly despair, to show them a way to find a personal meaning which could transform their apparently unrecoverable losses into personal human gains.[6]

It would not be exaggerating to interpret Frankl's story of the manuscript, at the beginning of the autobiographical account, as symbolic. It served as his marker. For him, personally, the loss of the book — the fruit of all his spiritual efforts — was a fateful moment. Through it, he gained his first insight into the dehumanizing meaning of a concentration camp, clearly grasping the existential level at which he must confront his personal trial. For him the destruction of the manuscript was a venomous humiliation directed against the core of spiritual meaning in his personal life. "Shit" was the answer of an inmate to whom Frankl appealed for help to save his book, and immediately he states the effect. "At that moment I saw the plain truth and did what marked the culminating point of the first phase of my psychological reaction: I struck out my whole former life."[7] If this culminating point of the first phase had been the end of the process, if he had been finally and decisively yielding, giving up his whole former life, meaning also his whole future life, clearly that would have been first his spiritual, and then his physical, death. But the story documents his clinging to the meaning which the book symbolized, clinging to its spiritual message. Thus, Frankl turned the brutal threat against the meaning of his personal life into his greatest achievement. He did this not only through a restoration of the destroyed book, but also through a deeper development of its redemptive message and a decisive proof of its truth. The story of the book became symbolically his own story, a story of life restored through the restoration of a truth. Indeed, the act of restoration and the conviction that it is always possible, even on the brink of death, is the conclusion of Frankl's confrontation with the Holocaust. It is the crucial message of logotherapy as it has been developed since his liberation.

The story of the destroyed and rewritten book is, therefore, a confession of fundamental importance. It contains an authentic element of initiation to a prophetic redemptive mission which clearly states its source of authority and its motivating power. This would appear to be the fundamental explanation for Frankl's need to substantiate his psychotherapeutic message by his personal experience in the Holocaust, a theme which reappears in almost all his books.[8] This is also the key to understanding the nature of his books which are a peculiar combination of the scientific and the popular, intended not only for professional psychiatrists, but for the wider public, and especially for the lonely, suffering individuals of our time. It is the affinity between the scientific and the prophetic that is most striking in his appeal and that makes his writing close to classical Jewish ethical literature.

To return to the question of sources: there is no direct biographical information about Frankl's Jewish education. The only way to answer this question is to study the evidence of his writings. Admittedly, that which Frankl cites from Jewish sources does not reflect a very wide or solid Jewish scholarship. Beside the Bible, Frankl cites the Jewish prayer book, and he reflects a general knowledge of Judaism which seems to be derived from secondary modern sources, such as the books of Martin Buber and Leo Baeck, which he mentions.[9] Though he does not mention them by name, the impact of Gershom Scholem and other famous Jewish scholars can clearly be detected in his philosophical and theological ideas.

However, the elementary, almost quintessential knowledge seems to have been deeply understood and internalized, becoming formative both for personal self-identification and toward shaping a personal religious experience. The facts here are sufficiently overt to be objectively proved and measured. As a psychiatrist Frankl uses, in addition to his own empirical research, all the available sources of scientific psychology and psychiatry.[10] But parallel to these general European sources, Frankl derives the main body of his Existentialist theology from Jewish sources. This means that to the extent that the impact of sources, in the traditional or cultural sense of the term, can be detected in Frankl's religious philosophy, they are mainly Jewish. Not that Frankl does not often quote Kierkegaard, Scheler, Heidegger and Sartre, but when what is unique in his religiousity is approached, the classical and modern Jewish sources are also implied. These reflect, quite identifiably, biblical, midrashic, ethical and Hassidic messages.[11] But beyond the centrality of religious and ethical ideas derived from Jewish literature in Frankl's writings, the most impressive phenomenon is his method of relating to his task both as a psychiatrist and a writer. This is recognizable in the content, form and style of his books. It may be unhesitatingly suggested that Frankl's works belong to the classical tradition of "ethical literature" (*Sifrut Mussar*). This writing was shaped during the Middle Ages and subsequently directly influenced the late ethical literature of Hassidism and the Mussar movement, as well as the Enlightenment and neo-Orthodox literature (especially Rabbi S.R. Hirsch's works). One cannot know if Frankl ever carefully studied such books as Rabbi Saadia Gaon's *Beliefs and Opinions*, Rabbi Bahya Ibn Paquda's *Duties of the Heart*, Maimonides' *Eight Chapters* or Rabbi Moshe Chaim Luzatto's *Way of the Righteous*, because he never refers to these best-known examples of Jewish ethical literature. But distinct similarities in content and educational-therapeutical task, as well as in form and style, can be pointed to.

What does the affinity between Frankl's teaching and classical Jewish ethical literature consist of? Paradoxically, it is found precisely in the direct, universalist claim and in its scientific, functional purpose. Unlike philosophers such as Buber and Baeck, Hermann Cohen in his last book, or even Rosenzweig in his systematic work, Frankl did not intend to write a specifically "Jewish" book. What he did write should be defined as an attempt to make use of his Jewish experiences and wisdom, together with other relevant wisdom, in order to solve an urgent human problem. Moreover, his interest has been defined on the functional-practical level of human behavior, and not on the philosophical or theological level. Frankl established a theory of therapeutic practice, proved its empirical success, and then developed his philosophical and theological work as part of a practical scheme with which to try solving painful, personal spiritual problems.

Traditional Jewish ethical literature in the Middle Ages was marked by these two characteristics. Its Jewishness required no proof. It was directly affirmed by the use of authoritative sources, thus itself becoming an integral part of the so-called "Oral Torah." Precisely because its Jewish authenticity was beyond any doubt, there was no need to answer questions regarding what was unique or specifically Jewish in its content. Such questions might have been raised in a polemic context, mainly with Christianity, but the first and immediate interest was to discover a truth which would serve as a guide toward a life worth living: a truth oriented toward goodness, perfection and meaning, for the sake of which every relevant truth, derived from any source, became sufficiently "Jewish" to be worthy of study. Its aim was not only theoretic, but it offered practical instruction on the ways and techniques to avoid sins which are damaging to the sinner; on correcting faults of personal character, feeling and opinion; on developing a good personality through a meritorious way of life; that is to say, it offered what was defined by this literature itself as "healing for the soul" (*refuat hanefesh*). This characteristic of classic Jewish ethical literature must be strongly emphasized. Its generic literary quality is defined by its functional purpose: to educate, first of all, the official educators of the Jewish community, the so-called "soul-healers" (*rofei hanefesh*), who, therefore, serve as models of ethical perfection;[12] to reach out through and beyond them to each individual in the community. This required the use of proper educational tools and didactic techniques based not only on the theoretical, but also on the direct impact of a didactic technique which was inherent in the structure and style of the books themselves.[13]

Is Frankl really unique among the modern teachers of Judaism, such as Cohen, Buber, Rosenzweig and Baeck, in adopting this semi-traditional approach? It is true that these Jewish philosophers were inclined to present Judaism as a guiding truth to religio-ethical perfection, intended for all humanity. Even more than their medieval predecessors, they were interested in proving the universal validity of Judaism because the Emancipation had provoked their need to justify the separate existence of Judaism by a claim of universal mission. Yet it was just this apologetic effort to justify Judaism that strengthened Jewish self-identity from within as well as defended its right to a separate, particular existence against external attacks. For theologians and philosophers such as Cohen, Buber and Baeck, the main problem to be solved, with tools of scholarship and philosophy, was — what is Judaism? What does it mean to be a Jew? What is the Jewish contribution to humanity?[14]

Solutions for such questions, of course, imply practical conclusions. Yet these discussions were on an intellectual level, intended to acquire historical knowledge and achieve philosophical understanding. The concern was not necessarily about the *halakhic* task of deciding norms of behavior and shaping a day-to-day way of life; even less were the psychotherapeutic dimensions of the confrontation with spiritual and moral crises engaged. That is, the theoretical solutions of such intellectual problems do not imply any confrontation with therapeutic problems which may result in a classical understanding of the "healing of the soul." To sum up, the teachings of Buber, Rosenzweig, Baeck and such others are educational only on the intellectual level, and, therefore, they may not be included in the category of classic Mussar literature, while Frankl's works, which use Jewish wisdom in terms of the practical treatment of suffering human beings, are both innovative in the context of modern Jewish thought, and traditional in the context of Jewish ethical literature.

It is necessary to substantiate these rather general observations through an analytical discussion of a number of Frankl's central ethico-theological teachings, comparing his main insights first to similar teachings in traditional Jewish ethical sources, and then to parallel teachings in the writings of those modern Jewish scholars and philosophers who were concerned with the "problem of man" in our age. The distinct religious quality of Frankl's logotherapy is the starting point, and here a delicate differentiation is necessary.

Frankl himself rejects the characterization of his psychiatric theory as "religious." According to him, his is an empirical theory which is to be validated, or refuted, by the use of regular "secular" scientific tools. The theory is based on a general anthropology and its conclusions should be valid for any human being, religious, non-religious or even anti-religious. Moreover, Frankl suggests there is a sharp distinction between the psychiatrist's professional task as a doctor, and the spiritual help which he, as a believing human being, may offer to certain patients whose sufferings are effected by their spiritual crises as believers. A psychiatrist, according to Frankl, may also be a religious person, and there are moments in which he should, if he can, offer his patient needed religious support which is beyond professional help. Frankl even states that there are cases in which this spiritual-religious support may be more important than the professional psychiatric treatment. Still, it should definitely be forbidden to mix up these two separate treatments or to blur the boundary between them. These are clearly separate disciplines which may complement each other but never serve as substitutes for each other, the relationship between them being similar to that between physical medicine and psychiatry. Physicians as well as psychiatrists should fully recognize and appreciate the special function of each of these three disciplines, each one of them in its proper realm. Neither the physician nor the psychiatrist should ever deny the validity of the other disciplines, neither should he reduce them to his own. Never should religious support be offered instead of psychiatric help, or psychiatric support instead of physical medicine, etc., because doing so will cause damage and mislead. The psychiatrist should first diagnose the sort of problem from which his patient suffers in order to determine which treatment, or treatments, are relevant, after which he should offer his assistance in the appropriate and distinctive realm.[15]

Without denying this explicit warning, the claim is made that Frankl's psychiatric theory is based on a philosophical anthropology which comprises a distinct, essential, religious component. Moreover, this religious component is implied in his "secular" scientific theory and, therefore, informs even his methods of psychiatric treatment, though it does not assume that every patient is, or has to be, religious in the simple meaning of this term. The personal conviction of a patient is, indeed, irrelevant from the psychiatrist's point of view. But even as a psychiatrist Frankl interprets the patient's human condition, his relation to the world and to himself, in terms which are essentially religious, and these essential religious presuppositions are implied in the psychiatric treatment itself. This complex argumentation will be clarified by a general review of Frankl's anthropology.

Frankl's logotherapy is based on the following main assumptions:

1. Man is inclined, by his unique human nature, to search for a transcendental meaning as his ultimate end, not for happiness, material satisfaction, or individual "self-actualization."

2. Man therefore is naturally inclined to accept responsibility before a certain entity which is beyond himself.

3. In the core of his soul every human being has an active individual conscience which directs him towards his specific transcendent source of meaning. (This conscience is the "Divine Image" in which man has been created.)

4. Through his transcendental personal responsibility, a man can endow even suffering and failure with meaning. Thus, the gate to personal redemption is never shut before him.

5. The basic question which man must ask himself, for the sake of his mental health and spiritual well-being, is not, what can I get out of my life? Rather he should ask, what does life demand of me?

What is my unique individual responsibility? Before whom and for what am I personally responsible?

These anthropological assumptions which we claim are essentially religious, without any explicit decision about the specific "identity" of the transcendent source of meaning or the specific direction of behavior which every autonomous conscience decides for itself. One need not speak of God as his transcendent source of meaning, nor choose religious observation as his specific realm of responsibility. Still, the basic nature of his relationship to himself and to the world will remain religious, that is, oriented toward a transcendental ultimate meaning.

Frankl himself accepts this characterization of his anthropology. Obviously, this is the foundation of the theological theory which crowns his intellectual efforts with the idea of "the unconscious God."[16] Admittedly, the belief in the existence of an "unconscious God" as an absolute truth does not necessarily blur the distinction between the religious and the non-religious. It remains both valid and important in terms of conscious life, world views, ethical values, ways of behavior, etc., which each man chooses autonomously. According to Frankl, the differences between world views and lifestyles are sufficiently important to substantiate a distinction between the secular responsibility of a psychiatrist and the religious responsibility of a believing friend or teacher, but the distinction is not valid on the subconscious level, at which each human being is religious, according to his own personal understanding. If that is so, it appears that there is no way out of the conclusion that logotheraputic treatment, though consciously secular, must contain a certain "unconscious" religious dimension.

In what follows we will try to clarify this claim, but as we are dealing with one of Frankl's fundamental ideas, it is useful to confirm and elucidate it in his own words:

> The concept of such metameaning is not necessarily theistic. When I was fifteen years old or so I came up with a definition of God to which, in my old age, I come back more and more. I would call it an operational definition. It reads as follows: God is the partner of your most intimate soliloquies. Whenever you are talking to yourself in utter sincerity and ultimate solitude, He to whom you are addressing yourself may justifiably be called God. Such a definition avoids the dichotomy between atheistic and theistic

Weltanschauungs. The difference between them emerges only later on, when the irreligious person insists that his soliloquies are just that, monologues with himself....I think that what counts first and more than anything else is the utmost sincerity and honesty. If God really exists he certainly is not going to argue with irreligious persons because they mistake Him for themselves.[17]

Thus circumventing the difference between the theist and the atheist, Frankl defines the secular dimensions of his work within the wider circle of his essentially religious teaching.[18] Indeed, in this wide circle of religious teaching, Frankl is attuned both to classic Jewish ethical literature and to the influence of some modern Jewish thinkers.

The first area in which a return to the classic stance of Jewish traditional Mussar literature is observed in Frankl's anthropology is his method of differentiating between body and soul. In this area, Frankl's departure from both the Freudian and the behavioristic schools should be emphasized.

As the dichotomy "conscious-unconscious" has become only a secondary issue, so the age-old psychophysical problem now proves to have lost its primary significance. It has to recede behind the much more essential problem of spiritual existence versus psychophysical facticity. This issue is not only a problem of greater ontological import, but also one of greater psycho-therapeutic relevancy. After all, a psychotherapist is continually concerned with spiritual existence in terms of freedom and responsibility, and with marshalling it against the psychophysical facticity which the patient is prone to accept as his fate. The awareness of freedom and responsibleness which constitutes authentic humanness must be set against this neurotic fatalism. But we must not neglect the fact that being human is always individualized. As such, it is always centered around a core, and this core is the person, who, in the words of Max Scheler, is not only the agent but also the "center" of spiritual activity. I would say that this spiritual personal center is encompassed by the peripheral psychophysical layers. Now instead of talking of spiritual existence and psychophysical facticity, we may speak of the spiritual person and "its" psychophysical overlay. By "its" we mean to emphasize that the person "has" a psychophysical overlay, whereas the person "is" spiritual. After all I am not really justified in saying "my self," not even "myself," since I do not "have" a self, but I "am" a self. If anything, I can "have" an id, but precisely in the sense of psychophysical facticity. Being centered around the existential, personal, spiritual core, human being is not only individualized but also integrated. Thus the spiritual core, and only the spiritual core, warrants and constitutes oneness and wholeness in man. Wholeness in this context means the integration of somatic, psychic and spiritual aspects. It is not possible to stress enough that it is only this threefold wholeness which makes man complete. In no way are we justified in speaking of man in terms of only a "somatic-psychic whole." Body and psyche may form a unity — a psychophysical unity — but this unity does not yet represent the wholeness of man. Without the spiritual as its essential ground, this wholeness cannot exist. As long as we speak only of body and psyche, wholeness has not yet come in.[19]

There is an astonishing resemblance between Frankl's argumentation in this passage and the peculiar blend of Aristotelian and neo-Platonic psychologies which is typical of medieval Mussar literature, especially that of Maimonides, which represents the more Aristotelian version, and Ibn Paquda's, which represents the more neo-Platonic version. In these two variations, one finds on one side the same emphasis of psycho-physical unity which marks the biological organism of man as an animal, interpreting all the activities of the body as psychological functions (the function of the "nutritive," "sensitive," "reactive" and "imaginative" parts of the soul in the Maimonidean theory, or the "vegetative" and the "animalistic" powers in the neo-Platonic theories).[20] On the other side, there is the uniqueness of the human soul as a supernatural, spiritual entity (the "logical" or "reasonable" part in Maimonidean theory; the "spiritual" power in the neo-Platonic theories).[21] Indeed, according to these medieval theories the real core or "essence" of the human soul (that which Frankl depicts as the "self" which cannot be considered as belonging to man because it is *the* man), is identified with the "separate," "distinct" core of the human soul, which is Reason according to Maimonides, and Spirit (*Neshama*) according to the neo-Platonic versions. According to these medieval theories, therefore, one may state, exactly as Frankl states, that the essential core of the human soul is wrapped in psychophysical "layers," and that the human personality is unified and becomes a perfected whole around its spiritual core because the other "external" layers of the soul are destined to serve the spiritual essence as their goal.[22]

There is here a basic similarity between two threefold ontological conceptions of the human personality: the body and the soul, which are functionally interdependent, and the spirit, which is distinct though it needs the services of the body and the soul, and a basic resemblance between the two theories according to which man is unified and perfected around the spiritual core which is identified with that which is essential in him.[23] Therefore, there is also a resemblance between the two theories which distinguish between physical medicine, related to the psycho-physical organism, and psycho-therapy, related to the activity of man as a spiritual entity, aiming to achieve the ideal of an integrated human personality.[24] The second topic is systematically grounded in the threefold ontology of the human personality: the peculiar qualities which characterize the uniqueness of the human spirit, as differentiated from its external, psycho-physical "layers" which are autonomy and an inclination toward a transcendental source of meaning.

First is the development of the assumption of human autonomy. Frankl's severest criticism of psycho-analytical and behavioristic theories is directed against their determinist attitude which necessitates a "mechanistic" method of treatment in the natural "drives" and cultural "conditionings" of the soul. Against this determinist conception of man, Frankl proposes a different conception of man.

> It sets another concept of man ever against the psychosomatic one. It is no longer focused on the automaton of a psyche apparatus but rather on the autonomy of spiritual existence. "Spiritual" is being used here without any religious connotation, of course, but rather first to indicate that we are dealing with a specifically human phenomenon....In other words, the "spiritual" is what is human in man....In fact, existential analysis interprets human existence, and indeed being human, ultimately in terms of being responsible.[25]

Parallel to this statement is the typical Maimonidean stance, which on this topic represents all the recognized authorities of Jewish ethics, almost without exception. Man, as a reasonable animal, has the power of will (autonomous decision) and objective freedom of choice. Man chooses not only between good and bad in his external social behavior, but he can also shape his own ethical qualities, which are his soul's attributes; therefore, he is responsible to his ethical character as well as to his conscious deeds. The centrality of this global understanding of the ethical responsibility in medieval Mussar literature must be emphasized because it has important implications for education and psychological treatment. A man is considered healthy as long as he recognizes his responsibility and shows adequate effort to fulfill it in his total activity.[26] The therapeutic conclusion from this assumption is quite clear: the psychotherapist acts mainly by the instrumentality of educational means. First and foremost, he must convince his patient, offering ideational guidance. As a soul-healer, his main task is to enable his patient to develop his personal understanding of ethical truth, through which he will understand the full range of his individual responsibility. The psychotherapist must guide his patient towards his unique transcendent goal, direct him in his behavior, and tell him how to fulfill his human potential, perform his duties, and serve the goal of humanity.[27]

One may claim that in order to assert the autonomy and moral responsibility of man, Frankl could return to Kantian or neo-Kantian humanism, which is part of modernity. Why should we, then, assume a return to a medieval ethical tradition? Our answer to this possible criticism is, firstly, that Frankl systematically grounded his concept of human autonomy in the previously described ontology of the psyche, intending to develop not only an abstract theory of law and ethics, but also an empirical-practical theory of psychotherapeutic treatment. (On the *a priori* idealistic setting of Kantian humanism, such empirical-practical theory is inconceivable!) Secondly, Frankl assumed a teleological causal relationship between the concept of moral responsibility and the existence of a transcendental commanding authority, as a source of moral duty and spiritual meaning. (This *heteronomous* understanding of responsibility contradicts the Kantian concept of autonomy, which is inherent in human reason.) In other words, the psycho-empirical quality of logotherapy, and its transcendental religious character, distinguish it from the idealistic version of modern humanism as well as from the main schools of modern scientific psychology, and place it back in a traditional religious setting. Actually, it is Frankl's concept of the conscience that is referred to here.

> The psychological fact of conscience is but the immanent aspect of a transcendent phenomenon, it is only that piece of the whole phenomenon which seeps into psychological immanence. If conscience is the voice of transcendence it is thus itself transcendent. Viewed in this light, an irreligious man is one who does not recognize this transcendent quality. Needless to say, the irreligious man also "has" a conscience, and he also is responsible; he simply asks no further — neither what he is responsible to, nor from what his conscience stems. But this is no reason for the religious man to become haughty....If Samuel failed to recognize that the call came to him from transcendence, how much more difficult it must be for an ordinary person to discern the transcendent character of the voice he perceives through his conscience. And why should we be surprised if he takes this voice for something that is rooted merely within himself? The irreligious man thus proves to be the one who takes his conscience in its psychological facticity. Facing it as merely an immanent fact, he stops — stops prematurely — for he considers conscience the ultimate "to what" he is responsible. However, conscience is not the last "to what" of responsibleness, but the next to last. On his way to find the ultimate meaning of life, the irreligious man, as it were, has not yet reached the highest peak, but rather has stopped at the next to highest. (This, of course, is the way the religious man looks at the irreligious.) And what is the reason the irreligious man does not go further? It is because he does not want to lose the "firm ground under his feet." The true summit is barred from his vision; it is hidden in the fog, and he does not risk venturing into it, into this uncertainty. Only the religious man hazards it.[28]

But traditional Mussar literature did not develop a theory of conscience in Frankl's sense.[29] It simply did not need it, being fully and directly grounded in its religious sources. With such religious thinking, inspired by a revealed Divine commandment, there was no function for an ontological "conscience" beyond reason, while Frankl really needs an intermediate rank of guidance between man and God in order to create a common denominator between the secular humanist and the religious believer. Unless he assumed the existence of a conscience as a transcendent "rank," which, however, is not identified with God, he would not have been able to apply logotherapy to the non-believer! According to traditional Mussar conceptions, human reason which emanates from the Divine Essence (the Maimonidean version) or the human spirit which is derived from the Divine spheres of existence (the neo-Platonic theories) elevate man to the status of an animal created by God in His own "image" or "form." The connection between this understanding of the relationship between God and man, and human responsibility before God as the authoritative source of ethical commandment, is achieved through the concept of prophecy, or revelation of Divine transcendence in the human soul. Reason, or the spiritual element in the human soul, which is derived from the Divine entity, is inward and absolutely faithful to its source. It is absolutely devout to its supreme transcendental origin, striving to return to its higher primal condition, or even to be reunited with the spheres of the Divine on high. Thus the traditional religious anthropology achieved an ideal unity between obedience to Divine transcendental commandment and faithfulness to the inner, "essential" self, or between "heteronomy" and "autonomy." This means that the function which Frankl attaches to conscience is fulfilled in the traditional Mussar conception directly by Divine inspiration, or by Divine presence in man. God and man meet in the act of prophetic revelation on the part of God, and prophetic internalization of the Divine truth and justice as his own autonomous will on the part of man. In this way human behavior reflects both man's autonomous grasp of the concept of truth and justice, and his absolute compliance to the authority of a revealed norm of behavior.[30]

Returning from this traditional conception to Kantianism, even in the neo-Kantian version of Cohen who developed the concept of "correlation" between human reason and the transcendent ideal of God, it definitely becomes clear that the idealistic philosophical conception of religion is essentially reductionist. Even when it strives to "save" religion for modernity, it does so by adapting the concept of religion to the philosophical horizon of the secular non-believer. In his retreat from Freudian and behavioristic psychologies, Frankl as a believer could not be satisfied with idealistic reductionism. He, therefore, reached back to the psychological ontology which could serve as a basis for a more "orthodox" understanding of religion. Indeed, in order to remain true to his vocation as a psychiatrist in its modern, scientific understanding, he had to accept a certain "compromise" with Kantian idealism, or to "tolerate" it, because only through its concept of moral duty could he apply his anthropology to the non-believer. Still, if Frankl's approach to the non-believer is carefully examined, it will be apparent that he incorporated the hidden religious dimension of his secular psychology in his concept of conscience, which is open — "unconsciously" so — to the call of a hidden transcendent authority. Thus, he could actually "tolerate" only the neo-Kantian version of humanism, because this was the only kind of humanism which remained open to the ideal of transcendence, before which man accepts his responsibility, and from which he draws a sense of direction and meaning. Even the non-religious "rank" of authority must at least be quasi-religious in order to accept logotherapy as a relevant treatment.

The third topic of comparison between logotherapy and traditional Mussar literature is also systematically connected to Frankl's anthropology: the redefinition of the realm of the spiritual "unconscious," in the context of a radical criticism on Freudianism.

> To take up once more the issue of "depth psychology" we have to extend the meaning of this concept, because up to now depth psychology has followed man into the depth of his instincts, but too little into the depth of his spirit. Since "depth" refers to the unconscious, it necessarily follows that the person in his depth, the spirit in its depth, or for that matter, human existence in its depth is essentially unconscious. This is due to the fact that spiritual activity absorbs the person as the executor of spiritual acts; that he is not even capable of reflecting on what he basically is. The self does not yield to total self-reflection. In this sense, human existence is basically unreflectable, and so is the self in itself. Human existence exists in action rather than reflection. Insofar as human existence cannot fully be reflected upon by itself, it cannot be fully analyzed either. That is why existential analysis can never be an analysis of existence, but can only be an analysis toward existence. Human existence remains an Urphenomenon, i.e., an unanalyzible, irreducible phenomenon. And this holds for each of its basic aspects, e.g., such human phenomena as consciousness and responsibleness. If these are to be illuminated, we have to transcend the ontic plane toward the ontological dimension. Within the plane of psychological im-

manence, both consciousness and responsibleness are and remain unsolvable problems. However, as soon as we transpose them into the ontological dimension they cease to be problems. For then they are taken as Urphenomena, constitutive of human existence, or in Heideggerian terms, they are "existentials," attributes that belong to the very foundations of human existence. To sum up, spiritual phenomena may be unconscious or conscious; the spiritual basis of human existence, however, is ultimately unconscious. Thus, the center of the human person in his very depth is unconscious. In its origin, the human spirit is unconscious spirit....However, the spirit is not only unconscious where it originates, that is, in its depth, but also in its height as well. In fact, that which has to decide whether something is to be conscious or unconscious is itself unconscious....In order to make such a decision, however, it must somehow be able to discern. Since both deciding and discerning are spiritual acts, again it follows that these spiritual acts not only can but must be unconscious in the sense of being unreflectable.[31]

The reader should be aware of the fact that this passage discusses the concept of conscience in the context of a scientific psychological theory, and not in a theological context. Frankl seems to be very cautious in his distinction between the concept of spiritual unconscious and what he has to say as a theologian on the "unconscious God," the God who is transcendent in human consciousness.[32] The statement in the last quotation refers to his claim that the human spirit is unconscious of the nature of its own self and, therefore, also unconscious of its exact ways of functioning: the way in which it selects, chooses, decides, etc. Of course, the human spirit can be aware of the dimensions of its own unconsciousness as a profound experience; it can even understand the ontological necessity of this condition. Do we do justice to Frankl's teaching if we claim that even here, where he uses distinct Kantian and post-Kantian philosophical ideas alongside modern, scientific, psychological conceptions, he is basically continuing an old medieval religious tradition? The inclination is to answer this question in the affirmative, though here a careful distinction between the ideational contents and their terminological garment is suggested.

For the sake of clarity, an implied observation should be added to the above-quoted passage. Frankl actually argues that alongside the realm of the "subconscious," which is the object of psychoanalysis, there exists in man a realm of the "above" or the "beyond" of consciousness, namely a realm which absolutely transcends human ability to know; this realm is, indeed, the spiritual unconscious.[33] Assuming this observation, it may rightly be claimed that traditional psychology was inclined to neglect the realm of the impulsive, animalistic subconscious. (However, let us stress that neglect does not mean denial.) Traditional psychology was indeed conscious of an animalistic, irrational realm of natural drives which can eventually be ruled but cannot be completely comprehended.[34] But, contrary to its lack of interest in the subconscious realm of the irrational, it was very much concerned with the realm of the "above" and the "beyond." As part of a religious philosophy it attached a great deal of importance to the denotation and illumination (as far as this is possible in philosophical terms) of this realm. Of course, the term consciousness in its modern connotation is not used, and therefore there is nothing about an "above-consciousness." But the content is there.

It has already been noted that traditional Mussar literature did not refer to the ontological category of conscience because it could rely on the revealed word of God. Obviously, in this reliance, it denoted the transcendent realm above human knowledge, though still directly related to man. Truly a mere denotation of a transcendent authority above man is not what Frankl means when he points to a realm above consciousness in man himself. But now Frankl's ontology of the conscience must be carefully reexamined because its exact position between the other faculties of the soul, comprising the spiritual faculties of consciousness, reason and will, seems to be quite unclear. Is it an inherent part of the human personality, or, being open to the transcendent, is it a separate entity beyond inherence, thus intermediating between the self and what is beyond the self? There is no clearcut answer to this question, and one can interpret Frankl's ambivalence on this point as an indication of a mysterious infinity in the human soul, which is both inherent and transcendent, both in and beyond man himself. It is, therefore, both known and unknown to man, making him aware of the hidden beyond, and unable to know the secret of his own spiritual self. If this interpretation of Frankl's theory is correct, then we have touched a substantial ground for religious experience which serves as the most profound point of meeting with the traditional theory of Divine emanation and Divine inherence in the human soul.

Let us return to the medieval theory of Divine emanation either of or in the soul of man. The same unclarity or ambivalence is confronted here as was detected in Frankl's theory. Here, too, one is reminded of a mystery, an infinity within human finality. The human Socratic endeavor to "know himself" ends, parallel to the human endeavor to know God, with an enigmatic "from where?" In its finality human reason stumbles on an unsurpassable limit, beyond which it can only be aware of the endless, the absolute, the eternal, the other which is itself. Eventually we are advised that these two infinite reflections are of one and the same subject, that is, man reflects on the mystery of God in his own soul when he reflects on the inner mystery of the source of his own soul. Man comprises fully only those parts or spheres of his soul which are manifest in this-worldly, secular functions. He knows himself as he is active outwardly in the world. When he turns inward to understand what the source of his existence is or to experience the inner essence of his self, he confronts the mystery of creation, or of emanation from a sphere beyond a sphere *ad infinitum*. Only by self-transcendence, which is an intellectual or emotional effort beyond finality, can he become aware of a source in the beyond, experiencing it both within and above his self-knowing self. In this way psychology played a central role in traditional theology. God is a spiritual entity. Can man grasp the incorporeal as an entity, a real existent? Can man have a concept of the spiritual as such? Normally our human intellect grasps only the corporeal existents and tends to identify the attribute of existence with corporeality, which is the source of the difficulty in grasping the pure idea of monotheism, or the source of the mistake of idolatry. A spiritual entity is beyond the grasp of our sense faculties, whereas through our this-worldly normal functioning we experience reality only through the senses, and therefore tend to define them as a sole source of knowledge, even in the realm of the sciences. Normally, then, men are inclined to deny the existence of a spiritual entity.

Traditional theology points to our inner experience of the soul in order to prove its claim that beyond the experienced "reality" of the sensual, which is only seemingly real because it is final and transient, there exists a realm of eternal, absolute existence, God being its supreme source. The soul is the source of every activity of the bodily organism. It activates the senses, yet it evidently transcends its own senses. The soul is, therefore, the evidence for the existence of spiritual entities. It testifies to the existence of God and as such it is also the primal way to come closer to the knowledge of God. There is at least a "similarity" between the transcendent dimension in the soul and God; at least, we say, because the resemblance is sometimes understood as inherence, the soul first inheres in God as its source, then God inheres in the soul as its hidden core. Therefore, self-knowledge, the knowledge of the soul, is the starting point for the infinite dialectical advance toward the knowledge of the Divine. The more we know our soul, the more we come nearer to God. It is an endless process of self-knowledge and self-transcendence.

The similarity between medieval theological psychology and Frankl's argumentation is here at its peak. There still exists though a dim difference between them because Frankl has no theory of emanation, so that his conscience seems to take place "in between," as a point of meeting and departure, the soul itself from one side, and God, the absolute transcendent, from the other side. As a believer, Frankl fights against all sorts of intellectual and psychological reductionisms. He approximates the traditional psycho-theological argument, and the affinity between his theology of the "unconscious God" and the psycho-theology of Ibn Paquda's "Duties of the Heart," or even of some of the most influential Kabbalistic books, is indeed astonishing.[35]

The discussion of similarities between Frankl's ontology of the psyche and classical Jewish Mussar literature alluded to a number of differences as well. These stem from Frankl's use of modern scientific and philosophical tools. When these differences are examined, however, in their full cultural context, yet another aspect may be observed of Frankl's relatedness to a Jewish milieu: his affinity to modern Jewish existentialism. Such an assertion requires careful definition. While a direct influence cannot be proven, it may be safely assumed that Frankl studied Buber's writings intensively and absorbed some of his ideas. It may also be assumed that he read something of Baeck's theological works and perhaps those of Heschel as well. Further, one may conjecture that Frankl studied some of Scholem's work with great interest, in addition to other books on Jewish literature by well-known scholars.

On the other hand, it appears that he knew nothing about A.D. Gordon or Rabbi A.Y. Kook. Thus, if despite this missing link an essential philosophical affinity between Frankl and Gordon and Kook is detected, it testifies to something more significant than direct influence. That something may be grounded in an inner disposition to a certain historical tradition, or to a common cultural subconscious. To comprehend this similarity is to understand a crucial element in current Jewish thinking.

First, it would be useful to expand on the differences between Frankl's teaching and the psycho-theological elements in traditional Mussar literature. Some of these differences were dealt with earlier. They stand out most clearly, however, when viewed from a different perspective.

Ontology: We have observed Frankl's views from the perspective of his critique of Freudian psychoanalysis and behaviorism. One recalls his admitted discipleship as a psychotherapist of the Freudian school, and the admission of his general indebtedness to modern scientific research in psychology. Yet Frankl's teaching is a critical synthesis of several schools of modern psychology and modern existentialist philosophy. Typically, he draws upon the positive contribution of every serious school in science and philosophy so as not to lose any worthwhile item of knowledge, or any fruitful method of treatment. Adopting a modern scientific method of research as a basic approach, Frankl could not but ignore the methodological aspects of traditional psychology. The resulting divergences are reflected mainly in the way he grasps the psycho-physical realm, and the way in which he defines the difference between mental and bodily diseases. To put it more exactly, it is in the way he differentiates between the mental aspects of somatic diseases and the somatic aspects of mental diseases. In all such aspects there can be no comparison between Frankl's empirical theory and traditional scholastic theories. This is not only the outcome of a vast accumulation of empirical knowledge, but as formerly stated, a result of using different methods of research. Moreover, it culminates in an ontological difference.

Since Frankl grasps the whole structure of relations between mental life and bodily functions in an entirely different way, of necessity he must also grasp the impact of bodily functions on mental processes differently. What is important for this discussion is the ontological-structural conclusion, namely, the centrality of the "subconscious" in the modernistic approach and the ontological division between the "super-ego" and the "id" as distinct realms in the hierarchical structure of the soul. This conceptualization of the soul's structure is not only vital for Frankl's ontological theory, it is of critical importance for his psychotherapeutic method of treatment. Traditional theories of the psyche lack an ontological basis for applying such modern psychological categories. This is a profound change which must impact on almost every topic relevant to psychology. Consequently, an expansion of the differences between Frankl's teaching and classical Mussar literature will illuminate an early and basic difference. In general terms the affinity between Frankl's theory and classical Jewish Mussar literature grows from similarity to an almost complete identity in the higher, spiritual spheres of mental life. But the correlation diminishes to complete otherness toward the lower realms of bodily activity and the mental functions which govern them.

At first glance there is no analogy between the differences of ontology, on the one hand, and the differences in understanding the spiritual autonomy and freedom of will, on the other. The primary cause of this relative obscurity is the impact of our modern age; first, the impact of scientific research, but over and above that, the impact of an individualistic secular ethos. However, when dealing with the psychological aspects of human ethical behavior one should assume some interaction between seemingly disparate elements: the social ethos, which guides and shapes the inner mental experiences and the inner conscious, or the subconscious; man's relations to himself and to his environment; and the methods and conclusions of scientific research. We have already noted that traditional ethics does not recognize the status of the personal conscience, which plays a very important role in Frankl's teaching. According to traditional theory, man discovers the eternal-universal principles of law and justice with his intellect. The application of these general principles to concrete specific conditions and the shaping of exact norms is the task of another relevant kind of intellect — that of the "practical" intellect,[36] which relies on the accumulation of experiences and the acquisition of skills to foresee the probable results of human actions. Yet, as even philosophers must admit, the intellectual assessment of changing material conditions never results in sufficiently certain practical conclusions.[37] There must then be a super-intellectual authority, that of the revealed law, or the Torah, in order to have a firm normative lifestyle. The Torah, as the revealed will of God, is then the supreme guiding authority, and not the personal conscience.

This divergence is grounded in a basic, ontological difference in the understanding of individuality, its source and its status. The following passage from Frankl's book illuminates this difference very clearly:

It is the task of conscience to disclose to man the *unum necesse,* the one thing that is required. This one thing, however, is absolutely unique in as much as it is the unique possibility a concrete person has to actualize in a specific situation. What matters is the unique "ought to be" which cannot be comprehended by any universal law. No generally valid law in the sense of Immanuel Kant's "categorical imperative" can get hold of it, but only an "individual law" in the sense of Georg Simmel. And above all, it can never be comprehended in rational terms, but only intuitively.[38]

And thereafter:

The "ethical instinct" is entirely different. In contrast to vital instincts, the effectiveness of the ethical instinct depends on the fact that its target is not anything general but something individual, something concrete. And just as the animal is at times misled by the vital instincts, so may man go astray, ironically, by obeying the precepts of moral reason which, as such, only deal with generalities, whereas the ethical instinct alone enables him to discover the unique requirement of a unique situation, the *unum necesse.* Only conscience is capable of adjusting the generally agreed-upon moral law to the specific situation a concrete person is engaged in. Living one's conscience means living on a highly personalized level, aware of the full concreteness of each situation. Indeed, conscience has comprehended the concrete "whereness" (*da*) of my personal being (*sein*) all along.[39]

As noted, traditional ethics is also informed by an awareness of uniqueness in every individual and every situation of life. There is no simple recurrence of exactly the same individual nor are there two identical situations. Therefore, an established norm is always a conjectured approximation which needs reapplication time and again. But when Frankl states that we must detect the unique demand of every life situation, his reference is not mainly to the changing elements in objective social situations. Rather his attention is concentrated on the subjective inner constellation of a particular concrete individual person, who becomes involved in changing objective situations. Ultimately, Frankl is preoccupied by his commitment to what is defined in Heideggerian terms as "the concrete whereness" of the individual. Every man has his own singular destiny. His ethical orientation must be decided by his unique existential inclinations. Therefore, he should not obey a general law. He must discover his own private task in each situation of his life. Here the ontological departure from traditional ethics is obvious. Traditional ethics does not recognize and never allows for an individual existence of this kind. There are indeed various philosophical ways to account for individuality, its source and status in its "genus."[40] Basically, however, it is assumed that there is only one universal, true, abiding ideal of human perfection, one universal human destiny which is derived from the eternal essence of humanity. Thus the differences between concrete individual representatives of humanity are grasped in terms of rank, of quality and quantity in the achievement of that human perfection. The ideal in its absolute, infinite perfection is represented by God through His revealed eternal law. God's laws contain the paradigm of His "ways," in which He guides humanity. The prophets embody and exemplify these ways by their personal qualities, character and behavior. It is the acme of perfection available to man; all other human beings must imitate the prophets, as the prophets imitate God.[41]

Ultimately, of course, individuals will only partially achieve certain specific aspects of the infinite ideal. Indeed, this accounts for individuality. Moreover, if a human being finds it difficult to obey the general law, if there is something within him which resists Divine commandment, this is due to the degree of his attachment to natural drives and instincts which are unbalanced, full of imperfections, or simply corrupted. Man is expected to overcome his natural drives, to subdue them under the command of his moral will, thus gaining true freedom for his pure soul. Therefore the "ironic" situation described by Frankl, in which a man may be diverted from his true personal destiny precisely because he complied with an eternal universal ethical law, is, according to the traditional understanding, an utter impossibility.

In a traditional ethical context, such statements have no meaning. In the context of a traditional philosophical background it would also appear unreasonable to speak of the existence of a "moral instinct," which, as Frankl puts it, guides and directs man to his destiny in an "irrational" manner. The Divine commandments are, indeed, in part, above human reason, but they are far from being either instinctive or irrational. They represent the authority of an absolute mind which is beyond the attainment of human final reason. In Frankl's theory, however, the irrational "moral instinct" represents the individual existence which is rooted in its own essence and "stands on itself" — alone. According to this theory every soul is in fact a singular, unique "monad." As such, it must discover its place and meaning in its surroundings. The fulfillment of this demand poses a dilemma for Frankl which necessitates the assumption of an irrational conscience, or a "moral instinct." This is because, along with his radical individualism, Frankl recognized the claim that the meaning of life should not be identified with individual "self-actualization," nor with the harmony of inner inclinations and outward conditions. Meaning is only to be achieved in the world, in society, in relation to others, in accepting responsibility before a transcendent being. A man should comply to a command from above in order to achieve meaning in the objective world outside himself. Yet, at one and the same time, he must discover in the commanded act a direct, unique response to his singular subjective destiny. Such "pre-established" harmony between the inner subjective inclination and the outward objective demand is hardly attained by reason. Man needs this sort of conscience which serves as a mediating agent between the self and the "unconscious" God. Man needs this "voice of transcendence," which contains within itself "a transcendent quality," and yet is inherent in man, acting in full harmony and as an instinct of his unique nature.[42] Indeed, there is no rational way to explain the activity of a "power" which is at once within the human spirit and outside it. Though an ontological construction demands an explanation, it cannot explain the source or the activity.

As a scientist, Frankl responded to this bewildering intellectual challenge by applying his phenomenological method to the empirical experience in the realm of inter-subjectivity and self-retrospection: the observation and analysis of a "fact" in the empirical data. But in addition to the empirical evidence Frankl believes that he can explain philosophically why it must be impossible to know how the conscience reaches decisions, and how it acts. His main argument contends that the spirit knows, but it cannot know the knowing subject itself, namely the subject who carries on the act of cognition.[43] Be that as it may, Frankl represents a radical type of individualism which characterizes the Western-modern ethos in democratic countries. This source of inspiration is indirectly indicated in Frankl's own reflections on modernity. The reference here is to his theory of "existential vacuum" from which, so he claims, many people are now suffering.

> Today we live in an age of crumbling and vanishing traditions. Thus instead of new values being created by finding unique meanings, the reverse happens. Universal values are on the wane. That is why ever more people are caught in a feeling of aimlessness and emptiness or, as I am used to calling it, an existential vacuum. However, even if all universal values disappeared, life would remain meaningful, since the unique meanings remain untouched by the loss of traditions. To be sure, if man is to find meanings even in an era without values, he has to be equipped with the full capacity of conscience.[44]

One may infer from this argumentation, which Frankl repeats in many books, that in our era the conscience, as specifically defined according to Frankl's theory, has been found behind the cover of authoritative tradition which formerly fulfilled the task of guidance. Only now, as the traditional authority establishment is collapsing and vanishing, can man fully realize his individuality. Still, together with the positive discovery of his uniqueness, man also discovers his loneliness in a society which cannot guide him. Therefore, man must delve deeper into himself to discover — in the depth of his loneliness — an inner guidance, a personal conscience, which may save him from disorientation, directing him towards transcendence.

But it would appear that alongside the phenomenon of "existential vacuum" there was another motivating reason for Frankl's halfway retreat from the one-dimensional, superficial ultra-individualism of modernity, and back to more traditional stances. Ultra-individualism destroys the common ground of moral responsibility to society and to other men. In itself, this bears the threat of a pernicious spiritual disease, serving wickedness and evil as destiny and a source of "meaning." An individual who has gone through the experience of the Nazi rise to power and the Holocaust will not allow himself to hide from this terrible danger in modernity. Humanity must, therefore, be saved from the dangers of loneliness, of spiritual vacuum and of the acceptance of evil as a substitute source of meaning, caused as they are by a negative type of egoistic individualism which alienates man, transforming his individuality into an

110

object for manipulation, pressing him to become a negligible atom in the multitude.

Previously noted is Frankl's theory of the spirit as separate from the psycho-physical "layer" of personality and as an agent that can communicate with outward, transcendent entities. In this context it is worthwhile to emphasize again Frankl's distinct rejection of the modern ideal of individual self-actualization and happiness:

> By declaring that man is a responsible creature and must actualize the potential meaning of his life, I wish to stress that the true meaning of life is to be found in the world rather than within man or his own psyche, as though it were a closed system. By the same token, the real aim of human existence cannot be found in what is called self-actualization. Human existence is essentially self-transcendence rather than self-actualization. Self-actualization is not a possible aim at all, for the simple reason that the more a man would strive for it, the more he would miss it. For only to the extent to which man commits himself to the fulfillment of his life's meaning, to this extent he also actualizes himself. In other words, self-actualization cannot be attained if it is made an end in itself, but only as a side-effect of self-transcendence.[45]

It is to this type of statement, which recurs many times in Frankl's books, that reference is made when we claim Frankl's "going half-way back" to traditional wisdom.[46] Here Frankl speaks about the experience of spiritual vacuum; at times he also refers to the moral dangers of ultra-individualism. Frankl is very much aware of the pitfalls of the Nietzschean "will to power." The instinct which guides man towards his personal end Frankl defines as a "moral" instinct, and though there is an obvious tension between Frankl's unique individual conscience and what he calls the "general law," Frankl never assumes a contradiction of principles between the two. It would appear that his use of the term "irony" to describe this quality of tension admits a full commitment to universal ethical laws, which should never be transgressed. Thus he says, "Only conscience is capable of adjusting the 'eternal' generally agreed-upon moral law to the specific situation a concrete person is engaged in." This means that the unique personal destiny is to be discovered within the general framework of universal morality, as a specific version of the universal; in other words, concrete morality demands an act of adaptation which is an individual

111

interpretation of a general law. To quote Frankl: "Living one's conscience means living on a highly personalized level, aware of the full concreteness of each situation."

Here we should add the psychological and ethical conclusions which Frankl drew from his experience in Nazi extermination camps with regard to the functionaries of the Nazis:

> We shall consider a question which the psychologist is asked frequently, especially when he has personal knowledge of these matters: What can you tell us about the psychological make-up of the camp guards? How is it possible that men of flesh and blood could treat others as so many prisoners say they have been treated? Having once heard these accounts and having come to believe that these things did happen, one is bound to ask how, psychologically, they could happen. To answer this question without going into great detail, a few things must be pointed out: First, among the guards there were some sadists, sadists in the purest clinical sense. Second, these sadists were always selected when a really severe detachment of guards was needed....Third, the feelings of the majority of the guards had been dulled by the number of years in which, in ever increasing doses, they had witnessed the brutal methods of the camp. These morally and mentally hardened men at least refused to take active part in the sadistic measures. But they did not prevent others from carrying them out. Fourth, it must be stated that even among the guards there were some who took pity on us....From all this we may learn that there are two races of men in this world, but only these two — the "race" of the decent man and the "race" of the indecent man. Both are found everywhere; they penetrate into all groups of society. No group consists entirely of decent or indecent people. In this sense no group is of "pure race" — and therefore one occasionally found a decent fellow among the camp guards. Life in a concentration camp tore open the human soul and exposed its depths. Is it surprising that in those depths we again found only human qualities which in their very nature were a mixture of good and evil? The rift dividing good from evil, which goes through all human beings, reaches into the lowest depths and becomes apparent even on the bottom of the abyss which is laid open by the concentration camp.[47]

In the final passage of this quotation Frankl assumes that, together with the moral instinct, the human soul is inhabited by contradictory or bad faculties. Further, he claims (in what seems a simplistic manner which is difficult to integrate into the totality of his system) that those human beings who are possessed by evil inclinations form a separate "race," a separate genus of human beings — the "indecent." Reading this strange theory one gets the impression that by "adapting" the outrageous terms "race" and "pure race," and by reducing his explanation of "radical evil" to this almost vulgar simplicity, Frankl is reacting in a fierce and bitter irony against Nazism, denying racism by excluding the racists themselves from his kind of humanity. Be that as it may, Frankl's prime explanation is hinted at in the first part of the passage quoted. Here he does not assume two kinds of human beings. Instead he explains the phenomenon of men who seem to be completely devoid of conscience or moral instinct, as a result of mental disease in the "clinical sense" of the term. He then distinguishes between two classes, or grades, of this kind of mental disease: those who are radically ill (sadists) and those who are "mentally hardened." The latter are men not devoid of moral instinct but who are corrupted, or numbed, by enforced work under the power of an evil regime, the causes of which Frankl does not try to account for in psychological terms. (In another place, he indeed hints at a more profound psycho-cultural explanation, but this transcends his psychological theory and belongs more appropriately to his existentialist theology of the unconscious God.) There is, then, only one kind of normal human being, all of whom are endowed with a moral instinct which life's circumstances, especially in modern civilization, can numb or corrupt. There are, of course, differences in individuals — not only in their grasp of personal destiny, but also in the strength of their ability to resist corrupting circumstances and so protect their inherent moral freedom. If this is a correct interpretation of Frankl's thesis, we may sum up with the contention that though he does not use the Kantian term "categorical imperative," he does assume an absolute human commitment to the universal principles of ethics as a "categorical" command, but in psycho-existentialist terms: those who do not take upon themselves this existential commitment deny their own humanity.[48]

This presents a difficult philosophical problem: how does Frankl bridge the gap between his radical individualism and his religious-universalist ethics? Factually, Frankl does not appear to be sensitive to the existence of a problem. He simply does not raise the question, which may be accounted for by his style of exposition. Frankl develops his thinking step by step, moving dialectically from one pole to the other in a consequential spherule movement.[49] Thus he seems to expose the integrative logic of his theory through its actual operation. Indeed, the implied response to the question may be found in the manner by which Frankl develops his theory of the spiritual "self" of man. Avoiding an overt reference to his philosophical source and refraining from a detailed amplification, Frankl seems to rely heavily on philosophical dialogism, especially on Buber's theory of "I," "Thou" and "It." The "self" is grasped in this existentialist theory as an on-going process of becoming between the "I" and the "Thou"; it is ever created in the sequence of interrelations and meetings. The spiritual self of man is not a finally defined existent; it is continually recreated, reexpanded. Of course, it is rooted ontologically in a certain unique beginning, which is referred to by the "I." But the ontological status of the "I" and its attributes are far from being clear even in Buber's much discussed exposition. Frankl exempts himself from even an attempt at definition, claiming that the spiritual self experiences its own existence but cannot know it as an object. Therefore, the spiritual self can be revealed to itself as to the other human beings only when engaged in a dialogue, or in a moral activity, in love. It inheres in its subject, the "I," as the capacity of self-transcendence.

To return to the sentences which conclude the passage about the absolute individuality of human personality: "Living one's conscience means living on a highly personalized level, aware of the full concreteness of each situation. Indeed, conscience has comprehended the concrete 'whereness' (*da*) of my personal being (*sein*) all along." As noted earlier, here Frankl uses Heideggerian terms, but the philosophical theory in its entirety is based mainly on Buber's ethical, social and religious teaching. For Buber, too, the problem of achieving a balance between radical individualism and radical responsibility before God toward all humanity is in the center of his ethical deliberations. Buber also considered it one of the most grievous problems of humanity in our age. He tried to solve the problem on the basis of a religious truth which was derived from Jewish prophetic and Hassidic sources, searching, thus, for an answer to both a general universal problem of humanity, and a particular problem of Jewish self-identity and sense of belonging.[50] Frankl, it seems, was never preoccupied with the particular Jewish aspect of the problem. Accepting his own bond to the Jewish people as a matter of fact, he confronted the universal problem in Buber's frame of reference.

One final note, in the context of this topic, relates to the question of Frankl's place in the study of Jewish thought in our era. Buber was not unique in his attempt to pose the problem of individualism versus absolute religious responsibility before God as a problem which emerges precisely from the conflict between Jewish faith and ethos and modern civilization. From the end of the nineteenth century to our own day there has not been one important Jewish thinker who did not relate to this problem as a major and central motif. Buber, though the best-known Jewish thinker in the first half of the twentieth century, especially outside Jewish circles, did not originate his own philosophical approach. He is but one of its creative representatives, and is himself highly indebted not only to the known dialogical philosophies of Hermann Cohen and Franz Rosenzweig, but also to the less-known teachings of Moses Hess and A.D. Gordon. More-over, precisely in the context of this problematic, there is a distinct common denominator between these thinkers and the most influential Orthodox Jewish thinker of our age, Rabbi A.Y. Hacohen Kook. Therefore, in considering the centrality of this problem in modern Jewish social and theological thinking, and the centrality of the dialogical school which responded positively to the demand for both faithfulness to Jewish identity and openness to universal culture, Frankl, the existentialist theologian, emerges not merely as a Jewish thinker who is partially influenced by some Jewish sources, but as a contributing participant in the debate on one of Judaism's principle contemporary issues. Of course, for Frankl it is not specifically a problem of Judaism and the Jewish people. Therefore, he never overtly defines his teaching by factual relatedness to Jewish sources. But even in this he does not differ markedly from most of the aforementioned thinkers, including Rabbi Kook. Universalism characterizes them all.[51] Further, precisely by posing the theoretical and practical problems which he actually confronted as a Jew, as part of Jewish religious culture, he reaffirmed his Jewish identity on the universal level. He made his uniquely Jewish contribution to general human culture without feeling any sort of contradiction or tension between the acceptance of his identity as a Jew and the universal significance of his thinking. The "truth value" of the claim regarding his position in modern Jewish thought depends on Frankl's

conscious relationship to man's position within his cultural inheritance and his particular religion.

Thus the third point of comparison: what are the differences
between the modern dimension of Frankl's teaching and the tradition
to which he half-way returned, from the perspective of the spiritual
"unconscious" as a ground for a religious worldview? Already noted
is the essentially religious character of logotherapy. The theory of
the "spiritual unconscious" as the "beyond" of consciousness and the
theory of conscience as a "moral instinct" posit the human spirit in
its own sphere of existence, beyond the psycho-physical bodily
organism, describing it as a representative, an image or a "voice" of
"transcendence," namely, of divinity. In Buber's terms it may be
said that Frankl understands the spirit as the sphere "in between," or
as the realm of meeting between God, who is for man the "Eternal
Thou," and the human "I." And, indeed, the religious belief which
Frankl proposes on the basis of his theory of the spiritual unconscious is similar to Buber's religious belief: a biblical kind of
personal religion. It may even be said that in Frankl's version, using
his psychological terms, it is much more concrete, simpler and popular
than Buber's abstract and misty expositions, thus coming nearer than
Buber to the suggestive simplicity and experiential evidence of the
original prophetic sources. From time to time Frankl's words are
reminiscent of Heschel's (sometimes even of Will Herberg's) emotional way of rendering the prophetic experience, especially in
Heschel's well-known book, *God in Search of Man.*[52] Frankl's unconscious God is the personal God who cares for man, whose call searches
for man in his hiding places, loving, commanding, judging. It is the
God before whom man can pray, a God who listens to the cry of
suffering man. It is the God before whom one atones for his sins, the
God that forgives and purifies:

> But just as drives and instincts cannot repress themselves, like-
> wise the self cannot be responsible merely to itself. The self
> cannot be its own lawgiver. It can never issue any autonomous
> "categorical imperative," for a categorical imperative can re-
> ceive its credentials only from transcendence. Its categorical
> character stands and falls with its transcendent quality. It is true
> that man is responsible for himself, but ultimately he is not
> responsible before himself. Not only man's being free, but also
> his being responsible requires an intentional referent. Just as

freedom means little, indeed nothing, without a "to what," likewise responsibleness is incomplete without "to what."...Just as I can only answer if I am first questioned, just as each reply requires a "to what" and such a "to what" must be prior to the reply itself, so the "to what" of all responsibleness must necessarily be prior to responsibleness itself. What I feel that I ought to do, or ought to be, could never be effective if it were nothing but an invention of mine, rather than a discovery. Jean Paul Sartre believes that man can choose and design himself by creating his own standards. However, to ascribe to the self such a creative power seem to be still within the old idealistic tradition. Is it not even comparable to the fakir trick? The fakir claims to throw a rope into the air, into the empty space, and claims a boy will climb up the rope. It is not different with Sartre when he tries to make us believe that man "projects" himself — throws himself forward and upward — into nothingness. It may be said that the psychoanalytic superego theory comes down to the contention that the ego pulls itself by the bootstraps of the superego out of the log of the id. However, the superego is not the only thing regarded as an (introjected) father image; the God concept too is interpreted in terms of a (projected) father image. Now let us for heuristic purposes play off the psychoanalytic view against the theological. A copernican switch would be the result. For theology, God is not father image, but rather the father is an image of God. In this view father is not the model of divinity, but on the contrary, God is the model of paternity. Biographically and biologically the father is first; theologically, however, God is first. Psychologically the relationship between the child and his father is prior to the relationship between man and God; theologically, however, my natural father, and in this sense my creator, is but the first representative of a supernatural father and creator of the universe.[53]

Buber's terms are dominant in the first paragraph of this passage, but in the paragraphs that follow it seems to be Heschel who directs the emotional music of expression, and the entire passage is very much involved in the movement of "return" which characterizes existentialist Jewish philosophy in the first decades of the twentieth century. It is best exemplified by Frankl's rejection of the "old idealistic tradition," to which — Frankl claims — Sartre still adheres,[54] and so the passage culminates in a typically biblical version of theological personalism. One should not conceal the impact of the modern "problem of man" which this theology of return not only confronts but also embodies as a basic constitutive experience. Frankl's individualistic psychology inspires his theology. The "Thou God" who inspires and confronts the conscience (it should not be forgotten that the conscience is an absolutely unique personal entity) is a personal God, not only from the aspect of relating to Him as a "Thou," but also from the aspect of the experience by which we come to know Him. In every case it is a concretely unique experience which is hardly transmittable to others. Thus, each person has his own individual, personal one God. According to Frankl every man arrives at his appointed meeting with God moved by his own individual spiritual unconscious; Frankl definitely rejects the current conceptions of an "immanent" divinity, including Jung's theory of the "collective unconscious."[55] At the same time Frankl rejects the claims of religious establishments to serve as models of authenticity.[56] Thus, authentic religiosity is, according to Frankl, a direct personal experience of each believing individual. Each man, it would appear, not only has his personal God, but also his personal religion. If this is so, the seemingly unavoidable conclusion must be that religion as a social common experience, and religion as an historical establishment which mediates between God and man and claims authority in teaching and transmitting commandments of values and norms, loses its tasks together with its spiritual legitimacy.

One can indeed interpret some of Frankl's statements in this spirit. But, on the whole, Frankl understood very well that presenting this position either too radically or too simplistically would be unacceptable. This is true, first of all, from an historic-empirical point of view. The fact is that all those who claim a direct religious experience testify to it within certain historical traditions. They are not simply believers. Rather they are Jewish, or Christian, or Moslem, etc. This is true for Frankl himself, who expressed his own experiences as a believer in clearly identified historical religious language, derived from Jewish sources. Secondly, from the point of view of the essential religious experience itself: faith in God is a relationship to an eternal "Thou" who cannot be known to man precisely because as the God of the believing individual He is the God of the infinite cosmos, the God of all humanity, the God of all those for whom the individual believer is responsible. Authentic faith in God is not a separating experience.

On the contrary, it creates interrelationships; it shapes a sense of belonging. Only in this way does it endow the believing individual with meaning.

How does Frankl integrate these two seemingly contradictory data in the same philosophy of religion? The following quotation is a telling exposition of his full thinking process on this topic. Frankl starts with the introduction of an individual "private" religiosity, contesting Jung's philosophy of religion, but he moves on toward his own solution.

For Jung, unconscious religiousness was bound up with religious archetypes belonging to the collective unconscious. For him, unconscious religiousness has scarcely anything to do with a personal decision, but becomes an essentially impersonal, collective, "typical" (i.e., archetypical) process occurring in man. However, it is our contention that religiousness could emerge least of all from a collective unconscious, precisely because religion involves the most personal decisions man makes, even if only on an unconscious level. But there is no possibility of leaving such decisions to some process merely taking place in me....If we respect the spiritual and existential character of unconscious religiousness, rather than allotting it to the realm of psychological factitiousness, it also becomes impossible to regard it as something innate. Since it is not tied up with heredity in the biological sense, it cannot be inherited either. This is not to deny that all religiousness always proceeds within certain preestablished paths and patterns of development. These, however, are not innate, inherited archetypes but pre-given cultural models into which personal religiousness is poured. These models are not transmitted in a biological way, but are passed down through the world of traditional symbols indigenous to a given culture. This world of symbols is not inborn in us, but we are born into it. Thus, these are religious forms, and they wait to be assimilated by man in an existential way, i.e., to be made his own. But what serves this purpose is not any archetype, but rather the prayers of our fathers, the rites of our churches and synagogues, the revelations of our prophets and the examples set by saints and tzaddiks. (In my book *The Will to Meaning* I have expressed my conviction that there is a dimensional barrier between the human world and the Divine world, a barrier that prevents man from really speaking of God.

He "cannot speak of God but he may speak to God. He may pray," I have said in this context.)[57]...Culture offers enough traditional molds for man to fill with lived religion — no one has to invent God. On the other hand, no one carries him in the form of an innate archetype.[58]

In proposing the concept of a transcendental God who is beyond our knowledge as an existential truth, and not as a psychological, subjective truth, Frankl is opting for an empirical, cultural-historical solution. For him, religion is a realm of shared knowledge, as well as a realm of a direct individual experience. Man begins with a given historical inheritance which is inherited in the same way that every other empirical knowledge from the "outside" is inherited, by learning and through a process of internalization. This is a natural process which is necessary for the development and spiritual ripeness in the religious realm of spiritual creative life. The religious man needs symbols, prayers, ceremonies and patterns of worship. He also needs an ideational and normative behavioral teaching. All these elements necessary for spiritual creativity are supplied by that religion in which the individual happens to be educated. Without the benefit of such environmental education the religious belief of the individual will remain undeveloped, "naive or childish." When one is deprived of religious education by an otherwise developed cultural environment, his religiosity becomes oppressed, hidden or distorted.[59]

Yet even a naive and childish belief is not awakened in a separate and detached soul. It can be stimulated only through a lively, direct interrelationship with a religious community. This is the reason that Frankl defines the historical religions, in contradistinction to political or social ideologies, as "organic" developments. Within this context, it is obvious that the concept of "organic development" replaces the concept of "establishment" in order to restore the legitimacy and educational authority of the historical religions after the denial of their legitimacy by the political-dogmatic establishments.[60]

What then is the relationship between faith as a personal individual attitude or decision, and religion as a cultural inheritance? The answer is given in the passage previously quoted, in one short sentence. "Culture offers enough traditional molds for man to fill with lived religion." And this short sentence testifies again to Frankl's relatedness to that group of Jewish religious-humanists which reaffirmed the full identification of the modern Jew with his particular religious culture, not as an enforced religious establishment, but as a continuous organic process which allows each individual to find his own choice through his specific experience, and also enables him to relate with full dignity and respect to other religions in other cultural milieux.[61] Of course the theory of religion as a cultural inheritance is not an unheard-of novelty; in itself it has nothing specifically Jewish about it. The innovation which was created by the great representatives of Jewish culturalism, such as Ahad Haam, A.D. Gordon, Ch.N. Bialik, and M. Buber is in the adaptation and integration of a typical humanistic concept to Jewish religious tradition. This occurred as a revolution which required much more than the development of a mere theoretical concept. It was a great challenge, a huge creative task. Not only did Judaism have to be reinterpreted, but it was also reproduced as a culture through major literary, artistic, scientific, social and political projects.[62] Frankl did not contribute anything of his own to the development of the theoretical framework of Judaism as a culture, but he did contribute his own creative achievement, his philosophical teaching, even his psychological and psychiatric theory and method. He entered into an already existing framework and used tools that were already forged. Thus, he could assume the existence of Judaism as an obvious historical fact. But this is precisely what is most significant. Here is an original, humanistic religious thinker whose identity as a believing Jew is distinctly clear without any conscious effort to justify or claim it. A careful reading of his work shows that his identification with his Jewishness as a peculiar religious tradition is completely factual. Therefore, he has no difficulty in presenting his individuality as a thinker or expressing his conclusions, which result from his personal and historic experience as well as his individual "spiritual unconscious," in the most self-assured manner. Neither does he find difficulty in relating respectfully, and on the basis of full equality, to other religions. His "organic," undogmatic method of relating to his own religion imbues him with this freedom, and his contribution to the universal milieu of religious and ethical thinking emerges out of a particular Jewish cultural inheritance, its traditional ethical wisdom, its religious sources, symbols, prayers and ceremonies.

The implications of Viktor Frankl's experiences in Nazi concentration camps on the development and reshaping of logotherapy were examined earlier. It will be instructive to conclude the same topic by considering the theological point of view.

Historical research on the Holocaust indicates that two types of radical responses were experienced by believers to the trials of the Holocaust: a radical despair and loss of faith because of God's "silence," and an astonishing strengthening of belief and faith as a source of power to survive and protect human qualities during the severest trials. Frankl's book *Man's Search for Meaning* is one of the most impressive and thoughtful examples of the second response.[63] Its peculiarity consists of an intention to establish, through a minute biographical account, a scientific theory which will serve as the foundation for a complete philosophy of meta-ethics and theology. Thus, Frankl's work is both one of the earliest and one of the most systematically developed philosophic-theological confrontations with the problems and consequences of the Holocaust.[64]

Parallel to the explication of logotherapy as a scientific theory based on modern psychological research, the development of the philosophical teaching of the unconscious God was based on a particular trend of twentieth century existentialist philosophical literature which attempted to understand some of the ethical and theological aspects of the Holocaust in the wider context of the "problem of man" in modern Western civilization; which is to say that the consequences of the Holocaust form a major problem area in Frankl's work. What is exceptional in Frankl's response is his attempt to discover, even in this extremist traumatic experience, messages which are not only of a negative character. The principle positive message is as follows.

Through his experiences in concentration camps Frankl ultimately came to the assumption that it is impossible to deprive man of his "essential" freedom because it is an inner infinite capacity of the spirit. According to empirical evidence of his own, even if a man is placed under total arrest, technically deprived of all his rights and freedoms, left only with the one open route to do whatever it is he is commanded to do by the aggressor, he can still choose his inner relationship to the outwardly enforced situation. By this choice of an emotional and intellectual inner attitude he not only can protect his inner freedom, but also save a positive and personal meaning for his life. Empirically, from his experiences in the concentration camps, Frankl came to the belief that man can discover a positive, personal meaning in every situation of life, including those which were initiated against him as a form of degradation and dehumanization. Last but not least, in the concentration camp Frankl reassessed his religious belief: faith in a personal God is the source of eternal, unshakable meaning; therefore, those who know how to reveal God's presence, those who rely on God's loving-kindness and recognize the perpetually open gates of prayer will protect the eternal value of their lives in any enforced life situation. It was precisely in the Holocaust that Frankl found the empirical subjective proof, the ultimate proof possible, for belief in a personal God. It is a proof that stands securely against empirical and philosophical doubts, that overcomes every disappointment.

> I myself went through this purgatory when I found myself in a concentration camp and lost the manuscript of the first version of my first book. Later, when my own death seemed imminent, I asked myself what my life had been for. Nothing was left which would survive me — no child of my own, not even a spiritual child such as the manuscript. But after wrestling with my despair for hours, shivering from typhus fever, I finally asked myself what sort of meaning could depend on whether or not a manuscript of mine is printed. I would not give a damn for it. But if there is meaning, it is unconditional meaning, as neither suffering nor dying can detract from it....The unconditional faith in an unconditional meaning may turn the complete failure into a heroic triumph. That this is possible has not only been demonstrated by many a patient in our days, but also by a peasant who lived in biblical times, somewhere in Palestine. His were granaries in the literal sense. And they were literally empty. And yet, out of an unconditional trust in ultimate meaning and an unconditional faith in ultimate being, Habakkuk chanted his triumphant hymn: "Although the fig tree shall not blossom, neither shall fruit be in the vines; the labor of the olive shall fail, and the fields shall yield no meat; the flock shall be cut off from the fold, and there shall be no herd in the stalls. Yet I will rejoice in the Lord, I will joy in the God of my salvation."[65]

But there is also an important negative conclusion: the empirically proven fact that the loss of faith, or its distortion, is the source of radical evil which threatens the future of humanity. We come back to a former discussion which began with a quotation from *Man's*

Search for Meaning. It is only in his later book, *The Unconscious God,* that Frankl proposed a full explanation of Nazi behavior in the concentration camps.

> Freud, in *The Future of an Illusion,* said: "Religion is the universal compulsive neurosis of mankind. Like that of the child, it derives from the Oedipal complex, from the relationship to the father." In view of the case history abstracted above, we are tempted to reverse Freud's statement and dare to say compulsive neurosis may well be diseased religiousness. In fact, clinical evidence suggests that atrophy of the religious sense in man results in a distortion of his religious concepts. Or, to put it in a less clinical vein, once the angel in us is repressed, he turns into a demon. There is even a parallel on the socio-cultural level, for time and again we watch and witness how repressed religion degenerates into superstition. In our century, a deified reason and megalomanic technology are the repressive structures to which the religious feeling is sacrificed. This fact explains much of the present condition of man, which indeed resembles a "universal compulsive neurosis of mankind," to quote Freud. Much of man's present condition? Yes — with one exception: religion. With special reference to technology, however, one is reminded of a dictum of Goethe: "He who possesses art and science also has religion." But today we know only too well where man would wind up if he had science and nothing beyond it: Soon the only thing that would be left of his science would be the atom bombs he possessed.[66]

The far-reaching significance of this explanation of radical evil reveals not only the motivating drive behind the development of logotherapy and the theology based upon it, but also one of the fundamental insights which informed Frankl's anthropological and theological teachings. Moreover, it is clear that because of such insights Frankl found it necessary to turn back to traditional sources, in an attempt to discover, in their neglected wisdom, a healing message to the sufferings of modern man. If so, one may raise the question, what was Frankl's response, if any, to the first extreme feelings of disappointment experienced by believers during the Holocaust? Had he any comforting message for those whose belief completely collapsed? Initially, there is the impression that Frankl's fundamental response is contained in his distinct avoidance of the theological problem of theodicy. At first glance it seems that this problem does not exist for him. In the previous quotation he indeed hints at it, but he does not explicitly articulate it, nor does he offer a theological solution. This cannot be incidental. It is rooted in his basic religious attitude. In spite of his theological personalism, Frankl's experience of an unconscious God does not allow for any expectation that God will intervene in the physical realm of human experience. God is confronted, according to his teaching, only in the spiritual and not in the physical realm. God, in Frankl's theology, is indeed a being before whom one prays. Moreover, those who know how to pray feel that God is present. He hears. There is a way in which one can feel a response, but it is, of course, not an "answer" in the "physical" meaning of the term. Here, indeed, we come nearer to Frankl's explicit theological explanation.

> But what about the issue at hand. Is God dead? I would say that God is not dead but silent. Silent, however, he has been all along. The "living" God has been a "hidden" God all along. You must not expect Him to answer your call. If you probe the depth of the sea, you send off sound waves and wait for the echo from the bottom of the sea. If God exists, however, he is infinite, and you wait for an echo in vain. The fact that no answer comes back to you is proof that your call has reached the addressee, the infinite.[67]

In other words, the questions for which Frankl searches out religious answers are those which man confronts existentially in his search for meaning, and not those with which he struggles trying to change his lot in physical life. Religion must answer the ultimate questions raised when man confronts his human fate, his finality, his unavoidable sufferings, trials and death. Religion is not called upon to explain why mankind suffers and dies as it does. This is already known to creatures of flesh and blood. Man is created as he is and the acceptance of the human situation as such is, it seems, the first move towards the opening of the heart to the comforting religious truth. Only beyond this first acquiescence to human destiny can man be redeemed by the religious answer to his cry of anguish. Therefore, for Frankl, the only relevant question in religious terms is: how should believers relate to the concrete experience of suffering, including the sufferings caused by radical evil? How is it possible to transcend suffering and death through religious faith? Putting it paradoxically, one may say that for Frankl the expectation of a change in man's physical destiny by the intervening power of God means expecting a non-religious solution from religion. Rather, if there is any agency by which man can change his physical destiny up to some given limit, it is to a secular agency to which he should apply his scientific knowledge. When man turns toward religion, the only legitimate expectation is that of a meaningful truth. With this as background, Frankl's message becomes understandable with the hint of a theological solution to the problem of theodicy: between God's and man's modes of being there is a dimensional difference, like that which exists between an animal and between a human being that is endowed with spirit.

On this theological assumption Frankl considers an idea derived from Buber's religious existentialism: man cannot say anything about God, he can only speak to God. In other words, man cannot know anything about the causal relationship between God and the physical world, just as man cannot understand the functional relation between our body and the spiritual part of the soul. Therefore man cannot explain physical destiny in religious terms. Through the intermediacy of the spirit, which transcends the body, man has, however, an experience of presence before God, the essence of whom is not to be known. Man relies on this presence, humbly accepting his inability to transcend human "unconsciousness." In a way it is a return to a particular kind of traditional philosophical response to the problem of theodicy — that which is best represented by Maimonides, for whom questions of theodicy are quite understandable from the emotional human perspective, but are intellectually illegitimate. Frankl is even more radical than Maimonides, rejecting the question on even the emotional-human level.

Man cannot break through the dimensional difference between the human world and the Divine world, but he can reach out for the ultimate meaning through faith which is mediated by trust in the ultimate being. But God is "high above all the blessings and hymns, praises and consolations, which are uttered in the world" as it is said in the famous Hebrew prayer for the dead, the Kaddish....The ontological difference between being and things or for that matter the dimensional difference between the ultimate being and human beings prevents man from really speaking of God. Speaking of God implies making being into a thing. It implies reification. Personification would be justified. In other words, man cannot speak of God, but he may speak to God. He may pray.[68]

One more essential difference can be inferred from this argumentation between Frankl's modern conception of religion, influenced by Buber, and the traditional conception of religious truth. Frankl's narrowing of the realm of religious truth to answers of ultimate existential questions of humanity is an unavoidable logical consequence of his radical individualism. His existential starting point for expectations in the ethical relationships between man and man, as well as in the spiritual relationship between man and God, is his consciousness of man being a separate, final entity, having no "source" in any existent entity beyond or behind him, either in nature or in an assumed transcendent level of existence. This singularity is the source of absolute human inner autonomy and the relative ability to influence his own physical destiny. But this is also the source of his ultimate loneliness, out of which he can be redeemed only by a religious self-transcendence, which reveals eternal meaning beyond and above him. To conclude, there are two main experiential foundations to Frankl's traditional, yet modern, religiosity: the humble acquiescence to suffering and death as necessary dimensions of human finality and loneliness, and the proud assurance of the ultimate ethical freedom of the human spirit, by which man can be redeemed in his earthly life, but also beyond the final limits of his earthly life, through meaning. On these two "Foundations of Faith" Frankl developed his answers to some of the critical ultimate existential and meta-ethical questions of the human being in our age.

Was Leo Baeck correct when he contended that Frankl's logotherapy is essentially an application of the teaching of Judaism? If Baeck's conception of *The Essence of Judaism* as a dynamic, continuously renewed teaching is accepted, the answer would be positive beyond any doubt. Obviously the similarity, in some areas even the identity, which Baeck could point to between his own understanding of Judaism and Frankl's psycho-existentialist wisdom inspired Baeck in his enthusiastic response to Frankl. And Baeck, it should be remembered again, represented an entire group of modern Jewish thinkers of his age. In his work, Frankl responded to the challenge of the "problem of man" as it was posed in the period after World War II and the Holocaust. He proposed his solution in a pattern which combined two seemingly opposite directions. In the first, there was the restoration of an old religious-cultural inheritance which had been rejected by modernity. In the second was the acceptance of new anthropological and religious existential insights which were developed mainly by this group of modern Jewish religious philosophers, who responded with openness to modernity but who were also able to relate critically to some of the great failures of modernity. From both these directions, Frankl's teachings stand in the center of Jewish thinking of our age. There is indeed a most significant message, a message which forms a unique contribution in content as well as in method: a new and modern version of traditional Mussar literature.

Notes

1. This discussion is based on four of Frankl's books, those which deal mainly with the existentialist theological aspects of logotherapy: I. *Man's Search for Meaning. An Introduction to Logotherapy* (first published in German, 1946. Revised and enlarged edition in English translation, New York and London, 1962). II. *The Will to Meaning: Foundations and Applications of Logotherapy* (New York and Cleveland, 1969). III. *The Unconscious God: Psychotherapy and Theology* (New York, 1968). IV. *The Unheard Cry for Meaning: Psychotherapy and Humanism* (London and Toronto, 1977).

2. Frankl admits Freud's major influence in almost all his books and papers. At the conclusion of his Introduction to *The Will to Meaning*, he presents himself as Freud's disciple. See Introduction, p. 12.

3. Dr. Reuven P. Bulka, who wrote prolifically on Frankl's logotherapy and its relation to Judaism, states that Christian psychologists and theologians were first to detect the religious dimensions of Frankl's teaching, and to claim its affinity to Christianity. The interest of Jewish scholars in the specifically Jewish religious characteristics of Frankl's teaching appeared much later, although Frankl neither hid the fact that he was a Jew nor his Jewish religious belief. Recently, however, numerous articles, particularly in Jewish periodicals in the United States, indicate that the interest of some Jewish scholars seems to have been awakened. The most important contribution is that of

Dr. Reuven P. Bulka, *The Quest for Ultimate Meaning* (New York, 1979). For a full English bibliography of studies about Frankl see *The Unheard Cry for Meaning*, pp. 163-182. These studies of Bulka and other Jewish scholars are mainly occupied with similarities between distinct ideas such as freedom of choice, moral responsibility before God, search for meaning as against striving for happiness, the possibility of finding meaning even in suffering and death, and between logotherapy and Jewish traditional sources (especially talmudic). In this way they are able to show that Frankl's wisdom is reminiscent, or even filled with echoes of the wise, profound sayings and ethical teachings of eminent Jewish sages, who were blessed with deep insight and empathy into the human soul. The principal weakness of such discussions is their random character, even when they are successful in gathering an impressive number of quite convincing single items. Each case of similarity is cited out of the entirety of its context, without any systematic attempt to examine the specific relationship between such psychological and ethical insights and the whole religious world view in which they were conceived. Moreover, such studies were done without any serious attempt to follow up Frankl's own attachment to a particular Jewish world view, or to trace in a systematic manner the impact of his experiences as a Jew on his world view. Yet it is likely that only through such systematic studies of the affinity between Frankl's existential, ethical and religious teaching as a whole, and basic outlooks or creeds, which may be identified as specifically Jewish according to established criteria, is it possible to prove or refute the characterization of logotherapy as a trend in Jewish thought. Which is to say that, at best, the results of the existing studies indicate a certain mental affinity that captures the attention and may fill the hearts of some apologetic Jewish scholars with a sense of pride. Yet if Leo Baeck's claim (according to Frankl's testimony, and see below) that logotherapy is a typical Jewish teaching is indeed to be verified, one must go beyond the phase of random, even impressionistic, research. What is required is an overall view of Frankl's ethical and theological teaching in order to ascertain its conscious or unconscious (in Frankl's own understanding of the term) relationship to Jewish sources and ideas as defined and recognized according to their own internal criteria. As I am convinced that Leo Baeck was correct in his far-reaching statement, namely that Frankl is not only echoing older ideas attributed to great Jewish sages, but develops a world view and way of life which may be defined as Jewish according to established historical criteria, I will try in what follows to complete some of what is missing in Dr. Bulka's (and others) interesting book and papers.

4.   *Man's Search for Meaning.* It should be emphasized that the author presents his book as "An Introduction to Logotherapy," and that this definition comprises the first and largest part of the book in which Frankl presents his account of "Experiences in a Concentration Camp." In other words, Frankl tells about his personal experiences in the Holocaust as a scientist, consciously preoccupied with his task as a scientist, in order to resolve or assess previously determined consequences which are to be applied in psychotherapy. This is the unique character of Frankl's story in the context of the vast testimonial literature on the Holocaust, but this is also what is unique about this book in the context of scientific literature. It is a biographical-historical experience dealt with in terms of a scientific experiment, the experimental dimension being the very decision to relate to his own fate as an experiment in overcoming a traumatic fate. This is exactly what Frankl tried to study in his remarkable book.

5.   *Man's Search for Meaning*, pp. 12, 106.

6.   *Ibid.*, pp. 80-84.

7.   *Ibid.*, p. 26.

8.   See also in Bulka, ch. 11, "Logotherapy as a Response to the Holocaust."

9.   Buber is mentioned by Frankl several times, together with Abner, as the founders of philosophical Dialogism. Frankl's fullest account of this topic is included in his *Unheard Cry for Meaning*, in the chapter entitled, "Critique of Pure Encounter." See especially p. 64. Buber's opinions are indeed criticized in this discussion, but the criticism itself reflects deep indebtedness. It may be added that in many passages Buber's influence is implicit without being mentioned. As to Leo Baeck, Frankl quotes his remark that logotherapy is essentially a Jewish teaching in his book, *The Will to Meaning.* Thus Frankl documents something more than personal acquaintance. The two of them had similar experiences in concentration camps and very much resembled each other in the way they responded to and overcame their trials, arriving at the same conclusions, though on different levels. This fact obviously had something to do with Leo Baeck's opinion of Frankl.

10. The way in which Frankl, not only as a psychiatrist but also as a philosopher, relates to scientific psychological literature, especially to the writings of Freud, Jung and Adler as well as to Behaviorism, is best exemplified in his book, *The Will to Meaning*, Part 1, Chapter 1,

"Meta-Clinical Implications of Psychotherapy," pp. 15-30. He accepts and adapts most of their data, but he demands an awareness to the dangers of "Reductionism" in the sciences as well as in philosophy. Thus he contends that the difference between himself and all other psychiatrists is rooted in his ability to avoid reductionism, and examine each realm of the psychological experience on its own terms. For Frankl, the anthropological-philosophical dimension is a necessary complement to the scientific study, and not merely a "cosmetic" addition.

11. In what follows we will try to show how much Frankl absorbed from Buber's writings. Our contention that Frankl's Jewish knowledge is mainly derived from Buber, Baeck and other modern Jewish scholars is based on his selection of texts (mainly the Bible and Hassidism) and on his method of conceptualization, which seems to point to these sources. But surely it is only a conjecture.

12. The term "Soul Healer" (*Rofe' Hanefesh*) as an attribute of the Jewish sage in his capacity as educator, especially when applied to personal behavior, the shaping of individual personality and the character of his disciples, is contemporary to medieval Jewish ethical literature. The source is the very influential and much studied ethical tractate of Maimonides, entitled, *The Eight Chapters*. See ch. 1 of this book. See also my study, *Reflections on Maimonides' Eight Chapters* (Hebrew; Jerusalem, 1961), ch. 1.

13. The classical, most popular Mussar books such as *The Duties of the Heart*, *The Eight Chapters*, *The Gates of Repentance*, and *Way of the Righteous*, and later *The Tania*, and the books written by Rabbi Yisrael Salanter and his disciples in the Lithuanian Mussar movement, were not studied simply as theoretical books for the benefit of intellectual enrichment. They were composed as guides for personal, practical behavior, and were used for this purpose by rabbis and teachers for their disciples. They were used as well by individuals who strived for personal perfection and were anxious to overcome inner psychological disturbances, flaws of character, bad inclinations, lack of faith, etc., which hindered them. In some educational institutions (*yeshivot*) which were especially devoted to Mussar, these books were even used as guides for exercises in personal ethical behavior. In this context special attention should be paid to the Mussar movement that was founded by Rabbi Yisrael Salanter which, like logotherapy, was very much engaged in the psychological phenomenon labeled by Frankl as "existential vacuum." (Salanter described it as a situation of spiritual dullness and inner fatigue, caused by the expansion of the "dark" or "dim" subconscious powers in the

human soul.) Indeed, it seems that much could be gained from a comparative study of logotherapy and the educational use of classical and new Mussar literature in the modern Orthodox Jewish religious movement.

14. The preoccupation of modern Jewish existentialist thinkers with the problem of "Jewish identity" is distinctly represented by Buber's Jewish works and in most of Baeck's writings. See Buber, *Der Jude und sein Judentum. Gesamelte Aufsaetze und Reden* (Koeln, 1963). Of special interest are those articles which were first given as lectures for a group of Jewish youths raised in assimilated families and therefore torn between their Jewish and German identities, who suffered from a feeling of vacuum regarding their Jewish belonging. Leo Baeck too started and culminated his spiritual enterprise as a Jewish teacher with books concerned with the content and meaning of a Jewish identity, namely, *The Essence of Judaism*, and *This People Israel*. The same characterization can be made for the Jewish works of Cohen, Rosenzweig, Heschel and their disciples.

15. See ch. 7 in *The Unconscious God* (on Psychotherapy and Religion). Frankl's approach may be described as systematically eclectic. He strives to find a realm of relevance and competence for every existing psychological school, but he also criticizes them all for their monistic reductionism. Applied to this topic it means that ethical-religious guidance, when necessary, should be considered as the completion of psychiatric treatment and not as its substitute. See also Bulka, ch. 3, "The Ecumenical Ingredient in Logotherapy."

16. It should be emphasized that in spite of Frankl's insistence on the distinct secular character of his scientific theory, he himself stresses the systematic connection between logotherapy and the theology of the "Unconscious God." In his words, "Now in its third stage of development existential analysis has uncovered within the spiritual unconsciousness — unconscious religiousness. This unconscious religiousness, revealed by our phenomenological analysis, is to be understood as a latent relation to transcendence inherent in man" (*ibid.*, p. 60). This statement indicates that the theological dimension was discovered by proceeding with the regular scientific study of the soul, using phenomenological tools of "existential analysis," as with other discoveries of empirical truth. One may almost claim, relying on such statements, that Frankl developed his theology in purely secular concepts and methods.

17. *The Unheard Cry for Meaning*, p. 63.

18. Frankl's attempt to discover the religious dimension in atheism by the use of existential analysis has already been referred to. Therefore, Bulka is correct in claiming that "It seems that the philosophy of logotherapy is a bit more than merely a borderline theology. I have referred to it in fact as a 'religion to the non-religious'" (*ibid.*, p. 57).

19. *The Unconscious God*, pp. 26-28.

20. See again Maimonides' *Eight Chapters*, ch. 1. Maimonides depicts there the Aristotelian division of the one soul into five "parts," according to its different functions. But he also refers to the Platonic division into three parts, or more accurately, three interrelated, distinct souls in each human person.

21. Maimonides proposes, in the last paragraph of the first chapter of the aforementioned book, the medieval Aristotelian distinction between the "potential" intellect of man, which is one "part" or "function" of his soul, and the "actual" intellect, which is united, through the agency of a transcendental "Active Intellect," with the eternal truth of metaphysics, thus acquiring a "separate" existence, independent of any corporeal subject, as a pure spiritual existent, like that of the angels. The Kabbalists went even further. They developed a theory of hierarchic order of souls, giving to each a specific Hebrew name: Nefesh, Ruach, Neshama, Chaya, Yechidah. Nefesh, and even Ruach, are dependent on the corporeal organism, as the inner source of activity, but Neshama is a transcendent spiritual entity, while the supreme, hidden, Chaya and Yechida, are in fact pure metaphysical entities emanating from the sphere of the Divine. See Yishayahu Tishbi, ed., *Mishnath Hazohar* (Hebrew; Jerusalem, 1961), vol. 2, Part 1, chs. 1-2, pp. 3-125.

22. According to Maimonides, man should unify all the energies of his soul and direct his whole activity in its realms toward the achievement of one goal: the knowledge, or the love, of the supreme metaphysical truth — God. This is the ultimate human perfection (see *Eight Chapters*, ch. 3, *The Book of Science* in *Mishneh Torah, Hilkhoth Deoth*, ch. 3, and *The Guide for the Perplexed*, Part 3, ch. 27). Other thinkers, like the author of *The Duties of the Heart*, who were as devoted to the ideal of intellectual perfection, defined the ultimate human goal in emotional terms of fear and love of God (see *The Duties of the Heart*, ch. 10). However, common to all these medieval schools is the assumption that man should strive to achieve perfection by self-transcendence.

23. According to Maimonides each human soul is one, its unifying pure essence (or the authentic "self," as we would put it) being the intellect (see *Eight Chapters*, ch. 1). Therefore, when man becomes a slave to his bodily needs and lusts he actually yields his true self to an outward interest. Only when he devotes himself entirely to his intellectual perfection is he truly working for himself (see *The Guide of the Perplexed*, Part 3, ch. 54).

24. See again Maimonides' distinction between the task of the physician and that of the "soul-healer" in *Eight Chapters*, ch. 1.

25. *The Unconscious God*, ch. 1, pp. 21-22.

26. Maimonides assumes the principle of human freedom of choice as a necessary condition for ethical responsibility. There is no rationale for a moral commandment, for punishment and reward, unless we assume free choice. Of course, freedom of choice is granted to man within the limits of his corporeal existence (see *Eight Chapters*, ch. 8). Frankl's explanation of human wickedness as a mental illness resembles Maimonides' way of explaining the phenomenon of a sinner who loses his freedom of choice as the result of an evil inclination which becomes habitual by practice, thus appearing as a "punishment" on the sinner's way of life. Then, even if the sinner becomes aware of the deadly damage caused by his sin to himself, he is no longer able to free himself from the bondage of his established evil inclinations. (This is how Maimonides explains the case of Pharaoh's compulsive disobedience to God's command despite the terrible damage done to himself and his people.) According to both Maimonides and Frankl it is impossible to deprive man of his inner freedom of choice through outward compulsion, but man can condition himself through certain behavior which he willingly initiates to the loss of his freedom. Yet even in this situation man remains responsible for his sins because he has only himself to blame for his loss of choice. Moreover, when a soul-healer begins his treatment of mental illness on the level of ethical behavior, he must first make his patient conscious of both his situation and his responsibility. The patient must realize his own inner freedom of choice and make an effort to use it, to create a new, healthy, goal-oriented habit of behavior. Here we detect an almost complete systematic analogy between Maimonides' and Frankl's definitions of the practice of "soul-healing" in the area defined by Frankl as "non-logical" mental diseases. This may eventually result in similar methods of treatment.

27. In the fourth chapter of his book, as well as in his "Book of Science," Maimonides offers some advice which one can define as a technique

of treatment, beyond the general ethical guidance. The same is more or less true of all the previously mentioned classical works of Mussar literature.

28. *The Unconscious God*, ch. 5, pp. 53-55.

29. The current Hebrew word for conscience (*mazpun*) indeed appears already in the Hebrew translation of *The Duties of the Heart*. But the intention there is to distinguish between commandments related to physical modes of behavior, the observance of which is clearly visible outwardly, and those related to thinking, knowing, believing and feeling, which are hidden in the hearts of men; therefore their fulfillment can be known only to the doer and to God. In this context, *mazpun* means "That which is innerly hidden." Only in the modern era has this term acquired the meaning of "conscience" in Frankl's sense.

30. The classic discussion of this subject is in the third chapter of Rabbi Saadia Gaon's *The Book of Beliefs and Opinions*. There, the Gaon offers his distinction between commandments of reason (*sichlioth*), and commandments which were heard from (Divine) authority (*shimioth*). The first category comprises all the ethical and political commandments. Depicting these commandments as derived from reason, the Gaon assumes the autonomy of the human intellect in the realm of inter-human and other worldly relationships. The Divine commandment is still needed in these areas: 1. To add the dimension of abiding authority, duty being a particular responsibility before a recognized authority. 2. For the sake of establishing definite norms of behavior which, as such, are essentially authoritative and cannot be applied by reason alone. Maimonides rejected the term "commandments of reason" (*Eight Chapters*, ch. 6) because, according to his system, practical deliberations are never logical in the strict scientific sense. Still, he recognized the category of normative social consensus, achieved by practical deliberations on the basis of accumulated experiences, namely, decisions of practical reason which are autonomous. Be that as it may, Jewish traditional Mussar literature as a whole shared the following common assumptions: 1. That God commands only what can be justified according to objective criteria of good. 2. That man, who has been created in the image of his Creator, namely, endowed with intellect and free will, knows the criteria for distinguishing between good and bad, and has the capacity to choose to abide by or to refuse outward authority. On these grounds it is correct to conclude that what is conceived by human reason as true and good is a message from a transcendent Divine source, which has been internalized by man through his intellect. In other words, the universal, objective human intellect functions here as the "voice of transcen-

135

dence," and, therefore, there is no place for nor need of an individual conscience.

31. *The Unconscious God*, ch. 2, pp. 29-31. There is a striking resemblance between Frankl's analysis of the spiritual unconscious in this passage and A.D. Gordon's characterization of "Life-Experience" as differentiated from "Consciousness." It is basically the same profound insight, leading to very similar conclusions. In Gordon's case the relationship to Jewish Hassidic sources is direct and the terminology overt.

32. See *ibid.*, ch. 6, pp. 29-31.

33. Frankl himself offers a very close equivalent to our suggested term for the Spiritual Unconscious: "Since I coined in 1938 the term 'height psychology' in order to supplement (rather than supplant) what is called 'depth psychology'" (*The Unheard Cry for Meaning*, p. 29).

34. The theory of dreams in medieval psychology is aware of unconscious drives, or of events in the body which man does not fully mind when he is awake, but whose impact may be responded to in dreams. A good deal of dream material is interpreted in such traditional theories, and accepted into Mussar literature, as the documentation of inner events which are hidden during periods of vigilance. The best summary of medieval scientific knowledge in this realm is Gersonides' book, *The Wars of the Lord* (see English trans. [Philadelphia, 1984], Book 2, chs. 1-3).

35. See *The Duties of the Heart*, Part 2, ch. 5; Part 10, ch. 1.

36. Maimonides adopted the Aristotelian distinction between the theoretical intellect, which grasps the objective truth, and the practical intellect which shapes opinions and judgments of good and bad, profitable and damaging. It is the first category of intellectual activity which motivates and achieves human perfection (in Frankl's terminology — human sense of meaning). But it should be remembered that for Maimonides the goal of human perfection is the ultimate criterion of good (*Eight Chapters*, ch. 6), which means that ultimately the knowledge of good is the highest intellectual achievement and highest goal of man.

37. Continuing what has been stated in the previous note, the inference is that there cannot be absolute certainty in practical moral judgments and decisions because conditions and situations never recur exactly.

What appeared to be good in one case may be proven utterly wrong in a slightly different case. Moreover, it is not possible to shape a precise rule, or norm, which will always fit the changing conditions of life. There is no exact measure of correct ethical behavior. This is why Maimonides rejected the term "commandments of reason."

38. *The Unconscious God*, ch. 3, p. 34.

39. *Ibid.*, p. 35.

40. The medieval Aristotelian view is that the essence, or form, of every existent is generic and therefore the same in all the individuals of the same genus. The differences between the individuals of the same genus are therefore "accidental," and effected by the changing qualities of matter (or body); the neo-Platonic conceptions of the Kabbalists attach more importance to individuality, at least in humanity. The soul of every man is created, or emanates, in its unique particularity. Yet all the souls are united as an organic whole, emerging from and striving to return to the same infinite source. Every soul has its unique "place" in the organic system, so that differing from each other they complement each other as members of one and the same corporeal body. Be that as it may, there is a common universal source for all individuals; therefore, there is a pre-established harmony between the universal and the individual good. Basically they are ontologically the same. Modern Jewish religious thinkers who still retained their attachment to traditional ontology, such as A D Gordon and Rabbi Kook, remained true to this assumption of pre-established harmony in spite of their profound respect for individuality. Obviously this is not the case with philosophers such as Cohen, Buber, Rosenzweig and Frankl.

41. According to the traditional conception, God, the creator and leader of the world, is not only the source of ethical commandment and the authority before whom man is responsible for his deeds, He is also the ideal model of ethical behavior. When God relates to humanity, humanity must imitate His ways or the attributes of His actions. To come closer to God means to make progress in the knowledge of His truth, and in the imitation of His ways. This idea complements the theory expressed in a previous note. The traditional concept does not recognize individual ethics. Ethics is a general, universal category. Perfection is achieved through transcendence not only in the sense of expanding individual existence in the direction of the beyond, toward God, but also in the sense of identification with a community, a nation, even with humanity as an ideal whole. The model of perfection is universal; therefore, he who approaches perfection approaches

the existence of a universal essence. This was considered possible by acquiring universal knowledge and doing what is universally good.

42. This is a typical example of Frankl's dialectical thinking, which sometimes seems to be full of contradictions. In the third chapter of his *The Unconscious God*, which is an "Existential Analysis of Conscience," he describes the conscience as "A true Urphanomen, an irreducible phenomenon that is inherent in the human being as a deciding being" (*ibid.*, p. 30). As against this, in the fifth chapter of the same book, which deals with "The Transcendence of Conscience," he states, "I can be the servant of my conscience only when the dialogue with my conscience is a genuine dia-logos rather than a mere mono-logos. This however, can only be so when my conscience transcends myself, when it is the mediator of something other than myself" (*ibid.*, p. 52). Moreover, in what follows Frankl states that "Conscience not only refers to transcendence, it also originates in transcendence. This fact accounts for its irreducible quality. Therefore, if we raise the question of the origin of conscience, there can be no psychological answer but only an ontological one" (*ibid.*, p. 55). We may then conclude that the conscience both inheres in man and transcends him. But obviously Frankl needs these two contradictory statements because only as both inherent and transcendent can conscience fulfill the dual task in Frankl's system.

43. See *The Unconscious God*, ch. 5.

44. *The Will to Meaning*, p. 64.

45. *Man's Search for Meaning*, p. 134.

46. See Bulka's book, the chapter on logotherapy and talmudic Judaism.

47. *Man's Search for Meaning*, pp. 84-87.

48. In his *The Unheard Cry for Meaning*, Frankl writes, "We must not let our belief in the potential humaneness of man blind us to the fact that humane humans are and probably always will be a minority. Yet it is this very fact that challenges each of us to join the minority. Things are bad, but unless we do our best to improve them, everything will become worse" (*ibid.*, p. 30). This is a typical characteristic of Frankl's moralistic realism. Yet it is important to note that "potential humaneness" is ascribed to each individual.

49. One must recognize in Frankl's discussion of this topic a continuous intellectual struggle because his messages are not always coherent.

On the one hand, he lays heavy stress on the particular and unique in man.

> Thus man is unique in terms of both essence and existence. In the final analysis no one can be replaced — by virtue of the uniqueness of each man's essence. And each man's life is unique in that no one can repeat it — by virtue of the uniqueness of his existence. Sooner or later his life will be over forever, together with all the unique opportunities to fulfill the meanings. I have nowhere found this couched in more precise and concise words than those of Hillel, the great Jewish sage who lived nearly two millennia ago. He said: 'If I don't do it — who will do it? And if I don't do it just now — when should I do it? But if I do it for my own sake only — what am I?' If I don't do it... This seems to me to refer to the uniqueness of my own self. If I don't do it right now... refers to the uniqueness of the passing moment which gives me an opportunity to fulfill a meaning. And if I do it for my own sake only... what here comes in is no more nor less than the self-transcendent quality of human existence" (The Will to Meaning, pp. 54-55).

This quotation from the sayings of Hillel is typical of Frankl's conscious reliance on classical Jewish religious sources, divulging and interpreting them in his own personal way. His quotation is not precise, nor is it a question only of his peculiar translation. Even the original order of Hillel's sentences has been consciously changed to fit Frankl's systematization. Moreover, the interpretation is very much informed by modern individualism which is far beyond the religious horizon of a rabbinic sage. But, side by side with this kind of individualism, Frankl speaks of the demand of self-elevation by complying with a commandment which is derived from a "transpersonal" realm. In such passages there is a hint of a common transcendent source which guarantees an objective validity to subjective values, so as to be integrated into something common to all humanity. "However, we must not forget that among these situations there are also situations which have something in common, and consequently there are also meanings which are shared by human beings across society and, even more, throughout history. Rather than being related to unique situations these meanings refer to the human condition. And these meanings are what is understood by values. So that one may define values as those meaning universals which crystallize in the typical situations a society or even humanity has to face" (*ibid.*, pp. 55-56). Frankl even speaks of a "hierarchical order of values" (p. 57) out of which every individual person chooses his own values. Frankl does not appear to sense a contradiction between these statements, placing them together here in the continuity of one long paragraph. The reader, however, may feel that a systematic integration of these two statements is not so easily achieved.

50. Buber's confrontation with this challenge of modernity finds a systematic exposition in his theory of the "interpersonal" realm in *I and Thou*. This is indeed the most fitting place to note that Frankl's criticism of Buber's theory of dialogue in *The Unheard Cry for Meaning* (see the chapter on "Critique of Pure Encounter") does not do justice to Buber's argumentation. Buber, as much as Frankl, interprets the relation of the "I" to the "Thou" as an act of self-transcendence. It is a mutual effort of self-transcendence between two "I"s which creates the "In-Between" beyond the narrow circles of the meeting selves. To state it in a somewhat radical way, Frankl uses a pretended polemic here to cover the fact that basically he has adapted Buber's approach.

51. See Hermann Cohen, *The Religion of Reason*, Chapter 10; Franz Rosenzweig, *The Star of Redemption*, Part 2, Book 2; Martin Buber, *I and Thou*; A.D. Gordon, *Clarifying our Idea from its Foundation* (Hebrew, in Gordon's collected writings, Vol. 2, *Man and Nature* [Jerusalem, 1951]); Rabbi A.Y. Hacohen Kook, "The Footsteps of the Flocks" (Hebrew), in *Eder Ha'yekar* (Jerusalem, 1967).

52. A.J. Heschel, *God in Search of Man* (New York, 1955).

53. *The Unconscious God*, ch. 5, pp. 56-58.

54. The criticism on the Kantian reductionist approach to religion, which grasped the concept of God as an ideal of human reason, is the starting point of twentieth century Jewish theology, beginning with Cohen's *Religion of Reason*. With his idea of "Co-Relation," Cohen transcended Kantian idealism, and took a significant step in the direction of religious existentialism. Rosenzweig and Buber went further in a process of recapitulating the personalist theology of the Bible. Frankl's approach joins this theological tendency and is, in fact, a variation of the same.

55. See *The Unconscious God*, ch. 6.

56. In a note to the previously quoted passage Frankl states, "Much of what is derogatively called 'organized religion' rather deserves the name 'organic religion' because it has grown organically instead of being fabricated and propagated as ideologies are" (*The Unconscious*

God, p. 64). In this definition, which, interestingly enough, is again very close to A.D. Gordon's use of the terms "organic religion" as against organized religion, Frankl hints at his derogative evaluation of organized religion. Indeed, in his postscript to the third edition of *The Unconscious God* (the first passage of the postscript, entitled "Logotherapy and theology"), Frankl expands his criticism using very strong words, which resemble Buber's sharp criticism of any kind of religious dogmaticism.

57. This is typical Buberian coin, yet Frankl does not mention his source, preferring a Heideggerian context!

58. *The Unconscious God*, ch. 6, pp. 63-65.

59. *Ibid.*, ch. 6.

60. Twentieth century Jewish existentialist theology from Moses Hess to Cohen, Buber, Rosenzweig, Baeck, Gordon, Heschel, etc., stresses the "organic" character of Judaism. In other words, Judaism is conceived as a folk-religion as against Christianity which is a church-religion. Moreover, the Jewish religion operates spontaneously in family and congregation, typical models of organic society. The organization or establishment, remained a marginal phenomenon, because Jewish religion is a comprehensive lifestyle of the whole nation. On the other hand, Judaism, though particularistic in its attachment to the Jewish people, is an ideal model for humanity. From all these points of view Frankl's theory is a typical representation of modern existential Jewish theology.

61. In note 56 there was an indication of Frankl's positive approach to organic religion. It is not at all astonishing that Christian theologians sensed an affinity between their conception of Christian morality and logotherapy. Frankl's religiosity is never captured in established patterns or dogmas. Tending toward a spontaneous individual expression of faith, Frankl is empathetically open to every kind of authentic religiosity, especially on the level of individual experiences. Any sort of non-fanatic religiosity is "legitimate" in his eyes, an attitude which does not contradict his matter-of-fact attachment to Judaism.

62. See my book, *Judaism and Secular Culture* (Hebrew; Tel Aviv 1981).

63. There are many testimonies of such cases. Some of them are referred to in the third chapter of this book, "Dilemmas of Ethics and Faith in Literature Written During the Holocaust." For bibliography, see note 3 of that chapter. A profound theological discussion of this existential

phenomenon is found in Eliezer Berkovits, *With God in Hell* (New York and London, 1979). A remarkable case of a religious awakening during the Holocaust which is especially significant in the context of studying Frankl's reaction to the Holocaust is E. Hillesum, *Het Verstudoode Leven* (Busum; De Haan/Unieboek BV, 1981). This is the diary of a young woman who reacted to the experience of Nazi persecution through a religious awakening. It was her own decision to be with her Jewish brothers in a concentration camp, to help them as she could. It is a striking example of discovering the ultimate personal meaning of life and of confronting the traumatic experience of persecution, dehumanization and death by transforming it into a personal victory over wickedness and death. Berkovits' book is equally remarkable as an analogical existential analysis of religious awakening during the Holocaust.

64. Though the emotional problems of faith in the terrible experiences of the Holocaust were raised early on, the philosophical or theological confrontation with it began relatively late. Eminent philosophers and theologians such as Baeck, Buber and Heschel, who were then in their full philosophical creativity, refrained from a systematic discussion during that period and well afterward. Emil Fackenheim, himself a survivor of the Holocaust, who now considers the Holocaust as the most crucial topic for philosophical confrontation in our age, did not realize his involvement with the topic until some twenty years after his escape from a concentration camp. Reactions to the problem were more poetic than philosophical. The best example of this is Elie Wiesel's prolific writing on the Holocaust, mainly from a religious point of view. From this aspect, Frankl's relatively early philosophical response seems, therefore, to be unique.

65. *The Will to Meaning*, pp. 156-157.

66. *The Unconscious God*, ch. 6, pp. 68-69.

67. *The Will to Meaning*, p. 154.

68. *Ibid.*, pp. 145-146.

Chapter 3

DILEMMAS OF ETHICS AND FAITH
IN LITERATURE WRITTEN DURING
THE HOLOCAUST

Much has been written on the problem of whether and how to conceptualize the Holocaust as an "unprecedented event" in the history of the Jewish people, as well as in the history of mankind. The participants in this debate generally take as their point of departure the characteristics of the Nazi "Final Solution" — that is, the plan, its conditions and its techniques of implementation. They then try to decide whether these characteristics are "extraordinarily unique," and if so, to depict the special "attributes" which should define "Radical Evil," that kind of evil which is symbolized by the "planet" named Auschwitz.[1] By implication this requires that an attempt be made to conceptualize the objective conditions of human reality which were created in the Holocaust, primarily through an analytical examination of the initiators' plans — their intentions, strategies and techniques, and of course the ideology, which "inspired" and guided them in all their deeds. "Radical Evil" is identified in this way by initiative, motivation, feelings and thoughts, and by the actual implementation of such feelings and thoughts into action. Therefore, to understand this unique manifestation of human wickedness, one should study its pathological, or demonological, motivating sources. This is an apparently convincing approach. The forcefulness of its conceptual and methodological assumptions cannot be denied, yet one may argue that something is lacking. The point of view of the victims must be taken into account. It was the victims who were exposed to Radical Evil. It was the victims who not only had to suffer it, but also to confront, reject, overcome and survive it. As they were the first not only to experience Radical Evil but also to try to understand its meanings and implications, this discussion would not be complete without including the thoughts of victims themselves: their conceptualizations of the experiences and the dilemmas they

143

had to face in their passive or active, intended and chosen or dictated and forced, responses to this "unprecedented event."

The intent of evil originated by man is generally characterized by a striving not only to cause suffering or to kill, but also to conquer, subjugate and manipulate to the point of penetrating into the victim's very existence, so as to shape him from within as an object of hate. Thus his annihilation is justified as a satisfying revenge or "fulfillment" of the evil motivation. Radical Evil the more so. It is radical mainly in its virulence to penetrate and subjugate its victims, trying to recast them absolutely into a passive reflection of its own vicious activity, not permitting them any remnant of selfhood or freedom. Viktor Frankl, however, has ample basis for his unrelenting claim that it is impossible to deprive a human being of his "ultimate" ethical freedom, which is identified with the spiritual core of the human personality. At the very least, a human being cannot be deprived of his freedom to decide on his inner relationship to conditions forced upon him, or to define their meaning from his point of view.[2] As long as he is alive, not only physically (or biologically) but also spiritually, as a person conscious of self, man can resist, through his own spiritual rejection — which is a kind of internal activity — the attempt to transform him into an object or functionary of an externally enforcing will. Therefore, the attempt should be made to understand the nature of evil not only from the standpoint of the perpetrator, but also from the standpoint of the victim, examining the dilemmas he is forced to confront by the attack of evil intentions on all levels of his active, conscious life: feeling, understanding, evaluating and judging, decision-making, keeping hope and faith. It seems reasonable to assume that a normal human being is not able or, properly, not willing to empathize with the demonic-pathological motivation of those who practiced Radical Evil. Precisely because of this emotional-intellectual limitation, it seems likely that the only way that remains for a normal human being to gain any insight into the nature of Radical Evil is to try to empathize with the situation of the victims. This applies of course to those who contrived to protect their "human image," who did not comply with evil by yielding to it through imitation and adoption of their persecutors' behavior; which is to say that the uniqueness of the Holocaust may be reflected in the extraordinary conceptualization of ethical, emotional and spiritual dilemmas by such persons.

It should be emphasized that in employing such a limiting qualification — namely, studying the thoughts of those victims who were determined to protect their "ultimate" inner moral freedom, who were anxious to save their "human image" — the dilemmas of the confrontation with Radical Evil are severely encapsulated; the more so because, as noted, Radical Evil is not "fulfilled" by external conditioning or by the use of an external compelling power. It is not fulfilled by even wild, cruel, relentless and unrestrained use of power against its victims in the effort to subdue and annihilate them from without. Rather it strives craftily to penetrate into the inner-most spiritual core of the victim. Surely, therefore, the "mere" decision to resist becomes the core of the victim's problem.

The aim of this study is to methodically examine the ethical, emotional, intellectual and existential dilemmas experienced and defined by some Jewish thinkers under the Nazi regime. Such a study is necessary not only for the sake of a better understanding of Radical Evil, but also for the sake of a serious philosophical examination of the Holocaust and its implications for understanding a culture in which such events were possible. The assumption, in fact, is that the dilemmas which confronted the Holocaust victims are immanent in Western culture, that they may confront us — though in disguised, covered and less acute ways — even in "normal," "peaceful" days, and not necessarily under the yoke of a totalitarian regime.

The literature to be studied is not principally philosophical in method and form, yet it is likely that no other reflective literature can rival its profitability in the process of detecting, posing and defining the problems raised by the Holocaust for a philosophical discussion.[3] Therefore, it is assumed that, methodologically, such a study is a necessary preliminary step for a serious philosophical discussion of these problems.

The first questions to be posed by the Nazi rise to power in Germany, and subsequently as new countries were conquered by Nazi forces, were, naturally, questions regarding an adequate "reading of the map." What really happened? What is going to happen? The technique of taking government and wielding power in Germany, the exceedingly cruel strategy of the Nazi military conquest achieved by the unrestrained use of formerly unknown weapons of mass killing which were directed at military forces and civil population alike, and aimed at a complete demoralization of the civil population, left no room for doubt that this was an unprecedented

145

insolent attack for which atrocity seemed to be an end in itself. But what was the purpose behind it? What kind of motivation is represented by such deeds? What is the character and aim of a regime that initiates them? What are its "ultimate" plans? And is it really determined to and capable of proceeding in the uninhibited implementation of its plans? How powerful, capable, prepared and determined are those who are expected to resist and fight against it? Or to put it differently, in what measure did those who were expected to resist remain resolved, unyielding and uncontaminated by Nazi power as well as by Nazi propaganda? To none of these crucial and pragmatic questions were there solid, well-founded answers. Obviously even conjectured answers were vital. One needed to know what to expect and how to prepare. Immediate responses, therefore, were necessarily grounded in a previous, anachronistic wisdom applied because no one knew better, because it was impossible to remain utterly passive though almost everyone was at least partially conscious of the fact that his reaction could not be an adequate one.

The first reaction of the Polish population to the trauma of Nazi conquest, and even more that of the Jewish population in Poland, was quite characteristic — flights of multitudes to nowhere and then the rush back to crushed and devastated homes. A syndrome of disorientation in its most concrete form was thus revealed.[4] People fled because they remembered World War I. They fled to escape the initial temporary disorder of the conquest assuming that the strategies, the processes and the tempo of the second war would resemble those of the first. Yet almost immediately they sensed that a qualitatively different war was upon them. No one could know exactly what it was, nor what the "right" way would be to survive it.

It should be kept in mind that this was just the beginning. Yet the Nazi regime was already determined not to let the civilian population settle into a "normal" stability under recognizable orders and rules. The Nazis never allowed the civilian population to acquire a sure orientation, especially the Jewish population. The effect of utter disorientation was a strategic aim, a method of wielding power. It was not merely a tactic. It represented the essence of the regime: intended ruthlessness, intended torture, intended breakdown of the dignity, self-respect and resistance of the conquered population. Therefore, before the overwhelmed population could rally its spiritual resources and attempt to decode the "secret" of the regime, only

146

too blatantly manifested in its deeds, most of their capacity to prepare an efficient defense was lost.

The question, "What is really going on?" continued to intrigue Jewish victims almost to the final stages of the Holocaust when at last the "camouflaging" effort became both impossible and unnecessary. From the victims' point of view this camouflaging was one of the characteristic manifestations of Radical Evil in the Holocaust: on one side, a blatant, consequential, unrelenting and resolute manner of execution. Every "action" carried out "to the utmost," directly, efficiently and ruthlessly. (Those courageous enough could, therefore, read the regime's intentions and plans from the stamp of its deeds.) At the same time, tactics of camouflage, misinformation and brutal lies were used in the same resolute, unresistant manner.* This was a simple course for the regime to implement, and from its point of view quite free of internal contradiction. In its insidious tactics, transparent because of their vulgar brutality, the Nazi regime benefitted by manipulating the obvious faults and weaknesses of its victims. In particular, the victims were vulnerable because of their lack of preparedness to understand (normal human beings could not ascribe such motives to a civilized regime!) or rather their being only too prepared not to understand what was actually in front of their eyes. They were ready and anxious to take hold of any illusion and accept as salvation every deceptive promise. Here, indeed, the wickedness of the Nazi regime was expressed to the utmost degree, turning the weaknesses of the victims against themselves, first to dehumanize, then to murder them. It was, therefore, absolutely necessary to grasp the nature of what was really happening in order to escape the trap of being unknowingly — or somewhat knowingly — seduced into cooperating with the totalitarian regime against

---

* A typical example in Kaplan's diary (3 #1). As early as his entry of 10 March 1940 he states that "The major catastrophe which struck Polish Jewry is not to be compared to anything, even in the darkest periods of Jewish history. In the first place — this depth of hatred." He observes the total rejection of Jewry and of Judaism by the German people, and states unequivocally: "This is the end of the tempest that aims to sweep us out of the world" (*ibid.*, pp. 201-203). Yet whenever a new decree against the Jews was promulgated he reacted with astonishment and surprise to the depth of Nazi depravity! Each time he thought that they had indeed reached the limits of their cruelty, only to discover again and again that much worse could be done.

one's own self. Comprehension and realization became the primary conditions for the fulfillment of that ultimate freedom which every human being can and should protect: the freedom of choosing his relationship to what is forced upon him against his will.

If, indeed, the question concerning the "nature" of an event includes within itself the question of how to react, at some level it may be claimed that understanding what was happening was the beginning of a cogent reaction: at the very least to refute the conqueror's cruel intention to deceive its victims and make them collaborators in their own destruction. For the victims a correct understanding was the beginning of their capacity to choose their own relationship to events, and to make decisions which would really be their own.

In this struggle it should be remembered that the victim found himself confronting not only external enemies, but obstacles as well from within the community of victims and even within himself. He had to overcome his fellows' inclination — and his own — not to see what they saw. This became more and more difficult because, in addition to the fear of confrontation with the formidable threat of annihilation, one had to overcome a certain form of crisis behavior which had already been established as a psychological or cultural pattern. Such response forms were part of the personal memory of many individuals, as well as the collective. They were the product, the accumulated wisdom, of former experiences which had been studied over and over again. Indeed, the use of such "inherited" models of reaction was almost a matter of instinct. They began to function even before there was time to deliberate their adequacy. In point of fact their adequacy was suspect, and one could sense the horrible risks. Yet the instinct for survival prefers any sort of "doing" to "not doing anything at all," and the remembered reaction appeared to be the only one available in the first traumatic moments. This traditional form of responding to collective distress was identified with the instinct of survival by the majority, both of individuals and of organizations. Those individuals who were conscious of the need for a critical examination — Is this indeed the right way to act? — had to "correct" something that was already operative, at times even arranged and established within organizations that were sponsored by the conquering regime. Moreover, it seems that in situations of direct threat and pressure, taking a position which is critical of what has been done for the sake of survival contradicts the instinct of self-defense. It seems better to obey the functioning leadership and so maintain a measure of stability and order in the on-going disorientating turmoil.* The psychological difficulty of rising to the position of a critic in such situations becomes clearer if one reflects

---

* The tendency to prefer a certain stable framework which hopefully would be able to keep order and maintain a routine of daily life in which one could know today what he could expect tomorrow was manifest every-where. This was desirable even if the cost was to obey the oppressive evil decrees which Jewish organizations had to see to on behalf of the German authorities. Those who contrived to act on their own initiative against the authority of the formal leadership which was recognized by the Nazis (the Judenrat) faced — in almost all cases — the opposition of the Jewish community, at times even its hostility. They were considered to be irre-sponsible and a threat to public security. The best examples took place in the Vilna Ghetto, and the traumatic testimonies, among them those of the leaders of the P.P.A. themselves, are well known. In terms of this study, the most significant item is the moral backing that a person of such spiritual authority and influence as the writer Zelig Kalmanowitz was prepared to give to the phenomonon of extreme public criticism. See his diary (3 #n, pp. 85-87). To cite here only the sharp conclusions to his remarks: "Let us hope that together with the tyrannic regime [the Nazi regime — E.S.] this group [The P.P.A. — E.S.] will completely disappear from the scene of our Jewish public" (*ibid.*, pp. 115). And he continues:

> It is impossible to think that our extremists really believe in their own victory. Were they really inspired by a feeling of responsibility for the collective they would have known that humanity has sufficient power to defeat the tyrannic regime, and that even if the end lingers for a while, it will arrive at last. So why should they break away with no profitable result? The captive has no power beyond his mere existence. The collective does not demand any action of him. He need only keep on living by any means. If within these considerations any other feeling intervenes there is ground for a suspicion that it is a feeling of fear, a failing of the will to live (p. 116).

In these sentences Kalmanowitz seems to have clearly articulated the "rationale" which identified the will to live with an interest in keeping a stable and organized community framework. (The Nazis, however, were careful not to let a feeling of stability prevail, while taking care to maintain the illusion that after each "Action" there would be a return to stability. Thus, they prolonged the Jewish population's faith in the rationality of obedience.)

on the nature of the "survival instinct." This instinct tends to be identified with the inertia of that which is already known, with established ways of behavior and activity which people consider to be proper expressions of their regular way of life. The continuation of this regularity now contains the whole meaning of existence, of life. Though one cannot expect the continuation of his normal, regular way of life under conditions of conquest and war, one at least tries to create a new continuity or, as far as is possible, a new regularity, adapting to changed conditions in an effort to maintain a semblance of normality in an abnormal situation. For this purpose one tends to use, first, certain commonly remembered stratagems of behavior for crisis situations. These may also serve as symbols of constancy and continuity in spite of the upheaval. Times of distress, crises, misfortune, and tragedy, situations which enforce deviation from regularity are, after all, also the components of ordinary life experience. One learns how to adapt to such situations so that life may go on — one escapes, hides, circumvents, contrives alternatives, attempts stratagems of appeasement against the enemy, etc.* Basically these responses are attempts to continue the ongoingness of regular exist-

---

* The following are Kaplan's instructive words:

It is a blessing that the conquerer did not realize Polish Jewry's character and vitality. Rationally thinking we should have already been dead; according to the laws of nature we are doomed to complete annihilation. How can a whole community be nourished if it has already lost all hold on life's resources. Evidently there is no profession or kind of work which remains open before us without restrictions. Yet even now we are not "equal" to the laws of nature. We possess a certain hidden force, a mysterious unfathomable one, which keeps us alive in spite of all the laws of nature. When we are cut off from the permitted resources, we live from the forbidden ones. And we should not be blamed for this. What is allowed or forbidden — these are rules based on certain agreements. For one who did not participate willingly in the establishment of an agreement, that agreement has no moral validity in his eyes, especially when we have to deal with commands of a barbaric conqueror who is shaping conditions of life in the image of his murderous and plunderous conceptions....The urge to survive under such terrible hardships which are our lot is an expression of a mysterious hidden force, the essence of which is still undiscov-

ence through the use of habitual stratagems in conditions of "emergency." Obviously a position critical of such accustomed behavior tended to be interpreted by most people as yet another threat to existence itself, which meant that those individuals strong enough to conquer the impulse toward habitual responses in themselves had to confront it in the reactions of their fellows.

Be that as it may, the question of how to react in itself contained an element of criticism regarding the reaction which was already operating: Have we done what we should have done? If not, what is the correct alternative? At some point, this question was even forced upon those who had stubbornly refused to acknowledge it, had tried to escape from it. In the public domain there came a moment in which a critical accounting was unavoidable. Efforts to reach a certain stability or regularity and quasi-normality, within the abnormal, had been continually defeated, in itself proving that such defeats were the only sort of regularity observable. Bitterness against the Jewish leadership, the only leadership available on which blame could be placed, was overwhelming. To be more exact, the bitterness of a "disappointed" public against its leadership did not necessarily signify a criticism of the principles of community organization and policy. It was a protest of personal dissatisfaction, of feelings of neglect or betrayal, of disappointment caused by the failure to achieve desired results. Generally speaking, this public criticism served as a "catharsis," the only way left to express feelings of panic, frustration, distress, rage and pain which had been unrelievedly accumulating from day to day. Pressing criticism and blame is also a typical reaction to situations of distress. The Nazi regime, the real source of the tragedy, remained "immune" to any sort of criticism. The Nazi authorities could not be expected to act in favor of the

---

ered. It is a wonderful maintaining power which only the strongest and the most immune communities of our people has been blessed with (*ibid.*, pp. 201-203).

Similar ideas can be found in Ringelblum's study of the relations between Poles and Jews. He describes the persistence of the Ghetto population as an economic miracle, and attibutes it to the success of the Jews in their efforts to circumvent restricting ordinances and cheat Nazi decrees that were formulated against the Jewish economy (see, 3 #d, vol. 2, pp. 300-327).

Jews; it was not possible to "get in touch" with these authorities. So, even if one dared to speak up against them, he could not experience the feeling of satisfaction that, indeed, someone had heard him and had been insulted. The only address left for criticism then was the Jewish leadership, which could not but fail.* Precisely because of

* The following are typical examples of criticism voiced against the recognized Jewish leadership. In the underground periodical of Hashomer Hazair, "Neged Hazerem" (Against the Stream), No. 7-8, Tishre 1941: "History, it seems, knows not of such examples of decline, of lowliness which reason cannot suffer, which is alien even to organizations of professional criminals. Of their own free will (even the Germans did not ask for it) this gang of robbers created their own national Gestapo ("The 13") in order to steal, to blackmail, to slander and to plunder their brethren, for their interests, joining in with the conqueror" (3 #a, vol. 3, pp. 399). Kaplan was especially quick to criticize the Warsaw Judenrat, particularly its chairman, Czerniakow. After Czerniakow's suicide Kaplan admitted that there was a "remnant" of morality and conscience in this man, but Kaplan still did not regret his former negative opinion. In Ringelblum's papers, naturally, the most severe criticism is reserved for the Jewish police:

> We are breaking our heads trying to understand how it is possible that Jews, most of them from the intellectual professions, former lawyers [the majority of the officers were lawyers before the war], take their brothers to the death sentence with their own hands. How is it possible that Jews capture children, women, elderly and sick people on the roads knowing that they will be taken to the slaughter. There are those who think that every society gets the police that it deserves, which is to say that the sickness of helping the regime slaughter 300,000 Jews has contaminated the whole society, not only the police, who are only an expression of society. Others are of the opinion that the police attracted the weakest types, those who were anxious to survive these hardships it any price (3 #d, vol. 2, p. 32).

In another paper Ringelblum cites the words of Aharon Einhorn, a journalist from the *Heint*: "The Jewish 'Public Order Services' have been transformed into a band of "Khappers" which terrorizes the life of the masses. The Jewish population has not withstood the trial. It has been left in its own hands in the Ghetto, and it functions so badly that worse is unimaginable, far worse than anyone else would have treated us" (*ibid.*, pp. 694-696). These extreme criticisms are not directed against the establishment as such, but rather against the way it functioned. About this topic in general, see I. Trunk, *Judenrat* (Jerusalem: Yad Vashem, 1979).

this situation of despair, the leadership was driven to self-justifica-
tion, or to drawing certain conclusions. Responsible leadership had
to put the blame on "impossible" conditions, dealing with the surrealistic situation in the only way it saw possible so as to at least
reduceor minimize the suffering.* Still there came a moment when
the leadership was deprived of even this defense.

To proceed with an analysis of the process which developed of
questions vis-a-vis reality, the form of reaction that was operating
needs to be examined because it was this that determined the method
of raising practical questions. What should the right reaction be?
What can and should be protected? How could it be done? Beyond
the tendency to maintain a regular, familiar way of life through
various strategies of adaptation and "arrangement," one may identify a certain model of organized public reaction which had crystallized in the Jewish community during generations of existence in
exile. It would appear that both the wisdom of survival and the
despair of self-defeated manifested in the behavior of the Jewish
community during the Holocaust point to this model.** The mainte-

* All those who served in a Judenrat justified their activity by an
inescapable necessity, or by its being the only way that remained to exist
in an impossible situation. The only alternative to "Self-Rule" in the
Ghetto would be direct government by the Gestapo, the effects of which
would have been, in the opinion of these leaders, much worse. It was a
controversial topic in the Ghettos, and the controversy continued after the
war. The best known exponent of extreme critical opinion was Hannah
Arendt in her well-discussed book, *Eichmann in Jerusalem* (New York,
1963). See ch. 5, "The Second Solution: Concentration," pp. 63-78. Her
views are very similar to certain opinions which Ringelblum cites as
current in the Ghetto (see 3 #d, vol. 2, pp. 37-38). However, the majority
of scholars who study the subject tend to reject this kind of criticism, and
agree basically with the opinion of the Judenrat leadership. See the above-
mentioned book of I. Trunk; see also the final chapter in I. Arad, *Jewish
Vilna in Struggle and Annihilation* (Hebrew) (Jerusalem: Yad Vashem,
1976).

** In addition to the above-cited passage of Kaplan, the following is
the testimony of N. Eck on the position of the eminent historian, I. Shiffer:
"Dr. I. Shiffer then stood up in the committee in mid-discussion, beat the
table and said, 'Stop all these arrangements and organizational prepara-

nance of a Jewish community in exile had served to condition its representative leadership (appointed through congregational institutions) to trust the central gentile government and to cooperate with it. They represented the interests of the congregation before it, petitioned for rights and the necessary sources of sustenance, sought the protection of governmental patronage. On the other hand, the congregation as an aggregate of individuals had to develop a variety of private tactics to circumvent threats, oppressive decrees and various kinds of trouble that a gentile government was "naturally" inclined to invent against them. Of course, cooperation with gentile authorities had its price, which could be quite high. The Jews were considered strangers, at best profitable "guests." The authorities had no preestablished commitment or responsibility toward the Jews.

---

tions. It will serve us no good. The congregation of Israel will save itself, as it always has, without these arrangements. Every individual will find a way of escape for himself. He is instructed to do so by an old inherited wisdom.'" And Eck adds his comment: "and the Ghetto, indeed, had self-same vitality and strength for the life instinct could also effect an aptitude to illusion and fantasy which had no basis in reality, and so convinced many to rely on German announcements and deliver themselves blindly to death. On the other hand, the talent and sagacity of individuals to find their own private solutions meant also caring only for themselves. This could result in a lack of solidarity, leaving the poor, hungry and sick to their fate. Critical notes on these subjects can be found in almost all sources, for example, H. Zeidman's testimony on the discussions between well-known persons in the Warsaw Ghetto, querying themselves as to why the Jews submitted so easily? Why did they not physically resist? Among other explanations he emphasizes the effect of illusion and fantasy, and in the trust that "we will find a way to escape, due to our Jewish sagacity" (see 3 #m, pp. 154-156, and also pp. 218-222). In a special paper, N. Eck describes the "hopes and illusions up to the last moment" (3 #s, p. 118). Also instructive is Ringelblum's paper entitled "The Ten Tribes," which describes various illusions in the Ghetto and their tragic effects (3 #d, vol. 2, pp. 42-44). In the paper mentioned above on A. Einhorn, Ringelblum cites Einhorn saying that "the feeling of mercy in the Ghetto has been completely corrupted. On one side coffee houses and places of entertainment flourish while on the other side men and women and children are lying in the streets swollen from hunger, and the dead are stretched on the pavements" (*ibid.*, pp. 694-696). Rabbi S. Huberband also describes a shocking lack of mercy and solidarity in the Ghetto in his study on "The Jewish Woman in the Years of the War" (3 #f).

They were not obliged by law to accept or to keep the Jews as their subjects. The basic assumption of cooperation was manifestly utilitarian, the only recognized motivation of the gentile government to "accept" the Jews under its protection being the direct and immediate satisfaction of egoistic interests: the Jews must be a source of continual gain. The government was then prepared to let them live according to their own religious laws and manners and to develop their economic activities, which were the source of their ability to pay the demanded price. This meant, of course, the payment of high taxes of various sorts, special taxes for Jews, irregular payments and various services to the government, some very difficult and most burdensome. The recognized Jewish leadership had to take care of the specific fulfillment of all these demands. It had to take full responsibility for the satisfaction of the rulers. It had also to be continually aware of the possibility that the government might plot against the Jewish community out of "special" reasons or needs, or sheer caprice. The recognized Jewish leadership had to be willing to pay as much as was necessary to make the existence of Jews and their activities "worthwhile" for the gentile governing authorities, yet they had to take care that the price demanded remained one which could be endured, that it not transgress a limit which they could approve as legitimate demands of a government. Once this limit was transgressed, an alternative form of activity would have to be employed — that of evading, escaping, circumventing or neutralizing the "unjust decrees" of the authorities. This was done by each individual as best he could,* but with the consent of the Jewish leadership, and within the highly valued social ethos of mutual responsibility (*Yisrael arevim ze laze*). This is clearly a model of "dual relationship" with the gentile government: both a positive

* Reference should be made here to discussions in rabbinical responsa on the problems of applying the principle of *Dina d'Malchuta Dina* (The law of the kingdom is the law). There is a clear distinction between a "law" of the kingdom, and "plunder" of the kingdom. According to the *halakhic* decision, those decrees of the gentile government which fall into the second category are not valid. One is allowed to circumvent or escape such unlawful decrees, and anyone who manages to do so should save himself. On the other hand, the congregation accepts the responsibility of fulfilling the demands which fall into the first category.

readiness for far-reaching cooperation and satisfaction of interests on the basis of a utilitarian "outward" morality, as well as a legitimation of every possible individual escape from cooperation (in response to "unjust decrees") within the framework of an inner Jewish morality of mutual responsibility.

This model of interrelationship could be maintained as long as the balance between a preferred interest of the government to accept the Jews as a protected alien minority, and the preferred interest of the Jews to convince the government that their acceptance was worthwhile, was not seriously shaken. But, as is very well known, that did happen; that very sensitive balance was shaken, and quite often. In such moments the Jewish community faced a cruel alternative: either to emigrate (assuming there were open options for Jewish emigration) or to suffer all manner of oppression and violent attacks of hate and murder, patiently waiting for better days. Thus they exhibited an extraordinary capacity to lean inward, to rely on certain religious values and hopes, to suffer and make great sacrifices of martyrdom, yet to maintain a trust in God that the majority of Jews would survive, that the nation would live forever, that those who merited it would see the coming of a redeemer.

The situation established under the Nazi regime may be defined as driving the Jews back to old conditions of exile, such as those in the period before Emancipation, while at the same time destroying entirely the balance of mutual interest. The Nazis quickly eliminated even the second alternative, that of confronting a crisis situation in exile, as there was no possibility of mass emigration, even when the Nazi regime did allow it. And, as the Nazi's far-reaching intentions were defined in terms of a "Final Solution," there could be no hope for "better days" to come.

Yet the Nazi regime did make a recognizable effort to maintain the illusion that a certain balance of interests still existed, that the alternative of suffering with the hope for better days was still operative. They encouraged the reappearance of the traditional Jewish pre-Emancipation model of crisis reaction by the reestablishment of the Ghetto along with a complete simulation of Jewish self-rule within it. They employed the Jews in the Ghetto in factories which provided supplies for the German army. After every "Action" in the Ghetto, they promised that it was the last one, thus encouraging the illusion that the process of mass murder had ended. Summing up these particular policies, one may characterize them by the extraordinary situation they created and the challenge that then had to be faced by Jewish leadership and public organizations. By encouraging a traditional Jewish model of response, the Nazi regime hoped to "enlist" the Jews and make them collaborators in their own dehumanization, degradation, and final annihilation.* The traditional reaction model operated almost everywhere under Nazi control and on all of its levels of activity. The "Judenrat" and the Ghetto organization tried everything possible to appeal to the Nazi regime, to convince it of the existence of a real German interest in maintaining a Jewish community, so as to gain minimal conditions of survival, at least for part of the community.** At the same time, many individuals really accomplished wonders in escaping, circumventing and refuting the "evil decrees" of the regime, especially against vital Jewish economic activity. Spiritual characteristics of leaning inward and relying on the eternal spiritual values of Judaism — religious, moral and national values — as sources of trust and hope, were revealed in all their strength. A heroism was exhibited of suffering and sacrificing individual life for the sake of the people — a heroism of devotion

---

* One precedent which may have been seen as a warning sign by many was the policy of Jewish congregational leaders in nineteenth century Russia to capture young Jewish boys and deliver them to the gentile government where they would serve for a lifetime in the army. Children of the wealthy and notable were allowed to escape their mobilization; instead the leadership snatched children of the poor. It seems a unique example of cooperation by a Jewish leadership in the execution of a cruel and *halakhicly* unlawful decree. It was a revolting "selection" which discriminated between blood and blood, and between soul and soul in Israel. Indeed, this chapter of Jewish history in Russia was both a result of and an enhancing factor in the demoralization and decline of the Jewish congregational institution in Eastern Europe during the second half of the nineteenth century.

** As noted, an analysis and summary of the deliberations of responsible Judenrat leaders can be found in the studies of Trunk and Arad. Eck tells of his and Geller's attempt — and their complete failure — to convince the leaders of the Judenrat in Czenstochow that the end of their entire congregation was very near. This account is important because it not only sheds light on rational deliberations, but also on the mentality and mood of leaders who were undoubtedly responsible and decent Jews, devoted to the interests of their community (3 #s, pp. 81-82).

to study and the teaching of Jewish sources and values, of strengthening Jewish identity and keeping a Jewish way of life, a heroism of
being prepared for martyrdom, a heroism of faiththat evil will be
broken, that revenge will not be late to come, that salvation is near.*

Yet there is no way to escape the bitter realization that in spite
of all this activity, the brutal and insidious Nazi regime achieved its
satanic aim of utilizing elements of the Jewish model of response to
turn it into a model of self-defeat. The hypnotizing power of illusory
hopes and the inertia which resulted from behaving within an established pattern of response proved so strong that the majority of
responsible leaders who survived postponed — virtually to the last
moment — beginning the process of sober, critical reevaluation, by

---

* Some of these reactions will be examined in subsequent discussions.
In this phase it is important to take note of attitudes which were given
community application such as the widespread, organized educational
activity in Germany, under Leo Baeck's leadership, from the time of
Hitler's rise to power for as long as was possible. Baeck continued his
efforts in the same direction while he was a prisoner in Theresienstadt; see
E. Simon's paper, "Jewish Adult Education in Nazi Germany as Spiritual
Resistance," in the *Leo Back Institute Year Book 1* (London, 1956), pp. 68-
104. Widespread cultural activity was also initiated and organized in the
Warsaw Ghetto around Ringelblum's circle, as was impressive educational
activity in the same Ghetto. See N. Eck's paper, "The Cultural Struggle in
the Warsaw Ghetto" (3 #s, pp. 37-40). There are similar impressive
testimonies on such activity in the Ghetto of Vilna and in other Ghettos. An
intensive cultural activity aimed at strengthening spiritual resistance is
reflected in the underground periodicals which represented the Zionist
youth movements. Rabbis and Hassidic leaders and many religious scholars were also intensively involved in teaching and preaching. For a detailed
documentation, see Rabbi E. Person and R. Guttman, "The Religious Life
in the Ghetto of Kowno" (Yiddish) in *Fun Letzten Khurb'n*, 3 #v, No. 9
(1948), pp. 36-51. In the same issue there is a description of secular
cultural activity in Kowno. See also Zeidman's description of religious
educational activity in the Warsaw Ghetto. Zeidman saw these activities as
affecting moods which worked both to strengthen and to weaken — the
strength of faith and trust that the Nazi regime would soon be defeated and
that redemption was very near was sometimes transformed into fantastic
illusion. Contrary to these spiritually elevating manifestations, there were
of course manifestations of spiritual weakness, abandonment of Jewish
identity and demoralization.

which time, the dimensions of the catastrophe having become completely clear, there remained almost nothing to be saved or changed. Only then did some Jewish leaders come to the conclusion that the established response model was mistaken, that even if the "tactical" use of partial cooperation with the Nazi regime was unavoidable and, therefore, justified for the sake of "gaining time" and preparing for a different reaction, the "strategic" conception should have been based on completely different assumptions and expectations so as to face reality and fight for an achievable moral aim at a completely different level. But here again it must be emphasized that the majority of scholars engaged in a study of the Holocaust tend to the conclusion that there was no practical option for a different "strategy," that the effort to gain time was the only possible strategy, and the hope for an early Nazi defeat in the war the only way out of an otherwise hermetically sealed death trap.*

For some very sensitive personalities, mostly from the younger generation, the futility of the established, traditional model of reaction did become a matter of growing frustration and distress, making it a subject of intensive thought. The major practical and moral problem behind their soul-searching deliberations was, What is the limit of cooperation with the Nazi regime, the limit of obedience to its demands, both on the collective and the individual levels? Are there orders which the collective as well as the individual should never obey regardless of the pressure and against any "costs"? Are there demands which should not be fulfilled even for the sake of a surviving remnant? Is it always justified to sacrifice one part of the collective on the chance that another part may be saved? Secularist

---

* In an article about the personality of M. Anielewicz (the commander of the Warsaw Ghetto revolt), Ringelblum writes: "The young man first intuited this truth when it was already too late, after the majority of Warsaw Jewry had been taken to Treblinka" (3 #d, vol. 2, p. 149). This is a key sentence. A similar opinion is found in Z. Lubetkin's testimony on the Vilna Ghetto (3 #j, pp. 27, 33, and 64). The same motif is expressed by such recognized young leaders as Kovner, Tenenbaum-Tamaroff and Drenger. We cite here only the words of Drenger: "We, the Jews, regretfully missed the right hour. The best part of our power has been swept out by the general gale of annihilation" (3#c, p. 69). See also his statement in the article on "The Jewish Partisan Movement," pp. 155-158. However, the reader should be reminded that scholars like Trunk and Arad believe that there was no alternative, that missing the right hour was enforced and unescapable.

Jews discussed these problems within the framework of their human-istic ethical world view; for religious Jews the problems were defined in *halakhic* terms. It appears to be typical of the extraordi-nary situation that occasionally even secularists grasped the problem in traditional *halakhic* terms. A number of their leaders were vitally interested in the *halakhic* viewpoint, approaching eminent rabbis with the question of how one should behave in such tragic dilemmas.*
Almost daily decisions had to be made on issues which were obvi-ously beyond any known ethical norms of behavior for even the most extreme situations of crisis, namely situations in which "normal" limits between the morally right and wrong, the permitted and forbidden, had been obscured or entirely swept away. Responsible leaders desperately needed a normative guiding authority to know where and when they faced a demand which should be defined in the *halakhic* terms of "let one be killed and refrain from any trans-gression." Let the whole collective be killed and refrain from any transgression? Maimonides' famous *halakhic* decision in the case of an enemy's demand to deliver certain Jewish individuals into their hands under threat that unless these individuals were delivered the entire Jewish community would be killed, was frequently discussed. Was his clear normative decision valid in the surrealistic situation created by the Nazis, a situation in which the only "interest" which the enemy had in keeping a Jewish community alive was to continue with its own orderly process of murder?[5]

The moment in which this was clarified beyond any doubt was of course the moment in which the objective meaning of cooperation with the Nazis was also clarified. Did this clarification necessarily signify the end of cooperation? For a leader such as Czerniakow in Warsaw, this was indeed the border which should not be violated, but

---

* One well-known example is the approach by Gans, Head of the Judenrat in Vilna, to the Rabbi from Usmiana, for the Rabbi's *halakhic* decision as to whether it is justifiable to deliver the elderly people of the town to be killed by the Nazis, in order to save the young Jews who remained. Kalmanowitz, referring to this event, comments, "The old Rabbi should be an eye opener for us. We must save whatever is possible" (3 #n, p. 86). Similarly, a group of rabbis were requested to decide whether it was permissible to transmit to the Nazis, on demand, a list of Jews in the community who were evidently to be murdered. See S. Globe, "Die Din Torah" (The Torah Decision) (Yiddish), in *Fun Letzten Hurb'n* (3 #x, no. 6, August 1947, pp. 44-47).

other leaders, such as Ganz in Vilna or Rumkowsky in Lodz, did not change their policy. They were prepared to go on as long as they were able to convince themselves and their followers that there was still some hope to save a remnant. For the sake of the remnant they were ready to cooperate even to capturing and delivering Jews directly into the hands of the murderers.

The same problem was raised on the personal level. What is an individual allowed to do in order to save himself or his relatives? What is the limit of cooperation with the enemy for the sake of an individual escape? This question was relevant first for those who were ready to serve as leaders in a Judenrat or in the Jewish police forces in the ghetto. But everyone was in daily danger of being trapped in a situation that caused him to face such dilemmas,* namely, that the only way to save himself would be — directly or indirectly — by condemning others to death. The Nazis created such situations intentionally, clarifying beyond any doubt or illusion that their only interest in Jews pertained to an orderly dehumanization and murder. Thus, the Nazis defined the meaning of "Radical Evil" on the level of daily life.

In its absolute extreme, the principle of "collective responsibility," as interpreted and enforced by the Nazis, became the background on which these ethical problems were posed. All the Jews as a collective, and every single Jew individually, were declared responsible before the Nazi authorities for the deeds of every other individual Jew, or every group of Jews. The Jewish collective was then threatened with cruel punishment for any "sin" committed by a Jew, the most severe "sin" against the Nazi regime being the "sin" of escaping dehumanization or death because German law demanded that the Jews willingly accept their own dehumanization and annihilation. Every act of self-defense, hiding, escape, even more, every

---

* Well-known and much discussed is the question which Rabbi Weinberg was approached to decide when he was a prisoner in a death camp. Is a father permitted to save his own child from death, knowing for certain that some other child will be taken to his death instead. The Rabbi refused to offer a decision, and the father interpreted the refusal as a negative response (3 #v). For a discussion of *halakhic* problems in that period generally, see Rabbi Dr. H.J. Zimmels, *The Echo of the Nazi Holocaust in Rabbinic Literature* (Great Britain, 1975).

attempt to revolt and take revenge, were immediately punished using the cruelest methods of collective or environmental atrocity. The ethical problem then was, are individual persons morally allowed to try to escape and hide, knowing that once their escape is revealed, the Nazis will take their revenge on other Jews? And beyond that, is it morally permissible to resist the Nazis in any measure by the use of force? Or, is it permissible to refrain from cooperating with the Nazis knowing that it may result in collective punishment? The uniqueness of the moral problem of "collective responsibility" created by the Nazi regime was grounded in the fact that not only could the effort of an individual to save himself be condemned as egoistic and morally irresponsible, even devotion to an ultimate moral value, such as the sanctity of human life and human dignity, which is based on faith in ultimate moral values, could be condemned as immoral. This formulation of the dilemma is not an abstract construct of a hypothetical situation. It was a daily experience. Every attempt to organize a resistance operation for self-defense in the ghetto had to confront this dilemma, expressed in an antagonistic public opinion which at times even included a bitter, moral condemnation of such uncalled-for "zeal." The criticism was made in the name of those who were to be defended, those who were expected to participate in the planned act of self-defense.*

* Cited above are the words of Kalmanowitz, but in this context the full history of the clash between the P.P.A. headed by Wittenberg and Kovner, and the Judenrat headed by Gans should be noted. The leaders of the P.P.A. faced a physical protest against their position when a majority of the Jewish population massed against them in the streets. It was clear that if they insisted on having their own way, they would be plunged into a fight against the Jewish community. So they were forced to give up their first plan to resist in the ghetto. In Bialestok the majority did not act against revolt, but neither did they respond to the call to participate. Instead they let themselves be led passively to evacuation. In Warsaw there was no clash, but this was only achieved because the resistance fighters deliberately waited for the final moment when the Nazis came to evacuate the last of Warsaw's Jewry. The problem of "Collective Responsibility" was a major consideration in all these internal debates and struggles. See, for example, the testimony of R. Kortchak (3 #i, p. 56). But the most important testimony is S. Drenger's long article: "In the Mischievous Circle — Is this Really a Collective Responsibility?" (3 #c, pp. 84-86). Drenger makes an impressive intellectual effort to break out of the ethical trap and to defend

Saul Friedlander laid bare the problem of "the ambivalence of good" from the point of view of an anti-Nazi German who was convinced that the only way for him to fight effectively against Nazi atrocities was to become an S.S. officer and act from within.[6] In the case of a German officer, what may be considered by many as an artificially created dilemma was an inescapable moral trap for every victim in a Nazi concentration camp or in a ghetto who was prepared to defend his sacred moral values through direct active resistance.

Two moral dilemmas emerge here which again concretize the meaning of being victimized by Radical Evil. There is the dilemma of being forced to participate in the Evil itself in order to survive; there is also the dilemma of refraining from active resistance to Evil in order to avoid responsibility for the suffering and death of others. Those among the leadership (as well as many private individuals) who made an effort to protect their moral freedom to choose a response toward that which was being forced upon them, were trapped by one or both of these dilemmas. Did they really have that "ultimate" freedom which Victor Frankl claims is "essential" to the human soul, and is therefore beyond any possibility of being taken? The answer may be "Yes," but if so, it is only through an extraordinarily heroic ascent in which one is consciously prepared to "pay" the ultimate personal, and even collective, "cost." It means choosing a way which incorporates within itself a grave ethical dilemma. There were those who came to the unequivocal conclusion that the Nazis were fulfilling a precise, detailed plan aimed at a total annihilation of the Jewish people, and that this plan, though insane, was within their reach. The Nazis, they concluded, were already on the brink of their "final" achievement which meant that they had the possibility of finishing their "enterprise" before their defeat in the war. (In fact, the more obvious and the closer their defeat became, the more the Nazis increased their efforts to accomplish the "Final Solution" against the Jews, signaling by their frenzy that this "accomplishment" had indeed become their ultimate goal.)

It was just such individuals then who could definitely reject any consideration in favor of cooperation with the Nazis and opt for an organized, self-initiated activity of resistance and defense, using all the means within their reach, including arms, in spite of their clear

---

the freedom to fight in spite of the "Collective Responsibility" imposed by the Germans.

knowledge that there was no chance to "win" in the physical senseof the word. In their eyes, the struggle itself signified a tremendous victory. They could even resolve the dilemma posed by "collective responsibility," by refusing to yield to the German interpretation of the term, attempting to reinterpret it according to their understanding of the situation. First, they pointed to the fact that when one deals with a process of total annihilation, the threat of "collective punishment" loses its binding moral significance. The fate of the collective, as the fate of almost every individual in the collective, has already been decided. At worst, the Nazi "revenge" would bring this fate a bit sooner. This consideration had to be weighed against the possibility that through resistance some individuals would survive. They went even further. In this extraordinarily unique situation one should define anew, and in an extraordinarily unique manner, the basic existential interest of the collective. At this moment, they claimed, the ultimate existential interest of the collective is resistance, not survival. Only by being prepared for unconditional resistance as the ultimate interest can chances be created for the survival of some remnant, whereas acting on the assumption that survival is the ultimate interest only pushes the individual and the community toward a dehumanizing annihilation which has less chances for survival. Obviously, this reasoning did not nullify the moral demand to take into account the threat of "Collective Responsibility" as it was enforced by the Nazis. Still, in the broad conception, the idea of survival was held as a "tactical" consideration. One should gain time so as to be prepared to choose the right moment for revolt, placing the responsibility for creating better chances for the collective to resist above the responsibility for the life of the individual. And, having once decided on the precedence of resistance over survival, the only conclusion possible must be that not only is resistance allowed, it is a moral commandment which may ultimately require individual and collective sacrifices.*

---

* In this context it should be emphasized that all the young thinkers who initiated and justified the idea of revolt — Kovner, Tenenbaum-Tamaroff, Geller and Drenger — were clearly and firmly committed to national responsibility. They saw the revolt as the necessary conclusion to a correct strategy for national survival. All of them realized that the Jews had to become "the masters of their death" (*Adonei Hamawet* — according to Kovner's expression), which meant that one should be ready to die in the

struggle when faced by the alternative of life without moral freedom and human dignity. In this way, one would regain moral freedom, actively choosing his own death. Yet it must be emphasized that while they articulated this courageous view, they were anxious to make clear that they did not prefer death as such. On the contrary, being ready to die, they opted for life, if not for the individual then at least for the sake of the collective, the nation, the forthcoming generations. Moreover, in every operation which they planned, even when the chances to get out of it alive were almost nil, they had an escape plan and searched out every possibility for individual survival. It was a matter of principle for them: one should always cherish the hope of life. Clearly any practical decision about if and when to start the fighting must consider the pros and cons from a collective, communal and national point of view. Had the moment arrived when readiness to sacrifice life was preferable from the collective's point of view? Only when it became clear that the community as a whole faced the last phase of annihilation, that on a practical level there was no justification for waiting any longer, did they consider it legitimate to begin a general revolt. As long as it seemed that by waiting it would be possible to save more Jews, they continued their preparations and waited, maintaining preparedness to fight as their hope and their source of inner freedom. This kind of deliberation was behind the P.P.A.'s decision to get out of Vilna, to give up the idea of fighting a Jewish national war in the ghettos. It was not only the opposition of the majority which they had to face; they also took into account the probability that the evacuation to "work camps," proposed by the Nazi regime, might offer a better chance of survival for more Jews until such time as the approaching defeat of the Nazis by the Russian Army. Though, as noted, when a revolt did take place, it was always in the final stages of the annihilation, it should be remembered that the firm decision to fight in defiance of the death threat had already been taken and the resolution to resist had been expressed strongly and effectively through intensive preparations, which, for the individuals engaged in them, were almost as dangerous as the fight itself. Moreover, once having decided on revolt, it became the strategic concept of a Jewish resistance, while other considerations were mere tactical deliberations. From the point of view of the resistance fighters, one may say that the revolt actually began with the decision to prepare for a fight. The decision legitimized the tactics of survival up to the moment which was ripe for war; waiting for the right moment was, in fact, a part of the war itself. This was the major difference between the ideology of the young fighters and the ideology represented by Kalmanowitz. Their revolutionary way of thinking was manifested on the strategic level and enabled them to justify the use of certain traditional ways of survival as part of an overall new conception. On this, see Reizl Kortchak (3 #i, pp. 53-56, 172, and 206-

For those who were able to sustain it, this position regained the freedom of moral choice against externally enforced conditions. But its severity should be fully comprehended. An extraordinarily unique courage was demanded to clearly define the situation and to understand the reality that had been defined, especially since the majority of the Jewish community — including its responsible leadership — contradicted this definition even after exposure to the full meaning of Ponar for the Vilna ghetto, and Treblinka for the ghetto in Warsaw. Even more courage was demanded of those who actually started to take action, who proceeded to organize an underground group and made preparations for a significant resistance under almost impossible conditions — all of this in the face of the traumatic realization that in most cases they failed to convince the majority of the Jewish population of their position. Instead, they met with critical antagonism, sometimes even in their effort to reveal the full truth about the Nazi camps. This was because some responsible community leaders hesitated, preferring not to share their knowledge with the Jewish population so as not to deprive it of the smallest hope that they might survive until the Nazi's defeat.* The situation

---

224); I. Ringelblum on Anielewicz (3 #d, vol. 2, pp. 141-150); Lubatkin (3 #j, pp. 64-87); Tenenbaum-Tamaroff (3 #g, pp. 50-84); Geller (3 #c, pp. 61-65, 101-103, 116-117, 217-220).

* It is difficult to differentiate between doubts about the final intentions of the Nazis and how far they were prepared to go with their "Actions" against the Jews, and doubts about disseminating information (which had been checked and tested) on the true situation in order to save the victims from fear and despair in the knowledge that there was no hope, assuming that indeed there was practically nothing to be done that could change their fate. Obviously, in deciding to make such information available, one had to be perfectly sure that his facts were precise. Such surety was beyond human capability. Here lay the internal obstacle which was also an external obstacle: it was almost impossible to be convinced of the credibility of such information. Then how could one be certain that he should disseminate it? And how could the public be convinced it was not simply a case of terror tactics? The doubts expressed by even a firmly committed man like Kovner are instructive: "The point that is vague in this debate" — he says to his comrades — "is the source of our assurance that we are facing total physical annihilation. Though for me it is perfectly clear, I know that I cannot convince the others....There will come a day

was more severe for those who felt that they should not act without the consent of the majority in actions against the Nazis because they would thus make the entire community responsible — against its will — as a result of their personal decisions. Yet, for them, resistance was a condition of life, an ultimate ethical commandment.*

---

when this knowledge will be recognized by all. Yet the most important thing is to take care that this general recognition does not come too late, when we are already utterly despairing and broken. Therefore, we are commanded to choose certainty in spite of our doubts" (3 #i, p. 55). Kovner chooses certainty in spite of his doubts. For him it is a matter of will, not merely of knowledge. If so, one must empathize with the feelings of responsible leaders who carried the formal responsibility and therefore were unable to choose such certainties as Kovner's. Indeed, they believed that they could not allow themselves to embrace such incredible certainties, that, unlike Kovner, they were commanded to be very cautious. So even when the evidence was before them, they did not permit themselves to know. Eck's story on his and Geller's attempt to notify the leaders of the Judenrat in Chenstochow of the approaching "Action" and the tendency to create hope through illusion and fantasy is relevant to this topic (see 3 #s, pp. 81-82, 118). Even Eck, who was aware of Nazi intentions, states in the context of the story that before the advent of the last stage, Nazi intentions were beyond credibility. "How was it possible, in September 1942, not to assume that Hitler had decided to annihilate only a part of the people and not the whole people? With our own eyes we saw that it was so. In every place from which Jews were 'expelled,' the Germans left a part of the Jewish population in the ghetto" (*ibid.*, p. 84). Even Czerniakow, who committed suicide when he finally grasped the Nazi design, did not make his knowledge public. As to a conscious decision not to spread information, the most famous case is that of Leo Baeck in Theresienstadt (see Albert H. Friedlander, *Leo Baeck* [London, 1973], pp. 43-48). Another well-known and much debated case is that of I. Kastner in Hungary.

* From what has been related, it becomes quite clear that doubts on this subject accompanied all the leaders of ghetto revolts. This was clearly demonstrated in the case of Vilna as the P.P.A. yielded before the majority of Jewish public opinion. In this context there were also internal implications related to the method of decision-making. In spite of the fact that these were semi-military underground organizations, the final decision for action was reached only after an assembly of the organization's active members engaged in a free discussion. All opinions were heard, and it was agreed that the assembly should reach a decision that would be acceptable to all, taking each opinion into account in the attempt to be as considerate

The confrontation with these dilemmas raised the ethical contest to an added height. A clear realization of the fact that the Nazis intended the total annihilation of the Jewish people, that is, the murder of every single Jew they could reach, would appear to be a definite answer to the question, What is happening? What is the "nature" of this unique historical situation? But, in fact, in order to arrive at this insight one had to grasp the full scope of the terrifying question, and only when its full background was realized could one begin the search for a correct answer. Those who refused to admit what they saw even in the terminal stages of the Holocaust — and it must be reemphasized that it was psychologically natural not to admit the existence of such events — stubbornly assumed that what was happening was a "repetition" of what had happened before and could be explained on the same historical background as known phenomenon in Jewish history. What was happening, though on a tremendously larger scale, was defined by such thinkers as a "pogrom," more intensively motivated but basically the same virulent anti-Semitism as in the past. Those who were able to grasp the total, absolute nature of the events faced something which was, indeed, beyond comprehension. What could motivate such events? How was it humanly possible? What could explain the decision of a government to plan and execute such deeds, and especially when it was clearly contrary to what appeared to be (in the eyes of any rational observer) against the best interest of the regime itself? Why were the Germans ready to give up the benefit of Jewish experts for the German war machine? Why were they ready to employ a considerable part of their army in the middle of the war, even when everything had turned up against them, for such an "unnecessary" enterprise? How could it be that hatred toward the Jews could become the ultimate concern of a nation and drive it beyond all limits of a civilized society? These were not merely theoretical questions. They

---

as possible. Kovner's speech, cited in the previous note, was delivered on such an occasion. A parallel testimony can be found in Lubetkin's book (3 #j, p. 87). The most instructive debate is reported in M. Tenenbaum-Tamaroff's diary. He describes in detail the debate in a general assembly of the kibbutz on February 27, 1943, in which other members of the movement also participated. Each person stated his opinion and after a long discussion the final conclusion took all the expressed positions into consideration (3 #g, pp. 77-84).

carried with them the anguish and fatefulness of painful existential searchings. But even beyond that, an answer was demanded for the sake of convincing others that this was what was really happening so that they would know how to fight against it "effectively."

To restate the case: It is no longer a fight for survival, even less a fight for victory. It is an act of resistance to Radical Evil. It is an act which strikes at the center of Evil, pointing to what it is and proving that though it may succeed in murder it will never overcome the spiritual core of its victims; it will not demolish their humanity or their Jewishness. Obviously, one must understand exactly what he is wrestling against so that the struggle will achieve its full spiritual meaning, first in his own eyes but eventually also in the eyes of the enemy. Let the enemy feel to the full his victim's sense of superiority and revenge.*

---

* A careful study of the underground periodicals and a good part of the diaries shows that there were two central needs which they were intended to satisfy. The first was to understand the meaning of the events through reliable information and sound analysis, and on the basis of certain ideological assumptions. (The second, as noted earlier, was to leave full documentation of the events as an historic record.) During the first phase of the war, efforts were concentrated on a dogmatic reaffirmation of previously accepted ideologics, but later the growing need for greater clarification becomes apparent. "The suffering makes it possible for us to recognize new truths. These are powerfully manifested before the eyes of the oppressed — the beaten, the hungry, the deprived. The child who is lying in the street and dies has recognized a great truth about life which we do not yet know. We must add this knowledge to Marx's 'Communist Manifesto' to renew and complement it with the power of this truth. From all our catastrophes we must emerge with a new 'Communist Manifesto,' a more complete one." This is stated in an article dedicated to the 1st of May, 1941, in the periodical of the Dror movement (3 #a, vol. 2, pp. 307-308). The contents of the periodicals affirm this statement with the main articles devoted to recent information accompanied by fresh analysis and comments. The diaries are also a medium of reflection. Kaplan's diary is typical of this. For him understanding is not only a means to an end, in fact it is his path of resistance. "Even in the most horrible hours, when Warsaw was conquered and the enemy's planes were showering death and horror from above, I did not forsake my pen. I felt the need to document the events for posterity. Above my head the angels of death were flying, and I concentrated on my sacred work. It was a sublime heroism...this is my

At this stage it was clear that explanations from previously accepted ideologies were irrelevant. Marxism, Borochovism, Gordonism, Jabotinsky's teachings, or the traditional religious conception of "the hatred of Esau to Jacob"* — none of these ideologies could account for such events; they did not contain any insight into the motivation behind the reality of the ghettos and the camps. No rational, economic, social, political or national explanation could account for the fact that anti-Semitism had been transformed from the status of a socio-cultural by-product into an end in itself. It became evident that absolute hatred was the essential psychological motivation for the war, and that this hatred was not a product or a projection of anything else, not even of religious fanaticism. Hatred is a self-destructive feeling because in itself it is a process of inner disintegration. It needs an outlet, and the outlet must be a victim into which it penetrates in order to utterly destroy it. Of course it must be

---

consolation and my therapy. Because I know that a political system which has not one grain of good in it, will not persist" (3 #1, p. 201). The need to document the events may be observed in this passage, but it also expresses the feeling that understanding the essence of Nazism is in itself a therapy; it becomes the basis for hope as well as for a feeling of superiority. Precisely because it was so important for him to understand the Nazi system, he subsequently became increasingly bewildered, experiencing the incomprehensible. "Full of oppressive impressions I returned home, an utterly broken vessel. I looked at the fanatic scenes in the streets of Warsaw and could not stop thinking, are we guiltier than any other people? Have we sinned more than every other nation? Are we doomed to complete oblivion? We should search the ways of the world: who has seen or who has heard of a similar event in which a whole people, the men and the women, the elderly and the children, are doomed to death?" (*ibid.*, p. 365).

* In following the ideological development which was reflected in the underground periodicals, three phases can be discerned. In the first phase, a stubborn affirmation of former ideological stances. Of course, the feeling that there is a need to restate and strengthen these ideologies points to a developing sensitivity. The "official" ideologues did respond to a growing suspicion that the validity of their movements' ideologies might be shaken or even destroyed as a result of the fate of the Jews under the Nazi conquest, the relationship of Soviet Russia to the Nazis in the beginning of the war, and the anti-Semitic behavior of the gentile society toward the

persecuted Jews. The following is a typical note, taken from the periodical of the Dror Movement:

> The darkest days of a renewed Middle Ages have come upon us, together with all its "equipment" of diabolical creatures, but in the modern clothing of the twentieth century....In spite of all, we, the Jews, and especially our youth, are obliged to overcome our bitterness and disgust toward European culture because of the terrible, barbaric deeds which have swept over European countries. We must understand that this is only a passing phenomenon in the history of mankind, a terrifying dream which is rooted in deeper causes, in the struggle of a collapsing Europe after the miserable first World War. A Europe which is entangled in the complexity of its social and economic contradictions. When we grasp this, when we are convinced that it is only a passing phenomenon, then we will be able to overcome our mood of depression, so as not to abandon our hope for a better future, which will surely come (3 #a, vol. 1, pp. 46-47).

Parallel to this, in the periodical of Hashomer Hazair: "In the meantime we, the Jews of Poland, are facing annihilation. The regime which is a hard hammering fist for the nations of the world, is a death sentence for us. In the thousands of years of our history...we did not know even an hour of such overwhelming torture and never was the attack so well thought out and directed." The writer then describes the great danger that, due to their oppressive experiences, the youth will yield to the Roman maxim, *homo hominis lupus est*. His final advice is: "It is a duty to think! It is forbidden to yield to reality; it is forbidden to give up hope and faith. We must use our clear thinking as a tool that will enable us to survive, not deteriorate. We must study! We must gather knowledge in order that we may be able to accurately analyze recent historic events....It should be understood that Fascism is a particular historic phenomenon through which the downtrodden class is trying to maintain its government by the use of force." Here, indeed, is the familiar Marxist analysis popular from the years before the war (*ibid.*, pp. 91-92). This pattern of thinking is to be found in all the periodicals, each movement, of course, referring to its own cherished ideology. In the second phase, the recognition that the established ideologies were inadequate, that they could not provide a convincing analysis of the historic reality, penetrated deeply into the minds and the hearts. It has now become commonplace that certain additions are needed to revitalize the old Communist (or other) Manifesto, though one still cannot find much evidence of new or creative thinking. In the passage cited in the previous note, the statement that attention must be paid to new truths discovered

a particular victim which the hater can shape as the carrier of all the characteristics he so intensively hates, characteristics which the hater projects out of his own insane personality, in order to feel the perverse satisfaction of a negative fulfillment.

It was natural to choose the Jew as the hated victim because the Jew served as scapegoat in European society for many generations. The background was indeed "traditional," but the phenomenon itself was new. Jews became the object of a new kind of hatred, hatred for itself, hatred as an ultimate value. For this purpose Jews were exhibited as the "emblem" of everything hated by the Nazis, the absolute negation of the Nazi conception of the ideal Aryan. In this way the war came to be, *ab initio*, the war of Nazi Germany against Judaism and the Jewish people. The Nazis had to destroy the Jews in order to fulfill themselves. This appeared to be the rationale behind the practical exposition of the Jew as Germany's main enemy and the resolution not to rest until the last Jew was seen to be dehumanized, and murdered.

Still, how can one account for such an extraordinarily unique phenomenon? There were, it seems, only two categories of explanation — either in terms of psycho-social pathology, or in terms of diabolical metaphysics. Full scientific accounts cannot be expected, of course, in the underground literature of the ghettos. But brief insights and hints are present in both directions. Clearly, these insights related to the phenomenon of Radical Evil; that is, Evil as an end in itself, Evil which must be rejected beyond any possibility of a negotiated compromise. Victims of such Evil must resist and fight against it in order to tear it out at its roots. Therefore, from the Jewish view, the meaning of the war was understood as an act which

------

through suffering only served as an excuse for another repetition of old truths. Not until the third phase — and this occurred almost in tandem with the realization of the nature of the "Final Solution" and its actual application — did the process of developing new insights really begin. Of course, it could not be fully developed. Drenger's original and thoughtful articles in *Hehalutz Halohem* are an astonishing exception which may be considered an exemplary expression of this new kind of thinking.

signified absolute rejection, and beyond that absolute reaffirmation of the values of Judaism and humanity.* Those who realized the facts

* To refer to Kaplan's entry in his diary:

The huge catastrophe which crushed Polish Jewry is not to be compared to anything else in Jewish history, even in its darkest periods. Firstly — the depth of hatred. It is not hatred rooted only in the ideology of a movement, created for the sake of politics. It is not a conjectural hatred; it is an emotional hatred which is caused by a psychopathic sickness. In its outward expressions it works like a physiological hatred, describing its object as a defiled body, or a leper which has no place within the camp. It is essential hatred that has been spread among the masses. An ideological hatred is above the head of the narrow-minded. Philosophy is strange to them, and they are unable to grasp it. So they have absorbed the teachings of their masters in the most concrete and corporeal manner: the Jew is foul, the Jew is a liar, a scoundrel. The Jew hates Germany and works against it....These are well understood concepts, the effect of which is immediately sensed in daily life. Yet the founders of Nazism and leading individuals in the party created a scientific theory based on deeper foundations. They developed a whole theory which penetrates into the depth of Jewish spirituality. Judaism and Nazism — these are two world views which cannot suffer each other, and therefore cannot exist together. Two thousand years ago Judaism captured all the nations of the world in its net and influenced them through its spirit and culture. Thus Judaism becomes the enemy of German paganism which came from a different source, developed a different culture, and blocked the spread of Judaism. Two kings do not use one crown. Humanity will become either Jewish or German-Pagan. Until now, it has been Jewish, Catholicism also being a daughter of Judaism, the fruit of the Jewish spirit, which inherited all its mother's faults. The new world which Nazism is going to create must represent ancient Paganism with all its "attributes." Therefore it is commanded to fight against Judaism to its complete destruction....This is the secret of the storm which threatens to sweep us out of the world (3 #1, pp. 201-202).

Nazism is explained here as both an extraordinary emotional pathology and the result of a penetrating world view. In what follows, Kaplan tends to emphasize the psychopathic element in Nazism without any "spiritual" dimension:

could not fully expound the psycho-social, psycho-political or psycho-cultural motivations behind them or analyze their sources, but once the level of "otherness" of this unique confrontation was identified, they could better define the level and meaning of a correct reaction.

Cruelty is a sickness, as is torture. The imagination of man's heart functions from his youth. The feeling of mercy is natural to him from the day of his birth. All of this is true for a normal human being. A man whose human emotions have been corrupted is not normal. A man who enjoys the torture of someone weaker than himself is suspected of being psychologically sick. We should pity the victim of cruelty, we should sympathize with those who suffer torture. Yet the cruel person himself is miserable, though he does not deserve mercy....From this point of view, the Nazi is also a miserable sick man. Until now, we have seen only individuals who are cruel. But with Nazism, cruelty became the sickness of a whole party, perhaps even of a whole nation. Once even the cruel individual had feelings of shame; cruelty was done secretly, not in public. But when Nazism came to the world, public shame disappeared; whoever multiplies his cruelty in the streets is acclaimed....The only consolation is that Nazism is madness....But how can it console a Jew who has been wounded to death (*ibid.*, p. 491).

One may describe Kaplan's attempt to delve deeper into an explanation of Nazism as the expression of a stage in which Kaplan partially changed his former ideology. Indeed, explanations which were rooted in the theory of a spiritual confrontation between Nazism and Judaism can be found in the writings of those who were engaged in reaffirming their old ideologies. Thus, in the underground periodical of the General Zionist party, *Shviv*, this explanation is found: "From what has been said we may conclude that Europe's spiritual life has always been influenced in a rather great measure by Judaism. It is not in vain that 'the yellow beast' is fighting against our people and its teaching. This beast knows that Judaism is a source of danger to the kingdom of evil and its wicked regime, which strives to subjugate all humanity....On the other hand the defense of democracy depends, spiritually, on the self-same ethical values which progressive Europe has absorbed from the Jewish sources" (3 #a, vol. 1, p. 242). A similar trend is revealed in Kalmanowitz's diary (3 #n, pp. 116-117). Leo Baeck also understood Nazism as an attack against the universal-ethical essence of Judaism.

174

"Once Jews were ready for martyrdom to sanctify the name of God. In these times they should sanctify their own lives."[7] This familiar sentence is attributed to Rabbi Isaac Nissanbaum from the Warsaw Ghetto, and is the subject of much discussion in attempts to characterize the Jewish response at its best. But how should one define, in a practical way, the distinction between the sanctification of life and the sanctification of the name of God? A major part of the answer was obvious, even agreed to by all concerned: finding and delivering life resources for the Jewish community in every way possible, creating lines of communication with the outside, gaining help from the outside, enhancing the feelings of solidarity and reciprocity inside the Jewish community, and continuing spiritually creative life activities to emphasize the inherent value of humanity and Judaism — all of which called for undertaking educational and cultural activity in their full magnitude, at all levels. And more, it meant strengthening Jewish self-identity, self-respect and pride in the superiority of Judaism over its persecutors, refuting the attacks of hatred and spite against the Jewish people, reaffirming hope and faith, and believing that the Nazis would finally be defeated and the Jewish people would survive and be redeemed.[8] In summary, it may be said that the practical meaning of the "Sanctification of Life" was grasped in terms of continuing the fullness of Jewish life. It meant wrestling for survival, not merely on the physical or biological level, but against Nazi attempts to reduce Jewish existence, in its spiritual dimension, to naught. This struggle, according to Rabbi Nissanbaum, was the response which was required to the Nazi assault; this was obviously the source of his distinction between the "Sanctification of the Name of God" and the "Sanctification of Jewish Life." In the past, when gentile nations tried to force Jews to desecrate the commandments or convert to another religion under threat of death, the Jews were commanded to refute the threats by their readiness for martyrdom. Now, however, when their enemy's aim was to annihilate Jewish life and its inherent values, the Jews were commanded to refute the "counsel" of their enemies by their devotion to Jewish life in its full spiritual ramifications.

But how was it possible to fulfill this commandment when the Nazis continued to tighten and narrow the situation in which conditions for survival meant giving up any option of physical resistance or protection of life's ethico-spiritual values, as well as collaborating against oneself in the process of murder, dehumanization and annihilation? Is it possible to "sanctify life" while complying with such conditions? It would appear that when the reality and severity of this question was fully grasped as a practical issue which touched each individual, thoughts about the "Sanctification of the Name of God" were reawakened as the only valid channel, in a meaning that was, however, essentially different than the traditional. A number of sensitive individuals who were unconventional thinkers now realized that for the sanctity of life as against Nazi attempts to degrade and void the inherent values of Jewish life, it would not suffice to cling stubbornly to survival, even to survival as Jews. It must now be recognized, and proved through personal activity, that there are absolute values beyond survival which are the source of life's sanctity. For the sake of such values, and only for their sake, is life worthy to be lived.

To reformulate the ethical dilemma as an existential paradox: for the sake of the sanctity of life one must be ready to give up his own life. Only those courageous enough to prefer death in the struggle against Evil to life under the yoke of Evil can defend the sanctity of their own lives and hold fast to the hope that they or some of their friends, but surely the Jewish people, will survive for a life that is worth living. In a situation of Radical Evil, being prepared to die in the struggle for values beyond life was the only way to attest to the sanctity of life.* Those who based their lives on this insight regained

---

* "A bright light will shine in our hearts when, into this hemorrhaging darkness, a recognition penetrates that we are the masters of our death. Then *our lives* will have had meaning." These are Kovner's words (3 #i, p. 56). Drenger says:

We do not worship a fatalism of death. If our words have created this impression, it is because of a lack of daring to see that the results of an armed struggle may be not only a life in which there is freedom, but also a death in which there is freedom. The enemy, in its tactics and propaganda, has pushed our people into the problematics of survival. To survive, to outlive all conditions — this has become a popular slogan. The cost of survival depends on the measure of flexibility of the individual conscience, or on possibilities which are attained by money. Contrary to this thinking we say: If survived, then only as free human beings. If this becomes impossible then let us die *as free human beings*. We want to live, and we know *what to live for*. This is precisely

their capacity to choose their relationship to the events forced upon them. They also regained the criteria for observing a clearly defined limit to "let one be killed and not transgress" in their relations with the Nazis, including the threat of collective punishment. This meant that cooperation in Nazi "Actions" against Jews, directly or indirectly, for the sake of delaying a greater catastrophe, was absolutely forbidden. They could ethically and legitimately direct acts of defense, even violent attacks against the Nazi forces, in spite of the threat of collective punishment. But of course there was one condition that was inviolate — the attack could not be merely the efforts of individuals for their own chances at survival, or even for their own ethical integrity. Rather it must be a manifest readiness for self-sacrifice on the part of individuals fighting in the battle of the people against its enemies. The principle of national responsibility was very strongly emphasized. The Nazi regime's plan to kill every single Jew aimed at the destruction of the entire Jewish people, so each Jew must consider his life as representative of the entire Jewish people. Only through this consciousness which carried with it its own limitations would the struggle against Nazism be ethically significant.*

---

the reason that we must fight, knowing that this fight brings with it more than life. Let all those people who are coming to join us only for the sake of life know that if life has an aim, it is possible to accept death in dignity and tranquility (3 #c, pp. 102-103).

Drenger continues on claiming that even the struggle for survival must be bound to an aim beyond itself, because survival is not an end in itself. "I have a duty to survive not only because *I want* to live, but precisely because as a Jew I have a *right* to live, in spite of the fact that I am deprived of this right" (*ibid.*, p. 116). (All emphasized words are so in the original — E.S.)

* The certainty that the people will be saved and will even gain something from the final result of the war, in spite of the terrible cost of blood, is a central motif of consolation and hope for the majority of these writers. They concluded that even individuals under threat should look for hope and meaning in the struggle for national survival. Those who dedicate their lives to such activity will find a source of personal hope. This was a central motif in the educational projects of Leo Baeck and his colleagues in Berlin, as well as in the activities of the youth movements, parties and

rabbinic leadership in the East European ghettos. Kalmanowitz clearly articulated this trend, "To mourn over the falling and the dead — certainly, this is natural, especially when one has lost relatives and kin. But it has nothing to do with the nation. One should not intertwine these different issues...spare your grief — the people will not be damaged. We have grounds for hope that they will emerge from this trial even stronger. This is what should fill our hearts with a feeling of joy and thankfulness to the Angel of History" (3 #n, pp. 96-97). Kalmanowitz based his firm opposition to the ideas of the P.P.A. on this kind of certainty, yet, ironically, the ideology of the P.P.A. leaders was not different from his own, at least in this area. They also emphatically negated a war for the sake of personal aims, either in the case of individuals or political parties. "Faithfulness to our movement today means sustaining the human dignity that is within us and preserving the dignity of our people by means of the struggle against the murderer. Is there a more sublime command than that — to change the people's oppression into an organized fight?" (3 #i, p. 56). This principle was the reason for the P.P.A.'s decision not to withdraw to the forests immediately, but to fight first in the ghetto. It was precisely for the sake of fulfilling a national purpose: an attempt to defend and save the Jewish community, or at least to save its dignity; it was not a fight for those individuals who were able to use arms for their personal survival. In this area, too, Drenger's thinking was the most developed and intellectually articulated. Like Kalmanowitz he stated, "Personally we are all lost. Our chances to survive are nil, and as long as we remain broken and separated from each other we do not have much hope for life. Yet even as we fall, together with all the Jews in Poland, we sense the historic meaning of this hour in the most tangible way, and say courageously that our death is not the end of the world. The history of mankind, and with it the history of the Jewish people, will continue, though the tombstone has already been erected on our mass grave" (3 #c, pp. 61-63). From this assumption he comes to a conclusion regarding the meaning and path of the struggle.

> Our every deed should pave our people's way to freedom and advance the building of our national homeland. Our revolt is a protest against the wickedness which engulfs the world. In retaliation to the aggression which smashed our people, we rise to fight for justice and freedom, for the sake of all humanity. We want to die in such a way that it is not seen as a shameful death of slaves by Jews in the future, so that no one will be ashamed of the memory of the Jews of Europe because they went like sheep to the slaughter and could not rise to the level of courage needed to face death in defense of their lives. Since we cannot participate in the constructive effort of building our homeland, let us at least fulfill our historic task here. We must raise the dignity of our

One must fully appreciate not only the measure of autonomy and courage needed for entering into any activity on the basis of such insights, but also the tragic sense of responsibility which was knowingly undertaken, actually putting into practice the newly adapted

---

dying people, erase the stain of slavery from its flesh, and include it among those peoples whose spirit is free (*ibid*).

Thus Drenger justifies the revolt against even the threat of "Collective Responsibility." In his view, the individual is not defending himself alone:

In our conditions, the death of other victims as a result of an individual's self-defense is a nobler death, as it serves a purpose. When hundreds of people are killed without reason, simply for the joy of barbaric human beasts, a death for the sake of freedom — even of a single daring man — which may contribute to the building of a new world, is a positive achievement....A person who does not understand this and tries to stop his friend in his flight to freedom, unconsciously becomes a partner to the crime. Moreover, one who consciously demands acquiescence to the principle of collective responsibility is himself a criminal — a hundred times lower than the murderer — because he is pushing his brothers toward an inhuman death for his own expediency and egotistic will to live even if it means walking over corpses (*ibid.*, pp. 84-86).

It must be emphasized that the rejection of the principle of collective responsibility is justified here in the name of a true ethical responsibility toward the Jewish collective and humanity! In what follows this paragraph, Drenger also demands an understanding from those who grapple for their lives by hiding, that their struggle will be meaningful and worth the superhuman effort only if they embody a national and universal human cause in their survival. "We must survive because to give up our right to live means escaping from the field of battle, means opening the way to aggression which will flood the world. Surviving we fulfill the function of a living dam which opposes the rule of wickedness, at least in that small portion covered by the life of one single man" (*ibid.*, pp. 116-117). Without such consciousness, Drenger thinks the terrible effort to survive for the sake of survival in the biological meaning, under such horrible conditions, is unjustified — even acknowledging the instinct for life — because such a life is worthless. Examining the problem from all aspects, Drenger concludes that the identification of the individual with the nation and the hopes of the nation is the only source of purpose, value, hope and meaning.

principle of "let one be killed and not transgress" while legitimizing a violent revolt against the Nazis on the same principle, in defiance of the threat of collective punishment. It was clear that every practical situation deserved special examination and a decision which had carefully weighed the pros and cons from the national point of view. It was not sufficient to state the legitimacy of a certain pattern of reaction. It was necessary to carefully observe when and in which way, yes; or when and in which way, no. Otherwise there was a danger that in taking upon himself the responsibility to fight for the sake of his people, an individual would find himself involved in a tragic private war against his own brothers for what he had considered to be his human or Jewish responsibility.*

Ethical dilemmas such as these which were concerned with ultimate topics of life and death, meaning and purpose, had meta-ethical implications. They posed questions of faith in God, faith in humanity, and faith in the Jewish people. In this context it should be

---

* This is implicit in what was cited in the previous note. The fighters in Vilna and Bialestok faced this practical problem precisely on the background of their nationalist ideology. Since they failed in their effort to convince the majority of the Jewish community to act with them, they might have been forced into a situation in which their struggle would have been interpreted as a "private war," entered into for the sake of their own decency and purity of conscience. This is expressed in Kovner's speech made after the escape to the forests to join the partisans. Kovner felt a need to justify this move which appeared to contradict the ideological decision which had been taken to begin the revolt in the ghetto, and to fight for the ghetto. On the contrary, says Kovner, in the actual situation which developed, starting the war in the ghetto would in fact have meant fighting a "private war." Therefore, the escape to the forests to fight against the enemy there was the only way to remain true to national responsibility. Kovner admits that "the most difficult thing is to witness the blindness of the Jewish masses in this last act." For him, the battles in the forest were a continuation of the former path, in a different way. "But we struggled not only for the sake of life. We struggled to achieve meaning in our lives, which had lost their meaning; those who remain alive will consciously or unconsciously be sanctified by this death. A cry which has not yet reached its climax calls to us from within the earth: Go on! Remember until the last breath of life. This was the message of the first proclamation, many, many days ago. Two years of bloody struggle. But we will continue until our last breath! and, perhaps, until the break of day!" (3 #i, p. 224).

remembered that decisions about problems which related to the limits of "let him be killed and refrain from transgression" or of starting an open revolt in the ghetto could not result in success or victory as such. There was almost no chance of being released or saved, and there was absolutely no chance to defeat the enemy in battle. In very rare cases there were grounds for hope that some of the fighters would survive, if they got the chance to carry on with partisans in the forests until the final victory over Germany. But this was, indeed, a rare and still dangerous chance. Basically, those who decided not to cooperate with the Nazis when it was demanded but to participate in revolt and defense realized that they would be killed, in most cases within a short time. The only possible victory was the moral victory which was identified with the decision and the actual act of resistance. The resistance fighter knew the exhilarating thrill of an act of direct revenge; a moment before his death he had the experience of being redeemed by attaining ultimate meaning, or of victory by achieving freedom through his own decision to resist and fight back.

Even then, the significance of the action was dependent on the possibility of transcending the passing moment and the subjective circle of individuality. Before whom does one stand and testify in his act of resistance? For whom is it important? Who will remember and justify it? Who will endow it with permanence? There were three possible answers: humanity, the Jewish people, or God.* This means that the decision to fight back was in itself an act of faith in humanity, in the eternity and destiny of the Jewish people, or in God — the personal God, the God who knows man, commands him, and loves him in his trials. Those who opted for resistance reaffirmed their belief and trust, each in his previously established *weltanschauung*. The time was not ripe for deep, systematic philosophical or theological reassessments. Each individual spoke using simple, elementary words in the language of faith he had known before the Holocaust. However, it is obvious that for each of them the decision to fight was

---

* The question "Before whom does one bear responsibility and before whom does one testify when he endures his trial?" is concealed within the answers to the previous question, since a particular answer to this "transcendental" question is the silent motivation behind every act of resistance. One acts and resists out of a certain belief. The fact that this question was posed and the attempts which were made to solve the problem it

not only a moment of victory over the fear of death, it was also the victory over despair and doubt. The confrontation with Radical Evil threatened to destroy the foundation of faith in the future of humanity, in the future of the Jewish people, in God. But in the moment of decision, faith was an entity which transcended the fate of the single individual. In his passing moment, the individual identified with the will to live. Those who were spiritually strong enough to fight for life on the threshold of death reaffirmed, together with their will to live, their faith in man, in the Jewish people, or in God. Thus, though the words were the same as those which had been spoken in the past, the meanings which emerged from the existential context were different, were related to a different sphere of experience. From the point of view of the religious believer, especially the Orthodox, the question was posed in its boldest form on the meta-ethical levels. There are quite early beginnings, starting during the Holocaust itself, of theological reflection. Perhaps these early reflections should be reviewed as a direct continuation of the old debate between believers and non-believers which began with the Enlight-

––––––

presents were first expressed by the strong drive to write in order to leave a documented testimony. Those who considered their death an act of religious martyrdom saw it as an expression of the strength of their faith in God, and, having overcome all doubts by their act, generally did not feel the urge to leave behind a written document. God, who sees all and knows all, surely knows and will remember their deed. Whereas secular and non-Orthodox believers saw themselves responsible to and standing trial before the Jewish people, or before humanity. They, therefore, were driven to an almost fanatic devotion to the documentation of their deeds. Indeed, persons like Ringelblum, Tenenbaum-Tamaroff, Kalmanowitz, Kovner, Kazenelson and many others like them, attached a meaning which borders on the religious to the acts of documentation and preservation of their testimonies. They considered their testimonies to be the "immortality of their souls" as individuals, as Jews, and as representatives of humanity. In a way, then, the documentation incorporated the question together with the answer: even when there was no hope of surviving the Nazi conquest, the certainty prevailed that the people of Israel would exist forever, and humanity, faithful to its moral destiny, would live forever. This meant that one bore responsibility before the transcendant idea of the Jewish people and of humanity most dearly in his mind and heart.

182

enment. Be that as it may, the theological question was consummated in the formulation of a *halakhic* question related to the norm of martyrdom: is the norm for "Sanctifying the Name of God" relevant under the conditions created by the Nazi war against the Jewish people? Does this religious norm relate to an attack against the physical existence of the entire Jewish people? Has it any meaning under such conditions? In order to avoid misunderstanding, it must be emphasized that, *a priori*, there is not necessarily a connection between this question and the question which was discussed under the title of "Letting oneself be led to extermination like a sheep to slaughter." The norm of "Sanctifying the Name of God" does not stand in contradiction to violent revolt against the enemy, nor is it necessarily an alternative to a violent revolt. Resistance by fighting until death may also be considered an act of martyrdom in which one sanctifies the name of God. Such cases abound in Jewish history;[*] such cases also occurred during the Holocaust.[9]

The sanctification of the Name of God basically means the absolute refusal to transgress God's law, readiness to die rather than yield to such a command from an enemy. It is obvious that fighting back in refusal to transgress God's commandment is within this definition. In fact, a Jew is commanded to "choose life" and to defend his own and his fellow Jew's life. He should not give up his

* The idea of the Sanctification of the Name as a public testimony to the reality of the kingdom of God in the world takes its origin in the exemplary act of Pinchas, the son of the priest, Aharon, in the story of Zimri. Its interpretation as an act of martyrdom is rooted in the resistance struggle of the Hassidim (the faithful ones) in the Hasmonean period against the Greek oppressors and their Jewish allies, who attempted to force a transgression of God's Law. It did not necessarily mean to die and so refrain from transgression, since the armed revolt of the Hasmoneans was definitely considered an act of Sanctification of the Name. Those who called themselves the Kannaim (Zealots) also considered themselves devoted to the Sanctification of the Name. Rabbi Akiva, who is included among the ten great rabbis martyred by the Romans for devotion to the Law, is held to be one of the greatest Sanctifiers of the Name. His support for the Bar-Kochba revolt against the Romans is well known. Even in the Middle Ages there were some Jewish communities which defended themselves by force of arms before they let themselves be killed as martyrs.

right to live without an act of resistance, which means that if he can, he must fight for his life. The question concerning the relevance of the norm of martyrdom was raised in terms of the religious meaning of complying with an unavoidable destiny of death in the Holocaust. Did the Nazis create a situation in which a Jew was put on trial with regard to his faithfulness to God's commandments? Was it a case of testifying for the absolute abiding force of God's commandments? Indeed, in the extraordinarily unique conditions which the Nazis created in the Holocaust the question of how the Jews decided to meet their fate became critically important even from this religious point of view. There are numerous testimonies from believing Jews, many of them great sages and rabbis, who accepted their fate in a spirit of resignation, believing that in that way they stood their trial, and testified to their absolute faith in God, "Sanctifying His Name" in public. These believers clearly articulated their understanding of the situation in words and prayers before their death. There can be no doubt that they and their community understood that they were dying as martyrs. No one can doubt the sincere conviction of witnesses that for these martyrs the moment of their death was a moment of inner illumination and religious elevation, a moment of trust in the redeeming presence of God. Beyond their traumatic anguish over their fate, which was religiously not understandable, they did testify to an experience of direct, absolute affirmation of their belief. Indeed, moments of martyrdom are essentially moments of primary religious experience, moments in which one "proves" the truth of his belief, thus testifying to the truth of the very experience out of which religion is born and renewed.* From this aspect, there can be no doubt that these were truly moments of martyrdom in the full religious sense of the term.

---

* One of the well-known stories of Sanctification of the Name in the Holocaust is about Rabbi Shmuel Shlomo Leiner, the Rabbi of Radzin. The story was the inspiration for an influential poem which indeed took on the quality of a mythos: "Dos lied weg'n Radziner" (The Poem about the Radziner) by Y. Kazenelson (3 #w, pp. 663-706). See, too, the introduction of the editor, Y. Scheintuch, *Areinfir* 35, pp. 660-662. Also well known is Hillel Zeitlin's "Last Way to Treblinka" — going to the Umschlagplatz in Warsaw wearing his prayer shawl and phylacteries. The meaning that he attached to this last way should be interpreted on the background of his prophetic experiences in the ghetto during the Holocaust. In his diary, Zeidman tells about an invitation that Zeitlin once sent to him:

From an objective point of view, however, a question is properly raised (as it was during the Holocaust) which relates to the *halakhicly* determined norm: was there a situation which demanded this religious behavior? In particular, could the way chosen by the majority of those who interpreted what was happening as a call to martyrdom — a humble, peaceful resignation without any attempt at violent resistance to death — be accepted as an act of martyrdom in its full meaning? In most cases the Nazis did not put their Jewish victims to

---

As the next Shabbat is the last Shabbat in this year, a year of emergency, and as this year of tav-shin-alef (701 according to the Hebrew calender —E.S.) is the Year of the Eve of Shabbat (tav-shin-bet equals 702 according to the Hebrew Calender, and also equals the Hebrew letters for Shabbat — E.S.) which is lost to us without any deeds of repentance for the sake of spiritual elevation, and without the necessary inner preparation for the forthcoming Year of Shabbat — which is for our benefit and our redemption — I think it is necessary that, at least on this last Shabbat, we reflect and search our souls. We do this in order to be spiritually prepared for the Year of Shabbat — which will certainly be a year of complete redemption — toward a spiritual elevation which is similar to existence in the next world, according to Maimonides in *Hilchot Deot*. Therefore, I am inviting a number of thoughtful people to my house on the forthcoming Shabbat, in order to discuss how we should properly receive the Year of Shabbat — as it is known to those who understand the hidden wisdom — for those who labor on the eve of Shabbat will feast on the Shabbat.

Then comes a description of the meeting which was opened by Zeitlin: "Jews, dear Jews of Warsaw, can you not feel the breath of the Creator, He that builds worlds and destroys them? Do you not see that the skies are blazing and the worlds are burning? Do you not hear the pace of a new era?" (3 #m, pp. 296-297). Zeitlin had a prophetic revelation and was sure that the supernatural messianic era must begin here and now. It appears that this faith was with him to his last moment. In a permanent state of devotion, his Sanctification of the Name was actually a gesture of directly going forth toward a mystical redemptive reunion. Nor is it the only testimony of a primary, immediate experience of religious revelation during the Holocaust. Also to be noted: the diary of E. Hilsum (3 #q); Leo Baeck's book, the first part of which was written in Theresienstadt (3 #z); also the diary of M. Flinker (3 #o).

a trial of faithfulness to their creed or to their religious laws. The Nazis did not demand conversion, transgression of a religious law or exclamation of disbelief.[10] The Nazis were interested in the extermination of the Jewish people. Every Jew was sentenced to death as a result of his being born to Jewish parents. Thus his faith, his world view or way of life, were, as far as the Nazis were concerned, completely irrelevant.* But the main point to be emphasized in this context is that by sanctifying the Name of God through peacefully accepting the fate of murder, the martyrs were doing exactly what their murderers expected them to do. They yielded to the will of their murderers. The response may be a blunt "so what?" Must religious Jews account for their enemy's depraved way of thinking? Their martyrdom was an act between themselves and God, as well as between themselves and the Jewish community. They yielded their bodies to the murderers and assigned their souls to the hands of God, their redeemer. Thus, they proved that the abominable sin against them could not really reach them. They were beyond the brutal power of their enemies. They were on a different existential level, one from which they could despise their persecutors and refrain from any relatedness to them, even the relatedness of responding by the use of violent means. Among the testimonies about acts of martyrdom during the Holocaust there is one story of a rabbi who appealed to the Nazi commander with a request for several moments of delay before the shooting, in order to prepare his congregation for death.

* To be more precise, Nazi ideology defined the Jews as a "lower race," thus their only crime was their total crime, namely, their origin. Every single Jew was condemned to death because of his "Jewish blood." However, in the entry cited above, the way Kaplan presents the Nazi theory is sound. Nazi ideology understood Judaism as a source of inspiration for all the spiritual streams that the Nazis despised and considered inimical — Christianity, Marxism, Communism. The radical aim of the Nazis was the physical elimination of the Jews, thus uprooting at its source the "evil spirit" which had caused the deterioration and degeneration of "pure" original European culture. It was, indeed, a total war against Judaism, not only against the Jewish people. However, the assumption that the spirit is a direct function of a racial, biological quality makes an examination of the opinion, view and behavior of every individual, or even every group, completely irrelevant. According to this theory, surely there cannot be any way to alter or "de-Judaize" the Jews by assimilation. A Jew is considered "foul" even after two generations of intermarriage.

His request granted, the rabbi turned to his congregation with words of comfort and trust in God. After the prayer and the recital of *Sh'ma* he said to the Nazi commander, "I have fulfilled my task, now you can fulfill yours."[11] It is obvious that the proud statement of the rabbi delineates the sharp distinction between the realm of spiritual freedom of the believer and the realm of brutal power and bestiality, which is where the Nazis reigned supreme. Yet, even if the rabbi's act is accepted as an expression of ultimate faith, can it be assessed as an act in which the name of God has been sanctified with exactly the same meaning as in the "classic" situation of martyrdom when Jews refused to transgress God's commandments or to convert to Christianity for the sake of survival? It is not only that in this situation faithfulness to God's commandment was not the issue. It is more that in the classic situation the victim's readiness to die to remain true to his religion meant the failure of the enemy to achieve his aim — the conversion of the Jew to the persecutor's religion. In the case just described, the Nazi commander achieved exactly what he wanted, namely a peaceful, orderly, extermination of the Jews which was, of course, the reason for his consent to the rabbi's request.

The question thus raised is, may a believing Jew completely disregard the meaning of absolute separation between the two realms as it is understood from the persecutor's point of view? Granted that the persecutor's ideology, or belief, had no significance in the eyes of the rabbi, does such a situation have no objective meaning which is significant before God and His chosen people, or for humanity? On the contrary, it would appear that the complete separation between the believer's realm of spiritual freedom and the realm where Radical Evil reigned supreme, reveals the unique problem of faith in a personal, commanding, leading and caring God as it is raised on the background of the Holocaust. Precisely because it was within the objective possibility of the Jew to interpret his suffering and death as a meaningful religious act, which he freely chose, one can detect the source of a convincing religious response to the problem of theodicy as it relates to the fate of the Jewish people in the past. When an objective option existed for an act of martyrdom in the traditional meaning of "Sanctifying the Name of God," that act contained within the deed itself the answer to the question of theodicy. For the martyr it was a great redeeming moment as he was sure of his spiritual reward in the world to come, but the significance of his act was not its importance to himself alone. Rather it was that through this act the Jewish population experienced the presence of God amongst them, and thus became stronger in the belief that their suffering was a trial, that it had meaning and purpose.

In such situations martyrdom really served as proof to believers that God truly reigns in this world too, that the moment of revenge and redemption is approaching and that God would soon manifest His sovereignty in the physical world. The martyrs died absolutely relying on this religious knowledge, preferring the reward of their martyrdom to any continuation of life. Still, it seems that martyrdom could only be understood in this way when the historic context was that of a struggle between the Jewish religion and a rival religion that also spoke the language of martyrdom in its struggle for universal recognition as the one and only true path. Obviously such a situation did not objectively exist when the Jewish people were not in the position of confronting an opposing religion in the same realm and on the same level of spirituality as Judaism. What the Jewish people now had to confront was the attempt to eliminate every Jew; and the Jews were caught utterly helpless in this death trap, completely alone, actually standing on the brink of total extermination. Could there be an historical situation better suited to the expectation that God would intervene directly, at least according to the Orthodox understanding of God as the Creator, the King who commands, the leader and the redeemer? Could any hour be better suited for God to prove that He is what His believers proclaim Him to be? How then can His faithful believers' readiness to die in complete resignation and according to the will of their enemies prove what God himself denied by His absence from history? In other words, it would seem that where there was a consummated threat of total extermination, there could be no validity to the theology of the "Hidden Countenance" of God (*Hester Panim*),* which was assumed to be the basis for the norm of the "Sanctification of the Name of God." In the context of the Holocaust, the "Hiding of God's Countenance" could not be interpreted as a situation of trial. It could only be interpreted

---

* The theology of "The Hiding of His Countenance" — which means that God punishes His people by "hiding" Himself, by refraining from any sort of direct intervention in the fate of Israel, and by allowing the gentile nations to act against Israel as they wish — is based on a previous assumption that God's providence and special care for Israel is eternal, as the Covenant between God and Israel is binding forever. Therefore, God

188

as a refutation of the Orthodox believers' faith, or at least as a dilemma which could not be resolved by any of the traditionally accepted justifications.

To reaffirm what has been hinted at: precisely in such moments of crying to God, *De Profundis*, it could happen that one would be blessed with a direct transforming experience of God's presence beyond the dilemma of His absence from history and independent of any theological solution to the problem of theodicy. Believers who were blessed with an inner illumination and knew that God was with them in their suffering, indeed, sanctified the Name of God though with a meaning which was essentially different from the traditional one. Such a phenomenon was experienced by many individuals during the Holocaust. In such moments, the faith of struggling believers who are hovering on the threshold of a spiritual breakdown is reassured through a direct experience, making (at least in the immediate situation and within the context of their individual destiny) the search for a theological solution completely superfluous. This was the personal truth for which they testified though they did not, and perhaps could not, feel the need to change the definition and meaning of the traditional norm of martyrdom.

Yet a feeling of crisis did exist, and some believers sensed that there was a need to understand the norm differently. A hint of this can be found in the previously noted insight of Rabbi Isaac Nissanbaum, namely, that in such a situation Jews should sanctify their own lives. There were some who went even further, declaring that when an attempt is made to exterminate the Jewish people, the "Sanctification of the Name of God" should become the sanctification of the name of Israel, meaning that acts of dedication to save Jews from death should take precedence. There were some Orthodox rabbis who came to the same conclusion,[12] but more often this concept characterized those religious thinkers who tended to iden-

---

never really forsakes His people, for God will never let His people perish in exile. If not directly through overt miracles, then indirectly through hidden miracles, there is no danger of a total annihilation. Obviously, such theology reflects a certainty. In antiquity, in the Middle Ages, and even in the great massacres of 1648-49, there was no threat of a "Final Solution." The Holocaust was, therefore, unique in the sense that it was an overt, concrete threat of total extermination which, of course, shook one of the basic assumptions of traditional theodicy.

tify their belief in God with a belief in the unique, spiritual destiny of Israel. Some, such as the poet Isaac Kazenelson, the writer Zelig Kalmanowitz, or, quite differently, the progressive theologian Leo Baeck,* even identified God with the unique spirituality that inheres within the Jewish people. Of course, by equating the act of saving the people with the act of sanctification, such thinkers expressed their belief in the spiritual and ethical greatness and unique destiny of the Jewish people because only through the Jewish people — His people — can God be present in history.

In the context of the Holocaust, what is the meaning of faith in Israel as a people? Were there really greater grounds for having faith in Israel than for having faith in a personal God? The answer emphasizes two aspects of the same idea. In the first instance, it is trust in a modern, nationalist understanding of the verse, "The Eternity of Israel will not lie..." (I Samuel, 15:29); that is to say, the

* Creative writers expressed their understanding of the Sanctification of the Name as the Sanctification of Israel both in the ideational content of their writings and in their devotion to their literary work. In their eyes, writing had the significance of a holy mission, a testimony and a testament. The poet Kazenelson dedicated his creative work during the ghetto period to elevating his murdered nation and cursing its murderers. He described the people of Israel as a holy people, in whose life a Divine ideal had been fulfilled, which meant that the ideal inheres in the spiritual activity of the people. (See his "Opening for a Bible Evening," and the poems "Jacob and Esau" and "On the Rivers of Babylon," 3 #w, pp. 145-233.) In his poem on the Rabbi from Radzin he presents his hero as a Sanctifier of the Name of Israel. He does so in protest against the silence of God who had forsaken His people, collecting the murdered Jews and bringing them to a Jewish graveyard. It is, of course, an expression of his own symbolic action, because as a poet, Kazenelson accepted the mission of "collecting" the memories of the murdered, and bringing them to the everlasting remembrance of the nation, through his poems. Contrary to God who did not fulfill His part in the Covenant, the Jewish people had fulfilled their part, so the people in Kazenelson's poem became holier than their failing God. A similar process is to be recognized in Leo Baeck's theology, though he was very far from Kazenelson's theological paradox. In the book that was written in Theresienstadt, Baeck moved from the abstract *Essence of Judaism* to the Sanctification of the eternal "People Israel," the people that represent God in the history of humanity. The book was written both as a testimony and a testament (see 3 #z, Introduction).

Jewish people will exist forever in spite of its enemies' attempts at annihilation. In the past, the Jewish people had overcome its ordeals in exile; the Jewish people will overcome its ordeal again, not merely by survival and existence but also by the fulfillment of an historic destiny. Therefore, those who devote their lives to their people's survival will live forever as their deeds take on significance in the collective memory of the Jewish people. Indeed, the seriousness attached to this belief is evidenced by the intensive efforts of the protagonists to document their deeds and words and those of their fellows, and by their care to preserve the documents so that they would surely reach their appointed readers. Though it sounds exaggerated, the survival of their documented testimonies seemed for some to be more important than their own survival. They profoundly believed that through their remembrance by the Jewish people they would gain eternity, thus attaching to their memorial an authentic religious significance.*

---

* The concise expression of this insight in Kalmanowitz's diary elicits its own empathy: "Your memory, people of the ghetto, will be raised to greatness by history. Every expression of yours will be studied. Your struggle for the sake of man will inspire poets, your physical debasement and your ethical lonliness will be an awakening challenge. Your murderers will be cast for an everlasting shame. The world of men will stare at them in trembling, and will become afraid for itself. Why did He (sic!) do this to this people?, they will ask. And the answer will be, this is what should be done to the wicked who destroyed the Jewry of Eastern Europe" (3 #n, pp. 96-97). This is a first reaction, but later one can sense a new dimension in his thinking:

> To be a Jew means to always be on an elevated stage. The suffering and hardships which the Jews experience have a reason and a meaning. These are not vain harassments, and they cannot diminish the Jew for the Jew is part of a tripartite unity: Israel, the Torah and God, that is, the Jewish people, the Ethical Law and the Creator of the World. This unity exists, and it works in history. It has endured trials and has been factually proved. Of course history is now tempestuous, a war is being waged against the Jews. But this war is not intended against only one part of the tripartite unity; it is intended against all of it: against the Torah and God, against the Ethical Law and against the Creator of the World. Can one doubt which side is the stronger? (*ibid.*, pp. 103-105).

The second aspect of the same nationalist idea was in reference to the Jewish people as the chosen people. Israel embodies the highest ethical-spiritual ideals of humanity. This is the first and the basic cause of their persecution by the Nazis who are the incorporation of the ultimate rank of wickedness and degraded humanity. Therefore, dedication to the rescue of Israel is in fact devotion to the aims of humanity and has universal significance. The fact could not be avoided, however, that the situation created by the Holocaust was the most serious attack ever on the validity of faith in the eternity of Israel. Against a "Final Solution" which was being effectively and inexorably carried out, was it not clear that the Jewish people stood on the threshold of extermination? Could one not visualize the void that the poet Isaac Kazenelson expressed in the shuddering simplicity of his words: "Nought is my people — my people exists no more!"?[13] Could one really sustain a belief in the spiritual destiny of the Jewish people while confronting the evidence of what had become of this people during the Holocaust? In the ideological debate which took place after the Holocaust, the opinion commonly accepted regarding the question, "Why did the multitudes of Jews let themselves be led to their death in complete passivity, like sheep to the slaughter?" was that its critical, almost accusatory nature was a characteristic response of Zionist movements in Israel. Especially this was said to be true of the younger generation that had been born in Palestine and educated in an ideology that called for the "negation of exile." The statement sounds reasonable, but a close examination of the literature written in the ghettos during the Holocaust puts its accuracy in doubt. The question was raised for the first time during the Holocaust by the victims themselves. Those who raised the question — in pain and profound feelings of guilt — were many and diverse: leaders, rabbis, writers, and ordinary people of the ghettos. It may well be the case that young people, educated in Zionist youth movements, were the first to articulate it, but subsequently it was a question shared by people of various ideological positions. It was, in fact, a question which could not but burden the conscience of many who survived and were driven to reflect on their survival.*

* From the abundance of expressions related to this topic in various literary works written during the Holocaust, the following is the summarizing testimony from Ringelblum's paper:

What is more, the actual formulation of the question (with its metaphor from biblical elegiac poetry) did not reveal the circumstances in their full depth; indeed, it served to partially mask them. In the situation created in the ghettos as a result of Nazi tactics of

---

It seems to me that people will not now go like sheep to the slaughter. The community (*Der oilam* in Yiddish — E.S.) wills that the enemy pay dearly for its life....The psychological law according to which a completely oppressed slave cannot revolt has been stated. Yet it appears that the Jews have come back to themselves after the great afflictions: they recuperated from their experiences, did a calculation and saw that going unresistantly to the slaughter did not lessen the catastrophe. On the contrary, it increased it. No matter with whom you speak, you hear the same voice: it is forbidden to capitulate to the "Aussiedlung." The Jews should have gone out to the streets, set the houses on fire, broken through the wall, and crossed to the other side. The Germans would have had their revenge, myriads would have been killed, but not 300,000. Now we are sunk in shame and abuse before ourselves and before all the world; our acquiescence did not profit us. This should never recur. Now we must resist (3 #d, vol. 2, pp. 27-28).

And in another place:

People began to tear the hair of men who let their dear ones, their wives and children, be taken from them without resistance. Loudly they rebuked those sons who let their parents be taken. Loudly they swore, the Germans will never again move us from our place without damage to themselves. We will be killed, but the conqueror will pay with blood for our blood. Our fate is sealed, they said. Every Jew carries with him his death sentence which was given him by the greatest murderers in history. Therefore we should not think of saving our personal lives — a very dubious aim — but about a dignified death, death with a gun in hand. And this oath which they took in memory of the dear Sanctifiers of the Name, they fulfilled. The ghetto began to arm itself and waited for the next blow (*ibid.*, p. 331).

It is important to point again to the fact that Ringelblum ascribed this reaction to the whole Jewish world (*Der oilam* in Yiddish) and not to a particular group, a certain movement or a special age. At the very depth of the reaction was the burden of guilt for those relatives and kin who were allowed to be taken to their death without any resistance.

extermination — that is, driving the victims to collaborate in the orderly process of their murder — it was impossible to avoid feelings of guilt on the part of a leadership that tried to save as much as it could through cooperation with the Nazi regime. Therefore, the leadership was generally opposed to plans which called for violent resistance. It was also impossible to avoid profound feelings of guilt and sorrow by individuals who saw their parents, wives or husbands, children, relatives or friends taken to their deaths with no attempt to protect them, fostering the hope that by refraining from futile, violent resistance at least a remnant would survive.

The dilemma which lurked behind the question of "Why go like sheep to the slaughter?" was the fundamental dilemma raised by forced negotiation and cooperation with Radical Evil, which could only result in degradation and deep demoralization as the victim was forced to reflect on his own behavior with the contaminating Evil itself. It was generally a situation that was brutally enforced and its demoralizing effects were perhaps completely unavoidable, but in the end it was impossible to hide or to avoid soul-searching retrospection. There were explanations, truthful and convincing in themselves: the Jews could not, physically, choose a different way. They were utterly powerless, completely separated, had no help from the outside and no physical base for serious, violent resistance. Moreover, comparing the behavior of the Jews under the Nazi yoke to the behavior of other groups in parallel though much better conditions, it is evident that the Jews resisted relatively more than other national groups, perhaps more than could be expected of them.* Yet even

---

* The discussion of the question, why did Jewish victims not resist the Nazi terror more often and earlier?, is intensively   dealt with in the literature. There were many who asked the question and searched for explanations during the Holocaust, and especially after the "Aussiedlung" in Warsaw. Ringelblum discussed it at length in his greatest paper, "Relations between Jews and Poles During the Second World War" (3 #d, vol. 2, pp. 327-329). Kovner discussed it in his speech before soldiers of the Jewish Brigade at their first meeting ("The Mission of the Last," 3 #h, ch. 1). Dworzezky did the same immediately after his liberation from the Death Camp (3 #k); also Lubetkin (3 #j, p. 190). In addition to expressing his own opinions in his diary, Zeidman tells about intensive discussions on the subject among leaders of the Warsaw Ghetto long before the revolt (3 #m, pp. 154-156, an entry from 12 July 1942, and also an entry on pp. 218-222). There is also Eck's contribution (3 #s, p. 84). This list is only partial.

these explanations, which were already fully expounded in the underground literature of the ghettos, resonated with profound moral regret because they admitted a terrible fact. They recognized that the Nazis not only succeeded in annihilating almost all the Jewish population under their control, leaving only a very small remnant; they succeeded as well in their satanic intention of enforcing total demoralization upon their powerless victims. Thus, the rage and the hate against the Nazis was mixed with a compulsive guilt.

It would seem that the need to discuss the problem again and again proves the claim that during the Holocaust itself the moral burden surrounding the problem of resistance was very heavy indeed. The explanations offered are generally the same in all the sources. There are only variations of stress and order: the fact that only too late the Jews grasped the real intentions of the Nazis; the illusions on one side and the Nazi deceit on the other; the lack of arms, lack of help from the outside and lack of a "hinterland" for effective underground fighting. In inevitable comparison, the sources also refer to the behavior of people from other nations under similar, even less harsh conditions. Yet one senses that in spite of these very serious explanations, the problem could not be settled, and an atmosphere of disturbance and unrest prevailed. The reason becomes quite clear from Drenger's blunt words:

> We kept silent when we were plundered, when we were expelled from our houses, when we were deprived of our freedom, when we were hunted from place to place hungry as dogs and in the cold, when we were forced to work threatened by whip and gun. We were silent when before our eyes our children, our fathers, our mothers, our brothers and sisters, were murdered, and when our innocent blood streamed like water. And today again we keep silent before a shameful death. With our own hands we set up gallows for ourselves, with our own hands we are digging graves for ourselves, we appoint the hangmen and flatter the traitors among us. What happened to us? What has happened to the healthy human instinct for life which commands a man not to capitulate but to wrestle to the last moment for any chance of life? What has happened to our human conscience? Where have we lost the dignity which protests against this shame? (3 #c, pp. 83-84).

These questions left the feelings of guilt deeply engraved within, despite all the very convincing explanations.

A harsh question was raised, an account demanded: "The love of Israel" — that notorious Jewish solidarity, in its most elementary, existential meaning — did it stand the trial? Did the Jewish people prove its spiritual and moral superiority? Did they remain true to their spiritual destiny?

It was precisely on the background of these heartbreaking questions that the newly shaped norm, according to which the "Sanctification of the Name of God" should actually mean dedication to saving Jewish lives, found its full meaning. Those who lived and functioned with hearts full of love for their people yearned to prove, by their deeds, a different truth, an inner absolute truth which went beyond both the apparent and the actual situation around them. This was neither an illusionary gesture of closing one's eyes to reality nor an attempt at self-deception. On the contrary, it was an heroic attempt to confront reality and change it by an exemplary act of self-transcendence to a higher level of existence. It was an attempt to make manifest an inner level of reality, to reach back to origins through historic memory, and to bridge the gap between the past and the messianic vision of the future by the strength of a committed action. The moral will thus discovered within itself a level of spiritual force which was experienced as super-individual, flowing from metaphysical-national resources. The existence of this spiritual force, contrary to external reality, testified that indeed "the Eternity of Israel will not lie." Moreover, as this faith was evidenced by deeds, it permitted the individual a degree of objectivity in his own subjective trust in the future of the Jewish people. He knew perfectly well that his chance for personal survival was close to zero, but the future of the individual seemed of negligible importance — living in the moment meant eternity. The only really important issue was the trust (irrational though it may have been) gained through total commitment to the belief that the Jewish people would survive, that in its inner core it would remain true to its unique spiritual destiny. It was only because of an eternal transcendant source of this kind that the super-personal power to resist could be explained.*

* Two sides of a very bitter controversy invoke empathy. Kalmanowitz wrote (in continuation of what has been cited from his diary in a previous note): "In a war it may happen that a troop is defeated, beaten and falls into captivity. The Jews of the ghetto must feel that they are such prisoners of war. But they must also remember that the whole army has not been

What is described here is obviously a kind of religious experience, but the same paradoxical renewal of faith coming out of traumatic catastrophe also occurred in the experiential realm of those who were educated as secular Zionists, humanists and socialists. In the first stages of the war, the need to preserve the hope of a better future in order to support the will to survive against the threat of complete extermination was expressed in a universal tendency towards ideological dogmaticism in all the Jewish movements, Zionist, Zionist-Socialist, and Communist. In their underground literature, it is possible to discern a persistent effort to describe and analyze the events of the evolving war, including the fate of the Jewish people, according to preconceived prognoses. The inescapable conclusion, of course, was that redemption — national, social, or national with social — would certainly take place according to the traditional historic process immediately after the war ended. Therefore, the political task required doing everything possible to enhance the historical process. For Jews under the Nazi yoke this meant, first of all, an educational program which would enable them to resist demoralization through solidarity and reciprocal help. It called on them to study, to observe and be aware of what was happening, to think profoundly and to be spiritually prepared for the moment when

---

defeated and cannot be defeated. The Passover of Egypt is the symbol of an ancient victory of the holy tripartite unity. Let it be granted to us that we will be found worthy to live and be present at a Passover of the future" (3 #n, p. 105). On the other side, there are the words of Drenger to those Jews who were hiding in order to survive. He calls them "the Marranos of our time." He fully legitimizes their means of resistance, but he calls upon them to recognize that if they succeed and survive, they will have a task to fulfill, for the sake of which alone their whole superhuman effort to survive will be considered worthy.

It will be their duty to reconstruct the Jewish world which they witnessed and experienced in its most difficult hours. If they are saved from this murderous fate which has befallen their nation, it is not in order to deny their responsibility for this people, but to prove, through their creative thinking, that their saved lives had worth and value. Therefore, when the violence and hypocrisy have passed, they must appear as Jews who fought for human rights in spite of danger, and struggled for their existence on the principle that the life of a Jew is equal to the life of every human being, that this right must be fulfilled and guarded (3 #c, p. 117).

Jews would again be able to take part in and be committed to political, national and social creativity.

But reality very soon transgressed the boundaries of these pre-war prognoses. It became increasingly difficult to see how "redemption" could spring forth from the physical and moral destruction of Europe in general, and from the Jewish people in particular. It also became increasingly inconceivable to explain the evolving reality according to the assumptions of pre-war ideologies. However, the most frustrating development seemed to be the moral crisis within the movements which represented these ideologies and which saw themselves responsible for proving their validity. Did the ideologies stand the trial of war? Within the national movements there was no way to avoid asking the painful question, Had they done what they could to sound the alarm, to awaken the conscience of free humanity, to help and to rescue? Had the organized Jewish community in the free world, especially in Palestine and North America, stood its trial? As to the organized humanist powers in the West, the question seemed superfluous. Even those nations that fought against Nazism and Fascism did almost nothing on behalf of the mortally endangered Jews. Why? In the Socialist world, one could point not only to the forsaking of the Jews, but to an active betrayal, even cooperation in the crime itself. How was it possible for the Communist U.S.S.R. to sign a treaty with Hitler at the beginning of the war? How could it be that virulent anti-Semitism motivated not only the masses in the socialist and Communist parties, but also their leadership? Why was material help almost entirely withdrawn even from Jewish partisans in the forests, while Communist powers were on the spot and could have helped? Such questions seem to have shaken the foundations of secular faith in Zionism, Socialism and humanism no less than the falling away of religious faith in God or the Jewish people. Therefore the statement of faith from those who chose to go the way of direct resistance reflected a decision to transcend the whole collapsing reality, not through illusion or self-deception but through the truth of their redeeming action. They strived to testify to a different truth, a different reality which they evidenced in their inner experience and proved by their deeds. The source of their super-rational faith was that Zionism, which symbolizes the Jewish people's hope of redemption, would overcome disappointments and be fulfilled and that the workers' class, which represents humanity's yearning for social justice and human equality, would achieve its aims in spite of errors and guilt, so that man would at last recover his commitment to the vision of humanity in spite of betrayal and failure. One must struggle for the sake of these visions and for the future, but the memory of those who committed themselves to these hopes, with no chance for personal survival, would never be lost because their sacrifice would point the way and prove its own truth.

Here again, then, the act of revolt was considered a testimony. It would not be an exaggeration to describe these testimonials and their concomitant activities during the Holocaust as deeds of sanctification — sanctification of Zionism and the Jewish people, of Socialism and the workers' class, of humanism and humanity. There was a simple common denominator manifest for all those believers who spoke — each in his own separate ideology, philosophy or theology — using elementary, existential "code" words, transcending their different world views. For all of them it was a time for acts of sanctification, testimonial acts of faith based on experiences which may be described as "revelations" in the religious meaning, grounded in a hidden spiritual resource of the will to live on a spiritual-ethical level. This was the source of their super-rational belief that physical death, human frailties and faults, and even radical, demonic Evil would not overcome the true destiny of humanity or the true destiny of the Jewish people. To put it differently: in the three previously described ways of confronting Nazism, the religious, the humanistic and the nationalist, the messianic "myth" which had been completely demolished in the war and the Holocaust, was rehabilitated and renewed through an historic symbolic act of self-transcendence, aimed at the symbolic opening of a path before the Jewish people, or humanity, which would enable it to return to its true destiny.

These were the burning points of religious, ethical and national thinking as expressed in the literature written in the ghettos of Eastern Europe during the Holocaust. They were also the principle existentialist insights achieved by examining problems which consciously remained unresolved, or even unresolvable. Thus, the underground literature of testimony and philosophical thought provided the foundation for a retrospective deliberation of the religious, ethical and existential problems of humanity which were raised by the Holocaust. Such a foundation is, indeed, necessary in facing some of the most urgent problems of our time which have been raised as a result of this extraordinarily unique experience. Retrospective observers enjoy the benefits of historical perspective, existential distance and a calm mind. At the same time they suffer from a lack of direct experience which enables insight, and a lack of moral authority to articulate and understand the implications of some of the most painful and crucial problems present in the confrontation with Radical Evil. Finally, such observers miss the experience of revelation, without which it may be impossible to regain faith either in God, the Jewish people or in humanity. Therefore, in order to formulate our questions and shape our orientation, we must return to these sources of testimony and thought. Only on this basis may we then be able to begin our own intellectual efforts.

Notes

1. There is an abundance of literature written on this topic. I have referred to it extensively in my article "Is the Holocaust an 'Unprecedented Event'"? (Hebrew; *Iyun* 37, Hebrew University, Jerusalem, 1988-1989, pp. 271-281); see also Alan Rosenberg: "The Philosophical Implications of the Holocaust," in *Perspectives of the Holocaust*, Randolph Braham, ed. (Boston, The Hague, London, 1983), pp. 1-19; Emil L. Fackenheim, "Holocaust," in *Contemporary Jewish Religious Thought*, Arthur A. Cohen and Paul Mendes Flohr, eds. (New York, 1987); Yehuda Bauer, "Essay on the Place of the Holocaust in History," in *Holocaust and Genocide Studies*, Vol. 2, No. 2, pp. 209-220.

2. Viktor Frankl states this idea over and over again. It is a central assumption of his theory of Logotherapy. Yet his decisive experiential proof was his own experience as a prisoner in Nazi death camps during the Holocaust. His testimony is included in his well-known book, *Man's Search for Meaning. An Introduction to Logotherapy* (London: Hodder & Stoughton, 1988 [First published in 1946]), pp. 64-93.

3. The literary material which underlies this study is comprised of essays in underground periodicals published during the Holocaust (1939-1944), diaries, testimonies which were composed during the Holocaust for the purpose of documentation (especially in the Ringelblum Archive), literary works written during the Holocaust, and memoirs and reflections which were written immediately after the end of the war (1945-1947). The following is the list of principal sources: a) *The Jewish Underground Periodicals in Warsaw* (Hebrew), 3 vols., Joseph Kermish, ed. (Jerusalem: Yad Vashem, 1980).

b) *The Underground Periodicals of Gordonia in the Warsaw Ghetto* (Hebrew), Arjeh Avnon, ed. (Hulda: Gordonia Hamakabi Hazair Archive, 1966). c) *Hehalutz Halohem* (The Fighting Pioneer) (The Organ of the Underground Jewish Pioneer Youth in Krakow) (Hebrew), August-October 1943 (Tel Aviv: Hakibbutz Hameuhad, 1984). d) Emmanuel Ringelblum, *Writings from the Ghetto* (A new complete edition) (Yiddish), 2 vols. (Tel Aviv: J.L. Perez Publication, 1985). e) *The Destruction and Revolt of Warsaw Jewry* (A second enlarged edition) (Hebrew), M. Neustadt, ed. (Tel Aviv, 1947). f) Rabbi Simon Huberband, *Kiddush Hashem* (Hebrew), N. Blumental and J. Kermish, eds. (Tel Aviv: Zachor, 1969). g) Mordechai Tenenbaum-Tamaroff, *Dapim Min Hadleka* (Pages from the Fire) (A new enlarged edition) (Tel Aviv: Yad Vashem, Lohamei Haggeta'ot and Hakibbutz Hameuhad, 1984). h) Abba Kovner, *Al Hagesher Hazar* (On The Narrow Bridge) (Essays in Speech) (Hebrew), S. Luria, ed. (Tel Aviv, 1981). i) Reizl Kortchak (Rozka), *Lehavoth Baefer* (Fire in the Ashes) (Hebrew), (Merhavia, 1946). j) Zivia Lubetkin, *Bi'ymei Ki- layon Vamered* (In Days of Annihilation and Revolt) (Hebrew), (Lohamei Haggeta'ot and Hakibbutz Hameuhad, 1979). k) Dr. M. Dworzezky, *Bein Habetarim* (Between the Pieces) (Hebrew), (Jerusalem, 1956). l) Ch.A. Kaplan, *M'gilat Yissurin* (A Scroll of Suffering) (A Diary of the Warsaw Ghetto) (Hebrew), (Tel Aviv and Jerusalem: Yad Vashem and Am Oved, 1966). m) H. Zeidman, *Yoman Ghetto Warsha* (A Diary of the Warsaw Ghetto) (Hebrew), (Tel Aviv, 1946). n) Z. Kalmanowitz, *Yoman Ghetto Vilna* (A Diary of the Vilna Ghetto) (Hebrew), S. Luria, ed. (Tel Aviv, 1977). o) *The Lad Moses: The Diary of Moses Felinker* (Jerusalem: Yad Vashem, 1958). p) A. Klonizky (Kalonimos), *Yoman Avi Adam* (The Diary of Adam's Father) (Lohamei Haggeta'ot and Hakibbutz Hameuhad, n.d.). q) E. Hillesum, *Het Verstudoode Leven* (Busum: De Haan/Unieboek BV, 1981). r) J. Kortchak, *Min Haghetto* (1939-1942) (From the Ghetto) (Hebrew), (Lohamei Haggeta'ot and Hakibbutz Hameuhad, 1972). s) N. Eck, *Hatoim Bedarchei Hamavet* (Hebrew), (Jerusalem: Yad Vashem, 1960). t) Rabbi Issachar Shlomo Teichthal, *Em Habanim S'mechah* (Happy Mother of Children) (Hebrew), (First published in Budapest, 1943; New York, 1969). u) Rabbi Klonimos Kelmish Shapiro, *Esh Kodesh* (Holy Fire) (Hebrew), (Jerusalem: Yad Vashem, 1969). v) *Sridey Esh* (Remnants of Fire) (n.d.). w) Yizhak Kazenelson, *Yiddishe Ghetto K'tavim*, Warsaw 1940-1943 (Yiddish), Y. Scheintuch, ed. (Lohamei Haggeta'ot and Hakibbutz Hameuhad, 1984). x) V. Frankl, *Man's Search for Meaning*, see note 2. y) Leo Baeck, *Dieses Volk. Judische Existenz* 1-2 (Frankfurt am Main, 1955-1957). z) E.H. Boehm, *We Survived* (New Haven: Yale University Press, 1949). za) D. Hadler, *The Jew (His Tragedy and His Greatness)* (London, 1947). zb) *Fun Letzten Hurban* (From the Last

Destruction) (A periodical about Jewish life in the time of the Nazi Regime) (Yiddish), J. Kaplan, ed. (Munchen, August 1946-December 1948). zc) Y. Spiegel, *Malkhut Ghetto* (The Kingdom of the Ghetto) (Yiddish), (Lodz, 1947); *Stern Ibern Ghetto* (Stars above the Ghetto) (Yiddish), (Paris, 1948); *Menchen in T'hom* (People in the Abyss), (Buenos Aires, 1949).

4. A faithful and instructive documentation of the first traumatic reaction immediately following the Nazi conquest of Poland can be found in the excellent essay of Rabbi Simon Huberband, "The War Experiences of a Jew" (see note 3 #f). Similar descriptions are to be found in all the memoirs and diaries which documented this period.

5. See I. Trunk, *The Jewish Councils in Eastern Europe Under Nazi Occupation* (New York, 1972), chs. 16-17.

6. Saul Friedlander, *Counterfeit Nazi — The Ambiguity of Good* (London, 1969).

7. Nissanbaum is cited by Eck (3 #s), p. 244.

8. Under the heading of strengthening the power of survival, a wide variety of activities which have been documented in earlier notes should be included: reciprocal help (such as the House Committees in the Warsaw Ghetto); maintaining communication between communities and with the centers in Palestine; contacting gentile individuals and organizations; arranging cultural activities; continuing a religious life style and fulfilling religious commandments in spite of the hardships, etc.

9. The main testimony concerns the participation of religious Jews in the revolt of the Warsaw Ghetto. See H. Zeidman's story in his diary (3 #m). Beside these we have reliable testimonies of individuals who refused to go to death without defending themselves as they could, and were killed in the struggle.

10. The Nazis did destroy and burn synagogues, they did profane, spoil and despise scrolls of the Torah, they did force Jews to do these deeds with their own hands, they did mock and cruelly tear out the beards of religious Jews, etc. But there was no intention to effect conversion by these atrocities. The aim was to denigrate and break down the victims, spiritually as well as physically, before their death.

11. The source of this story which is retold in several books seems to be Rabbi Huberband's article, "From the Religious Life in the Days of the War" (3 #f).

12. See Huberband's paper in note 4. Rabbi Nissanbaum's saying, as cited by Eck, is in the same spirit; and according to his diary, Zeidman, too, was of the same opinion.

13. Isaac Kazenelson, "Halom Halamthi" (I had a dream).

Chapter 4

THE EXISTENTIAL AND MORAL DILEMMA OF ARMED RESISTANCE IN THE GHETTO: SHIMSHON DRENGER'S REALISTIC-IDEALISTIC THOUGHT

In this chapter, as well as the one that follows, a number of the theories and explanations previously dealt with will be examined more closely through a detailed analysis of two original and outstanding doctrines that were created during the Holocaust. The first is the doctrine of a young, secular thinker, Shimshon Drenger,[1] who was referred to earlier as one of the few ideologues to fully come to terms with the reality of that period and dared to confront the conclusions that had to be drawn from it. The second doctrine was formulated by Rabbi Issachar Shlomo Teichthal, an ultra-Orthodox rabbi who underwent a Zionist change of heart during the Holocaust.

Shimshon Drenger's thought, which was expressed in the pages of *The Fighting Pioneer*[2] in the period from August-October 1943, is of particular interest in three respects: 1) his sober and realistic analysis of the situation of the Jews under Nazi occupation and throughout the world; 2) a precise separation and definition of the existential problem, on both personal and national levels, faced by those who tried to survive within the unprecedented conditions of the ghettos and death camps; 3) his conclusions concerning the practical reactions called for, including a thorough response to the complex ethical problems involved. In the following pages, each of these areas will be examined in turn.

What was happening, or, more precisely, what was the Nazis' motivation in their abnormal attitude toward the Jews and what end result were they working toward? How did they operate? How effective were they? And, from the other side, could the Jews defend themselves? What resources of power were at their disposal? What possibilities did they have to maneuver in order to prevent, or at least delay, the annihilation? Could they rely on outside help from the non-Jewish society or from the Allies fighting the Germans? These

205

questions preoccupied the leadership elites of the Jewish people with particular intensity at the outbreak of World War II.

From the literature of ghetto underground movements, it is apparent that these questions were given priority, whether for the dissemination of information which was considered vital to survival, or in the context of analytical and discursive articles written from ideological and political viewpoints. The fervent and widespread practice of keeping personal diaries was also intended to fulfil these functions, along with the primary goal of leaving a testimony.

The writers of diaries wrote first and foremost for themselves. The act of writing every day about what they had seen and heard served them as a process for coming to terms with reality, facilitating the internalization of the fact that such was the direction events were taking, that such things were actually happening. Secondly, their writing was marked by a constant effort to understand the motives behind the unexpected moves, to predict what this held for the future and, to the extent possible, be physically and mentally ready in order not to be caught unprepared. In reading these diaries, which were written during the course of events, one realizes with certainty the level of continuing frustration caused by this process of coming to terms with reality and understanding the "rationale" of the surrealist situation in which the writers found themselves. Each day it seemed that the Nazis had reached the depths of their evil and that their final intentions had become clear; yet again and again their victims were surprised to discover that behind each evil lurked a still greater evil. Their imagination, drawing on the accumulative experience of the past, does not appear to have enabled them to correctly understand their murderers' motives, even though events would seem to have spoken for themselves. It was an indication of how hard it was, even for those not bound by dogma, to internalize the "rationality" of madness.

In this context, Shimshon Drenger's ability to coolly analyze the situation, without illusions, is all the more remarkable. Drenger wrote a succinct message in the main article of *The Fighting Pioneer*, issue 29, of 13 August 1943.[3] The article was entitled "Through the Looking-Glass of the Future," a title chosen, no doubt, to reflect a backdrop of hope without which it would have been impossible to examine such a desperate present with a modicum of impassion. Indeed, the overall impression of the article is that the writer was sober and realistic regarding the future. His description of the future was free of any signs of the ideological historicism which held out the realization of a future vision as the necessary result of "historical development," and he clearly did not attempt to justify the catastrophe in terms of any of the range of historical or messianic explanations that were found in accepted ideologies prevalent in his surroundings. On the contrary, on the basis of his experience, he predicted a difficult struggle which would continue after the war, until the Jewish people was able to obtain suitable means of defense.

"In the light of the tragic reality of the Jews," he wrote, in a guileless style devoid of pathos, "when the existence of the individual is dependent on chance and the existence of the aggregate has long since reached a nadir, it is more important than ever to examine the situation from a broad perspective. The personal viewpoint has no reality — this is quite clear to everyone. From the personal point of view, we are all lost. Our chances of survival are negligible; destroyed and alone we will not be able to place much hope in life.

This, in summary, was Drenger's considered assessment concerning his fate, the fate of his comrades and of all the Jews who would survive the Nazi regime. It is worth stressing that while it was important to Drenger to persuade his readers that this assessment was true, he was much more concerned that it be recognized and internalized. This would appear to have been his intention in claiming that "it is more important than ever to examine the situation in a broad perspective." For Drenger, being aware of the overall nature of the situation was the only way to escape complete despair and reach a degree of self-transcendence, without illusion. At the same time, he was well aware of the all too human tendency to escape from reality by means of denial. He saw that not as a healthy measure of faith but rather as a serious danger, a sign of weakness and degeneration and perhaps even a subconscious form of surrender. His main goal was to reverse such a tendency; but how could this be achieved? It was clear to him that denial — which fed on despair — could only be combatted by revealing a source of hope which would enable people to rise above subservience to the oppressive present, yet without denying reality. It explains why his detailed analysis of the situation was prefaced by the following short remark: "But as we, and all of Polish Jewry, fall as one man, we must realize the historical significance of these times and say courageously that our death does not mean the end of the world, that human history — and along with it, Jewish history — will continue to move along its path, even though the mass grave will already have been sealed."[4]

While there was no hope of life for the individual, there was hope for the people. For those individuals able to identify with the people, therefore, there was hope, and there was also a purpose which would enable them to come to terms with their fate as individuals while utilizing the freedom of choice still available to them concerning their response to this fate. Even if they could not be saved, they could give their response a national significance. In this way, Drenger found hope in what might be termed "spiritual survival," although it must be emphasized that the national hope on which Drenger based his response was not of a messianic nature. He did not speak of future redemption, only that human history along with Jewish history "will continue to move along its path."

It must be noted that for Drenger this restraint was most important, not only in terms of the hope that the vision would be realized, but also in terms of present behavior. Even in his vision of the future, Drenger did not seek an escape from reality, but remained true to his piercing realism: "The situation of world Jewry will be miserable after the historic bloodbath is replaced by peace." That was how he opened the comforting vision in "Through the Looking-Glass of the Future." Admittedly, the Jewish people had undergone many slaughters and murders, "but never have we known such total destruction. Never have we been caught in such a trap, and never has the mob set out to fight the Jews armed with the latest technological innovations, as it does today. Out of the sixteen million Jews in the world, there will probably be barely nine million alive after the war. Above all, the Jews of Europe — who until now were the healthiest section of the people — will be missing."[5]

In order to concretize his vision of post-war reality, Drenger turned his efforts to describing reality on the brink of the war's end. In fact, it was clear that he was preoccupied with the present which he examined "through the looking-glass of the future." He surveyed each of the different Jewish communities in turn. Regarding the Jews of the Soviet Union, whom he estimated to number some two million, he commented firstly that it was impossible to know how many of them had fallen and would yet fall in the war; secondly, from the point of view of the future of the people, they were "a negative number on which the Jews of the world could not rely." This would seem to be because they had undergone a process of deliberate destruction and far-reaching assimilation under the Communist regime. Polish Jewry, in his opinion the main source of creativity and national life for the Jewish people, had been destroyed completely. There followed a systematic and sober description of the process of destruction and annihilation.

Finally, he expressed the view that "within the borders of the 'General Gubernman' there are at most two hundred thousand Jews." Drenger's description of their condition was shockingly sober."Hungry, emaciated, decimated, and despairing, they drag their feet along with their last ounce of strength, vulnerable to disease and starvation, living like ghosts, brutalized by the enemy, and as a consequence their spiritual state is poor. Having been disfigured by the enemy and having absorbed the spirit of slavery, they shake with fear and are unable to think decisively or to see the overall picture. Like hunted animals, they strive only to live one more day, even if it is under the most appalling conditions."[6] Once again, note that the emphasis is on the vital need "to think decisively, to see the overall picture." For Drenger, this was the only way to free oneself of the oppressive and debilitating yoke of the calamity.

The trenchant comments made by Drenger, almost as an aside, will be discussed below, but first it is necessary to complete the description of post-war reality as he saw it. Polish Jewry will have been destroyed, as well as Romanian Jewry, the second largest center. The centers of Western and Central Europe were also being rapidly destroyed: "The Jews of Hungary still cling on, but they, too, are starting to fall. The Germans, disappointed with their Italian partners, will not allow the Hungarians to maintain their freedom for much longer, and will ensnare their country in the trap of terror. This situation raises serious misgivings for the fate of Hungarian Jews."[7]

Apart from limited remnants which would have managed to survive, then, European Jewry would disappear completely from the map of the Jewish people by the time the war came to an end. What would remain were the five million Jews of the United States. But did they represent a source of hope from a national point of view? Drenger's answer to this question was unequivocally pessimistic: "Nothing can change the fact that their almost idyllic attitude toward 'business,' the lack of organic, personal contact with the Jewish people's tragedy and their philanthropic approach to the Jewish question will prevent them from seeing national goals and the need to build Israel."[8]

Having read this gloomy analysis of the post-war reality, the reader may well ask in what sense Drenger offered any hope or consolation. The answer is embedded in Drenger's realistic, indeed pessimistic, assertion that "Zionism has never been so clearly vindicated as in the present situation." The hope of Emancipation led to assimilation, and was followed by great disappointment.

> Once more the truth of our isolation has been reaffirmed. We will bear this isolation until the end of the generations, and this truth leads to the watchword of self-emancipation as the only true rallying cry. We can only rely on ourselves; any other political perspective is a lie. We have paid the heaviest possible price for having allowed ourselves to be anesthetized by the affluence of Europe, for having deluded ourselves with false hopes of redemption from outside, and in this way we failed to see the basic perspective and wasted our strength in foreign enterprises, instead of building our own independence. Who knows what the nature of Jewry would be were it not for the settlement of half a million Jews which consolidated itself in the Land of Israel prior to the outbreak of war, and which has already reached one million souls. This sapling of the Jewish state is the only guarantee for the resurrection of the people, and it enables us to believe that the Jews will once again be independent, and, as is their custom, the carriers of deep spiritual values.[9]

The Jewish community in the Land of Israel is, therefore, the only hope; it guarantees the ability of the Jews to defend themselves in their own land. Once again it must be realized that for Drenger the main implication was not for the future, but his deductions concerning the present. "It is easier to die when one knows that there [in the Land of Israel] the pulse of Jewish life still beats; in this one corner of the earth, we are not aliens or destined to die in isolation or for no reason; it is easier to die knowing that when we are no longer alive, they will be the only ones who will bear our memory with genuine compassion."[10]

It is evident, then, that the purpose of the point of view in "Through the Looking-Glass of the Future" was to facilitate an understanding of the present, and to draw conclusions regarding the present. Moreover, the analysis sought not only to describe the facts which had already been irrefutably established, but also, and more importantly, to provide an understanding of the historical "rationale" of what the current reality was. Only in that way would it be possible to define real choices and work in a concerted and appropriate direction toward an achievable target. Certainly a particular level of courage was required, as the real choice which remained was not between life and death, but between death and death; nevertheless, it still enabled one to find meaning and hope beyond the utter slavery and despair.

What was Drenger's understanding of the rationale behind this desperate reality? The answer can be found in three key assertions of his that warrant extended discussion.

The first concerns the behavior of the Nazis. As if in passing, during the main thrust of his comments about the destruction of Polish Jewry, Drenger says,

> The situation must be soberly assessed. The enemy will carry out its policy of annihilation to the full extent. Since it is incapable of giving the German people victory on the battle fronts, it will have to seek glory in these home-front victories, and in line with its demagogic and bombastic policies it will destroy the Jews to the very last one. This is the enemy's final attempt to save its honor, and it will carry this out even as it is at the point of withdrawal. When the time comes for the enemy to withdraw from the territories it has occupied, it will not balk at striking the last blow against the remnants of the Jews; its shameful path of retreat will be marked in our blood and thus it will also prevent revenge. Nothing, then, will save the Jews of Poland, and all the delusions in this respect are no more than signs of panic at the prospect of death.[11]

These astute comments show that Drenger managed to go beyond the various ideological wrappings in which some of the leaders of the Jewish movements tried to present, in class or national terms, the historical "rationale" of the Nazis' racial hatred of the Jews. Because he was not trapped, as they were, in the intellectual tools of their previous world views, Drenger realized what most of the Jewish intellectual elites could not — that Nazism did not see the destruction of the Jews as a means. For the Nazis, destruction was one of the supreme goals of the war, perhaps even *the* goal which for them symbolically expressed the entire meaning of the war. Therefore, when the Nazis would begin to understand that they had lost the war, they would not halt or even slow the pace of destruction; on the contrary, the destruction would continue as the only one of their supreme goals which could still be achieved. It would also serve as a way to erase the direct evidence of their responsibility for the crime.

What, then, was the basic explanation for this motivation? Drenger apparently saw this as a degenerative pathology of the human spirit. He makes this particularly clear in a short comment incorporated in a description of the process of the destruction of Polish Jewry. "In the labor camps, or in the few ghettos which are the most appalling concentration camps, the Jews endure their fate which lies in the hands of the degenerate murderer who kills people for the sake of amusement."[12] Unquestionably, he does not see any causative "rationale" behind this crime. The rationale is inherent in the crime itself: an expression of senseless hatred, cruelty, abuse and murder. Such goals as these can also move the wheels of history. A people which seeks to survive must keep them in mind and learn how to defend itself against such possibilities. At the same time, Drenger did not ignore the global human dimension of the phenomenon, nor the specific attitude which existed toward the Jewish people.

The second of the key quotations reads,

No one reached out to the starving Jews, no one tried to give them assistance, not even by helping Jews escape from annihilation. They observed our extermination as one would observe the eradication of insects, as if a people replete with cultural values were not dying before their eyes. Even their hatred for the Germans was assuaged when the question of the Jews was raised. They expressed solidarity with the enemy as long as they could celebrate the downfall of the Jews; only a few maintained human dignity, and even they did not dare to express this publicly. The truth of our isolation was once more confirmed — an isolation we will bear until the end of the generations.[13]

Drenger emphasized the lesson to be drawn from the isolation of the Jewish people, namely the Zionist lesson: a people can only rely on itself. It is important to note the universal way in which the lesson is phrased. While the axiom may be expressed explicitly in terms of the particular weakness of an exiled people scattered among the

212

nations, Drenger applies it as a general assessment of human behavior. In his opinion, hatred of the Jews cannot be explained by any individual quality of the Jews, either positive or negative. His assumption was that during World War II, a pathological manifestation of a general human tendency was attested to about which there ought not be any historical or messianic illusions. Neither individuals nor peoples developed solidarity with the weak and persecuted; on the contrary, they were inclined to develop solidarity with the strong. For this reason, a weak people must not rely on solidarity, but must overcome its weakness and defend itself with equal force. This is the ethical responsibility it bears to itself, and perhaps to humanity as a whole.[14]

Drenger's analysis of the self-interested rationale underlying the position of the Allied forces in their war against the Nazis will be discussed further on. It is clear, however, that he saw this as a standard response of both individuals and nations, simple self-interest being the determining factor for most people. Racial hatred, abuse, and murder are indeed pathological manifestations, but they are less alien to "human nature" than one might like to believe. In reality, human nature is closer to these concepts than to the ideal moral sentiment which only a few individuals actually act upon at those times when it is put to the test. These insights were the underpinning of Drenger's consistent conclusions based on his analysis of the situation:

> Therefore, even in the face of inevitable death, our heart is with them [the Jews of Eretz Israel] in their struggle for the future. Every step we take paves the way for the freedom of the people and advances the building of an independent homeland. Our stance is a protest against the evil engulfing the world. In response to the violence which has crushed our people, we are enlisting in the struggle for justice and freedom, for the benefit of the whole world. We want to die in such a way that in the future Jews will not be burdened by a death of slaves, will not be forced to remember with shame the Jews of Europe who went like lambs to the slaughter and were not able to muster sufficient courage to die while defending themselves. Since we are prevented from participating in the constructive work of building, in this way we can at least fulfill our historic role. We must raise the banner of

this dying people, remove from its flesh the stain of slavery and place it among the free-spirited peoples.[15]

The final part of the passage was a call to pure ethical idealism as an act of sanctifying the name of the people. Freedom and meaning are derived from the realm of faithfulness to the absolute ethical values of humanity. Though it may seem so, this was neither a contradiction nor a paradox. Once again, the call to idealistic self-sacrifice in preference to an effort to survive at any price is not based on an idealization of human nature, nor on an idealization of the unique nature of the persecuted people, nor even on an idealization of the future. It is based on an utterly detached realism, an assessment of reality and a definition of the actual choices available. The choice that remained, as noted earlier, was not between life and death but between a death that bore witness to the value of human life or a death in which this value was completely lost. From within his complete realism, paradoxically, Drenger drew the strength of his faith in the value of justice and freedom as the sources which gave meaning to human existence.

Two more issues which Drenger discussed in detail are important here. First, an analysis of the policies and goals of the Allies in World War II; secondly, an analysis of how the Nazi apparatus of evil functioned. On both questions he demonstrated the same radical realism, proving that such a position could serve as a lever for freedom.

On the first topic, Drenger wrote a long article which was printed in three segments in issues 30, 31 and 32 of *The Fighting Pioneer*. In addition, "Zionism in the Light of the Political Situation" in issue no. 33, includes conclusions that Drenger felt the Zionist movement should draw from an analysis of the situation. Mention should be made first of the conclusion he reached in a still earlier article, printed in issue 29, on "The Third Stage of the Second World War."

"Nothing, then, has changed in the historical sphere," he declared, having analyzed the separate military strategies of the Allies and the links between these strategies and the imperialist interests of each of the Allied Powers. "Despite the tens of millions of victims of this bloodiest of wars, the cynical and insensitive 'national interests' of world imperialism deny all the hopes that tortured humanity bore for the coming of peace. The special interests of Great Britain, the United States and the Soviets are the factors which determine the future of the people, not democracy and justice on earth. The latter are no more than formal values rooted in politics, not a living idea which could influence the soul and direct it toward creative work."[16]

Naturally, these blunt comments had painful ramifications concerning the expectations for immediate salvation, by the remnants of Jewry, as the end of the war in Europe approached, and for the Jewish community in Eretz Israel after the war. National interests were clearly Drenger's priority so that he went into some detail regarding the global interests of the Allied Powers and his assessment of a post-war community in Eretz Israel. His realistic, supra-historical assumption was presented in the opening lines of an article.

The present war — as we have already noted here — is not being undertaken for values of freedom or for social values. As is the case with all wars to date, its roots are realistic and derive from the economic assumptions of the imperialist nations participating in the war. We have discussed several times the interests of Germany and her partners, and it is therefore appropriate that we should now discuss the real goals that bind the Allied Powers together in the present world crisis. These goals have undergone many changes (like the war itself), since the more one eats, the greater one's appetite grows. What was seen in a rising curve of Hitler's demands as Germany's army advanced victoriously is now being demonstrated in the growing and changing political aspirations of the powers on the other side of the lines. We are concerned here with the present circumstances of these demands, and we will try to describe the interests of the various nations.[17]

An analysis of the basic position expressed above discloses an apparent similarity to Marxist ideology. It should therefore be emphasized that this similarity applied only to the pragmatic realism involved in linking the war to material interests rather than to ideals. On the other hand, Drenger's assumption allowed for no historicist beliefs and no historicist dialectic. In particular, he did not identify the interests of any party with motives of national or social progress. In the context of the various streams which existed at the time in both Jewish and non-Jewish circles, Drenger's realism is particularly striking with respect to his position toward the Soviet Union. He points to the imperialist motives behind its positions and does not ascribe any ethical significance to them. He rejected Marxist-historicist claims that World War II was the "final conflict" between capitalism and the working class, that it would bring in its wake the victory of Communist social justice. In the same way, he rejected the claim of Nazi ideology that the war was a conflict between "young" and "old" nations, against outdated imperialism. Indeed, as he saw it, each of the competing imperialisms had been updated according to its own power base.

Britain, which, he felt, had suffered from her dominions being excessively far flung, was now aiming for "territorial concentration, and along with this, a centralization of the nation's economy, taking every corner over in order to ensure non-dependence on the interference or the policies of others, even if this meant losing territories in the remote dominions."[18] Britain was being careful to create a united and defensible block of colonies outside Europe and was therefore limiting her expansion within Europe. Her military tactic was dictated by these interests, and thus those politicians who expected an English and American invasion of Europe in order to protect the continent from the Soviets would do so in vain, as this would be contrary to the interests of both countries. Which was to say, neither ideals nor finely-defined pursuits were what determined policies during the war.

In articles that followed, Drenger devoted similar analyses to the interests and particular forms of expansionism of the U.S.A. and the Soviet Union. Once again, he showed the connection between the interests and the military strategy of these powers. Although the details of his theses reflect both deep knowledge and impressive powers of observation, what is relevant for this study is the central question which relates to the conclusions Drenger drew from his analysis concerning the future of the Jewish people and Zionism. The conclusion that was drawn concerning the remnants of the Jewish people under Nazi occupation should be noted first. Drenger's comments in this respect were not overtly phrased but they complement clear comments in earlier articles. The Allies did not undertake the war as a mission to save the victims of Nazism, and therefore it was an illusion to believe that they would place a priority on the liberation of the European countries from the occupation. Simply put, that meant that the chances of survival of those still alive were negligible. But the fact that he himself would not live to see the continuation of the building of Jewish life in Eretz Israel did not in the slightest diminish his vital interest in the chances of realizing Zionism and in the policies which should be adopted for this purpose. It was, after all, the continuation of the life of the people in Eretz Israel which gave meaning and hope to the resistance which must continue against the Nazi occupation.

It does not come as a surprise that Drenger opened with a demand that policy should be dictated by a viewpoint analogous to that of the Allies — i.e., that of Jewish national interest.

> If we really want to draw the proper conclusions and come out of the current period, rich in political and social changes as it is, as a whole, live people, the complex political situation requires us to assess our position realistically. Despite the defeat and annihilation of the Jews in Europe, we must evaluate our situation calmly and unemotionally. Let us not submit to the delusions which can be generated by the abnormal conditions of our present life, and let us maintain our historical perspective, as is necessary for the sake of our responsibility to the entire Jewish people.[19]

In this context, the main question that preoccupied Drenger was to which camp, among the participants in the war, the Jewish people should belong when the war was over. In other words, where did the best chances lie for the realization of Zionism? The demand that the Jewish people should take an unequivocal stance against the Nazis and the Axis Powers seemed axiomatic. Yet Drenger felt the need to consolidate this demand, given the fact that even the world Zionist leadership had hesitated in declaring war on Fascism "because of a mistaken desire to take into account their responsibility for the Jews of Germany and Austria, and out of fear of reprisals against these Jewish communities, which, by the way, were not large."[20]

Against this deception and, perhaps, against the attempts made by Zionist leaders to negotiate with the Nazis in order to reach agreements which would save Jews, Drenger called for a complete and uncompromising opposition which he himself had implemented in the underground and which he demanded should be equally implemented in the position of the Zionist leadership as a whole toward Nazi Germany. In his opinion, no compromise was justifiable in this matter since the struggle against the Nazis "is not only a logical result of the spirit of Zionism as a liberation movement linked to general progress, but above all an expression of the needs of the Jewish people in its attempt to establish a Jewish national home in the Land of Israel. Under the conditions imposed by Nazism, there is no chance of Jewish national construction and the development of a free society; the only prospect offered is physical and spiritual loss and annihilation....There can be no peace, not even a tactical peace, between Zionism and Fascism. This is a war of life and death."[21]

The practical question that arose after he had taken an unequivocal position in favor of the Allies was, to which of the two existing ideological groups within the Allied camp should Zionism adhere: the group of the Western democracies or the group led by the Soviet Union?

"To which of these groups do we have a greater affinity, and what is our position vis-a-vis the opposing interest?" The answer to this question began with what appeared to be a central motif in Drenger's realistic assessment of the situation. "Here, too, our national interest, correctly understood, must serve as the starting point." It is important to emphasize the two words "correctly understood" which were intended to point out from the outset not only the need to define what the national interest was, but also to emphasize the importance of an independent stance by the Zionist leadership, or, in fact, by Jewish leadership as a whole; the importance of an independent initiative that focused entirely on realizing Jewish interests as such.

Jewish interest "does not contradict in the slightest the general interests of progress — this must be clearly stressed — and is no more than a segment of this progress. Zionism is a force which corrects a deficiency in general progress, namely the injustice toward the Jewish people and its place among the nations of the world." However, the very act of stressing the correlation between "the general interests of progress" and the Jewish "national interest" is designed to emphasize the duty of the Jewish people to concentrate on its own affairs and to defend these alone.

No feelings of empathy or understanding will grant us the status we deserve in the post-war world. No realization of social ideas, no solution of general problems — social or political — will get us out of the impasse we have been forced into by hypocrisy and hatred, or by false interpretations of our rights. We cannot

218

simply wait passively for change to occur in the world, and woe betide us if we wait for the Communist vision of world revolution to grant us the Land of Israel in return for the services we pay this revolution now. If we do not muster sufficient courage to create the proper conditions for our national existence — even if this apparently requires us to participate in the general efforts for progress — nobody will grant us these conditions; moreover, no one will even recognize us as an independent people from a cultural or social point of view. Our struggle, therefore, is an intrinsic part of general progress at our own national level. And in the interests of this progress, we will seek allies wherever it is possible for us to fully realize our goals.[22]

The ethical duty of the Jewish people to rely on its own efforts in order to realize its just national interests led Drenger to the simple conclusion that Zionism should ally itself with the democratic countries. It bears emphasis again that this conclusion was the result of concentrating on the national interest of the Jewish people, not on considerations of "general progress." Drenger therefore avoided — consciously, it would seem — any judgmental attitude toward the Communist idea. Certain emphases in his writing suggest that he was not one of "the many in our camp who appreciate and admire the social achievements of the Soviet Union." Unwilling, however, to enter into a pointless argument at a time which required unity in the anti-Nazi camp, he concluded that "everyone generally sees in Communism an expression of general progress." Perhaps so. But what really counted for Drenger was the "attitude of the Soviet regime to the Russian Zionists who were accused of being enemies of the revolution and exiled to Sakhalin, or who died in great numbers in Soviet jails; and the persecution of the Zionist movement in western Galicia and in Lithuania." It is hard to imagine that these comments betray any particular enthusiasm as to the contribution of Stalinism to "general progress," but Drenger confined himself to the direct Zionist conclusion: there was no chance of convincing the Soviet authorities of the right of the Jewish people to its own land and of the justice of the Zionist cause. "Only the facts will manage to overcome misunderstanding and misconceptions concerning us...and if it is really the case that Communism and progress are synonymous, we will undoubtedly meet up with it at the end of our construction and proceed hand in hand."[23]

Just as he did not feel it necessary to negate Communist ideology in order to justify Zionism's independent path, neither did Drenger feel he was required to idealize the ideology of the democratic nations in order to justify his decision to join their camp.

In the meantime, we must look for our realization within that camp that does not chain us with monolithic positions, and whose interests happened to coincide directly with our own: namely, the democratic camp. We are well aware that present-day democracy is far removed from ideological truth, and that political hypocrisy stokes the fires of the imperialist engine. But we must not forgo the possibility that this allows us to build the Land. In the struggle to win our claim to Eretz Israel, our weapon is construction, and this is not possible without Jewish capital. Only within the world of liberal democracy can we make free use of our national capital, which, despite what we might wish, rests in the hands of the propertied Jewish class; only through the struggle of democratic imperialism for world control can we exploit the chance to build Eretz Israel and achieve the vital political consolidation of our project. In the light of these possibilities of realization which must be the central issue for any fighter, all the commonplace differences pale into insignificance. Moreover, these differences are of significance only to us — they do not affect the Allies in the slightest. Let us attempt to lay the foundations of our free existence, and we will undoubtedly find a common language with the genuine issues of human development.[24]

Drenger's supra-ideological philosophy of radical realism was expressed most consistently in its considered and deliberate decision not to attempt to present itself as a competing ideology or world view. This is once again that realistic idealism, or, if one prefers, idealistic realism, which consistently adheres to its specific values and purpose. It is true that Drenger's realistic idealism was rooted in the unique world view of the Akiva movement,[25] but it was brought to its logical conclusion and consolidated through Drenger's own experience as a young leader grappling with the reality of the Holocaust.

As to the second question — the analysis of how the Nazi apparatus of evil functioned — the conceptual significance of this subject lies not in factual findings but rather in the meaning attributed to the spiritual or emotional readjustment to these observations. The relevant comments are made in a series of articles that were printed in *The Fighting Pioneer*, issues 32-36, under the title, "I Was in Montelopi (Observations)." The content is a cool, dry, detailed, pedantic and systematic — almost scientific — review of the structure of the prison, its organization, regulations, characteristics of the prison staff, and the processes of life and death dictated for its victims. Naturally, the observations are based on Drenger's personal experience, yet the style is deliberately impersonal and technical. He does not even hint at his personal experiences nor does he express emotions or assessments, although it is hardly difficult to imagine the deprivations that prisoners in such conditions must have experienced.[26] The description does no more than reflect reality, as if through the lens of a camera. Why did Drenger adopt this position? He does not focus on this question, but the short opening passage leaves no doubt that the style was consciously chosen to represent a particular emotional and philosophical position.

> I cannot claim that the specific numbers quoted here are completely accurate, but they are more so than any kind of generalizations since they were collected through first-hand observation, quite broad for a political prisoner. For the individual who is free, they will serve to create a window in the wall of mystery which surrounds the most dreadful of all the political jails, and a window as well into that system which uses this mystery as a psychological weapon in its war against any undesirable awakening of the enslaved population. This is the standpoint from which this series of articles, set according to a particular sequence, should be approached.[27]

There can be no doubt, therefore, that the publication of these observations, both in content and form, was intended to foster defense through resistance. For potential prisoners, the articles served as preparation for facing the system that would be imposed against them if they were caught, particularly in terms of psychological guidance. Drenger attempted to demystify the demonic evil by presenting a rational assessment diametrically opposed to that which was instinctive to a prisoner. He was able to do this because of his realization that the Nazi system exploited the prisoner's instinctive reactions, turning them against himself in order to oppress him and break his spirit.

The Nazi system was based on keeping the prisoner in a permanent state of anxiety, terrified of something unknown and unexpected that would be still more terrible, so that he was anxious, depressed and humiliated, or, alternatively, in a passive and hallucinatory state of denial. Whatever the case, he would be emotionally and functionally unable to cope with the situation — still less to resist it, even passively. In other words, the prisoner became a creature controlled by his persecutors, devoid of initiative, devoid even of the ability to use his internal mental facilities. In order to escape this evil trap, it was obviously imperative not to become detached from reality through repression, evasion or delusion, but it was also vital not to become mentally enslaved to evil. The instinctive tendency of the prisoner was to do both these things simultaneously. What was necessary, therefore, was to restrain the instinctive reaction, replacing it with an emotional stance which indeed appeared from the outside to be not only a serious alienation from external reality but also from the ego and its spontaneous emotions. The ego thus became, as it were, a looking-glass reflecting expressly and with detachment the objective reality. It was precisely in this way that the necessary distance was achieved to free the prisoner and enable him to use his mental powers by himself, not in accordance with the dictates of others. From his detached and objective observation point, he could then choose his own methods of defense, albeit at the cost of his internal attitude toward what had been imposed on him from the outside.

Drenger certainly believed that objective and up-to-date information might also give the prisoner the chance to exploit an opportune moment for escape, or to reach an effective position of self-defense, even to attack and take revenge on the system of evil, as happened to Drenger himself. The most significant factor from his viewpoint, however, was to enable the emergence of a psychological position which protected individual autonomy, moral freedom, and human dignity in situations of the most serious oppression and degradation. In this respect, the objective and distanced observation point was in itself not only a form of defense but also a way to neutralize the efficiency of the system, and thus it constituted a real victory over Nazi evil.

These comments lead directly to the second issue: the abnormal existential decision which Drenger saw as a prerequisite for any attempt to resist the attack of absolute evil. According to his realistic assessment of the situation, the small number of Jews still left under Nazi rule had no serious prospect of survival. Certain individuals might survive, but this would be no more than accidental; there was no effective action which could increase even slightly the chances of survival. In such a situation, the real choice was not between life and death, but between death and death. This had to be acknowledged, although doing so raised the problem discussed in the analysis of the prisoner's position in Montelopi prison: in order to gain the freedom which enabled genuine resistance to the attack of evil, the individual must apparently resist the natural life instinct, even reverse it.

Drenger was not the only person who grasped and internalized this fact. In one way or another, the same point was expressed by most of those who chose the path of armed resistance to the Nazis, despite the certain knowledge that this form of resistance offered no chance of victory in the normal sense of the word. This awareness was clearly expressed, for example, in a pragmatic comment by Abba Kovner, "A great light will shine in us when into this bloody gloom comes the realization that we are the masters of death. Then our life will have meaning."[28] The paradox of going open-eyed toward death in order that "our life will have meaning" embodied the existential dilemma underlying this decision. As noted, all the fighters clearly faced this realization, but Drenger dealt with it consistently and with surprising depth, not only on the emotional plane but also on the intellectual plane and, it should be emphasized, not after the event nor from the perspective of distance, but in the very midst of the struggle. No greater example than this could be found of spiritual mastery over death.

Within the struggle, the problem of the attitude toward the value and sanctity of life was, unquestionably, the most pressing existential and ethical problem that arose and required ideological discussion. The supreme importance and vital dimension of the ideological discussion of this problem was shown by the significance attached to it from the point of view of the non-religious Jew. Of course, even religious Jews, such as Rabbi Yitzhak Nissenbaum, reached the conclusion during the Holocaust that when the oppressor seeks the very life of the Jews, and not their faith, the greatest commandment is not that of *Kiddush Ha-Shem* — "Sanctifying the Name," but rather of "Sanctifying Life."[29] This was even truer of a believing but non-religious Jew such as Drenger for whom the highest value — in the name of which he fought the murderous evil attacking him — was that of the sanctity of human life. And since the Jew was the chosen victim of absolute evil, the absolute value for him was the value of a Jewish life.

In this context, what is to be made of the position which Kovner called "mastery" over death — i.e., the position that simply put means that one should behave with complete disregard for the fear of death, indeed, in the clear knowledge that the result of one's actions will almost certainly be death? Does such a position not contradict the value of the sanctity of life? Could one not, in fact, see this position as a form of suicide? Abba Kovner addressed this question, attempting to prove that the opposite was true: "mastery" over death was for the sake of life, and therefore it was the only way in which it was possible to sanctify life in the context of the reality imposed by the Nazis.

Drenger took the same avenue of thought still further. In an "Open Letter" published in *The Fighting Pioneer*, issue 31, Drenger responded to a number of criticisms leveled at the path of struggle chosen by his movement. The last of the criticisms discussed was, "Why is your viewpoint colored by fatalism? Why do you incessantly speak of death as though there were no other way out than through death?" His answer to this criticism was characteristically terse.

We certainly do not worship the fatalism of death. If this is the assumption reached from our comments, it suggests that we have not been clear enough in our insistence that the result of the armed struggle may not only be a life of freedom but also a death of freedom. Through its tactics and propaganda, the enemy has forced our people to deal with the problems of survival. To survive come what may is an aphorism of popular lore. The price of survival depends on the flexibility of the individual conscience, or the possibilities offered by money. By contrast, our position is that if we are to survive, it is *only as free people*, and if this is impossible, than we shall die as free people. We want to live, and we *know what we want to live for*,[30] but precisely because of this we must fight, and this fight does not bring with it only life. Those who flock to our ranks for the sake of life alone should know this: death can be received with honor and serenity, if it is a purposeful death.[31]

This was an initial response. It was not exhaustive, but it laid the intellectual foundations on which Drenger built elsewhere. Above all, the goal of the struggle was without doubt life, not death. It emerged, however, that in order to live in the context of the reality imposed by the Nazis, unconditional willingness to die was required, in order that life — for as long as it continued — might be a life worth living, a life of value. For Drenger, the desire to live under any conditions, in any way, out of a fear of death which dictated all facets of the individual's behavior, implied a desecration of life, not its sanctification. Such a position was clearly based on a distinction between survival — the maintenance of life in the biological sense of the word — and the sanctification of life as a human value. For Drenger, too, the supreme value was synonymous not with life in the former sense but rather in the latter sense alone. Thus, for the sake of the sanctification of life, it was certainly legitimate to jeopardize life in its survival sense, even in the knowledge that this endangering of life was absolute, since the value of life would be kept even through death if it were a death consciously chosen to sanctify life. In the face of a death which came in the protection of the value of human life, every moment would embody this value.

These ideas served as a motif woven into articles in *The Fighting Pioneer*. The first example is from an article entitled, "First Exploit and Then Destroy" that appeared in issue 30.

They say to us quite clearly, "First we will exploit you to the full. We will torture you and enjoy your suffering. Afterwards, we will cruelly eliminate those who have no strength left, having been stripped of all health and humanity." We were silent when we were thrown out of our homes, when we were deprived of our freedom, when we were chased, starving and freezing, like dogs from place to place, when they set to work on us with whip and gun; we were silent when our children, our fathers and mothers, brothers and sisters were slaughtered in front of our eyes....We have been preparing our own gallows, digging our own graves, choosing the hangmen, ingratiating ourselves to the traitors among us. What has happened to us? Where is the natural human instinct for survival which urges us not to surrender but to struggle to the last for the slightest chance of survival? Where is the human conscience, where is our honor which cries out against this shame?...What still bonds us to these blood-chilling graveyards; why are we still deluding ourselves; why are we still waiting for yet more sophisticated forms of murder? Are we really so eager to have a few more days of cancerous rot? Underneath the debris of the shattered hopes of happiness, underneath the destroyed lives, there still flickers the weakest ember of genuine humanity. We must fan this ember and transform it into a flame which can redeem us from humiliation, save us from death, purify the conscience and encourage our spirit. Let us not forget this flame. Let us nourish it before it is extinguished.[32]

Note that Drenger called on the Jewish public which had survived to participate in an armed uprising that would lead to almost certain death on the basis of "the natural human instinct for survival which urges us not to surrender but to struggle to the end for the slightest chance of survival." Here, it would seem, was the strongest expression of the existential paradox: what was this "slightest chance of survival" to which he referred, given that he had just stated with certainty that there was no chance of survival, certainly not in the decision to fight? The answer, quite simply, was that the chance to live was the chance to allow the tiny ember of real humanity — that is, human conscience and dignity which protested the humiliation — to be fully expressed in an uprising on the threshold of death. Fanning this ember and transforming it into a flame offered redemption from humiliation, encouraged the spirit, purified the conscience and even preserved from death. It would seem impossible to understand this position unless one interpreted the concept of preservation from death as relating to spiritual death — the elimination of the human and Jewish spirit.

It is interesting, however, that Drenger could have employed the same logic in addressing those whom he termed "present-day Marranos" — those who invested superhuman efforts in survival by hiding and disguising themselves, even if it meant living under the worst possible conditions of persecution, conditions in which existence, as Drenger understood it, went beyond the impulse of the human instinct for survival. He did not choose the "Marrano" route, but since their survival was not at the expense of any form of collaboration with the Nazis, but through a superhuman effort to break their laws, he was willing to see this, too, as a form of sanctification of life. On condition, however:

Whoever has seen at first hand the fate of the present-day Marrano; whoever has seen him isolated from the world in the mountains and forests, his fate dependent on his resourcefulness and stealth alone, in the sun, rain, storm and cold, at the mercy of a farmer who brings him an occasional loaf of bread; whoever has seen him legally registered under an alien name, without his finding in this any room to breathe while he constantly quakes in fear of being recognized; whoever has seen him in an environment drenched with anti-Semitism, forging a path for himself not through the laws of justice but through lies; whoever has finally seen him a nervous wreck, falling into the hands of the police and still trying to protect himself — must despite himself have respect and admiration for anyone who is capable of struggling for his life in such a way. Indeed, these anonymous people are intensely heroic, fighting as they do a silent battle and leaving the world in silence, defeated by human hatred.

It is hard, however, to ignore a problem which arises along with these feelings of admiration. If what is represented here is a struggle for life, for biological existence, then it is hard to idolize an instinct common to every living being, regardless of its role within nature or the role it can forge for itself. It would seem to go without saying that the more numerous the hostile agents, the more powerful the instinct for survival which primes the organism to stand up to ever harder conditions (and we might add that in the paradoxical situations we now face all the time, things have reached the absurd point where we feel particular admiration for a Jew whose instinct for survival is to function properly). Nevertheless, we must free ourselves from unnatural criteria and assess the phenomenon according to normal and standard scales.

On the other hand, there is a definite limit to the ability to resist, and more than once we see that under the present conditions Jews have already broken this limit with superhuman efforts. One might ask: why is this struggle, beyond the human power of resistance, being carried on? If it is for the sake of life itself, it would be easier to die than to live in a state of panic without a moment's peace, dying from hour to hour. Someone who finds it worthwhile to live in such a way, just as long as he does not die, is surely acting according to a subconscious instinct, one of the laws of nature, and thus cannot be criticized. The same does not apply to someone who struggles for life in accordance with a guiding objective. Here it is easier to understand from where he draws inner strength, and this is the central point at stake.[33]

This long passage is important primarily because of the clear distinction made between an unconditional preservation of biological life and a human life which is worth living. Moreover, Drenger goes further by examining the benefit of life from the point of view of the biological instinct for survival. This instinct drives the human being to find a way to survive in any situation, and it becomes more pronounced as the conditions of existence become more difficult. But was it really unconditional? Was it really the case that existence in any situation reflected the healthy instinct of life? Might there not be situations in which a human being would instinctively prefer a one-time death to a continuous death? It would appear that Drenger's personal (instinctive?) answer to this was that there must be a limit. He believed that the instinct for survival did not drive the human being to continue life beyond what was worthwhile from the point of view of conditions, and the inherent content made possible by these conditions. This, it would seem, was one of the main reasons why he preferred the path of armed resistance to the path of the "Marranos," although he could respect their readiness to struggle for life even beyond the border of what was worthwhile, attributing this to "subconscious instinct." Whatever the case, this concluded his explanation of the existential decision that the sanctification of life in its human sense required a readiness to die with honor. For Drenger, this commandment derived not only from the meaning of human existence, but also from the natural-biological instinct for survival.

Following this distinction, what did Drenger himself have to offer in order to justify within his system the heroic struggle for survival of the "modern-day Marranos"? He stated that "this is the central point at stake." What exactly was "the point at stake"? A clue can be found in what has already been quoted above. "The same does not apply to someone who struggles for life in accordance with a guiding objective." From the point of view of the sanctification of individual life, and from the point of view of the individual, Drenger seemed to believe that any moment of life is worth living only for the sake of positive human values which are expressed in it. Therefore it was worth living only in moral freedom, only in conscience, only in self-respect. For this purpose it was even worth exposing oneself to certain death.

It emerges, however, that as a believing human being and a Jew, Drenger did not find this sufficient. Closer study shows that even in the definition of what was included in the concept of "human life" there was a proviso which expressed itself in terms of loyalty to humanity and to the people, since the ability to cope with ethical responsibility toward family, friends, community and compatriots was an indivisible part of human honor without which there was no point to life. In any case, the meaning Drenger attributed to human life which defied death was not confined to those moments of struggle when the feeling of moral freedom and human honor were fully expressed, but also related to the meaning that those acts had from the human and national viewpoint, after the death of the fighter, for those who continued his path through human and Jewish values of life and honor. The values of affiliation to and identification with the human and national collectivity were essential elements conditioning the significance of the existential decision to fight in the face of personal death.

Note the profound way in which Drenger posed his position.

I must survive not only because *I wish* to survive, but because as a Jew *it is my right* to live, even though this right is withheld from me. This must be the guiding thought of every person who escapes the ghetto and embarks on the difficult struggle for physical existence. We must survive, since any compromise on our part is a form of desertion, opening the door to the violence which fills the world. Through our very existence, we are fulfilling the function of a living dam holding back the flood of evil, at least in that small sector that is the life of one person. Clearly, this struggle is no substitute for active combat which must come first in our war for existence; it is, however, a parallel form of passive resistance, a way of breaking through the net of hell which the enemy has cast around us, an action against a racist categorization of a population so that enemy forces are diverted into looking for disguised Jews, and it gives a sound feeling to the person who refuses to be crushed.

Thus far, the emphasis has been on the effort to attribute to this form of personal survival the quality of passive resistance, to the point of including it in the general war effort against the Nazis. But the main point is still to come.

All their struggles to survive take on a broader significance when they are able to help in the task. Then their existence is not just a reflexive clinging to life, but a conscious existence for the human good. We often see in these Jews a support, a symbol of Judaism which, although it is being tragically lost, still clings on here and there and does not deviate from its path.

Many hidden Jews have an appreciable chance of survival. However, even this thought of survival must have a deeper import. Under no circumstances must they forget what they have seen and what they have undergone. If they stay alive, it must not be as though they have been saved by a miracle, but as a living chronicle of these historic events. They must not forget how they are to greet the coming dawn.

They will bear the responsibility for the reconstruction of the Jewish world, whose hardest hours they experienced and witnessed with their own eyes. They were not saved from the deadly fate of their compatriots in order that they might afterwards reject their people, but in order that they might bear witness to the value of the lives saved through their creative thought.[34]

These comments are parallel to those that were quoted earlier at the conclusion of his article "Through the Looking-Glass of the Future." "Even as we face inevitable death, our hearts are with them in their struggle for the future. Each act of ours paves a road for the people's way to freedom and advances the building of the independent homeland. Our actions are a protest against the evil flooding the world. In revenge for the violence which has crushed our people, we are enlisting in the struggle for justice and freedom for the sake of the entire world."

To sum up: when undertaken in a spirit of identification with all humanity and the entire people, and for their sakes, this resistance to the aggressive evil which imposed itself on its victims was an expression of life, and although it would lead to a certain death for individuals, even for these individuals it carried the connotation not of death but of life. The tragic death of the individual fighter was, from the viewpoint of humanity and of the people, a painful incident, but it did not reflect the general fate. Life went on and would continue to go on, embracing the contributions of all the individuals who acted and died for it. Therefore, even from the point of view of the individual who died in the course of resistance, life on the brink of death was charged with a historic dimension of meaning which surpassed the frontiers of death. Such life gained the quality of eternity.

However, the interpretation which attributed the sanctification of life to the existential decision to oppose total evil through exposure to certain death raised the dreadful ethical dilemma involved in its practical implementation. A person who acted out of conscious identification with humanity and with the people, and out of a desire to contribute to their future, could certainly not ignore the immediate ramifications his actions might have on the fate of his friends and neighbors and on the fate of his community. He knew with absolute certainty that his actions did not endanger his own life alone. The Nazis would take revenge. They would do so immediately, and their cruel revenge would fall on all Jews in the surroundings. Many might pay with their lives for his actions. Was he therefore entitled to do this? Was he allowed to respond to the "healthy instinct for survival" of the preservation of human dignity which pulsed within him? Was he allowed to buy his freedom and dignity at the price of the torture and cruel death of his compatriots?

These questions raised one of the most serious aspects of the examination of total evil, an evil which obligated its victims to collaborate against themselves, and even imposed on them, against their will, its own fiendish values. The dilemma thus created was absolute, at least at first sight, since whether or not the individual decided to rebel, the result would ostensibly be the same: one would be collaborating with the Nazis who used any pretext in order to destroy the Jews and erase their human image!

Drenger could not ignore the harshness of this dilemma which became apparent as soon as the decision to found the underground was taken. The first stages of organization and preparation already involved exposing those in the surroundings to a serious danger. This was underscored by the vigorous opposition to the underground organizations on the part of the leadership and any others in the Jewish community.[35] The initial solution was to organize and fight under a Polish disguise, outwardly masking their Jewish identity. Indeed, such a step was required not only out of consideration for the Jewish community, but also because of the need to function without encountering immediate and generalized hostility from the non-Jewish environment. However, from the viewpoint of the fighters whose principal motivation was the desire to defend their honor *as Jews*, this already involved a serious dilemma. They accepted the necessary disguise, but they did so reluctantly.[36]

From a practical point of view, it was equally clear that the disguise could only be a temporary solution and it was obvious that even when it was successful, it was only a partial solution. The terrible danger to which first the embryonic and later the active underground exposed those in the surroundings was serious and immediate.

With characteristic profundity, Drenger approached the task of resolving this crisis of conscience. As usual, he discussed the problem both from the point of view of the individual acting in accordance with his own conscience and from the general point of view of the whole. His conclusion was unequivocal: Jews must not fall into the ethical and existential trap which the enemy set for them by accepting the Nazis' distorted interpretation of the lofty ethical concept of the responsibility of the individual for the whole. If the Jews adhered exclusively to the original and authentic meaning of this concept, they would understand that it was actually their duty to defy the will of the Nazis and not take their evil distortions into consideration. To do that would be to collaborate in their own destruction, and moreover to accept Nazi "morality." The rebellion against Nazi law had a high price, as did any war for a just cause, but when one compared the price of avoiding rebellion with the price of rebelling, and when one considered the Jews' chances of survival in any case under the Nazi regime, the decision was clear: from the point of view of the individual and of the collectivity, resistance was an absolute imperative. The immediate ramifications of resistance had to be taken into account in deciding when and how to act. Under no circumstances, however, could it be imagined that these considerations represented a moral principle equal to the imperative of resistance.

Discussion of this issue continued, from various aspects, in the regular column of *The Fighting Pioneer,* entitled "In a Vicious Cycle." The most important article published in this column was "Is this Collective Responsibility?" which appeared in issue 30. Drenger opened by clearly pointing to the paralyzing effect that the distorted concept of "collective responsibility," which had been imposed by the Nazis, had on the occupied peoples in general, and on the Jews in particular. It is worth noting that he chose to present his discussion of this distortion and its dangers from the viewpoint of a person who had been motivated to take part in the resistance. The reason for this is clear. In the conditions created in the ghettoes and camps, the decision to rebel was essentially a personal one, the result of an awakening of the instinct for life, or the result of the distress of personal conscience. Such a decision came under immediate pressure from the notion of collective responsibility which was naturally applied not only by the Nazis, but also by the Jewish public and by immediate neighbors who bore the brunt of the sudden danger. Whatever the case, the initial burden of the decision fell on the individual conscience. The individual had to decide on his own while in a position of considerable isolation.

At the same time, from his opening sentences in which Drenger made efforts to find a moral justification for action based in the will and conscience of the individual, it was abundantly clear that he placed a clear emphasis on the duty of the individual to consider first and foremost those factors relating to his responsibility to the collectivity.

"What is genuine collective responsibility? Any ill-timed action — if it is not demanded by an ideological imperative — leads to numbers of casualties out of proportion to the importance of that action; in such a case, it is permissible to delay the action on the grounds of collective responsibility. But when the collectivity is in the shadow of a destruction which cannot be removed by any power, what relevance is there to fine points?"

Thus it can be seen that, from the point of view of the individual, the responsibility to the whole was of overriding importance. Then, however, the difficult question was raised of the right or ethical obligation of the individual to act in accordance with his instinct for survival or his human conscience.

Let us not allow our natural and healthy psychological response to be distorted. In the unending conditions and pointless death of "Katurga," collective responsibility means to escape from that place, even if this escape hastens the death of others. Not only is it permissible to shake off the yoke of slavery, it is essential to do so unless we wish to descend to a depth where the human image is eliminated and an unnatural state begins which cannot even be called animal-like, but is of an almost vegetative nature.

If we agreed even for a moment to such a thesis, we would have to forbid escape from the prison or concentration camp. There would be no way out of captivity since we would be bound by this distorted concept of collective responsibility in whatever circumstances we found ourselves. If we accepted this, we would have to allow ourselves to be led to the gallows and to the murderers' firing squads, for there would be no limit to the weakness of man's will.

No one doubts the right of every person to live a life of freedom. The natural response is that anything which leads to the fettering of this freedom should be smashed, even at the highest price which must be justified. In determining the justification of the price paid, the decisive factor is personal human responsibility, and the danger the individual takes on himself. The human being does not win freedom through the price of his fellow, but through the price of his daring decision and his boundless drive for freedom.

The death of others caused in this case is a more honorable death, since it has some purpose. In a place where hundreds die for no reason save for the enjoyment of unleashed human beasts, death for the sake of the freedom of even one brave individual who can help restructure the new world, is a positive achievement. In the light of this recognition, each person must overcome the fear implanted by terror and struggle to shake off the shackles of slavery.

The person who fails to understand this and tries to stop his comrade's escape becomes, through this act, an unconscious partner in crime. Someone who intentionally calls for adherence to the principle of collective responsibility is himself a criminal a hundred times more contemptible than the murderer since, for his own comfort and out of his selfish desire to live, he will even stride over corpses and push his comrades toward an inhuman death.[37]

The extreme severity of the claim made at the end of this article served only to emphasize a major point. Drenger indeed supported the right and obligation of the individual to oppose the terror overtaking him and to escape to freedom, but the norm he advocated was not the individualistic norm of the person fighting for his life, nor even for his personal dignity. On the contrary, it was the norm which had to be accepted by the collectivity as it fought for its life, with regard to both the intrinsic benefit of each individual and the intrinsic benefit of the whole. Through the way in which he defined his own benefit, the individual also had to define his comrade's benefit and the benefit of the collectivity. Moreover, he had to represent these, too, in his struggle. It was based on these notions that Drenger felt the need to present clear criteria according to which the individual had to weigh his actions. The healthy instinct for survival which required loyalty to human life, freedom, and self-respect was seen by him as a "categorical imperative," but since this related to loyalty to human life, responsibility for others and for the collectivity, it was an inseparable part of the considerations that granted this commandment its binding force.

It was absolutely imperative that the escape to freedom not be achieved at the expense of someone else who would be sacrificed instead. In such conditions, was it permissible to endanger others in the clear knowledge that the Nazis would take their revenge on them for the person who had fled to freedom? Drenger preferred to answer this point by rephrasing the question: was it permissible for the people who would indeed be endangered by the person who escaped to freedom to oppose and prevent such an escape? His unequivocal answer to this question was that not only were they not allowed to prevent the escape, but it was their duty to accept it and to assist. This position was derived both from the absolute right of the individual to freedom and from the good of the whole. It was from this standpoint that he reached the harsh conclusion that those who behaved otherwise, supposedly out of an insistence on their own right to live or on the responsibility for the good of the whole, were doing no less than implementing the evil morality of the Nazis and they should be condemned as criminals.

The second criterion concerned a practical consideration of the result of any act of resistance within the circumstances to which it pertained. Drenger had no doubt that the overall "strategic" position should be to resist the Nazis. But the question of when and how to act had to be examined according to the circumstances. In this context, it was important to realize that refraining from taking action in order to channel resistance toward a particular point was an integral part of the overall strategy of resistance. In any case, it is clear that the same demand Drenger made of the "present-day Marranos" was made of those who embarked on armed resistance against the Nazis: only if their battle was for the honor and future of the people, and not for themselves alone, or for their individual clean consciences, would the battle be meaningful and justified.

In order to assess the importance of Drenger's ideological contribution to this question, it is worthwhile comparing his opinions with those of two important philosophers who attempted to address this dilemma after the Holocaust, Emil Fackenheim and Victor Frankl. Emil Fackenheim accepted the definition of the Holocaust as Radical or "absolute" Evil, basing this definition on the claim that the Nazis imposed their own evil on their victims. The Nazis left no possibility for ethical escape from the existential dilemma they created for their victims since they allowed for no significant possibility of choice on the part of these victims. In any way they might choose to act, apart from passive acceptance of their fate, the victims would seem to be collaborating with the Nazi evil that was directed against themselves. In this way, the Nazis murdered their victims' humanity before bringing them to the point of physical death.[38]

Viktor Frankl, whose views were the product of his own experiences as a prisoner in a Nazi extermination camp,[39] claimed that, despite everything, it was impossible to deprive a human being of his freedom to choose to resist internally, a freedom based on human conscience which defines the meaning of human existence, even in situations where the human being is deprived of freedom to act in accordance with his conscience. Even spiritual or internal resistance alone was sufficient in terms of saving the meaning of human existence when the human being had no possibility of external action. In this way, too, internal freedom was maintained.

If these views are compared to those of Drenger, it can be seen that he would agree with Frankl concerning the claim that an individual can overcome and maintain his inner freedom even in the

236

context of the terror of Radical Evil. Drenger would not agree, however, that this was possible by means of an inner gesture in a situation where even passive acceptance of the slaughter was, in practice, to be interpreted as collaboration with the evil directed against the person and his comrade. Freedom could be maintained only if two conditions completely absent in Frankl's analysis were maintained: first, unconditional readiness to pay the supreme price; second, complete identification of the individual with the whole of humanity and with his people, before whom the individual carried complete ethical responsibility and to whose future he chose to devote his life.

However, in addition to this qualitative contribution, it is highly significant that Drenger believed that there was a vital need, indeed a supreme moral duty, to engage in such a profound ideological effort in the very midst of the Holocaust. This was in order to convince his comrades — and justify beyond all possible doubt in the eyes of the coming generations[40] — about the decision of those individuals who chose to resist the Nazi evil in the name of their healthy instinct for survival and in the name of the absolute ethical commandment embodied in this instinct. For Drenger, beyond a doubt, the ideological struggle was an indivisible and vital part of the overall struggle. This was true both in its positive dimension, in consolidating the path of armed resistance to the Nazis; and in its negative dimension, in opposing the dictates of the Nazis' distorted morality which took control of its victims and sought to imprint itself on their entire human selves.

In concluding this study, therefore, it can be said that this insight was the principal message which Drenger sought to impart to his immediate comrades in their battles; to the remnants of the Jewish people, all the members of which were still fighting as best they could to resist the Nazi obsession for their lives and the lives of their people; but no less than for the coming generations. It was true that the struggle against the absolute evil that humans were capable of was primarily a struggle for physical existence, but it was also a spiritual and ideological struggle. Absolute evil could be defeated only if it were opposed on these two planes simultaneously. The "morality" in the name of which the Nazis acted and which they tried to impose on their victims had to be rejected before the physical resistance to the existential situation that they created, for without spiritual and moral liberation from enslavement to evil there could be no resistance. This was undoubtedly the reason why Drenger devoted himself to an intellectual examination that bordered on the edges of philosophy — which indeed at times transcended those borders — while under conditions of existence that for most people would appear to exclude such a discussion from the realm of what was humanly possible, perhaps even from the realm of what was necessary. For Drenger, spiritual consideration, with its realism in assessing the situation and its idealism in terms of ethical preparation, was essential precisely because resistance to the aggressive and engulfing evil seemed to be beyond human capability. This reflection was the primary tool to be used in enlisting the necessary resources of strength for the struggle.

Beyond any other conclusion, this is the most important lesson to be learned from Drenger's cohesive thought in terms of a message for humanity and for the Jewish people who will continue their path through history. In this way, they may be able to participate in the continuing struggle against the human potential for evil in conditions of freedom and on the basis of their own political and military strength.

Notes

1. Shimshon Drenger (Shimak) was born in Krakow in 1915. At the age of 13 he joined the Akiva movement, and later became one of its key leaders and educators. He was first arrested by the Nazis in 1939, after the occupation of Krakow (along with his lifelong partner Gusta Davidson, author of *Justina's Diary* (Tel Aviv: Hakibbutz Hameuhad, 1953; 2nd ed., Lohamei Haggeta'ot, 1978), an eye-witness account of the Jewish underground in Krakow). The experience of this arrest brought home to Drenger what the future held for the Jews of Poland under Nazi rule. After his release, and after police surveillance was lifted, he returned to his activities in the movement. He was one of three leaders of the underground specializing in the preparation of forged documents. He also edited the underground paper, *The Fighting Pioneer*, and wrote most of the articles. After the movement's large-scale attack in "Tsiganaria," he was caught and imprisoned in Montalopi jail, but he managed to escape (along with Gusta) and continued his work, including publishing *The Fighting Pioneer*. He and Gusta were eventually arrested in November 1943, and the two disappeared. On his personality, see Rivka Koffer, "On the Character of Shimshon Drenger (Shimak)" at the beginning of *The Fighting*

Pioneer. He was a leading character in Gusta Davidson's descriptions in *Justina's Diary.*

2. *The Fighting Pioneer* — Organ of Pioneering Jewish Youth in the Krakow Underground, August-October 1943, introduction by Rivka Perlis: "The Fighting Jewish Organization in Krakow and its Journal." Pub. by Rina Kallinov; trans. from Polish by Zvi Dar (Beit Lohamei Haggeta'ot and Hakibbutz Hameuhad, 1984). Only issues 29-38 are extant; all other issues were lost.

3. *The Fighting Pioneer,* pp. 61-65.

4. *Ibid.,* p. 61.

5. *Ibid.,* p. 62.

6. *Ibid.,* pp. 62-63.

7 *Ibid.,* p. 63.

8. *Ibid.,* p. 64.

9. *Ibid.,* p. 65.

10. *Ibid.*

11. *Ibid.,* p. 63.

12. *Ibid.,* p. 62.

13. *Ibid.,* p. 65.

14. It should be emphasized here that in his comments about the complete isolation of the Jewish people, Drenger did not ignore the willingness of non-Jews to save Jews, even at the price of endangering their own lives. As a leader, however, his main interest was in the organized behavior of non-Jewish movements and parties. His comments about individuals related to certain leaders who expressed personal sympathy but did not use their influence within their own movements for any practical purpose. Drenger saw Jewish insistence on fighting for their rights as their fitting contribution to the general welfare of humanity (as will emerge from quotes given below).

15. *Ibid.,* p. 65.

16. *Ibid.*, p. 68.

17. *Ibid.*, p. 80.

18. *Ibid.*, p. 83.

19. *Ibid.*, p. 135.

20. *Ibid.*, p. 136.

21. *Ibid.*

22. *Ibid.*, pp. 136-137.

23. *Ibid.*, p. 137.

24. *Ibid.*, p. 138.

25. The influence of the original and unique ideology of the Akiva movement which strongly stressed factors of cultural and traditional Jewish nationalism is clearly present in Drenger's positions. The emphasis of the duty of the Zionist movement to take overall responsibility for the Jewish people and to focus above all on just Jewish interests is undoubtedly drawn from the general nationalist heritage of Akiva. On the ideology of Akiva, see *The Doctrine of Agudat HaNoar HaIvri Akiva,* ed. and trans. Rina Nazar (Tel Aviv: Masua, 1987).

26. Gusta Davidson related to these experiences in *Justina's Diary.* A parallel reading of chapters from the diary and Drenger's observations in *The Fighting Pioneer* is very enlightening and brings home Drenger's pedagogic orientation.

27. *The Fighting Pioneer*, p. 122.

28. Quoted in Reizl Kortchak (Rozka), *Fire in the Ashes;* see ch. 3, note 3 #i, p. 56.

29. Quoted in Saul Esh, "Sanctification of Life within the Destruction," *Iyunim B'Kheker Hashoah* (Jerusalem: Institute for Contemporary Jewry, Hebrew University, 1973).

30. The emphasis is in the original.

31. *The Fighting Pioneer*, p. 102.

32. *Ibid.*, pp. 83-94.

33. *Ibid.*, pp. 115-116.

34. *Ibid.*, pp. 116-117.

35. Cited in note 5 above.

36. Gusta Davidson emphasized this existential problem and saw a central dilemma in it. She stressed the existential and ethical difficulty involved in the transition from the youth movement experience to the underground experience in terms of the human relationships involved. See *Justina's Diary*, pp. 117-118.

37. See *The Fighting Pioneer*, pp. 84-86.

38. *The Jewish Thought of Emil Fackenheim (A Reader)*, Part Three, Section 1, "Radical Evil and Auschwitz as an Unprecedented Event" (Detroit: Wayne State University Press, 1987).

39. Viktor Frankl, *Man in Search of Meaning*.

40. It is reasonable to assume that the articles written for *The Fighting Pioneer* were not only intended for the small group of underground fighters still alive at the time. They were also undoubtedly intended — perhaps primarily — for those who would be able to study them after the war. Drenger was certainly well aware that at the time they were written and published it was already too late for them to have any great influence.

Chapter 5

THE ZIONIST THEODICY OF RABBI ISSACHAR SHLOMO TEICHTHAL

When Rabbi Issachar Shlomo Teichthal's book, *Sefer Em HaBanim S'mechah*, was first published in Budapest during the Holocaust,[1] it both excited enormous agitation and drew critical attention.[2] It is conceivable, however, that its ideological-theological thrust was overshadowed by the dramatic polemic of the book and its trenchant criticism of ultra-Orthodoxy's anti-Zionist leadership on the part of an ultra-Orthodox, anti-Zionist rabbi who had himself undergone a change of heart.

The reader is confronted in these pages by a rare and genuinely spiritual experience, one of the few theological reactions to the Holocaust written by an ultra-Orthodox leader. Though the work, as noted, contains a stinging critique of ultra-Orthodoxy's anti-Zionist leadership, Rabbi Teichthal's greatest divergence from his colleagues is expressed in his own spiritual awakening which resulted in an unflinching encounter, at the highest spiritual-religious plane, with the contemporary crisis of the Jewish people. The willingness to enter into such a spiritual contest was, in general, rare in all sectors of the people, but in Orthodox circles, particularly among the ultra-Orthodox, it was unusual to the point of deviance. Rabbi Teichthal's was a twofold audaciousness: the emotional and intellectual difficulties involved in the encounter itself, as well as the challenge to the fanatic conventions of his own community.

Indeed, this may explain an inherently belligerent motif which appears at the beginning of his book and reappears throughout the work. In anticipation of the fanatic attacks which he knew would come, Rabbi Teichthal sensed the need to justify himself. His tactic was that most effective of defenses, the counterattack. Even before presenting his thesis, he accused his prospective assailants of disregarding their grave responsibility as leaders of their community by responding to criticism with demagogic arguments rather than addressing a discussion in the prescribed negotiating manner of valid, substantive *halakhic* reasoning. He predicted that this was how his

243

claims would be treated and assured his readers that he, for one, would not pay attention to such unthinking demagoguery, nor should they. Unlike others, he understood the gravity of the situation and the weighty responsibility of his station as a spiritual leader.

> Until now "I was planted in the house of the Lord," a recluse, encased in the confines of *halakhah*, fortunate to be allowed to study and teach, to write essays which were well received by the luminaries of the generation. I never took the time to interest myself in issues that pertained to the life of our holy people for that was a worthy deed that could be discharged by others...but now in the midst of the great upheaval which has overtaken us, when it is no longer possible to concentrate on talmudic disputations of the ancient Sages... (p. 27).

He expatiated at some length about unsuitable leaders who by not performing their duties properly under the circumstances that prevailed actually delayed the redemption. Consequently every Jew ought to "observe the condition of his fellow Jews and attend to their needs." The Sages had called for such conduct

> even in ordinary times when peace followed its natural course and tranquility reigned in the world; all the more now should each Jew examine the current situation of the Jews when the fortunes of the people are at their lowest ebb, when they are looked down upon and reviled, their lives and their property as unprotected as fish of the sea; at such times the obligation incumbent on every Jew to care for the needs of his fellow Jews, to aid and succor them, is redoubled. He must do this by whatever means God granted him — advice, instruction, knowledge — so as to illuminate the road the Jewish people must take to escape their predicament (pp. 27-28).

Unlike those leaders who might dispute his views, Rabbi Teichthal confined himself to *halakhic* argumentation. Once again he claimed that all the topics he raised, including the expected redemption and the steps that ought be taken to hasten its coming which he believed to be the salient issue at stake, were decidedly *halakhic* subjects. The topics must therefore be addressed in keeping with the rules of *halakhic* deliberation.

Clearly, the resort to a polemic was a defensive tactic, not the substance of the work. The primary goal was posited in the long quote cited above: "to care for the needs of his fellow Jews, to aid and succor them....He must do this by whatever means God granted him — advice, instruction, knowledge — so as to illuminate the road the Jewish people must take to escape their predicament." In other words, Rabbi Issachar Shlomo Teichthal emerged from the protective shell of the study hall to propose a comforting truth to his people, a truth that would help them withstand their suffering and bring them closer to the redemption.

What was the comforting, guiding truth that the rabbi wished to declare to his people in the darkening eclipse of that time? Ostensibly the matter was simple: to direct their gaze to the light of redemption shining from Eretz Israel. Dispersed as they were in all lands of the Exile, shadows had descended on the Jews, but in Eretz Israel the omens of redemption were perceptible. Although in his book he did not refer to Rabbi A.I. Hacohen Kook by name, Rabbi Teichthal did recount Rabbi Kook's unmistakable signs and portents of redemption — resettlement of the land, cultivation of the barren places, and the ingathering of the exiles.[3] Therefore it was incumbent upon all Jews to return to their land as soon as the road was open, thus bringing the "end of days" nearer. But in 1943, could such a message serve the Jews — trapped as they were in the Nazi dungeon — as a beacon, a light to illuminate the road they must take to escape their predicament? Did it seem at all likely that they would ever see the road to their land open before them? And if it was possible, what were they supposed to do to expedite it? This was, after all, the most urgent question on their agenda!

A thorough study of Teichthal's book reveals that he sought to answer the question by assiduously examining the significance of the situation that had emerged in the Golah; it was through this profound exploration that he developed a theological answer to his question concerning the vindication of God in the light of what was then occurring. Could a scholarly man like Rabbi Teichthal who had spent his entire life in the study halls of Torah save his people by means of political direction? In fact, his guidance could be heeded only on the spiritual-religious plane, an assumption that Rabbi Teichthal appeared to embrace, and it was on this plane alone that he believed a practical solution could be found. Deliverance could be ensured solely by observing contemporary events so that the religious truth embedded in them would be understood, and by whole-heartedly and decisively accepting the spiritual conclusions drawn from these observations. It was precisely for this reason that a man such as he was called upon to carry responsibility in that critical period.

An examination of Teichthal's Zionist doctrine is needed at this point. The doctrine was based on the theories of Rabbi Zvi Hirsch Kalisher, the distinguished forerunner of Zionism, as they were presented eighty years earlier in his book *Drishat Zion*. In the midst of desperate circumstances, Issachar Shlomo Teichthal, the ultra-Orthodox rabbi, discerned the light and realized that Kalisher was speaking the truth. Teichthal understood that the time had come for the Jewish people to make efforts on its own behalf, that the redemption had to come by means of a force exerted by the Jews themselves; only then would God's supernatural reign be revealed in the world. He spoke at such length, citing proofs from ancient as well as later sources, that one might almost think Teichthal was merely restating Kalisher's thesis — as a solution to his own generations's plight — without the addition of any original notions. Could the matter conceivably be presented in such fashion?

Much had occurred since Kalisher had written (or Rabbis Elijah Guttmacher and Akiva Joseph Schlessinger, on whose works Rabbi Teichthal had also based his approach). In the interim, the ultra-Orthodox opponents of Zionism had raised objections and voiced disagreement. Could their arguments simply be dismissed without answer? Furthermore, the views of the proto-Zionist forerunners had been sounded at a time of brightening horizons. There had been intimations of an improvement in the attitude of gentiles toward Jews, hints that the gentiles would aid the Jewish people in the return to their land. In any case, the way had seemed open for Jews to leave the Exile and make aliyah. But by the time Rabbi Teichthal perceived the truth of the matter, the Jews were already embroiled in unprecedented straits. Even if in Eretz Israel there were signs that appeared to usher in the redemption, in all other areas of the world circumstances totally discredited the notion of deliverance, and escape routes were sealed off. Rabbi Teichthal felt obliged to respond to all these objections, and in recounting the message of his predecessors, he was, in reality, underscoring his own innovations.

First, Teichthal dealt at length with the question that arose in the wake of Kalisher and Guttmacher's concepts: why were Zionism's foremost spokesmen impious atheists who rebelled against the authority of the Torah? He answered the grave charges leveled at Zionism by its ultra-Orthodox opponents, and in his refutation had recourse to Rabbi Abraham Isaac Hacohen Kook's arguments (although here again he made no explicit mention of Rabbi Kook). Teichthal added his own polemic as well to demonstrate two points. 1) The *mitzvah* of settling the land was being fulfilled, and it was a mitzvah even when it was not performed as a religious precept. 2) People who dedicated their lives to this virtuous aim could not be viewed as sinners. The full religious response would not materialize until after the redemption; it would emerge from the potential inherent in Eretz Israel — not the other way round. For a variety of reasons, whether connected to the here and now, or whether theological and mystical in nature, the redemption had perforce to be conducted in the outer garments of ugly impiety. Nonetheless, if masses of the faithful had only undertaken the *mitzvah* of personally resettling the land, the reality in Eretz Israel would long ago have been immeasurably improved. (And the Holocaust, too, would have been forestalled.)[4]

Secondly, in varying degrees of intensity Teichthal was involved with the charges made by Zionism's opponents concerning the "three vows" which God had extracted from the Jews and the gentile nations; in particular, the oath that the Jewish people would not arise en masse to return to Israel before the advent of the messiah. Rabbi Teichthal was at pains to show that the return to Israel was not a transgression; on the contrary, aliyah was a direct response to God's call.[5]

Thirdly, Teichthal was anxious to prove that British and Arab opposition to the Jewish community in Eretz Israel was part of the Divine scheme for the onset of the redemption. This slowly unfolding reality would accelerate in response to the needs of the situation and to the extent that the pious would heed the call. Should they participate in the process, ensuring that the country was settled in accordance with the laws of the Torah, no obstacle would arise.[6]

But the gravest and most important question that occupied Rabbi Teichthal was the dilemma which centered on the vindication of God in light of the terrible reality of the Holocaust. "Why should God do this to us, bring the messiah by means of great problems? Was God incapable of delivering us without adversity? Could not our Deliverer appear gently and beneficently?" (pp. 61-62). What were the more sublime reasons for the Holocaust and what was its intent from God's standpoint? And what could the Jewish people, enmeshed in its travail, do for its own deliverance?

To answer these questions in relationship to Rabbi Teichthal's approach, one must first grasp the way in which he perceived the events of his time. In the 1942 preface to his book, it is clear that he already viewed prevailing events in eschatological terms, but these were general formulations such as "pangs of the messiah" or the "end of days." By the time the second preface was written a year later, the focus had sharpened into a specific observation of what the author believed was a historically unprecedented reality.

> Broken in spirit I speak of the tribulation that has befallen our people at this time, a time when Exile has waxed unbearable and has become as a dungeon. The all-encompassing nature of Galut has been traditionally subsumed in the phrase: "in which all of us are immersed." It is the Mishna's interpretation for the verse in Jeremiah (43:11): "such as are for death to death, and such as are for captivity to captivity, and such as are for the sword to the sword" with every development worse than the previous one. This is expounded in *Baba Batra*, IV.5 (see Rashi's commentary on the meaning of "captivity"). Israel's ray of hope is cut off; not since the beginning of Jewish history has there been such misfortune. Admittedly, the Jews have experienced difficult periods in the past, but these occurred in various places at varying times so that our ancestors had places of refuge. This sweeping, universal crisis afflicts all European countries; exactly those Jewish centers from which the great Jewish leaders and sages of the last few hundred years have come are now utterly destroyed down to their very foundations. There is no escape because all the gates of all the countries have been slammed shut. There has been no equivalent predicament since the days of the malicious Haman who also decreed a general massacre of the Jews within his domain — as is explained in the midrash (p. 26).

The description of the contempory situation in terms of its being unprecedented, along with the comparison to Haman's period, was undoubtedly meant to serve as the basis for an interpretation of the theological significance of the Holocaust.

Going beyond a detailed exposition of the gravity of the persecution, Rabbi Teichthal placed the emphasis on its vast scope. This time, the entire people had been caught, individuals could find no escape. Though he did not obscure the fact that the calamity befell Jewish concentrations in Europe, he made this admission almost as an aside. Teichthal spoke of the "Jewish centers," the places from which the great Jewish leaders of the past few hundred years had come. Moreover, even those countries where Jews were not persecuted were not open to Jewish refugees. In one instance he recounted the "destruction that was visited through manslaughter, murder, and all methods of brutality wreaked upon infants and children and the elderly; the annihilation of communities, some quite large in numbers, with scholars and sages, writers, and children flowering in Torah and awe of Heaven, all of them driven out naked and impoverished to perish" (p. 80).

Here, unexpectedly, he mentions the open-handed piety of American Jewry who to the best of their ability extended support and help at a time of need, thus explaining why misfortune had not overtaken them as well. But, he adds:

> Actually our distress does effect them as well, if not to the same extent as ourselves, it nonetheless assails them, too....In any case, we see that there are many kinds of Galut so that I would say about our brethren in the United States and other countries who do not experience the full force of what we endure, some attenuated suffering is theirs as well. They share our afflictions and together with us lament our fate because their honor has been impugned with ours. You can well understand that when their gentile neighbors read the papers or hear on the radio about the degradation that we here undergo, their honor, too, is debased. Do these gentiles not say, "See how they are humiliated there?" Consequently their own self-image is devalued.
>
> When they support us they are, therefore, participating actively with us, only under much less severe conditions. But even the light process of purging from impurities that they undergo is a comfort to us, while for them it is a partial Exile. It flows from this that they, too, are involved in the pangs of the messiah and that they have acquitted themselves as noted (pp. 82-83).

Rabbi Teichthal's reason for stressing the singularly worldwide nature of the afflictions taking place in his time is clear: in his opinion this was proof that these torments did indeed presage the coming of the messiah. Following the passage quoted above, he notes: "Be assured that we have come to the time of redemption as foretold in the *Zohar*; we are merely required to begin a spiritual awakening and God will complete the process to our benefit."

Furthermore, the pervasive aspect of the predicament validated the main thrust of his theological thesis that a situation now existed which left the Jewish people with but one option for its survival, a return to its land. This very renewal was the element God required so that he could deliver his people. "And the most important act is that we should bestir ourselves to return to our sacred land for it is only because of exile that these tribulations which I have described at such length have befallen us" (*op. cit.*).

In other words, Rabbi Teichthal grasped the extraordinary and unprecedented dimensions of the Holocaust as a circumstance which meant the total elimination of the Exile, insofar as it was an exile, a situation that left the Jewish people without an option. None of the old exilic paths remained; one clear-cut fate awaited the Jews — annihilation. The only escape left was Eretz Israel. There, in contradistinction to Galut, a preredemptive process had begun. It was therefore impossible to mistake the intent of Divine providence; since the Jewish people had not roused itself in time to return of its own volition to its homeland, it would be propelled there by a massacre so pervasive and so all-encompassing that it left no alternative.

Was this an instance of fundamental theodicy with recourse to notions of reward and punishment for Israel's sins in order to explain the Holocaust? Ostensibly it is the kind of fundamentalist theodicy that the extreme ultra-Orthodox made use of even before the Holocaust years, and all the more vigorously during the Holocaust and its aftermath. That is, horrible persecutions were decreed from on high because of the rampant sin of atheism, especially the transgressions of the Zionists, in which even the faithful are punished for the inequity of the majority.[7] Outwardly, it would appear that Rabbi Teichthal merely reversed the formulation. The zealots of his community blamed the Zionists whereas he condemned the anti-Zionists, holding them responsible for the calamity. The terrible criticism Rabbi Teichthal leveled at the leaders of his community, accusing them of culpability because they were responsible for the deaths of those who could have been saved, seems to bear out this supposition. Yet a careful examination of his words shows that this is an oversimplification not to be imputed to such a man. Regarding atheistic Zionists, he wrote,

> Everything I have ever written about the builders of the country, calling them "sinners," heaven forfend, was a quotation of the fanatics who refer to them in this fashion. I also wrote that the zealots erred, even if seen from their own perspective. They held themselves aloof from rebuilding the country because they did not approve of the builders. But I view things differently. In my eyes the builders are not wrongdoers, rather they are a true seed, the seed of Abraham, Isaac, and Jacob, a choice seed. Their only shortcoming is that they are like children captivated by idolaters. As I noted earlier, it is required of us to love them, to welcome them, and to draw them closer....This ought serve as a moral to those numbers of people who so lightly hold that the Israelis are sinners (pp. 125-126).

If Rabbi Teichthal disassociated himself in this way from the concepts of retribution held by the zealot community, and this was his conception of atheists in Israel, it does not stand to reason that he would easily portray fanatics of his own community and several of its rabbis as such transgressors that the Holocaust would be a suitable punishment for their wrongdoing.

It bears emphasizing that there is a substantive difference between Rabbi Teichthal and the bearers of fanatic anti-Zionist theology in how each understood the idea of reward and punishment. The Jews are indeed punished in Teichthal's view for not having made aliyah to Eretz Israel in a volitional response to the previous call to do so; but it would never have occurred to him that God's punishment could be construed as revenge for its own sake, certainly not such a cruel revenge. The only aim Rabbi Teichthal ascribes to his God is the deliverance of the Jews from Exile; there is no other motive. The massacre was not decreed for any reason other than to impel Jews to leave the Galut which means that an aperture existed. Rabbi Teichthal was persuaded that an "escape hatch" remained open even at the worst moments — a hidden exit to safety through Israel. And, he believed, it was precisely this understanding that underscored the grave transgression of opponents to Zionism. Had they seen the situation in its true light, they could have saved many of their fellow believers. The responsibility he placed on them was palpable, supported by obvious facts rather than based on general theological assumptions: there was a direct relationship between what the ultra-Orthodox leaders declared about Zionism and the fact that many who could have made aliyah, and thereby saved themselves, actually perished in the Holocaust. Similarly, his exoneration of atheist Zionists was based on the explicit fact that they, on the contrary, preserved themselves and many other Jews with them.

In this context, the consistency of Teichthal's understanding of Divine retribution also bears note. In response to the question of why among impious, atheist Zionists there were no observable signs of regret or of a return to religion — although ostensibly such signs had to manifest themselves as a precondition of redemption — Teichthal explained that, indeed, it could not have been otherwise. The trials and tribulations of Exile could not, of themselves, be expected to cause Jews who had renounced the Jewish religion to suddenly embrace the yoke of belief and practice again. People who did not regard themselves as "sinners" could draw but one conclusion from the ordeal of Galut — they must return to their homeland through their own efforts. This they did, and it was a return (*teshuva*) to their people. More specifically, it was an early stage of return. For a complete return to religious awe could not be a result of persecution, but would come only when God's grace manifested itself in the full redemption.[8]

Rabbi Teichthal did not believe that the impact of the exilic situation and its attendant punishments would cause the impious, contemporary generation to revert to piety; on the contrary, it could only reinforce renunciation and defection. Moreover, his understanding was that one could not write off their conduct as that of persons "seized" by assimilation in their early childhood with no experience or knowledge of things Jewish. The conclusion was clear to him. Because he did not accept a theology of punishment for the purpose of retribution, but rather a theology of punishment for corrective purposes, he held that the only justification for the tribulation Jewry was undergoing was in the sole positive result that one could detect: bringing the Jewish people to a condition from which they could be delivered. Only then would the miracle of a complete return be effected.

Still, a profound quandary remained: did all this offer any comfort to those caught in the noose of the Holocaust? Was there a way out of the death siege tightening about them? If it was to be compelling, Rabbi Teichthal's Zionist theodicy depended on the answers it could offer to these fateful questions.

As noted earlier, Teichthal had taken it upon himself "to care for the needs of his fellow Jews, to aid and succor them...by whatever means God granted him — advice, instruction, knowledge — that can illuminate the road they must take to escape their predicament" (pp. 27-28). The title of his work, *Happy Mother of Children*, which is evocative of jubilant tidings in the midst of catastrophe, testified to his spirited optimism. One notes that "joyous mother" is a sobriquet for Eretz Israel, and that the mother's joy is delight at the redemption that occurs within her provinces. There is no mistaking the author's intention in the title of the book — to comfort and gladden those lost in the darkness of Galut and to show them a passage to rescue:

> I entitled the book *Happy Mother of Children*, a derivation from the Jerusalem Talmud, *B'rakhot*, end of the chapter, "If he was reading...," where Eretz Israel is equated with the mother of the Jewish people and the countries of the dispersion with a stepmother; we also know from the Sages that our mother, Zion, weeps and laments over us for languishing in Exile, and she awaits our return.
>
> I was witness to the wonders of God in 1942, in Slovakia. Just before Passover, a harrowing decree was ordered by the accursed authorities to seize young Jewish women, 16 and older, to be transported to an unknown fate at an unnamed destination. To this day no one knows what happened to thousands of pure Jewish souls that had previously been taken to the same place, may God soon exact our revenge for them. There was great trepidation in the Jewish quarter at that time. A Jew who wanted to save his young daughters from that pit attempted to steal across the border with them. It was during the intermediate days of Passover, and he promised his wife that he would notify her by telegram of their safe arrival on the other side of the frontier. The mother sat at home anxiously waiting for the expected message. Instead, they were caught almost immediately and imprisoned in a town close to the frontier. They were in immi-

nent danger of being banished to some horrifying fate as there was an added punishment for fugitives. Meanwhile, the mother discovered what had happened and her early joy at their escape turned into grief. The Passover Festival became a dirge as she sat weeping with anguish for she knew what awaited her husband and daughters.

The great scholar, Head Judge of the community of Neitra, Rabbi Shmuel David Ungar, spared no effort until, at great financial cost, he obtained the release of the prisoners and they were able to return home without obstacle or incident, on the last day of Passover. The distraught mother was informed by phone of the joyful turn of events; there is no need to describe feelings. She now breathlessly looked for her family's return. Unable to remain in the house, she sat outside straining to catch the first sight of them. When the moment came, her weeping burst out in a loud cry for she was unable to restrain the feelings of her heart and she was unable to articulate in words her gratitude to God for the miracle He had performed for her and for them. Not to have seen the moment of reunion with the daughters after the terrible incarceration or hear the mother's sobbing as they came back to their home — the "mother of children in her joyousness" — is never to have seen an expression of delight.

What I have learned from that event which occurred in our own time is comparable to what I imagine must be the exhilaration of our mother, Eretz Israel, when we all return to her bosom after our terrible captivity in these hours; the miraculous happiness of the "mother and her children" — which is to say Eretz Israel — will be overjoyed with us, and we with her.

That is why I have called my book *Happy Mother of Children*, hoping that God will enable me to use it toward the goal of returning the children to their borders and to their mother's bosom, so that the expression will be realized in our time and we ascend to Zion in joy. Amen, so God has spoken (pp. 35-37).

The passage above was quoted in full in order to substantiate the author's emotional impulse to extend immediate consolation to parents in distress. Indeed these words of consolation and solace were not hollow pious hopes but a genuine expectation on Teichthal's part "to use [my book] toward the goal of returning the children to their borders and to their mother's bosom."

What, then, was the result that Rabbi Teichthal hoped his book would achieve? The answer appears at the very beginning of the work, in the 1942 preface to his book, stated in clear and concise terms which subsequently acquired theological amplification. In the author's opinion, the fundamental innovative interpretation of the book is found here: "I observed the 1802 letter of the Tanya [Rabbi Shneour Zalman of Ladi] written to Rabbi Levi Isaac of Berdichev, may their virtue stand us in good stead, when the Tanya was informed of his release from prison in Petersburg" (p. 21). Rabbi Teichthal's reference-text for his own significant, liberating innovation follows: "the Tanya ascribed the sole reason for his deliverance 'to the merit of the holy land and its inhabitants, which have invariably saved us and which will deliver us from all oppression'" (*ibid.*).

"And from his saintly words I learned something really new that I had neither been aware of nor read any book, that whenever a Jew is in dangerous straits he may be rescued by virtue of Eretz Israel and its inhabitants" (*ibid.*).

These brief words of Rabbi Shneour Zalman of Ladi struck Rabbi Teichthal as a great innovation, bordering on prophecy, which he had not encountered in the past. But he then turned to the Sources where he found "a truthful source in the sacred Torah itself" which was interpreted by the Sages to mean that "the merit of Eretz Israel is superior to all other virtues, and even exceeds our ancestral merits" (*ibid.*). After supporting this notion with additional early proofs from the *Mekhilta* and from the *Zohar,* Teichthal arrived at a modern conclusion: "Consequently, since we are now in great distress and afflictions coil themselves around our necks, multiplying not only day by day but hourly, so that were I to enumerate them all there would not be ample pages, and I must leave that to future chroniclers...consequently we are in urgent need of the merit of our sacred country which will preserve us and safeguard us and deliver us from torment" (p. 22).

But could the merit of Eretz Israel be so expanded that it covered the Golah, too? The affirmative answer to this question was the essence of the consoling truth revealed to Rabbi Teichthal. From Jacob's vow when he fled to the Golah away from his brother Esau's wrath, and from the commentary on that vow by the Sages that, "from this we deduce that one takes a vow when one is in distress," Rabbi Teichthal drew a *halakhic* conclusion with reference to himself.

I, too, will take a great vow to the God of Israel and pray as our ancient father did on behalf of all Israel; if God should be with me in these times of extreme affliction, and safeguard me from harm, and grant me food and clothing; and if the merit of Eretz Israel should stand me in good stead as protection so that no harm befalls me or my household, nor any damage, injury or maltreatment until the advent of Israel's collective redemption and my personal deliverance along with it, in the name of all Jews I beseech that the merit of Eretz Israel be employed on our behalf to save us, and declare that our afflictions are at an end...and that our hallowed land will ensure that we be quickly vouchsafed deliverance and mercy" (*ibid.*).

It bears emphasis that the novel intelligence which was revealed to Rabbi Teichthal was integrally connected to the very writing of his book. Admittedly, until then he had been spared, but the exact date of the redemption and the manner of its coming were unknowable, and in order to ensure the right to live until the salvation:

Therefore I will take a vow upon myself like the pledge made by Father Jacob. Immediately after God frees us from the yoke of our enemy I will compose a book, a book of homage dedicated to the honor of Eretz Israel, to search out all her splendid particulars and praise her and expound her virtues, that every Jew should make efforts for the reconstruction of our blessed country, for our whole salvation depends upon it....With God's help I shall explain all this in a book which will be dedicated to God's honor...and my regard for Eretz Israel shall be my support to liberate us from oppression so that I am enabled to discharge my pledge fully and competently, speedily in our days. Amen. (p. 23).

Writing a book about the preeminence of Eretz Israel and the obligation which devolves upon Jews to return to it and contribute to its renaissance, served as a partial fulfillment of the vow. It was by means of that vow and the seriousness of his intent to honor it that Rabbi Teichthal hoped to extend the protective merit of Eretz Israel to himself and to Jews enmeshed in the whirlwind of the Holocaust. It followed from this that it was also the consoling truth which the book heralded as a spiritual-pragmatic road for the preservation of the Jews. While yet in Exile, persecuted Jews in danger of extermination could be saved by invoking the virtue of Eretz Israel to themselves, as a shield. As the author had done, they should follow the example of the Patriarch Jacob and affirm an oath to return to their country as soon as the way was opened. They should dedicate themselves with all their might to the reconstruction of Eretz Israel, and to exalting its name. And if they were to undertake this vow now, they would at once be able to effect the merit of Eretz Israel which would sustain them!

Clearly, the book's main thrust was to prove, from a variety of perspectives, that the redemption was indeed dependent on the merit of Eretz Israel. In order to be redeemed, all Jews must strive to have that merit apply to them by resettling and rebuilding the land, and by doing so to the best of their ability, an aperture to redemption would open for them. Truly, even as the sword lay upon their necks in the darkness of the Galut, even as it appeared that there was no possible escape — there was still a practical-spiritual way out.

Of course, these ideological affirmations necessitated a theological foundation. Systematic exposition was not Rabbi Teichthal's natural province, yet if one follows the flow of his ideological motifs — though they, too, were not models of sequential discourse — they can be synthesized into a comprehensive theological doctrine focusing on the ontological meaning of Eretz Israel, the Jewish people, their history and how the three interrelate. The infrastructure is kabbalastic and its closest derivation is, once again, in Rabbi Kalischer's book. The development of the formulation, however, was closer to Rabbi Kook's doctrines regarding Eretz Israel and the Jewish people. The primary notion is that the essences of Eretz Israel and the Jewish people become ontologically harmonized. Their discrete and mundane tangible presences are but shadows of a single sublime presence for in that lofty sphere the "the Jewish collective" and "Eretz Israel" become as one. This impacts directly on the status of the country as well as on the position of the people in their terrestrial sphere. Eretz Israel is not merely the destined locale for the people but the heart that animates it. In one of Rabbi Teichthal most striking sentences he evokes Maimonides' view in *Sefer HaMitzvot* (in order to prove that according to Maimonides, as well, the commandment to settle the land holds contemporary applicability!).

If we were to assume, for example, that the inhabitants of Eretz Israel were to absent themselves from Eretz Israel, may God never bring such a thing to pass for He promised that He would never utterly obliterate the evidence of their existence from the land, but if they were all to be ejected from the country, there would be no [*halakhic*] court there; nor would there be a [*halakhic*] court in the diaspora invested, by a rabbinic court of Eretz Israel, with authority to confer jurisdiction, and all our efforts to get around such a difficulty would be to no avail, for it is written..."The Law shall go forth from Zion."

Rabbi Teichthal understood the passage above to mean that in Maimonides' opinion,

If Jews do not dwell in Eretz Israel that spells the end of the people, Heaven forbid. Such a predicament petrifies the human mind, and in my view this is because Eretz Israel is the heart of the nation, as is set out in the pious work, *Ohr Ne'erav* (*Twilight*), of Rabbi Moshe, the man of God from Cordoba. As I have noted above, and in this I quoted the Haham Zvi: "no creature can live without a heart." Consequently, should the Jews be dispossessed of Eretz Israel they would be bereft of their heart which would be tantamount to the termination of their national life. There is, furthermore, the commentary of the Sages on the Torah portion of *Re'eh* in *Midrash Tanhuma*, where God speaks of the Israelites as His portion, as in the verse, "For the portion of the Lord is His people, Jacob the lot of his inheritance" (Deuteronomy 32:9). And Eretz Israel is His inheritance, a land for which God is constantly solicitous, "Let my portion dwell in My inheritance..." which means that the Jewish people's bond to God is actuated expressly by Eretz Israel (p. 152).

The conclusion to be drawn from the Jewish people's link to God as mediated exclusively by Eretz Israel is that when the people are exiled from their land they lose the status of their nationhood and of God's providence. The people are scattered and dissolve as an entity. Not only are their independence and physical collectivity affected, but also their internal cohesion and external fate. God is now unable to guide them directly and overtly precisely because the direct contact between the people and their God is broken. The people are under the jurisdiction of natural forces that hold sway outside Eretz Israel. Admittedly, God continues to watch over them but only from afar and through the intermediacy and functioning of the natural forces. This was Teichthal's radical exegesis of an aphorism of the Sages that "anyone living outside of Eretz Israel is like a person bereft of God. And you should take cognizance of this for it is predicated on a foundation of truth" (*ibid.*). In other words, the truth of the statement is based on the foundation stones of a kabbalistic axiom — in the sense that in Exile, the Jewish collectivity and its individuals lack Divine guidance and even the direct presence of God. God is not with them and it is in this sense that they are godless. Only in Eretz Israel does God's *Shekhina* dwell as a Divine emanation. Therefore, when the people reside in their land, even in the absence of a Temple, God is an actual presence among them, which is not the case in the lands outside Eretz Israel

Still, there is some small comfort even in Exile. While under the sovereignty of natural powers, the exercise of free choice is not completely absent. In humans, the exercise of choice is a natural force and man's condition under the sway of natural powers depends on his own initiative and the choices he makes from among options. Exile, then, is not only God's decree, or judgment, against the transgressions of His people (which they committed while still in their own country), it also exposes the root of the offense for which the punishment of Exile was meted out. The decision to resign themselves to Galut or strive to extricate themselves from its bonds and return to Eretz Israel depends primarily on the people. According to Rabbi Teichthal's theological outlook, the people can retain their connection to God through the mediating force of their land even while they are still in Exile, or evoke the merit of Eretz Israel and apply it to themselves even when in Galut. If they reconcile themselves to Galut and opt for continued existence there, then that submission consists of a complete severing from their land and their connection to God by means of the land. But if they do not abdicate and if they give practical expression to their resistance by uniting around a common goal to return to their home, then the bond is maintained — even if from afar — and a redeeming Divine leadership can then become manifest by means of the unification.[9]

It is therefore evident that while in Galut, "spiritual attachment" alone is insufficient to maintain the people's unity and their connection to the land.[10] There was nothing to be gained by prayers, benedictions, professions of the unity of God, or by intentions: "Accordingly, one can understand the quotation 'and after that the Israelites sought God and David their King'; that is, they did not seek by prayer alone but they attempted to find them by means of concrete acts. This is perhaps better understood by the translation into Yiddish: 'they will actively search for the road which can return them to Eretz Israel'; they will not suffice with prayer but take some effective action, for one is ineffective without the other, and only then will they be granted a favorable omen" (pp. 103-104).

In a more radical formulation, toward the end of the book:

The four species (citron, palm branch, myrtle and willow that make up the etrog and the lulav) are intended to demonstrate faith in repentance — the choice is ours — to repair all our trespasses through a complete atonement that is composed of mending our thoughts, speech and action...to become such a great truth that it will set aside the decree...and if the question is asked, what moral is to be drawn from the belief that we are at liberty to choose repentance, the answer is *"any belief that is not accompanied by a deed cannot prevail and bear fruit"* (pp. 314-315, author's emphasis).

In other words, just as the condition of the people and land's spiritual emanation has an influence on their physical-terrestrial condition, so too, tangible-worldly deeds have an influence on the spiritual essence of their condition. The symbiotic link is absolute and cannot be avoided. Consequently, only when the people, by means of its individual members, brings its tangible presence to bear on its affinity to a temporal-material Eretz Israel, only then will the sublime influence be revealed in discernible miracles.

Again, it must be stressed that in the rabbi's view this derives from the nature of the emanations, on one hand, and from the basic quality of Creation, on the other. Tangible-worldly deeds stem from the determination of temporal human beings. God cannot force the people's will, but similarly He cannot redeem them before they arrive at the place where God's providence dwells. It is the nature of the temporal world and the essence of emanations that the historical and mundane stage initiated by mortals should precede the revelation of God's mercies to the people. Consequently, there is no alternative. Although God wants to redeem His people, and that has always been His sole intention, His will can be realized only when the people put themselves under his jurisdiction, in the place from which He can reclaim them, at which time His plan will come to fruition!

This is the theological key to understanding the situation of the Jews during the Holocaust. To their overwhelming misfortune, the Jews had distanced themselves from redemption, isolating themselves from it in an ever-deepening Exile. Besides a widespread, growing dispersion in gentile lands, there was also disunity, and the tragedy was that the cause of the disharmony and conflict was precisely the element that should have served as a unifying and redemptive factor — the renascence of Eretz Israel! Only a handful devoted themselves to the reconstitution of Jewish life there, whereas the majority held aloof, even opposing the venture. Indeed, if God were inclined to hasten the redemption by recourse to miracles, the people obstructed the recovery through their deeds. The historical process remained the only avenue available to God, a procedure which overshadowed the supernatural mode and was perforce long and drawn out. Moreover, detours and retreats were unavoidable along the historical route. In retrospect, one realizes that destroying the Galut was a precondition to motivating the Jewish people to return to its land of its own volition; or minimally, to prompt it to admit its obligation to its homeland. That is to say, for the sake of redemption there was no alternative to the destruction of Galut.

When the reason for the situation that came about is understood without ambiguity, the remedy advocated for its relief is also comprehensible: a willed initiative by the people to attach themselves to their land according to their own natural abilities in order to gain for themselves the merit of Eretz Israel! The theological foundation described above is what makes this possible, but here a further development is called for. Just as supernatural redemption is dependent on the people's attendance in a temporal-mundane frame which enables the operation of sublime spiritual forces, so these powers can become activated only when the people demonstrate a pragmatic readiness for movement in the correct direction. Clearly the ideal venture would be aliyah to Eretz Israel and participation in its restoration. That would constitute a material, tangible deed with sublime spiritual significance.[11] But if such involvement was thwarted due to circumstances indirectly caused by Divine will, it was sufficient for those incarcerated by the Holocaust to articulate their duty

toward Eretz Israel and undertake a personal obligation to make
aliyah — accepting the supremacy and preeminence of Eretz Israel
— and to do everything in their power to unite the people around the
goal of restoring Eretz Israel. This would be sufficient to have the
merit of Eretz Israel bear upon the Golah, even in a period of
devastation. In turn, this would empower God to rescue his people in
a supernatural manner. The light of redemption would burst forth as
soon as the majority of the people sincerely repented, that is, overtly
demonstrated its desire to return to its land. It is entirely evident
from Rabbi Teichthal's words throughout the book that he truly
awaited redemption at any moment.

To summarize: Rabbi Teichthal clearly perceived of the extraordinarily unique nature of the Holocaust in Jewish history. He acknowledged its scope and severity as the worst annihilation ever
experienced by the Jews. Nonetheless this assessment did not undermine his faith in the notion of Divine providence in its traditional and
fundamental sense: it was God that had decreed the elimination of
the Galut after forethought and deliberation. Indeed, this realization
was reinforced in light of the mounting severity of the tribulations.
Toward the end of his work Teichthal writes:

> Our obligation is redoubled in these times to bestir ourselves and
> awake from our slumber and indolence, for now there is ample
> readiness for action by those who have eyes to see and ears to
> hear the severe trials which have befallen us in these times; an
> oppressive four years which the chronicler of generations could
> designate as the "massacres of 1940, 1941, 1942 and 1943," just
> as the wicked times of the crusades were called the "massacres
> of 1096"...and everything that occurred was in accord with the
> Almighty's will because of our many transgressions....As I ex-
> plained in my commentary to *Lamentations*, they asked Rabbi
> Joshua Ben Levi, "Where is God?" and he replied, "In the great
> metropolis of Rome." Yet everyone knows that the true explana-
> tion is that in the days of Rabbi Joshua Ben Levi, Israel was
> sorely oppressed and the destruction of the Jews seemed immi-
> nent, so that the demand to know God's whereabouts was in
> effect a demand to know why God remained silent in the face of
> the atrocities being inflicted on the Jews. (This is not unlike what
> one hears from the masses in our time, "Where is the Jewish
> God? Why does He keep silent?") When Rabbi Joshua Ben Levi

answered, "in the great metropolis of Rome," he meant that all the massacres stemmed from Rome which was the seat of the rulers and their advisors, hence the source of anti-Jewish statutes. Rabbi Joshua Ben Levi asked his interlocutors, "Do you imagine that these massacres were decreed without God's knowledge? No! He was also there — in a manner of speaking — at a meeting of the ministry when the harsh laws were promulgated; everything was done in accordance with His will because it was consistent with His thoughts." And I replied in a similar vein when I was in the kingdom of hell, to the many who inquired of me "Where is the Jewish God?," with the rejoinder, "He is in the palace of the minister and He agreed with the proceedings" (pp. 284-285).

Once again it is important to be precise. Teichthal does not regard the decrees as Divine retribution but rather as a totally necessary means for expediting redemption. The Jewish people's transgression consisted of postponing the redemption (that had begun to manifest itself) because the choice of the majority was to remain in Exile. They had thereby held back the starting point for the beginning of deliverance by Divine intervention. When the interrelatedness of these aspects is assessed, the comforting truth that deliverance is imminent even in the depths of the annihilation can be seen. Its omens are clear, not only in Eretz Israel but in Exile as well, in the extraordinary universality and prodigality of the phenomena that testified to the fact that Galut had come to an end, and that the Jewish people had no other refuge but Eretz Israel. Moreover, far from being regarded as a punishment, the Holocaust should be regarded as a corrective operation; neither should it be seen as an irreversible judgement. Though it was true that the Jewish people had failed to act at the opportune time so that all paths to Eretz Israel that had been accessible prior to the Holocaust were now closed off, a way remained that was at one and the same time mystic-spiritual and also pragmatic-worldly.

The Jewish people could acknowledge the redemptive truth emerging from Eretz Israel. It could overcome the schisms regarding the notion of the Return to Zion that had split the people, reuniting the nation on the foundation of a common endeavor to do everything feasible toward advancing the practical rebuilding of Eretz Israel.

The people would then be rescued and given the opportunity to carry out its decision to come on aliyah.

Thus Teichthal again begins with a precept that is to be drawn from the terrible massacre rather than a justification of the Divine judgement. He concludes with the following spirited message:

> When we disregarded Eretz Israel, trials and tribulations descended on us, and having already dealt with this matter there is no need to recapitulate at length. In any case, now, in our time, there has been a momentous awakening in the struggle to return to our beloved homeland. So my brothers and comrades, arise! awake! come forward! unite! We shall be robust and strong in the name of God and our people, and the cities of God, and on behalf of our Torah. We shall be as one person and of one heart for the time has come for everyone to make aliyah and to help in the aliyah of others; according to all the signs, redemption is close at hand, therefore each person should energetically contribute in support of the *mitzvah* of aliyah and reconstruction" (*ibid.*).

In other words, despite the Holocaust, the Jewish people was still sovereign over its own will and articulate with regard to actions that were in its control, and not subject to approval by external forces. Thus, the people extended the merit of Eretz Israel so that it applied to them as well; the decree would then have achieved its purpose and be rescinded, and the redemption dependent on God's direction would shine forth and be revealed.

It may be said that Rabbi Teichthal articulated an ultra-Orthodox-kabbalistic version of the Zionist theory that was held by the pioneering immigrants to Eretz Israel. Indeed, he considered the composition of *Happy Mother of Children* and its publication at the nadir of the Holocaust an act of Zionist realization, the only deed a man such as he could accomplish at that time, surrounded by his people, in order to have the virtue of Eretz Israel apply to himself. In the midst of those awesome days, it was an action meant not only as a tiding of hope, but as a way to explicate and give voice to the joy of a merciful mother who beholds her children returning to be rescued from captivity.

Notes

1. *"Sefer Em Habanim S'mechah (Happy Mother of Children)* was composed by me, Issachar Shlomo Teichthal, in Budapest, 1943." A photocopy of that first edition was reisssued in New York in 1969. All quotes in this chapter are from that second edition.

2. J.J. Cohen, *Mekorot V'Korot* (Sources and Events) (Jerusalem, 1982), pp 273-277; Rivka Shatz, "Vidui Al Saf HaMisrafot" ("A Confessional at the Crematorium's Door: An Ultra-Orthodox Rabbi's Repentance"), *Molad*, no. 217 (1966): 18-24; Mendel Piekarz, "Remarks of the Rabbanit of Strikov on the Promise by the Rabbi of Belz, and Two Conflicting Views on the Lesson of the Massacres" (Hebrew), *Kivunim*, no. 24 (Summer 1984): 59-75.

3. *Sefer Em Habanim S'mechah*, p. 118. Rabbi Teichthal cites the same Gemarah alluded to by Rabbi Kook as heralding the evident End of Days, not by means of arcane mysteries but through recourse to palpable historical facts — the settlement and cultivation of the land.

4. Rabbi Teichthal frequently returns to this theme in his book, and most of the second chapter is devoted to it; see particularly pp. 119-125.

5. See pp. 247-249.

6. It bears noting that despite the rabbi's defense of secular settlers, he felt that ultimately the existence of the country depended on fulfilling the commandments and living in complete faith. The Jewish people had been punished and exiled from its land because it had breached God's law. It was clear to him that in the initial stages of the return which was totally dependent on the initiative of the people, there was much value in the return of the irreligious elements.

7. This is the widely known view of Rabbi Joel Teitelbaum, former leader of Neturei Karta, in his book *Va'Yoel Moshe*. With reference to Rabbi Teichthal, there was a similar disputation between Rabbi Teitelbaum and Rabbi Mordekhai Rokeach, brother of the Rabbi of Belz. See note 2, M. Piekarz's excellent article.

8. A notable part of the first chapter of *Happy Mother of Children* deals with this topic, e.g., p. 66.

9.   Rabbi Teichthal explains that uniting for the reconstruction of Eretz Israel does not call for suspending the independent structures of the ultra-Orthodox community, especially not the educational institutions. They can participate in the joint undertaking while retaining the integrity of their separate life style and schools. He describes the unifying arrangement as a manufacturing plant where there is an overall formation which contains separate departments. See p. 335.

10. Similar expressions have already been noted in this work. But it bears emphasis that in one of his references to this matter, Rabbi Teichthal approaches Ahad Haam's idea of a "spiritual center": if the Jewish people in its entirety would accept the authority of the Jewish community in Eretz Israel, then the merit of Eretz Israel would extend to all of them and the people would cease their exilic state. See p. 291.

11. This is again a radical approach on the part of Rabbi Teichthal who believed that any material volunteering for the benefit of Eretz Israel, or physical endeavor on behalf of its reconstruction, had a sublime spiritual significance. See p. 291.

PART II: PROBLEMS OF FAITH AND ETHICS VIEWED AFTER THE HOLOCAUST

Chapter 6

FAITH, ETHICS AND THE HOLOCAUST: THE JUSTIFICATION OF RELIGION IN THE CRISIS OF THE HOLOCAUST

There is a long-standing tradition of discussing the question before us in theological terms, as a question of the "justification of God" (theodicy). This same tradition formulates the question, is it possible, or how is it possible, to maintain a belief in Divine providence based on justice and reward, after what happened in the Holocaust? Is it possible to believe that the Holocaust was the result of Divine will and providence, and if so, how is it possible to justify this belief? If it is impossible, then where was God during the Holocaust? Why didn't He intervene? How can one justify His "hiding?" Or the question, is it even possible to believe in God at all, in a God who watches, commands, judges, and rewards the individual; how can one believe in such a God after the Holocaust?[1] This essay will deal with this basic recognition on the part of most discussants of this subject that the Holocaust raised the problem of faith to an unprecedented level of severity that negates most traditional solutions and calls the rest into doubt. It can be argued that this change is based on the fact that for believers, as well, the issue has moved beyond a religious struggle with the question of the justification of God or faith, and has become a struggle on the part of the believers with the question of the justification of religion.

Let us open the discussion with a certain empirical determination that requires a response as background to our argument. A thorough study made on the outlooks of Holocaust survivors before, during and after the Holocaust,[2] indicated two radical reactions to the Holocaust — an absolute loss of faith versus a strong reinforcement of faith. The Holocaust itself, for the most part, did not give rise to an essential turning point in the faith of believers or non-believers; the belief or unbelief already existed before the Holocaust for most individuals as a formulated stance, or at least as a clear inclination. The Holocaust itself strengthened preexisting views. While the

269

Holocaust caused a crisis of faith for some of the respondents in the study, most of them returned to their faith following the Holocaust.

When in the light of this finding we examine the ways in which believers struggled with the question of the "justification of God" during the Holocaust, we find that there is a small group of radical believers who stubbornly stuck to the fundamentalist traditional belief that the Holocaust was, indeed, the will and act of God as a terrible punishment deemed appropriate by Divine considerations for a great sin that the people had sinned before God, and that because of this sin the Holocaust was entirely justifiable and now demands soul-searching and repentance. Yet, in contrast to this minority of ultra-pious believers, whose views took shape even before the Holocaust in the face of the Zionist sin, on the one hand, and assimilation and religious reforms, on the other,[3] most of the believing public agrees that it is possible to understand the Holocaust only as a "hiding of His Countenance" (*hester panim*), and that this concealment is beyond comprehension. The Holocaust revealed acts of human wickedness and absolute evil beyond any evil that had yet been seen in history. No sin attributable to the Jewish people could justify a punishment like the Holocaust. On the contrary, if any situation has ever existed that required, from a traditional religious viewpoint, Divine intervention for salvation, it was indeed the situation of the Jews during the Holocaust. While the believers face a terrible enigma, this time they cannot accept the explanation that serves as a "last resort" in theology — "the ways of God are wonderful and beyond man's comprehension." Under these circumstances, their faith exists as a protest, a rebellion, or a cry of confusion. It is clear that this stand not only breaks away from the traditional theodicean framework in terms of solutions offered for the question, but it also calls into doubt whether the same question stands before us; i.e., it is uncertain that the same theological foundation upon which the question was formulated in the past still exists.[4]

On the basis of this empirical finding, perhaps the aforementioned distinction between the question of "the justification of God" and the "justification of religion," which is the established system of faith and beliefs, mores, commandments, and education as these values affect the relationship between man and God, becomes clearer. Is it possible to distinguish between these two questions? At the outset the obvious answer is negative; i.e., God and religion are two

270

sides of the same coin; religion justifies God, His role in history, His commandments and judgments. If religion proves to believers that God is justified, religion has also justified itself, and if it fails in its struggle with the question of theodicy, then it has also failed as a religion, for loss of belief in God is also a loss of religion. Indeed, the question of theodicy always appeared as a question testing religion — does religion have the power to offer the believer, shaken by large tragedies, especially evil human deeds, a solacing truth that will sustain his belief in his heart? Can religion guide and help him in contending with the tragedy that has occurred, and with its consequences, in a way that will enable him to return to a full life? Yet, we can distinguish between justification of God and justification of religion in at least two contexts. First, concerning the question of the justification of God, we can claim as believers that religion has failed in its mission without identifying this failure with the failure of God; and second, possibly religion as an established system sinned against God and thus caused the "desecration of God before the multitudes."

Individuals versed in these matters know that such criticism of religion has accompanied the history of religion since earliest times. In a certain way, this criticism is the focus of the controversy between religions, especially similar religions competing for the souls of the same believers. A substantial portion of the literature on the controversies between Judaism, Christianity and Islam is just an attempt on the part of each of these religions to justify itself against such criticism and to blame its rivals. In these interreligious debates, there is no comprehensive critique of religion, all religion as such, nor is there a critique of the religion by those who remain believers despite their criticism. We find a comprehensive critique of religion in general in the West in modern times. The modern denial of all religions, and not just of one religion in favor of the truth of another religion, is an expression of criticism of the phenomenon of religion and not of God. God does not occupy the thoughts of individuals who have denied Him, and the question of His justification is meaningless for them. What exists for them concretely in this world is the religion of churches and sects that presumes, indeed, to speak in the name of God. Their mission is to test the truth in religion's claims, its role in the social and political education of the individual, and the results of actions in these areas. For in this way, deniers of religion may recognize, as did Spinoza, for example,[5] the positive ethical value of

271

religion, but they are particularly aware of the damage that it causes. In extreme cases, such as Marxism,[6] they declare war against religion, presenting it as a deceptive, paralyzing fraud, and they blame religion for every offense and fault in society, in the state and in culture. To balance the picture we should mention counterevaluations by nonbelievers, especially after the wave of militant heresy had passed and the churches' interference in social and political life had been forgotten. Whereas the emotional and intellectual vacuum that resulted from the decay of faith had become clear in its entirety without being filled by any other content. Thus nonbelievers may recognize that religion fills a central social and psychological role in the life of man, and the loss caused by the undermining of religion is great and may be even irreparable.[7]

There can, therefore, be an argument among nonbelievers on the question of the guilt and justification of religion, whether it be an argument on the level of psychology, anthropology, the social sciences, or ethical philosophy, which is substantially different from the theological argument on the question of "theodicy." From the point of view of believers, of course, all of the reactions to both the critique of religion and its justification remain within the traditional framework of theology, for the attack on religion appears to them to be an attack on God Himself and on His will as revealed through His commandments. For the believers, change will occur only when there will arise a challenge forcing them to be critical of the religion that they embrace, the same religion that they see no chance of exchanging for another. For thus, religion turns into the central theological issue which separates the believer from his God. And this, it seems, is the new problem that arose out of believers' struggle with the Holocaust.

The failure of religion before God and man, from the point of view of the believer within the same religion, is particularly prevalent among contemporary Christian theologians for whom the Holocaust constitutes the central challenge.[8] Believing Christians who have internalized Christian religious ethics and whose religious-ethical sensitivity has been sharpened by the conflict between their religious morality and the very problematic ethical reality created in modern Western society cannot ignore the fact that Christianity failed in the Holocaust. Christian theologians want to understand the Christian message as one of salvation for civilization and society which, in their opinion, are sinking into ethical chaos because of their loss of faith. In other words, because the circumstances of modern Western history following World War II have reinforced their faith in the Christian message and in its necessity for the salvation of humanity, these theologians cannot ignore the ethical failure of Christianity as a religion when tested by the Holocaust.

The reasons appear very clear — Nazi ideology, the basis on which the Nazi regime planned and implemented the "Final Solution," may have been anti-Christian, but Nazism developed in a country with Christian culture. Many Christians became Nazis, and many of them, including clergymen, justified the judgment against the Jews as deserved because of their sins against the "messiah." No doubt there were exemplary Christians who risked their lives to save Jews, but most Christians either cooperated with the Nazis or, at least, did not object and did not try to help the victims, Even more serious, neither the Catholic nor the Protestant church fought against Nazi ideology and the "Final Solution." Most critical of all is the fact that lies at the foundation of these points — the dogmatic relation of Christians to Jews and Judaism, an essential component of Christian theology, contributed a decisive element of hatred, discrimination, pogroms and disturbances against the Jews over the centuries of Jewish exile among the Christians. Hence, the hatred of Jews that is rooted in Christianity is one of the central components of modern anti-Semitism, upon whose basis Nazi ideology took shape. In conclusion, Christianity failed on two accounts — it did not educate its believers to refuse to cooperate and to actively oppose the horrible acts of the Holocaust; and it made a significant contribution to the demonological hatred of the Jews.

These circumstances are enough to cause believing Christians to deal with the Holocaust, out of the depth of their Christian beliefs, as a frightening failure of their religion. It appears, however, that the roles of Christian dogma and of the Christian salvation myth in the demonological hatred of the Jews constitute a basis for a deeper criticism not only of a certain element of the Christianity in themselves. It is clear that the Nazi ideology underlying the hatred was not anchored in rational philosophy. It was basically irrational and fed by sick, dark, spiritual impulses that took on mythological expression and justification, and that were spread by dogmatic indoctrination techniques. These points apply especially to the dehumanization of Jews through anti-Semitic stereotypes. The Jews were perceived as subhuman creatures, embodying the foundation of evil and corruption in the world, which the Nazis were fighting against in order to save the forces representing the good and light. The thoughts behind the planning and implementation of the Final Solution could not have arisen, of course, without such a mytho-demonological "logic," and anyone dealing with the Holocaust must investigate not only the source of the hatred of the Jews, but also the source of this special form of hatred and its mytho-demonological character.[9]

Anyone dealing honestly with the Holocaust cannot ignore the fact that the Christian contribution to anti-Semitism was crucial at this level. Christianity was both a source of hatred of the Jews and a direct source of the mytho-demonological stereotypes of Jews. It is also impossible to ignore the fact that this stereotype is not a marginal element in the Christian myth; on the contrary, it represents an essential element in the structure of a religion based on the myth of a dichotomous struggle between holy and profane, good and evil in the world. Before us, therefore, is a fundamental element that Christianity cannot overcome without undergoing an essential change that touches not only its specific relation to Jews, but also the internal structure of its myth, as well as the perception of human reality that underlies it. Let us put it as clearly as possible: the fact that the Nazi ideology is not only influenced by Christian hatred of the Jews, but also seems to reflect the Christian salvation myth and to copy an essential element in it, is what arouses anguish and demands criticism. Indeed, it is a twofold criticism — of the demonological elements in the Christian salvation myth underlying the dehumanization of the Jews, and of the dogmatic and mythic conception itself, whose danger lies in the overpowering of man's rational understanding and autonomous ethical judgment by irrational impulses.

In consequence, the Holocaust concretized, for those Christian theologians who were moved by their deep belief in the ethical-redemptive mission of Christianity to come to terms with the Holocaust, the need to be aware and critical both of certain elements of Christian theology and of the basic conception of the Christian salvation myth, and perhaps even of the dangers hidden in the religious stance itself that is anchored in this myth. The believer apparently must be alert to the fact that his very stand on the foundation of the myth of revelation, Divine guidance and messianic salvation contains great danger; that what appears to be the goodness of a superhuman revelation is liable to embody troubled elements stemming from man. In other words, the religion that expresses the relation of man yearning for light and good to Divine, messianic truth is liable to express the depth of evil in man as well as to force him into terrible sins.

Does the self-criticism required of Christianity touch Judaism as well? Do questions penetrating beyond the justification of God to the justification of religion arise in Judaism too? At first glance it appears clear that the same judgment does not apply to the religion of the persecutors as to that of the victims. Christianity has a part in the blame, whereas Judaism is blameless, and it appears that Jewish believers are faced only with the questions of justification of a God who conceals His countenance as the test of their religion. Yet, a second look shows that the matter is not so simple and unequivocal. The first doubt is related to the general characteristic of the Christian salvation myth. If the guilt of the Christians lies in certain components and characteristics of the Christian salvation myth, and if the demonological hatred of the Jews is anchored in Christianity, and its source is the basic structural internal relation between Christianity and Judaism, then there is room to ask the question — is Judaism entirely clean of components and characteristics like those that caused the historical-ethical failure of Christianity, despite the fact that this failure was expressed as persecution of Jews and Judaism?

Certainly there are no simple answers to these questions. Yet, it is a fact that they are also asked by Jewish theologians. The most prominent theologian asking these questions is Richard Rubenstein, for whom the Holocaust and the phenomenon of genocide in the twentieth century altogether are primary and central.[10] Rubenstein sees a close relationship between the development of modern Western civilization and the crystalization of historical elements pushing towards genocide. These elements also provide genocide with the necessary technological and administrative tools, and with the ethical-ideological justifications. He also identified within the basic development of modern Western civilization the process of "secularization" that he believes began with the monotheistic religions — the expropriation of the holy from earthly nature by negating pagan pantheism; formulation of a transcendental concept of God; and turning earthly existence, including man himself, into an object of human utilitarian-authoritarian manipulation. According to Rubenstein, this process of usurping the fear and honor of the holy form "godfull" nature is already present in the Bible, and Western civilization inherited it from Judaism and then developed it in its own way.[11]

If, thus, one sees the Holocaust as outside the framework of the special fate of the Jews among the nations and sees it as one of the climactic expressions of the typical, generic phenomenon of modern civilization, and if one examines within this context the contribution of the religions that participated in the shaping of Western civilization for which genocide is a typical phenomenon, then Judaism must accept not a small portion of the blame. Rubenstein, at least, did not hesitate to draw this conclusion. His religious demand is to give up monotheism totally, including Judaic monotheism, and to return to the pagan pantheism that in his opinion requires a relation of holiness to everything in the universe.

We must admit that criticism of Judaism from this perspective is rare, and it is possible to counter it with the more widespread opinion that the Nazis saw in Judaism, and not in Christianity, the great mythological enemy of their world view. Judaism was the mother of Christianity in their minds, and it symbolized the humanistic-universal ideals that in their opinion destroyed pagan European culture. From the point of view of creating a redemption myth with demonological foundations and a tendency to dehumanize religious enemies, or from the point of view of inflaming religious fanaticism, it would certainly be possible to find these tendencies also in the history of the Jewish religion. However, as a dispersed and persecuted nation, the Jewish people were unable to expose these tendencies in acts of religious persecution towards non-Jews. In any case, among Jewish believers who examine the Holocaust as a spiritual religious problem, one finds not much critical reflection of this kind in relation to their own religion. At most, a question is sometimes raised regarding the existence of a motive for the command to exterminate a nation in the Bible, but mainly this is rejected outright because it involves a motive that lost its actual validity in ancient times, perhaps during the period of the Bible itself.

But here we must raise the puzzling question — was there really no support for Jewish believers, who died trapped in the ghettos and death camps in Europe, to feel not only that God betrayed them, but also that their religious doctrine, both its beliefs and its commands, as it was handed down to them by their religious leadership, led them astray, blinded their eyes from clear vision, or stifled their efforts to find a timely way to save themselves? Does this not provide a background for Jewish believers to see the Jewish religion, as it formed in the diaspora, and even more as it has formed in modern Orthodoxy, as a factor in the tragic misunderstanding of moral self-responsibility placed upon the Jewish people throughout its history, especially in modern times? Do not modern historical circumstances require a completely different understanding from that which formed during the generations of exile, regarding the place of the Jewish people among the nations, regarding the relationship between Divine providence and human initiative, and regarding the way in which God's will is fulfilled or violated in history through men? In more emphatic words, was it not Judaism's very great sin in its traditional mold as formed in exile, that it allowed Jewish believers to put faith in the expectation of the miraculous, saving Divine guidance of history, rather than teaching them to see clearly that the active initiative of the Jewish people struggling for its existence and destiny, as one who bears responsibility before God his commander, is the only way in which God can be present in His history and can influence its fate?

It can be easily argued that the source of these questions is in Zionist criticism of Jewish religion as it formed in exile.[12] Furthermore, even before the Holocaust this criticism was already being accepted by a portion of the religious Jewish public. The religious Zionists accepted this criticism, at least in part, and determined that the time had come for the Jewish people to repent in the national sense; that is, to return as a nation to Eretz Israel, to take independent action, and to found a new national life in its homeland. Based on interpretation of the signs of the times and historical trends, thinkers such as Rabbis Kalischer, Reines and A.I. Kook claimed this was God's will for his nation, meaning that the religious leadership that refuses to take "grassroots" national action for the redemption of the nation has failed and caused failure.[13] The big question, therefore, is — did this criticism gain strength in religious Zionist philosophy in the face of the Holocaust and did it arise also among those who had opposed Zionism in the past for religious reasons? Is there an obvious and recognizable expression of thought that says that the fact that the Jewish people was trapped without deliverance in the Holocaust borders on failure of the religion to fulfill its function in interpreting God's will and guiding the people? And the answer, it seems, is positive, and appears still clearer when non-Orthodox religious streams are considered.

We mentioned religious Zionism above. Its movements and leadership are usually thought of as part of the sector defined as "Orthodox" in their relation to *halakhah*. However, in its adherence to Zionist-nationalist ideology in the modern sense, and in relation to modern civilization, "secular" studies and professional employment in secular spheres, we have before us a clearly neo-Orthodox movement. Thus, on these two interconnected levels of deviation from ultra-Orthodoxy, there is an expression of recognition that the Jewish people must not only adapt its methods of education, finance, and political and cultural integration with its surroundings to fit the modern age, but it must also essentially change its outlook on its relationship to other nations and to God. The diaspora period has come to an end, and while the diaspora is indeed a "hiding of His Countenance" in terms of God's providence towards His nation, it is also a "hiding of His Countenance" of the nation itself in terms of the responsibility that the nation took for its own fate. If so, the Jewish people must first "reveal its countenance" by "returning to history," i.e., by initiating a return to national life in its land. If a very large part of the people, and especially a large part of the Jewish true believers, did not see properly the opportunities of the new age, and did not see the terrible dangers; if they did not understand what the Jewish people could do to redeem itself with the tools of modernity, which allow man an unprecedented level of control over his fate; and if they did not understand what other nations could do to them utilizing these very tools of the modern age, especially if the Jewish people did not obtain these tools for itself and become skilled in their use, then before us we have the large and difficult problem of justifying the religion.[14]

Religious Zionist thinkers, however, did not generally dare to expressly raise such a claim about the Holocaust. Yet, we can note several thinkers whose stands regarding Zionism were complex and fluctuated to extremes, and who, just before the Holocaust and some of them even during it, dealt with the severe failure of their religion to guide the people in the face of the great opportunity and frightful danger of the new age. We especially mention three original personalities among pre-Holocaust Orthodox leaders — Dr. Nathan Birnbaum,[15] Dr. Isaac Breuer,[16] and Hillel Zeitlin.[17] The first two very sharply opposed secular Zionism, but they had criticism very close to Zionism's of the ultra-Orthodox religious movement, among whose leadership they were counted. They blamed it for its unwillingness to present an initiative-taking and active national-religious alternative to Zionism. Hillel Zeitlin heaped very severe criticism on the social and national degeneration of Eastern European ultra-Orthodoxy. But we find theology focusing on criticism of religion through and after the Holocaust most prominently, on one hand, in the work of Rabbi Issachar Shlomo Teichthal, author of *Happy Mother of Children*,[18] who came from the heart of the anti-Zionist ultra-Orthodox community in Hungary, and examined himself and his community on the question of their relation to Zionism in the face of the Holocaust, and, on the other hand, by Rabbi Irving J. Greenberg,[19] who made the same self-examination after the Holocaust, and after marking the trends of ultra-Orthodox Judaism towards the modern State of Israel.

A parallel self-examination exists in the reactions of the non-Orthodox religious philosophers of "liberal Judaism." From its outset, Liberal Judaism took the stand of obligatory integration into the surrounding Western society and culture even to the point of forfeiting the people's social, political and cultural characteristics. The uniqueness of the Jewish people is its monotheistic religious-moral mission, a universal mission in whose name Liberal Judaism struggled both against Orthodoxy and against Jewish nationalism and Zionism.[20] Already in the beginning of the twentieth century, in the context of growing modern anti-Semitism in Europe and the turbulance that reached its peak in World War I and the Russian revolution, Liberal Judaism began to move toward Zionism, and this movement continued to grow stronger. We should note in this context the complex relationship between Zionism and philosophers such as Franz Rosenzweig,[21] Max Wiener[22] and Leo Baeck.[23] They also noted the fact that the Jewish religion failed in leading the Jewish people in the face of the prospects and terrible dangers of modern times. Indeed, they meant not only the failure of the Orthodox religious leadership, who, in their opinions, did not understand the demands of the times, but also the failure of Jewish theologians who also grappled with the problem of justifying their religion, not God, as the primary front of theological struggle.

In the light of these comments, we can now examine in more depth the reaction of fundamentalist Orthodoxy. On the surface, anti-Zionist ultra-Orthodoxy revealed an extraordinary level of immunity to religious self-criticism, to the point that it completely ignored the theodicy question in the special context of the Holocaust. The fundamental religious explanation is completely acceptable to ultra-Orthodoxy, without any admission of the Holocaust as an exception to the previous destructions that befell the Jewish people. The Holocaust, according to the ultra-Orthodox, was a punishment in accordance with the magnitude of the Jewish people's sin — Zionism and religious reform. It is the sin of deviating from the tolerable national norm of exile religiosity, that is, the audacity of Jews to take political initiative in order to be saved from the exile. In this respect, the Zionists and the religious reformers sinned, as did the Orthodox Jews who called for Zionism or the Emancipation. Why, then, were the believers who held fact to their extremist views also victims of the Holocaust? Surely because they were "caught up" in the collective guilt of the whole people, and certainly they were destined to receive the whole portion due to them in the next world or when the true messiah will arrive.[24]

It seems, however, that this extremism bordering on absurdity in magnifying the severity of the "sin" embodied in Zionism, even to the point of offering it as a theological explanation for the death camps and the other atrocities of the Holocaust, shows evidence that its attack is actually a form of defense, and the aggressiveness hides the confusion in the face of difficult, unanswerable questions, not only in the realm of theodicy. We mentioned above Rabbi Issachar Shlomo Teichthal's criticism in his book, *Happy Mother of Children*. What he saw revealed by history, the vindication of the Zionist prediction and the total failure of the anti-Zionist ultra-Orthodox prediction, many believers also saw, and even if they did not dare to vocalize the question, certainly it secretly weighed heavily on their hearts. At any rate, the Zionist leadership are not the respondents to whom fundamentalist criticism of the Zionist sin is addressed, and the accusations that Zionism is the sin for which we were punished by the Holocaust are not directed to the ears of Zionist circles, secular or religious. (It was clear to the ultra-Orthodox leadership from the start that they had no chance of convincing the Zionists!) Rather, it is the ultra-Orthodox public to whom the claim is directed in the extreme, in order to suppress the terrible question before it is vocalized or even felt in their hearts.

In spite of this fact, one may claim, there is apparently no external recognition of a crisis and no theological change resulting from the need to justify the religion. Is this really so? If we examine the struggle of traditional Jewish thought with the theodicy question in the presence of the waves of discrimination, persecution, expulsion and pogroms that befell the Jewish people in the Middle Ages, we can argue that the explanation based on the actual sins of the Jewish people was, for the most part, secondary. Although moralists used this explanation in order to educate the people and demand repentance, in the trying struggle with a hostile environment in a well-defined religious context (Christianity and Islam), it was nearly impossible to present the Jewish people's sins as the primary explanation for their cruel fate.[25] In comparison with the nations and religions that persecuted the Jews, it was impossible to give such weight to the Jews' sins against God. The conclusion is that already in the Middle Ages it was clear to most rabbis and thinkers that there is no "reasonable" relationship between the "sins" of the Jewish people and its sufferings. Two completely different explanations, based on recognition of the values and virtues of the Jewish people, rose instead to prime importance: a. Understanding the exile situation as one of a "hiding of His Countenance" as it relates to God's direct miracle-wielding guidance among His people, meaning that the Jewish people is abandoned to its fate among the nations, and the nations that persecute them out of the evilness of their hearts are also guilty and destined to be punished appropriately. b. Understanding the exile condition as a situation that demands martyrdom from the Jewish people, for the sake of God.[26]

Furthermore, explaining the suffering and persecution of the Chosen People as a test in which the people are collectively martyred opposes, and even contradicts, the explanation that suffering is punishment for sin. The Jewish people actually proves its righteousness and its supreme virtue among the nations and before God, thereby bringing closer the revelations of God's kingdom in the whole world, because through Jewish martyrdom all the nations will recognize the one true God.

While facing persecution and discrimination in the context of interreligious polemic and with an open path for Jews to save themselves by exchanging their religion, and with no direct physical danger of genocide (medieval Jewish thought was characterized by the certainty that God guarantees the existence of the Jewish people in exile despite all the suffering and persecution), martyrdom offered a means to justify Judaism in the argument with Christians and

Moslems. It was a sort of comforting truth, imparting exalted meaning to the suffering and obligatorily embracing the promise of reward and the absolute certainty that this suffering draws redemption closer, so that the sacrifice of martyrdom was a fitting way of dealing with the threat. We should take this traditional way of thinking as a basis for understanding the fact that with the Holocaust as an expression of racist anti-Semitism, and facing the danger of total annihilation, explanations along the lines of the "hiding of His Countenance" or martyrdom became secondary, to be replaced in anti-Zionist ultra-Orthodox circles by the fundamentalist idea of direct Divine leadership in Israel's history and of punishment for sin. It is the novelty that embodies, in a paradoxical manner, the trauma of fundamentalist theologians facing the ultra-Orthodox establishment's failure not only in guiding the entire people, most of whom had thrown off the yoke of religion (a sin, of course), but also in guiding its core of believers. It is possible to comment on this focusing — if the theodicy of the "hiding of His Countenance" and of martyrdom religion, whose strength was in guiding the people, was required to justify God, then in the theodicy that explains the Holocaust as a due punishment for a national sin, God was required, so to speak, to justify religion by claiming responsibility for deeds which are beyond justification from any ethical point of view.

The research findings presented above, that the Holocaust caused most Jews to reinforce their pre-Holocaust religious stands, serve as the basis for the assumption that belief in or denial of God is not dependent on religion's success or failure in providing a convincing theological explanation of what happened to the Jews in the Holocaust. Those who strengthened their denial of God only received reinforcement of their previous experience of human existential isolation. Over and over they saw that man can rely only on his own limited strength, on his resourcefulness and his talents, or on his morality and his social conscience in his struggle to exist and to preserve a trace of humanness.[27] Those whose belief was strengthened felt reassured that God was present for man, even, or especially, during his most difficult hour. Furthermore, without the feeling of the close presence of God, there was no reason for their existence and they could not survive physically or spiritually in the face of their sufferings. For these individuals, the fact that they succeeded in existing without losing their humanity, despite everything happening to them, was the supreme proof that God was with them in the bitterness of their suffering.[28] These primary experiences had no direct ties to the theological questions — is it possible to understand how God "allowed" these atrocities to occur? Why does He not reveal Himself and save the sufferers? Believers' testimony during the Holocaust shows that they cried out unanswered, maybe even certain that their questions had no answers, but their cry expressed their unshakable belief — despite everything. They could be angry at God, protest against Him, and even curse Him. Yet, in order for them to dispel the strength of their pain in these protests, they "had" to believe. Again we must emphasize — the types of belief expressed in diaries and other documents written during the Holocaust are within the realm of primary experience, beyond all theology, and from within this experience theology was not entreated. The attempts made to develop these paradoxical belief indicators into post-Holocaust theological teachings (literary creations, especially the lectures of Elie Wiesel, are the clearest examples of this "existential theology") did not succeed philosophically and failed to establish their religious world view as an educational message.[29]

The analysis proposed above interprets this fact as follows — the believers' faith existed even in the trial of the Holocaust as a miraculous spiritual strength from within the crisis of religion and despite it. The revelation of the faith attested to itself without providing explanations for the events that religion failed to explain. Religion, in the form of the Torah and personal and social leadership, was saved from the confusion by the great manifestations of faith of the individual. Not only did it fail to offer an explanation that served as a consoling truth from the world of the Holocaust, but it also failed to direct the suffering believers and to show them a way to deal individually and collectively with the cruel historical reality besieging them. To be exact — there is a close tie between the ability to offer a convincing solution to the theodicy problem in the form of consoling truth, and the ability to offer direction that enables individuals and a collective to cope appropriately and realistically with their cruel fate. This situation existed during the destruction of the First and Second Temples, during the failure of the Bar-Kochba revolt, and during the pogroms and persecution of the Middle Ages. The theodicy of the "hiding of His Countenance" and of martyrdom was convincing in those days because it offered meaning for the events and suffering, and it also provided a way of behaving that enabled the Jewish people to understand their situation in terms appropriate to the terms of those dictating their historical fate, and it enabled them to respond according to this understanding in a way that proved itself through the people's continued existence as the chosen people, even in exile.[30]

In this context, we will allow ourselves a general comment regarding philosophical struggle with the phenomenon of the Holocaust. The repeated claim that the Holocaust was an absolute anomaly, an event that is impossible to comprehend because it is impossible to give it meaning, stems basically from the fact that for the generation that survived the Holocaust it was, almost from the beginning, beyond the limits of probability. Even for those who foresaw the coming of terrible disasters, the Holocaust surpassed all that could be humanly expected or deemed possible.[31] Thus, when the Germans began to realize the "Final Solution," most of the victims could not comprehend the events or even realize the fact that they were happening. Moreover, they could not offer a personal or public response that could be described as adequate or "realistic." It can be said, without exaggeration, that there was a general breakdown in ideology and leadership. But apparently religion's breakdown as a leading and directing factor was particularly severe, especially if one considers the position of religion among the Jewish people throughout the historical processes preceding the Holocaust.[32] Religion was revealed as impotent, although, as stated, it was possible to note astounding expressions of impassioned belief. It seems that this fully explains non-Orthodox Jewish philosophers' recognition that the traditional answers to the problem of justifying God no longer suffice. If we delve into this claim, we see its intent. The religion that offers these explanations is incapable of guiding the Jewish people in its teachings, and individuals who continue to seek religious guidance as individual believers and as a people in modern reality must search not only for other explanations, but also for another mode of religious thought.

We must recall, however, that all these things were said from a viewpoint very close to the Holocaust as it occurred, almost from within it. The believer seeing these events or contemplating them, even after the passage of considerable time, is dumbstruck and his thoughts are silenced by the fact of the occurrences. Such actions, from within and without, seem to have no theological explanation, and it is doubtful that there is a convincing explanation in any other

284

moral world view. Yet, one must consider the fact that most of the systematic theological reactions to the Holocaust were written a relatively long time after the Holocaust,[33] and they reflect thoughts that were crystallized not only in the light of memories of the Holocaust and historical research on the topic, but also in the light of what has happened to the Jewish people and the European nations since the Holocaust. This fact is closely related to the problem of religious criticism and justification of religion. First, let us note the fact that religious thinkers from all streams of Judaism tended to delay as long as possible the publication, and possibly even the formulation, of their thought regarding the Holocaust. The decision to delve into theological discussion of the Holocaust, and the more so to publish works, involved an act of great boldness for most of the thinkers who eventually expressed their thoughts. They felt that they had to overcome very difficult intellectual and emotional obstacles and to burst the barriers that were virtually "taboo." The same recoiling on the part of the believer from approaching the realm of the holy and from saying anything about God, who is beyond comprehension, was carried over to this issue. Every approach to it approached the holy and dangerous, "Do not come closer. Remove your sandals from your feet, for the place on which you stand is holy ground" (Exodus 3:5).

It is easy to understand these inhibitions. The believer risks standing face to face with the doubt and the vulnerable points of the religious world view on which he was educated, and with the need to admit to the impotence and the flimsiness of many of the claims on which the religious view is based. He knows well that the very formulation of some questions is like a challenge of faith, even more so when searching for answers to these questions is an adventure into the realm of the unknown. Clearly, then, only the recognition that the theological struggle with the theodicy question is extremely vital and cannot be avoided can justify the theological boldness. The critical recognition is being awakened after a generation due to educational need. Whoever wants to impart the Jewish faith and religion to coming generations must answer their questions, and those individuals born and educated religiously after the Holocaust certainly will not be able to keep their questions trapped inside. A convincing answer will perhaps be their precondition to faith. But it seems that the boldness to struggle with the theological problem of the Holocaust after nearly a generation[34] came not only from feeling the need, but also from estimating that certain historical developments after the Holocaust "balanced" the terror, thus opening the positive struggle not only with the theodicy problem but perhaps foremost with the problem of justifying the religion.

For Jewish theologians from all streams other than the ultra-Orthodox, balanced development took the form primarily of the State of Israel's establishment, but also of the flourishing of Western Jewish centers that survived the Holocaust. Of course, the establishment of the State of Israel after the Holocaust did not answer the questions that arose during the Holocaust, and it must be emphasized that most of the theologians discussing the subject stood firmly on this point. Despite this, the establishment of the state provided the comforting truth that is to be found in returning to life. Furthermore, religious-Zionist thinkers who viewed the state's establishment as "the beginning of the growth of redemption," and connected it in this way to traditional theology, could find in the approval given to the Zionist principle an amendment to the problem of religion's justification and authority in the religious world view. The existence of the State of Israel thereby allows the restoration to the Jewish religion of leadership authority that copes correctly with reality. The establishment of the State of Israel after the Holocaust proves, from the religious-Zionist viewpoint, that there is help from above for the independent national redemption initiative, and that it is the Jewish people's obligation in these times not to expect God's mercy, but rather to take national responsibility and to act. But more importantly, the state gave religious Zionism a clear realm of leadership and a range of opportunities for the struggle to return the Jewish people to living under religious leadership, according to the Jewish faith and the Torah.

Thus, the events that approved and strengthened religious authority for religious Zionists intensified the religious dilemma for the anti-Zionist Orthodox. How could they see in the state's establishment the beginning of the growth of redemption? In their methodology, a secular state in the Holy Land was the victory of heresy, or in their reading, a certain sign of religion's failure! Clearly, the sharp attack on Zionism in general and on religious Zionism in particular was, as stated, self-defense against the difficult dilemma that they faced as religious leaders. But it is very doubtful if it were possible to emerge from the dilemma and to reestablish the shaken authority by venomous anti-Zionist attacks, were it not for the socio-economic, socio-political and socio-organizational rehabilitation processes of the Orthodox community in the State of Israel and the diaspora after the Holocaust. It became evident in the more favorable conditions for the Jewish people after the Holocaust, and in the light of the deep spiritual-moral crisis that befell secular Western culture, including the secular culture that developed among the Jewish people after the state's establishment,[35] that the ultra-Orthodox movement had revived and was able to offer its community frameworks, lifestyle and world view as valid answers to spiritual distress and to several of the soul-searching questions of individuals disappointed with the secular cultural vision, and maybe also from the realization of the Zionist vision. Beyond impressive community, political and economic consolidation, two phenomena at their climax today, attest to this — the phenomenon of growing "religious extremism," which strengthens the power of the anti-Zionist ultra-religious over the different varieties of neo-Orthodoxy, including Zionist neo-Orthodoxy; and the phenomenon of "born again Jews" (*baalei teshuva*), which strengthens the power of the religious, especially of the ultra-Orthodox, over the secular streams. Indeed, the phenomenon of "born-again Jews" fulfills a very vital function in Orthodox religious thought because it contains a "weighted answer" on ultra-Orthodoxy's losses to secular movements, and to the deep crisis that it underwent before and during the Holocaust. Among other things, it seems that in the cultural-historical circumstances that were created after the Holocaust and after the State of Israel's establishment, Orthodoxy succeeded in rehabilitating its spiritual and existential force, and to answer convincingly in the eyes of many the problem of "justification of religion," something that was denied it in the first half of the twentieth century. Against the religious success, ultra-Orthodox thinkers can, therefore, be bold and cope anew in their own way with the problem of justifying God in the Holocaust, and it is easy to argue that the "authority" behind these claims, which are difficult to digest yet full of extraordinary self-confidence, is none other than the recognition that in the battle over justification of religion against its critics from within and without, the ultra-Orthodox now feel they have the upper hand.

It is highly doubtful whether this is the final word. There is also doubt as to whether the success of Zionism in establishing the state, on the one hand, and the success of Orthodoxy in reviewing itself, on the other, exhaust the possible results of the great shock that overtook Western culture and the Jewish people in the second half of the twentieth century in terms of the status and authority of religion. Moreover, it appears that the basic questions regarding the issue of critique of religion, and the theological issues influenced by critique of religion, remain as difficult and decisive as ever. The answer, however, even when given out of renewed self-confidence and in the context of consciousness of the great weaknesses of the critics of religion, are doubtful and partial at best. There is no doubt that institutional shocks, confrontations, leadership, dilemmas and the distress of undermining faith still await the people of Israel and its religion, due both to historical events and to ethico-social and intellectual challenges that the religion has not yet proven its ability to overcome, nor even its innocence in the face of them.[36] There is thus no doubt that the problem of theodicy in the crisis of the Holocaust will continue to occupy Jewish theology for a long time to come.

But come what may in the future, it seems that the primacy and priority of the problem of the justification of religion, both from the point of view of its believers and within established religious frameworks, is as prominent today as it was in the first half of the century. This was and still is the source for the special, exceptional severity of the theological problem that arose in the light of the Holocaust. It is also the source of the widespread recognition that to return to the traditional solutions to the problem of theodicy is possible today only if one ignores totally their original historical context, on the one hand, and the uniqueness of the Holocaust as an event exemplifying the most awful negative processes of the modern era, on the other. Consequently, a proper understanding of the connection between the problem of the justification of religion and the problem of theodicy is still a necessary first step in dealing convincingly with the problems of theology in our time.

Notes

1. We have brought a "bunch" of questions that, in fact, present several different approaches to the subject. Only a portion of these questions present the problem of theodicy as it is discussed in traditional theological thinking. A question such as "Where was God during the

Holocaust?" deviates from the traditional context. Traditional theology focuses on the well-known question of the prophet Jeremiah, "Why do the wicked flourish?" or in a later formulation, how is it possible that "the righteous man suffers while the wicked man flourishes?" Nonetheless, those questions that point up doubts concerning both Divine justice and God's mastery and leadership of the universe remain within the framework of traditional discussion.

2. R.R. Brenner, *The Faith and Doubt of Holocaust Survivors* (New York, London: The Free Press, 1980).

3. The process of formulating these views is reflected in a long list of works written from within this intensifying struggle of the ultra-Orthodox and Agudat Israel believers against Zionism, especially religious Zionism. A representative collection of such works is *The Influence of the Holocaust on Jewish Thought* (Hebrew), Gershon Greenberg, ed. (Jerusalem: Akademon, 1987). Two more books that summarize and update these stands on the Holocaust have recently been published: Rabbi Yoel Schwartz and Rabbi Yitzhak Goldstein, eds., *The Holocaust* (Jerusalem: Davar, 1987); Rabbi Nisson Wolpin, ed. (New York: Mesorah Publications, 1986).

4. For the sake of exactness, we must note that the claim that the ways of God are hidden from human comprehension is reiterated in theological thought dealing with the Holocaust, especially from Orthodox and even neo-Orthodox points of view. Except for the radical ultra-Orthodox reaction that presumes to "understand" the terrible punishment, this claim is not accepted as a solution capable of halting the protest and the anger. This fact already embodies a questioning of the traditional theological perception of the relationship between God and man, but of course only theologians who have left the Orthodox framework can allow themselves such a clear formulation of the changes in the understanding of the concept of divinity and of God's relationship to the world and to man. Two interesting cases are those of two thinkers who stand in both worlds — Orthodoxy and yet beyond Orthodoxy theology: Irving Greenberg, "The Third Great Cycle in Jewish History," *Perspectives* (September 1981); Andre Neher, *The Exile of the Word, from the Silence of the Bible to the Silence of Auschwitz* (Philadelphia: Jewish Publication Society, 1981).

5. Spinoza's views on religion, its positive functions and its great dangers are presented in his famous work, *Theological Political Tractate*. See especially ch. 19 of this book.

6. There are those who claim that Marxism itself spread as a sort of alternative religion and hence the intensity of its battle against religion. While there is a certain parallelism between Marxism and religion, this identification is exceedingly simplistic. In any event, Marxists see religion not only as a fraud of the priests, but also as one of the major obstacles to the spread of class consciousness among the proletariat, and thus as an obstacle to social revolution. See Karl Marx, *On the Jewish Question*, in Karl Marx, *Selected Writings*, David McLellan, ed. (London: Oxford University Press, 1977), pp. 39-63.

7. In our time, this mood is stronger and more prominent than the mood of doing battle against religion. This is one of the results of the ethico-spiritual crisis that has overtaken secular culture, particularly since World War II. We emphasize, however, that this is truly a "mood," and not fully crystallized world views, since world views built upon this mood lead logically to attempts to return to faith and religion, and such attempts are, it seems, manifold and well-known. We mention the well-known work by Victor Frankl, *Man's Search for Meaning* (Boston: Beacon Press, 1968).

8. A considerable amount of literature exists on the subject. We shall mention just a few: *When God and Man Failed*, ed. Harry James Cargas (New York: Macmillan, 1981); *Auschwitz: The Beginning of a New Era?*, ed. Eva Fleischner (New York: Ktav, 1977); *Human Responses to the Holocaust*, ed. Michael D. Ryan (Lewiston, New York: Edwin Mellen Press, 1981); *The Holocaust: Ideology, Bureaucracy, and Genocide*, Henry Friedlander and Sybil Milton, eds. (Millwood, New York: Kraus, 1980).

9. For a study of this issue, see Fleischner, *ibid.*

10. See his collection of essays: Richard Rubenstein, *After Auschwitz* (Indianapolis: Bobbs-Merrill, 1966).

11. This perception of monotheistic religions as religions removing the holy from nature and opening the way for unlimited manipulative human control over nature is influenced by the secular perception developed in the Protestant theology of Harvey Cox. See Harvey Cox, *The Secular City: The Biblical Sources of Secularization* (New York, 1965), pp. 17-30.

12. Secular Zionism openly attacked the diaspora view that the Jewish people must bear their fate of exile and advance the redemption only by prayer and fulfillment of the commandments, in the expectation of

miraculous redemption. This is a basic motif in classic secular Zionist writings, and a central element in the theory of "negation of the exile." See Yehezkel Kaufmann, *Exile and Foreignness* (Hebrew), vol. 2 (Tel Aviv: Dvir, 1961), ch. 10.

13. Rabbi Kalischer abstained from open criticism of the religious leadership. After the problem of Zionism became a focus for sharp confrontation between anti-Zionist Orthodoxy and the religious Zionist movement, however, the criticism was made in a very open manner. Rabbi A.I. Kook, for example, saw the way in which the Jewish "Law" (*Dath*) had crystallized as a clear product of the exile, and although he justified this process at its inception, he saw it as a corrupting factor in the modern era. He thus adapted for himself the critique of religion of the secular proponents of the "negation of the exile." Particularly interesting in this respect is the article: "To the Course of Ideas in Israel" (Hebrew), in *Orot* (Jerusalem: Mossad Harav Kook, 1961). Also see E. Schweid, *The Land of Israel — National Home or Land of Destiny* (New York: Herzl Press, 1985), Part IV, ch. 4, pp. 171-187.

14. On this problem in general, see Ehud Luz, *Parallels Meet* (Hebrew) (Tel Aviv: Am Oved, 1985).

15. As is well known, Dr. Nathan Birnbaum (Vienna, 1864 – Scheveningen, 1937) went through several ideological metamorphoses before he finally became one of the spiritual leaders of Agudat Yisrael. But even when he had "stabilized" in his religious-Orthodox world view, he was not deprived of his critical independence. He was one of the first to warn of the dangers threatening the Jewish people in Europe immediately after World War I and the Russian Revolution. He understood that the Jewish people was liable to pay the price of the unsolved national and social problems, and demanded unification and organization for national salvation. In this context he not only criticized the complacency of the leaders of other movements, but also criticized Orthodoxy for not understanding the signs of the times and not leading the Jewish people as required in the correct direction, the brave venture toward redemption. It is clear that to him this was a severe problem, requiring in itself what we define as "critique of religion." I have dealt with this matter extensively in my article, "Toward Investigation of the Thinking of Dr. Nathan Birnbaum on Zionism" (Hebrew), to be published in the book from the conference on "Zionism and its Opponents," held at the Hebrew University in December 1987.

16. Dr. Isaac Breuer (Papa, Hungary, 1883 – Jerusalem, 1946) was even sharper than Dr. Birnbaum in his criticism of the established Orthodoxy in Agudat Yisrael. On one hand, he saw it as the sole representative of true Torah Judaism. On the other hand, he blamed it for lagging behind secular Zionism in understanding the messianic meaning of the historic hour (between the two World Wars), both in terms of seeing the dangers lying in wait for the Jewish people and in terms of the possibility of renewing the Kingdom of Israel in Eretz Israel according to the Torah. He demanded of Agudat Yisrael, in fact, that it take upon itself the role that Herzl Zionism had taken, thus again internalizing Zionism's critique of religion. See Isaac Breuer, *Concepts of Judaism*, ed. Jacob S. Levinger (Jerusalem, 1974).

17. Hillel Zeitlin (Korma, Russia, 1871 – en route to Treblinka, 1942) expressed from the start of his career as a publicist the fear of a great disaster about to befall the Jewish people. This fear was what diverted him during a certain period toward the idea of Uganda and Jewish territorialism. He never ceased to seek ways to save the people and its Torah faith. His final articles contain, together with enthusiastic devotion to the original Hassidism, very severe criticism of Jewish society as a whole, including the religious community and leadership. Here, too, there is a clear motif of critique of religion by one of its devoted and enthusiastic sons. Indeed, the history of Hillel Zeitlin's toils and troubles for internal renewal of the Jewish religion in order to save the Jewish people and for the sake of its Torah is worthy of a comprehensive study which has not yet been written.

18. This book, *Em Habanim S'mechah* (*Happy Mother of Children*), was first published in Hebrew in Budapest in 1943. A second edition was published in New York in 1969 and a third in Jerusalem in 1982. Pesach Schindler has prepared an edited, annotated English translation (forthcoming). In order to understand the important meaning of the book, one should note when it appeared, three months before the Nazi conquest of Hungary, and its author, a great scholar and head of a yeshiva in Budapest, and a Hassidic follower of the Rabbi of Munkacs. In other words, he was a scholar rooted in the ultra-Orthodox, anti-Zionist public, who had done his own reckoning with the ultra-Orthodox stance toward Zionism in light of the Holocaust. The book generated a great tempest within the ultra-Orthodox community on account of its critical nature, and it undoubtedly contains a piercing critique of religion.

19. Rabbi Yitzhak (Irving) Greenberg is one of the outstanding thinkers representing the "Left" in American neo-Orthodoxy today. The Holocaust and the establishment of the State of Israel are two of the

fundamental themes in his theology. In his opinion, the Jewish people have entered a new era, which requires a far-reaching change in the understanding of the relationships between God and man and between God and the Jewish people. This change imposes responsibility for history upon the nations, and among the nations upon Israel. Consequently, religion as it crystallized in the era before the Holocaust and before the establishment of the State of Israel no longer explains reality correctly and does not lead the people down the correct path. See his article mentioned in n. 4, as well as his article, "Cloud of Smoke, Pillar of Fire: Judaism, Christianity and Modernity after the Holocaust," printed in the anthology edited by Eva Fleischner, n. 8 above.

20. This episode is well known and extensively researched. A typical example of an anti-Zionist stance from a Jewish Reform point of view can be found in an article by Rabbi Henry Berkowitz, "Why I am not a Zionist," in the *Yearbook of the Central Conference of American Rabbis* (1899). An in-depth, theoretical formulation of the anti-Zionist stance can be found in the writings of Hermann Cohen, gathered in the second collection of his articles, which was published in Hebrew under the title, "Studies in Judaism and the Problems of the Generations" (Hebrew) (Jerusalem: Bialik Institute, 1978). On the theoretical background of this stance, see my book, *History of Jewish Thought in the Modern Era* (Hebrew) (Jerusalem: Kibbutz Hameuhad and Keter, 1978), ch. 7.

21. Researchers of the thoughts of Rosenzweig (Kassel, 1886 – Frankfurt, 1929) have tended to depict his stance as anti-Zionist, and close to that of his teacher, Hermann Cohen. Afterwards, they have pointed to a change in his stance after he became close to Martin Buber and became familiar with the cultural Zionist views of Ahad Haam. A study of his letters and journals, however, shows that even at the beginning of his return to faith and a Jewish way of life, he related sympathetically to certain basic elements of Zionism. His criticism of Liberal Judaism isolates a tendency in a Zionistic-spiritual direction, since Rosenzweig's concept of Judaism stresses greatly the aspect of belonging to the nation. See recently, *Franz Rosenzweig: Selected Letters and Journal Passages* (Hebrew), ed. Rivka Hurvitz (Jerusalem: Bialik Institute, 1987).

22. Max Wiener (Oppeln, Germany, 1882 – New York, 1950) was known particularly for his scholarly study, *Judische Religion in Zeitalter der Emanzipation* (Berlin, 1933). But within the framework of Liberal Judaism, he formulated his own view, which was distinguished by its piercing criticism of the Liberal Jewish approach both to Jewish

nationhood and to *halakhah*. His clear turning towards Zionism can already be seen. See Yehoshua Amir, "Max Wiener and his Work" (Hebrew), in the introduction to the Hebrew translation of the above book (Jerusalem: Bialik Institute, 1974).

23. Leo Baeck (Lissa, Poznan 1873 – London, 1956) was the outstanding spiritual leader of German Jewry during the period of the Holocaust. In his first great essay, "Das Wesen des Judentums," published in 1905, the importance of belonging to the nation is already recognized. After the Holocaust, however, this trend was strengthened still further, as his final work, *Dieses Volk*, which was published in 1955, attests. This book, indeed, attests to his drawing very close to Zionism.

24. The motif of the eternity of the soul and the rewarding of the righteous in the world to come is, of course, a central foundation of the theodicy of the ultra-Orthodox, who emphasize this motif greatly. In their view, this belief "neutralizes" to a great extent the horror of the destruction from the point of view of the innocent victims. This point is keenly felt in the essay, "The Holocaust," n. 3 above.

25. This motif of inability to accept the explanation found in the sins of the people, when its deeds are compared with the deeds of other nations who conquer and flourish, can already be recognized very clearly in Jewish literature after the destruction of the Second Temple. The book of *The Vision of Ezra* (*Hazon Ezra*), from the Apocrypha, is typical in this matter, but these things can also be recognized in Rabbinic writings. As for the Middle Ages, the explanations of Rabbi Judah Halevi in his book, *The Kuzari*, and the writings of Maimonides in the "Epistle to Yemen" should be emphasized. Despite the many differences between them, neither emphasizes the sins of Israel, but rather the great struggle against idolatry. In other words, the Jews' suffering is explained in terms of the idolaters' search for ever more severe ways to struggle against the truth to which the Jewish people attest.

26. "Hiding of His Countenance" (*hester panim*) is, of course, punishment. It is expressed, however, in God's "abandoning" His people and not saving them from the cruelty of their persecutors, who yet bear responsibility for their cruelty and will be called to judgment for it. It should also be emphasized that even in conditions of "hiding of His Countenance," the "hidden miracle" is maintained — the nations will never succeed in wiping Israel out, and an opening to salvation will always be found for the Jewish people in its troubles. As opposed to "hiding of His Countenance," the ideal of martyrdom offers a

positive explanation. In their very suffering, the Jewish people give testimony to its faith and thus bring nearer the spreading of the knowledge of truth and redemption among humankind.

27. A clear, exhaustive expression in this vein is the work of Jean Amery, especially *Radical Humanism* (Bloomington: Indiana University Press, 1984). See also the work of Reeve Brenner, n. 2 above, which provides answers of Holocaust survivors to these questions.

28. One of the outstanding testimonies to burning faith in the face of the Holocaust is the diary of Etty Hillesum, *Het Verstoode Leven* (Bussum: De Haan/Unieboek BV, 1981). There are many such testimonies, e.g., R. Klonimus Kelmish Shapiro, *Esh Kodesh* (*Holy Fire*) (Jerusalem: Yad Vashem, 1969); Rene Weill, *Yes, I Remember* (Jerusalem: WZO, 1983).

29. The theology of rebellion and protest has great charm, but it does not appear to be possible to base on this sort of theology a religious education that brings about a commitment to a religious way of life. For this reason, it is the fate of such theologies to remain expressions solely of the personal belief of individuals. Proof of this fact can be provided by examination of several theological essays written after the Holocaust proposing a basis for religious education, whether from the Liberal stream or the neo-Orthodox. For such movements, two solutions are possible — either in that man is wholly responsible for his fate on earth, and Divine providence can come about only in the sense that God's command is fulfilled in the deeds of men; or in "hiding of His Countenance" and the limitations of man's ability to understand, such as in the well-known work of Rabbi Eliezer Berkovits, *Faith After the Holocaust* (New York: Ktav, 1973).

30. The clearest proof is that the concept of martyrdom took on not only a theological and moralistic expression, but also a consideration, determining normatively how the collective and the individual must behave in situations of repression. All these discussions weighed well the prospects of survival both for the collective and the individuals in exile.

31. Several of the greatest leaders of Zionism foresaw an unprecedented disaster, based on an analysis of the historical processes, and there were people who spoke the language of prophets of doom, such as Zeev Jabotinsky, Uri Zvi Greenberg, Hillel Zeitlin and others. But that which actually did happen, the systematic destruction of six million in the death camps, no one could have imagined before the actual events.

32. It seems that it could be determined that from the last decades of the nineteenth century and throughout the first half of the twentieth century, the Jewish religion in its Orthodox forms was in a constant process of retreat. The secular public grew continuously. A large portion of the sons who had grown up in religious families threw off the yoke of religion, and it was the non-religious or non-Orthodox movements that actually led the Jewish people on the social or national level. This was the basis for the self-assured forecast of the secular movements that the hour of religion had passed, its disappearance a necessary consequence of the processes of cultural advance. This fact, of course, influenced the self-image of the religious public, which saw itself as besieged and helpless. See the chapters collected in the source book edited by Prof. Gershon Greenberg, n. 3 above.

33. During the last decade, a very broad body of theological literature has been written dealing with the Holocaust, especially in the United States, and it could be said that interest in this subject is currently at its climax. This is, however, an explicitly reflexive reaction, belated and delayed, and even thinkers who passed through the Holocaust, outstanding among them is Emil Fackenheim, did not begin to crystallize and express their thoughts on the Holocaust until about twenty years after it.

34. The term of "a passing generation" is possibly the explanation for the phenomenon cited in n. 33. Setting aside the understandable emotional need to delay the theoretical reaction and to defer it before the more pressing need to give testimony, the awakening of theoretical reaction stems from confronting the questions of the younger generation.

35. On the roots of the crisis that overtook secular culture in the State of Israel, see my book, *Judaism and Secular Culture* (Hebrew) (Tel Aviv: Hakibbutz Hameuhad, 1983). See particularly ch. 8 of this book. In general, it should be noted that actually after the Holocaust and after the establishment of the State of Israel, there was a marked revival in the Orthodox religious movements. Now religious believers are not alone in the view that in the "crisis of values" visited upon secular Western culture, the humanistic movements have lost their authority, and only religious movements are capable of offering authoritative answers and leadership.

36. The issue of the "innocence" of religion as a cause of ethical and social distortions apparently ceased to be a subject for discussion due to the crisis of values in secular culture, particularly after the ethical consequences of Communist-Marxist rule became clear. Today, how-

ever, with the rise of extremist religious movements in Islam, Christianity and Judaism, this issue is again coming under discussion. Among the Jewish people and in the State of Israel, this discussion now focuses on contending with the messianic basis of extreme religious Zionism, on the one hand, and on the other, with the non-Zionist, non-humanistic or non-democratic bases that show up in the struggle of Orthodoxy for influence in the State of Israel. It seems, therefore, that there is a basis for the prediction that this issue will come up again, and not only in debate between religious and secular camps, but also as a debate within the religious community and among its various streams.

Chapter 7

THE SPANISH EXILE AND THE HOLOCAUST: A STUDY IN JEWISH SPIRITUAL RESPONSE TO CATASTROPHE

Jewish scholars and philosophers who deal with the subject of the Holocaust are in general accord that it is not valid to compare that event to any other persecution of the Jewish people in generations past. Several years before the Nazis began to systematically carry out the "Final Solution," many recognized that the Jewish people was facing a calamity unprecedented in its history so laden with suffering, destruction, exile, expulsion, and pogroms. This realization was confirmed after the reports of what had happened in the ghettos and the destruction camps were verified.

It is true, nonetheless, that many Jews tried to assuage their anguish by recalling the endurance of their people in times of past catastrophes; religious Jews in particular sought both solace and strength in this fashion. Rabbi Leo Baeck, the leader of the Jews of Germany from the time of Hitler's rise to power until Baeck was sent to the Theresienstadt concentration camp, compared the Nazi decrees to those of the Spanish expulsion. At the first meeting of the Reichsvertretung (representative body of German Jews), of which he was chosen president, he asserted with conviction: the history of the Jewish people in Germany has come to an end. The "end" he envisioned may be inferred from a letter that he wrote some time earlier. In his opinion, the Jewish people was facing the same alternatives it had confronted after the destruction of Betar and after the expulsion from Spain. "The Jewish people have ancient eyes," he said to a friend, expressing his certainty that the people which had experienced many dire calamities in its history and had overcome them would surmount this one as well. For Baeck, this was not empty rhetoric; he formulated his policies as the leader of German Jewry on the basis of that forecast.

It would seem that Baeck was not alone among the Jewish leaders of this generation to reach this conclusion. Even those who understood that this calamity would be far greater than its predecessors, saw the difference in terms of quantity but not of quality. However, when war broke out and the Nazi army overran Poland, it was apparent that this was an event without precedent. All the responses made by the Jews, based on their memories of times past, including the period of World War I, proved to be useless encumbrances. The Nazi conquerors had no intention of permitting the conquered populations, particularly not the Jews, to return to any form of normal life. No one could anticipate what the next decree would bring, or how one should prepare for it. If at the beginning of the Nazi conquest the situation seemed unbearable, each day that passed actually increased the burden. It is not surprising, therefore, that when the results of the Holocaust became apparent, a consensus was reached that it was not to be compared to any earlier attempt at genocide.

Although debate continues regarding Emil Fackenheim's view of the absolutely *sui generis* dimensions of the Holocaust, sensitivity regarding comparisons that lead directly or indirectly to the dwarfing of the Nazi crime and to its "normalization" as a military or just another political crime, is too great to permit any easy comparisons to be made. Comparison with an event like the Spanish expulsion is even more difficult, for the latter was not an utter destruction. The kings of Spain and Portugal did not suffer Jews in their lands, and sought a "ritual solution" to the "Jewish question" which had been of concern to the Crown, the Church, and the people of Spain for several generations. The suffering of the exiles, many of whom died during their wanderings, was indeed appalling — but they were given real choices to live, either as converts or as exiles. And many of them survived and rebuilt their lives in countries which offered them a refuge.

If we seek an event in modern Jewish history that may be compared to the Spanish expulsion, and attempt to analyze the responses of the Jewish people to each of them, we would, it seems, have to choose the deeds of the despotic regimes in Russia in the time of the Czars, and in the days of Lenin and Stalin. These led, on one hand, to the forced migration of millions of Jews, and on the other hand, to the creation of a population of millions of involuntary "converts" of a new type. But on what basis would we compare the expulsion from Spain and the Holocaust? It would seem that one could only point to differences!

Having reached that conclusion, we may suggest that a comparison may perhaps be made on the basis of category. One could say that the expulsion from Spain and the Holocaust could be grouped with such calamities as the devastation of Eretz Israel in the days of Bar-Kochba, and the destruction of the First and Second Temples. All these events share a common national criterion — each destroyed the largest and perhaps the most influential Jewish center of its time, and resulted in undermining the faith which sustained the people's hope for a stable existence among the nations. In other words, these were not merely severe catastrophes; they marked the dissolution of the very basis of nationhood, and effectuated a total change in the status of the Jewish people within the society on which its existence was dependent.

One can, nevertheless, argue that, even in terms of such broad classification, a comparison of the national situation following the expulsion from Spain and that which prevailed after the destruction of the First Temple, the subjugation of the Bar-Kochba revolt, and certainly after the Holocaust, still remains questionable. The expulsion from Spain did not change the framework that determined the status of the Jewish people under Christian or Muslim rule. Similar events had occurred previously; the Jewish people could truly look upon that expulsion with "ancient eyes." It is true that it was the largest expulsion of all, but others had preceded it. For several generations the Jews had lived under the tension of the struggle for their continued residence in Christian Spain. During that entire period they had not been permitted to forget for even one moment their legal and political position under the Christian regime, that is, the conditions under which they were "tolerated" by the Crown, and what threatened them if they became more bothersome than useful. Thus, they could not look upon their expulsion as something surprising or unforeseen. The events that led, finally, to expulsion were of long duration, and the expulsion of Jews, who were considered to be chattels of the rulers, was not considered an illegal act in the medieval European Christian world. Quite the contrary, from the viewpoint of the Church it was an act of piety, in addition to serving the interests of the Crown. The fact that the decree of expulsion uprooted a large population that had been integrated in Spain for centuries, was well-rooted in the economic, political, scientific, and cultural life of that land, and had many achievements to its credit in all those areas, made it particularly upsetting and destructive. However, since several new diasporas opened their doors to the exiles and permitted them to rebuild their lives, one could claim, in the end, that it was but another dark chapter in their history — perhaps one of the darkest. But, again, we must return to the comparison with the Holocaust. Despite the fact that the Spanish expulsion did not effect an essential change in the political-religious status of the Jews in the Muslim and Christian diaspora, the exiles were required to take particular stock of themselves. There were many reasons for them to do so. Why? First, for the very reason that the expulsion had followed earlier ones; because the expulsion of Jews was a permanent element in the policy of Christian rulers toward Jews; because the Jews knew that they had to avoid making mistakes that might lead, in the end, to a similar result; because they struggled, ostensibly with open eyes, with the complicated problem of their relationship with the surrounding society, and invested in and made an extraordinary contribution to the interests of the country in which they resided — particularly to its ruling class — while they simultaneously strengthened their position and developed their own creativity; because this tremendous effort seemed so close to achieving impressive success, and despite this it ended, once again, in such a complete and crushing failure. For all these reasons, it was impossible to respond to this expulsion in the hackneyed terms used in the past. It constituted a shattering crisis of leadership, pointing to a serious error or great sin. Once again it was clear that the Jewish leadership had not learned its lesson, and had not adequately foreseen what was happening. The Jews, therefore, had to take stock lest, after the rehabilitation of the exiles in the new lands of their refuge, the catastrophe would reoccur.

* * *

A study of the literature written by the sages among the Spanish exiles, such as R. Joseph Jabez, R. Isaac Abravanel, or R. Solomon Ibn Verga, indeed reveals such efforts. This is reflected in the words of rebuke and admonition of Jabez that reflect a heavy sense of guilt about the sins of the wealthy and educated Jews who had cast off the burden of Torah and commandments. One may say that there was nothing new in such a reaction; it was merely a continuation of the severe criticism of the intelligentsia and of those who presented themselves as philosophers, students of Maimonides, that was expressed by the rabbis in Spain. But R. Solomon Ibn Verga, author of the influential *Shevet Yehudah*, reveals a different critical approach that evinces elements of a sociological, political, and even psychological analysis. One must note that Ibn Verga does not come up with his innovative, ironical explanation of the expulsion because he viewed it as an unprecedented event. Quite the contrary. His primary concern is to confront his readers brutally with the knowledge of how very foreseeable their fate was, on the basis of innumerable precedents. The ironic criticism is self-evident. The people, persecuted, exiled, and suffering, continue to behave as in the past.

The question that concerned Ibn Verga was truly innovative: What is the social and political source of the hatred of the Jews? In what way does the behavior of the Jews cause this? What is their mistake? And why do they so stubbornly refuse to learn their lesson? Evidently he hoped that this time the lesson would be thoroughly learned. Indeed, the innovative, even modern, element in Ibn Verga's words was also apparent in the writings of other contemporaneous Jews, particularly among those who were influenced by the Italian Renaissance. Ibn Verga was moving, in his response to the expulsion, toward the approach that would be adopted by the Jewish philosophers of the Enlightenment period and thereafter, who had enough of the traditional Jewish responses to repeated discriminations, restrictions, decrees, and pogroms, who were aware of the uselessness of all those responses, and who sought to escape the magic circle of repeated tragedies by learning the correct responses, and who sought to escape the magic circle of repeated tragedies by learning the correct historic lesson. Nonetheless, while this comparison brings us closer to the modern syndrome of struggling with the "Jewish problem" against the background of the Holocaust, there is still no analogy with the events of the Holocaust, and with the response that was required after that trauma.

We shall, perhaps, come closer to a fruitful comparison if we analyze the responses of R. Shlomo Ibn Verga, R. Isaac Abravanel, and others more thoroughly within the specific historic situation in which the expulsion from Spain occurred. We know that the rulers of Spain decided upon the expulsion primarily, but not solely, because of their unwillingness to permit Jews who openly identified themselves as such to remain in their land. The expulsion was to bring about a final solution to the problem of the Marranos. In order to ensure that Jewish converts would wholeheartedly accept Christianity and become true Spaniards, it was necessary to uproot the Jewish communities, for it was clear that as long as these continued to exist in Spain, there would be financial aid and psychological support for those who converted but continued to identify secretly as Jews.

The Jews had penetrated deeply and extensively into the economic, social, political, cultural, and even religious networks in Spain without losing their separate identity, and without giving up their reservations and estrangement from the religious core that was so central to Spanish (and to Jewish) identity. Those who remained openly Jewish succeeded in penetrating more deeply into the non-Jewish society in Spain than in any other Christian country of that period. Those who converted in great numbers were even more successful in this sense, and the fact that they continued to remain alien to Christianity in secret, despite all the Inquisition's efforts to find, punish, and compel them to be proper Christians, was intolerable to the secular and ecclesiastical rulers of Spain, as well as to the population at large. It was the conspicuous prominence of the Jew as the "other," who appeared critical and threatening within the sociocultural life of the Christian majority, that led to the desire to reach a "final solution."

This perception allows for a comparison to be made with the syndrome of Jewish-German relations that constituted the background for the anti-Semitic, racist ideology of the Nazis, and with the blatant Nazi goal to extirpate the Jews from their midst. (It must be remembered that for some time the Nazis were prepared to content themselves with expelling all the Jews from their land, and until then the above-mentioned prognosis of Leo Baeck was not groundless.) Several relevant factors contribute to this comparison:

1) The successful integration of wealthy and educated Jews is evident in the central and influential roles they played in the economic, political, and cultural-scientific life of Spain, and particularly in the numbers of converts who soon became subjects equal to the other urban subjects of the Spanish Crown and Church. This syndrome to some extent conjures up the Enlightenment, the struggle for Emancipation, the endeavor of the Jews to breach the ghetto walls and achieve acceptance in the open society, and the fact that despite their willingness to pay the price of converting without inner spiritual conviction, they remained "other" and surrounded by hatred.

2) Hatred of the Jews assumed a new dimension in Spain, bearing some similarity to racial anti-Semitism. It was a hatred rooted in

religion, but the stubbornness of the converts to remain Jews in secret generated a racial metamorphosis which was given clear expression in the denigrating epithet "Marranos" (pigs). It seems that one who was born a Jew, remained a Jew; not even the baptismal font had a beneficial effect on him. Jewishness was an inherent trait, and it appears that it was, in essence, characteristic of an inferior human being.

3) Because of the number of Jews in Spain, the extent of their integration, and their failure to assimilate despite the desire to strike roots in the country, the problem of the Spanish Jews, like that of the German Jews, became an issue which was overly burdensome to the Spanish people and rulers. At a certain point it seems that, primarily because of ideological-religious motivations, the Spanish regime assigned the highest priority to the solution of this problem, to the extent that it was even prepared to sacrifice other essential interests of the Crown, in order to rid himself of this problem once and for all.

* * *

All these factors, which certainly influenced the response of the Jewish people, may point to the relevance of a comparison between the Spanish Expulsion and the Holocaust; but we must again emphasize the essential differences in the *effects* of these two traumatic events, which contributed importantly to the formulation of the differing responses. We have noted that the rootedness of the wealthy and educated Jews and the integration of the Marranos in Spanish society conjure up the Emancipation. But is it correct to appropriate that term when discussing pre-expulsion Spain? It is a borrowed term and may be misleading. From the viewpoint of the rulers, that is, of the law, there was no change in the status of the Jews; this is evident in the widespread phenomenon of converts. There is, indeed, something similar about the desire of wealthy and educated Jews to escape the limiting and degrading position imposed upon them, but their status remained unchanged. Any thought of change on the part of the Christian society was focused entirely upon the search for effective ways to impress the views of the Church and the Crown upon the Jews. The success of individual Jews (and they *were* individuals, although not so few in number) in achieving economic, social, political, and cultural positions beyond that which was permitted by the Church, was in effect an illegal act or the circumvention of a law that was not fully carried out or properly observed. The rulers, for reasons of their own, tended to permit this as long as it was to their interest, but the Church watched like a hawk, protested, pressured, and encouraged pogroms against the Jews, and the Crown eventually gave in to the ecclesiastical demands. It would thus be absurd were we to present the forced conversion of many Spanish Jews as a form of "emancipation." The Jew who converted, for the most part against his will and not out of free choice, remained a "New Christian," and as such was under suspicion, under supervision, and in effect persecuted. In any event, the masses of Jews in their communities remained in their basic condition of exile — dependent upon the good will of the king, restricted, disadvantaged, and debased. There is no emancipation without a change in the law which defines the status of the Jews. This is also true with regard to the inner process of emancipation. A limited social group sought to acquire a general education that would be socio-economically functional within the Spanish society, but the masses of Jews retained their loyalty to the rabbinic leadership, to traditional religious education, and to a lifestyle of Torah and commandments.

An important element influencing Spanish Jewry's response to the tragedy that befell them was the fact that the traditional Jewish community in Spain preserved its inner strength and remained the sole basic organizational form of Spanish Jewry. This was of crucial importance to the converts who wished to retain their identity as Jews. It is true that the Jewish *kehillot* in Spain were shaken by tremendous social and spiritual struggles. It is also true that the *kehillah* underwent organizational changes in its internal leadership, in the face it presented to the general society, and especially in the forms of inter-*kehillah* organization for the purpose of contacts with the rulers. But the fact that the community remained the framework which encompassed all the Jews who did not convert, that its legal authority remained binding upon all the Jews, and that it was the only arena for Jewish social and spiritual-religious activity, was a determining influence in Spanish Jewry. No competitive framework appeared, and the efficacy of the *kehillah* was fully recognized. Furthermore, within the *kehillah* the leadership remained constant — the same traditional-religious rabbis and scholars who observed Jewish law. Although they had to struggle against the pressure of wealthy Jews who occupied public positions, in the eyes of the Jews at large the role of the rabbis as leaders of the community was not undermined. This was a factor of great importance before, during, and after the exile. The consolidated *kehillah* was the framework which responded as the representative of the Jewish people. It must be emphasized that this was also true of the *kehillot* in the lands which helped to settle and rebuild the lives of the exiles. The *kehillot* created a viable network of structures for the Jewish people; the rehabilitation of the exiles was accomplished by revitalizing the community organizations to which they had remained absolutely loyal.

This was not true of Jewish life in Germany, nor even in Eastern Europe, before, during, and after the Holocaust. It is recognized that the destruction of the traditional *kehillah* was one of the first results of the struggle for emancipation. In place of that all-encompassing framework, new local, national, and international institutions were created, whose functions grew in importance in the struggle for pan-Jewish interests. Only the selective, closed, sectarian framework of the ultra-Orthodox remained as a complete way of life. The forced return of the Jews to the old *kehillah* frameworks — in Nazi-created ghettos — only underscored the severity of the destructive process. People who were strangers to one another socially and culturally were forced to live together within a crowded and oppressive framework, under an imposed leadership which did not represent them, and which was not meant to serve Jewish life, but to carry out the sadistic and bloodthirsty goals of the Nazi rule. One must also note that the response of the Jews who lived outside the area of Nazi conquest was not channeled through the *kehillah*; other frameworks represented the Jewish people and directed its response. Although in the end the *kehillot* were also required to make their contribution to the absorption of the refugees, they neither initiated nor channeled the Jewish people's response to the Holocaust.

Yet another element differentiates the motivations, ideology, and purposes of the regime which decreed the exile from Spain from that of the Holocaust. In both cases extreme hatred of the Jews was apparent, based on the desire to eject the stranger who had penetrated within; in both cases ideological hatred made the "Final Solution" the priority goal of the state. But one cannot ignore the fact that, despite the quasi-racial designation "Marranos," in Spain the religious factor was decisive. It was precisely in order to absorb and assimilate the converts that those who remained Jews openly were exiled — and even they were given the choice of conversion.

307

Moreover, the Jew remained a human being in the eyes of the Spanish Christians; not even the Church had the right to murder Jews without a trial. The moral constraints applied to Jews were not the same as those applied to Christians, but they were not completely abandoned. That is to say, in addition to practical considerations, moral-religious constraints limited the only final solution that could be considered to that of exile, rather than destruction. To this we must add that the bulk of the Jews were permitted to leave Spain with part of their possessions, and that they immediately found countries of refuge which helped them rebuild their lives. Thus, we may assuredly say that the relations between Jews and non-Jews (Christians and Muslims) at the time of the Spanish exile cannot be compared with those apparent during the period of the Holocaust, when a noose of hatred and alienation was tightened around the Jews.

In summation: while the situation of the Jews in Europe, particularly Germany, was temporarily improved by the Emancipation, this was not true of Spanish Jewry before the exile. The Jews of Spain did not pay the price of the loss of their *kehillah* and Jewish identity, as did the Jews of Germany, and the change in the condition of the Spanish Jews following their exile was not as extreme and decisive as it was after the Holocaust.

That the elements which gave the Holocaust the characteristics of an event without precedent were not present in Spain is testified to in the way the Spanish exile was retained in the historic consciousness of the Jewish people — not as an unusual event, but as another one of the persecutions or destructions which befell the Jewish people in exile. Nor was it considered as an event that marked the end or the beginning of a period in Jewish history. No one suggested that a particular day of remembrance should mark the Spanish exile, and certainly no one thought that the memory of the exile should become an element in historic Jewish consciousness throughout all generations. The memory was retained, and was transmitted from generation to generation as part of the genealogical record of a large Jewish community which remained proud of its origins and glowing past. For the members of that community, their origins in Spain (but not necessarily the fact of their exile) was an element in their Jewish identity, and at times even became a justification for their snobbish differentiation from all other Jews. In any event, it was pride in their honorable origin, and not the pain and wound of the exile, that became a factor in the personal sense of identity of part — and a large part — of the Jewish people. This attitude is absent from the attitude developing within the Jewish people with regard to the memory of the Holocaust.

* * *

The difference in the responses stems, however, from a more basic differentiation. How do we identify the responding entity? Of whom are we speaking? The natural answer would be, *the Jewish people.* But the precise meaning of this term may be subject to diverse interpretations. In the case of the Holocaust one may point to an organized group response, namely, the response of all the Jews, not just the victims and the saving remnant of the Holocaust. Because of the political and communications networks of the twentieth century, all the Jews were involved in the knowledge of what was occurring and in reacting to it — each segment of the people in accordance with its particular situation and fate, and against the background of its ideological and political orientation. Furthermore, the Jews were already represented by a network of organizations, parties, and movements, some local-national, the greater number international in scope. Under these conditions, the question of how the Jewish people responded is, in a certain sense, relevant, even when the response was a blunder or silence; for these too were responses. Long before the Holocaust, and certainly during it and thereafter, the persecuted sufferers asked: what is the Jewish people doing? What are the Jews in Eretz Israel, the Jews of America, the Zionist movement, the Joint doing? Of course, the leaders of those communities and organizations were asking themselves similar questions. Expectations and demands were directed to specific frameworks which marshalled the Jewish people and assumed overall responsibility in its name.

This was not the case during and after the exile from Spain when the responses to that event were formulated and conveyed to following generations by the exiles themselves, by the communities which gave them refuge, and by individuals who had influential contacts with the authorities and voluntarily assumed responsibility to aid the exiles. It is true that there were certain expressions of collective Jewish activity, and a call for the Jewish people throughout their dispersion to coordinate assistance for the special needs of the exiles. Attempts were also made to reach all the *kehillot* and arouse some collective fervor for the redemption of the Jewish people. But these were the initiatives of individuals, and there was no organization which represented the entire Jewish people, nor an address to which one could direct claims in the name of the Jewish people. The awareness that "all Jews are responsible one for the other," and a rather tangible concept of "catholic Israel" did exist, but it did not find an organizational expression; it was purely symbolic. And the only symbol under which well-established Jewish activities were concentrated was the local *kehillah*.

If we consider the broad complex of events, emotions, and ideas conveyed to us through literary documentation, and the widespread dissemination of the literature reflecting the memories and expressing the direct and indirect responses of the Spanish exiles, we can certainly speak of the response of "the Jewish people" to the exile from Spain. But clearly this, and the response to the Holocaust, are two very different types of "people's responses," both in their essence, and in the formulation and transmission of the response as an educational message for future generations.

We have already noted that the traditional *kehillah* was the cell that activated the process of the exiles' self-rehabilitation. The medium of that self-rehabilitation directly embodied the initial response and message, both emotionally and intellectually. It was the spiritual response of individuals within the interpersonal network of the *kehillah*, and within the framework of inter-*kehillah* relations. Moreover, it was formulated in the religious, emotional-conceptual, and behavioral language that was still common to all those who responded as Jews. (We are not speaking here of the converts who did not return to Judaism.) The message that was conveyed to the Jewish public in the traditional religious language which united the *kehillah* and all its members, was absorbed and exerted influence. Therefore, even where there were conceptual differences — and one can discern a variety of spiritual trends that expressed the shared experiences of the Spanish exiles — the literature that documents their response appears to us as an organic expression of the mind-set of a leadership that was closely linked to the people; the expression of a people that may not have been united in an external framework but still shared a common inner spiritual world.

In contrast, the response of the Jewish people during and after the Holocaust — as against the many responses of individual Jews —

was a formal response in the political-social-existential as well as conceptual sense (mediated by the ideologies of movements, parties, and groups). It was not expressed in a common traditional language, and it is therefore very difficult to identify the message which emerges from within it or, in the highly significant metaphor, the "voice of the people's souls."

One may be more precise and say that, organizationally, the Jewish people speaks in the post-Holocaust period in a clearly heard voice, on subjects and at a level of deliberation which can be expressed and discussed within national and party frameworks; but the voice of the people itself, of its individual constituents, is still not heard. I would not say that the people is silent, although there was a period of silence and even of muteness; but I will say that the language in which individuals speak as members of the Jewish people, in diaries, memoirs, poems, stories, works of art, even in philosophical studies, is not the language which records the "establishment" responses of the nation or of its parties — it merely "embellishes" it. There is a wide gap between the hidden message within the personal responses of individuals, and the public educational message conveyed to the younger generation by the institutions which make such decisions. The latter tell the people what it should feel and what it should think, and there is good reason to question whether this message truly reflects deep mutual consent. I would not ignore the importance, even the necessity, of the role of that message, but we should be aware of the fact that it is covering and even subduing the voice of many hearts which hide their fears and bury their doubts.

We may now consider another issue, namely, the degree of satisfaction derived by the people from the manner of its response, both while responding and thereafter. There is a reflective element within the responses to such events — do they seem appropriate? Do they meet expectations? It is difficult to say anything clearly in this respect with regard to the expulsion from Spain, for we have no way of judging the "public opinion" of those days. Indeed, it is doubtful if there was a "public opinion" then in the sense that we understand it today. But we can say that even if there were responses of disappointment and bitterness, they were not transmitted from generation to generation, and certainly were not studied as they are today. Moreover, from the beginning, responsibility for rehabilitation fell first and foremost on the communities of exiles themselves, and the level of individual responsibility (relative to public responsibility) was incomparably greater than it is in our own time. If we add to this the difference in the nature and intensity of the two catastrophes from which the Jewish people had to recover, that is, the unprecedented severity of the Holocaust, the response to the latter leaves a deep, inconsolable, and incurable pain.

The responses of the Spanish exiles expressed feelings of guilt regarding the behavior of some of the Jews before the exile, and interpreted the exile itself as a punishment. But, as far as I know, there was no iota of guilt on the part of the Jewishly faithful leadership, nor were those leaders blamed by their communities for their activities during and after the exile. They did what they could, and what they did was accepted. As we well know, this was not the case with respect to the critical reflex appearing in the first response to the Holocaust — did the Jewish people meet the challenge? Did those who personally experienced the Holocaust stand up to the test? Did the Jewish centers in the free world respond to the demands upon them? Did the Jewish leadership do so? These questions haunt us to this day. Even those who are certain that it was not possible to do more than was done, are sure that the leadership should have done more than was possible! And there are many who believe that it was indeed possible to do more before, during, and after the Holocaust. Thus, a heavy sense of guilt regarding the response of organizations, and perhaps of individuals, is a central characteristic and essential component of the Jewish people's response to the Holocaust.

* * *

The question of the spiritual response to the exile from Spain and to the Holocaust touches mainly upon the significance of those events for the future vigor of the Jewish people, their faith in the beliefs for which they were suffering, being persecuted and slaughtered, and their determination to continue to identify themselves as Jews despite their suffering. In other words, the key question is how these traumatic events influenced the self-identity of the Jewish people and their will to survive, and how they were introduced into their consciousness as Jews both as individuals and as a group.

When we study the literature documenting the Jews' response to the Spanish exile, we must recognize, first, that this is a literature wholly characterized as religious thought. Even works which include some secular elements were considered to belong within that framework. The language of tradition and religion, of the written and oral law, of the commentaries and other writings which developed from that law directly and indirectly, is the language through which the writers seek to guide the people and to speak on its behalf. Second, despite the fact that a philosophic trend influenced by neo-Platonism existed in Italy, the literature written by and widely disseminated among the exiles and their descendants was, for the most part, kabbalistic writing which consciously turned its back upon the philosophical rationalism abhorred by observant Jews, and sought to review the faith of the Jews through the redeeming power of prayer and observance of commandments, and the belief in imminent redemption.

The strengthening of Jewish faith in the impending arrival of the messiah became a key motif in the response of the Jews after the exile from Spain. If one were to apply descriptive criteria to the various types of messianic beliefs which found expression during specific historic periods of Jewish history, the salient feature of the messianism of the generations following the exile may be said to be the motif of "renewing our days as of old." The restoration of a glorious past through repentance and atonement, that is, by a renewed obligation to cleanse oneself through the commandments, would be expressed in all aspects of the individual's and the *kehillah's* way of life. The significance of this approach is that the exiles tended, for the most part, to interpret their expulsion and sufferings not as a miscarriage of heavenly justice but, quite the contrary, as a punishment merited because of communal transgression which they could point to and define with precision. In addition, they viewed this as a form of pre-messianic trial, not only because of the degree of their suffering, but also because they could discern in the various political phenomena of their time signs of "Divine intervention" having messianic significance. There was great despair among those who suffered, but their leaders saw historic signs testifying to the fact that God had not abandoned His people even during its great misfortune.

Three factors — memory of lost glory, despair permeated with a sense of religious guilt, and hope based on both future possibilities and realistic socio-economic and political processes — influenced a response that might well be defined as "renewing our days as of old" in several areas: a) the immediate process of rehabilitation of the exiles in the countries which absorbed them, both as individuals aspiring to regain their previous status, and as communities seeking to retrieve the brilliant success enjoyed in Spain; b) correction of the religious lifestyle, both individual and communal; and c) the renewal of the nation which longs to return to its original holy land and its previous status as a nation led by God. It must be stressed that all this was expressed through creativity that was evident not only in writing and in study, but in a way of life that included a new expansion of the religious leadership and of elements inspired by the coming redemption. These elements were apparent in the establishment of Safed as a great and flourishing spiritual center in the century after the exile from Spain, and in the still influential spiritual message transmitted from that center throughout the diaspora.

Does the emotional and conceptual-educational response of the Jewish people to the Holocaust contain similar or parallel elements? Perhaps it does in its externals, but the inner mindframe is very different. One must note, first of all, that the response expressing the solidarity and national identity of the people is not religious in nature and does not rest upon the language and content of classical Jewish texts. There was and is, of course, a certain religious response couched in the language and content of the sources; indeed, echoes of this language and content were also incorporated in nonreligious Jewish responses. But communication among the segments of the Jewish people which jointly recall its destruction and mourning did not and does not depend on this language and content. The very establishment of a special memorial day for "the Holocaust and for heroism," as well as the continuing disagreement regarding the establishment of such a day, testify to this. The name and the date that were chosen leave no room for misunderstanding — the Jewish people after the Holocaust no longer speaks as one in the language of its religion. It attempts to express the shared memory which it bears as an open wound in language which began to take shape two or three generations before the Holocaust. This fact indicates that this response is not one of "renewing our days as of old."

* * *

Two historic phenomena require our attention in this connection. The first has the most far-reaching and widespread implications, namely, the establishment of the State of Israel. The second is relatively much more limited, but it has great importance for that part of the people whose numbers and influence are increasing, namely, the remarkable revival of the ultra-Orthodox communities, particularly in Israel and in the United States. Can these two phenomena perhaps be interpreted as a post-Holocaust "renewal of our days as of old," although in two different senses and in two completely different directions?

Without going into the question of the link between the establishment of the State of Israel and the Holocaust, which is subject to differing views, we may suggest the following as acceptable to all Jews, including the anti-Zionist, ultra-Orthodox group which, despite its strident proclamations against the "secular state," flourishes within it and with its aid: the rehabilitation of most of the survivors of the Holocaust within the State of Israel, the closing of all Jewish ranks around the state upon its establishment, and the messianic fervor which Israel has generated and which has not been dissipated despite being clouded by wars and domestic disagreements — all these express an emotional and conceptual reaffirmation and strengthening of Jewish identification, and hopes for future independence, freedom, and the full self-expression of the Jewish people, after all that had happened to it during the Holocaust.

The Zionist movement saw in the establishment of the state after the Holocaust the creative response of the Jewish people — not a response of revenge, but one of self-affirmation and rebuilding. The Zionist movement also saw in Israel's establishment after the Holocaust the lasting proof of the validity of its program, not only in the national-political sense of saving the Jewish people, but also as the new understanding of Jewish identity possessing the "normal" national-cultural-historic characteristics of a nation-state. In this sense, too, most of the Jewish people rallied around Zionism after the establishment of the state. Thus the Holocaust and the establishment of Israel were held to mark the beginning of a new period in the history of the Jewish people — the end of exile and the beginning of independence. Emil Fackenheim spoke for many when he enunciated the "614th commandment" which emerged from the ghettos and camps of destruction — not to give Hitler a victory after his defeat, that is, to revive and preserve the people which he sought to destroy. In practical terms this means establishing the state in order for the Jewish people to protect itself, express its cultural identity to the fullest, and live as a nation in every sense.

Should this be understood as a "renewal of the days of old" in the sense apparent in the responses of the Spanish exiles and their descendants? When answering this question, let us not ignore the tragic truth — the establishment of an independent State of Israel is certainly much more than the Spanish exiles were able to achieve in Turkey where they found ample opportunity for material and spiritual rehabilitation, or even in Eretz Israel whose community they strengthened. Moreover, despite this achievement which, in Maimonidean terms, in itself has a "messianic dimension," we cannot but be saddened by the fact that the State of Israel was not, unlike Turkey to the Spanish exiles, the refuge for the Jewish people that was anticipated when its existence was first conceived. It arose as a response *after* the Holocaust; only the victory of the Allies saved the last few remnants of the Jews of Europe. The State of Israel was not the haven for exiles on the verge of destruction, but the opportunity to save the remnants, after the diaspora had been destroyed together with overwhelming numbers of those whose coming to Israel was to have established its identity as a state of Jews and as a Jewish state.

To this one must add the simple fact which the religious public, both those who identify with the state and those who do not, cannot change, despite the weight of its presence therein — the Zionist movement established the State of Israel in Eretz Israel in an effort to constitute a presence within the continuity of Jewish history, but not as a return to the ancient point of origin of the religious tradition which united the people throughout the generations. Rather, it sought to create a new apolitical and nontraditional platform of "normal" secular nationalism for the Jewish people's continued existence. This approach is the source of the debate between those who approve of Zionism and those who deny it with ideological fervor. Indeed, this fateful disagreement, which creates a deep inner schism, is also one of the outstanding characteristics of the renewed identity of a pluralistic people for whom the terms of the covenant uniting it have changed and are no longer traditional-religious terms.

Similarly, the relatively widespread revival of the ultra-Orthodox groups and yeshivot reveals a purposeful and peculiar ambition to restore the ultra-Orthodox communities that had been destroyed in Poland and Lithuania to their supposed pre-Holocaust glory. A question we need not consider here is whether those days were really so glorious. Of greater importance is the question whether what we are witnessing today is really the result of the will to "renew our days as of old" in any other than a surface sense. In order to answer this question we must consider, first, the spiritual-religious conformation developing in these communities, and then, how these communities integrate into their post-modern secular surroundings.

A comparison of the spiritual-religious development of the post-Holocaust period with the tremendous creative revival found so impressively in the kabbalistic writings of the Spanish exiles and their descendants, a ferment that expressed the need to restore religious life through a spiritual return to the sources from which faith is renewed, points to two surprising differences:

1) The current socio-economic reconstruction of the religious community projects a religiosity focused on the dimension of *halakhic* observance, that is, strict observance of commandments as the outstanding symbol of authentic Jewish identity, without any dimension of spiritual-religious creativity, or of delving into the depths from which man renews his awareness of the presence of God.

2) The contemporary Jewish community lacks a sense of religious guilt and a strong urge to repent in the wake of the Holocaust. The *hozrim b'teshuvah* movement, which has been organized by the ultra-Orthodox communities in particular, points to this more than anything else; the *haredim* do not seek their own repentance, but the repentance of those Jews who had been brought up for generations outside the lifestyle of Torah and commandments. The significance is clear. The ultra-Orthodox community — and in this it exhibits a stance characteristic of all of Orthodoxy — does not feel a sense of guilt before God in relation to the Holocaust. Religious ideologists who explain the Holocaust as a punishment for the sins of the Jewish people proclaim in the most blatant fashion that it is not to their own sins or to those of their community that they refer, but to the sins of the Zionists, the Reform Jews, the assimilationists, etc. They demand the repentance of those who have lost the faith that enables one to feel religious guilt! The need to make *teshuvah*, which is so emphasized in the religious writings of the Spanish exiles, is entirely lacking in the Jewish people after the Holocaust; and in the absence of this impetus for *devekut* and devoutness, what will encourage spiritual-religious creativity?

Instead of immersion in religious-spiritual creativity, we find an impressive investment of emotional and intellectual effort in the socio-economic rehabilitation of the *haredi* communities, together with the effective discovery and utilization of the resources and possibilities open even to segregated ultra-Orthodox groups in Western democratic societies, particularly in Israel. Without going into a detailed analysis and defense of this statement (I have done so elsewhere), I will merely conclude that the rehabilitation of the ultra-Orthodox communities in our time, despite an external similarity achieved by nostalgic superficial imitation, is not a renewal of the "days of glory" of the pre-Holocaust communities of Poland and Lithuania, but a socio-economic, organizational, political, and cultural post-modern phenomenon. It expresses a strong desire to be rebuilt through the "normal" means and according to the "normal" criteria made possible in the secular societies of the free world after World War II.

There is, thus, a remarkable common denominator shared by the religious and the secular response to the Holocaust. Without the classic religious sense of repentance, even among the Orthodox, there is no mood of "renewing our days as of old" in its original religious meaning. The messianic ideology is common to both the religious and secular publics, each according to its own interpretation. But religious messianism, even that of the anti-Zionist ultra-Orthodox, expresses no less than the secular messianism of the Zionist movement the criteria of "normalization." That sort of pragmatic messianism guides the Jewish people today, both in its state and in the diaspora. The purpose is to merge quickly and successfully into the socio-economic and political fabric of the nations of the free world, and to benefit fully from its advantages. Even those who stress the singularity of the Jewish people among the nations, and the uniqueness of Judaism among the religions, have the same goal — to preserve the special identity of the Jews without having to relinquish "redemption" in its socio-economic and political sense. Furthermore, from the viewpoint of the religious sector today, religion in its Orthodox form is seen to contribute yet another advantage for achieving "normalization" in the secular society. The stubborn insistence on following an uncompromising religious-traditional way of life, which made the normalization of the ultra-Orthodox community so difficult in the pre-World War II period, now grants it a clear sense of security, stability, and support within a secular society which admits that the lack of these values constitutes a threat to the normalcy of its own life.

We certainly cannot explain these characteristics of the Jewish people after World War II solely as responses to or as a result of the Holocaust. They are the result of historic processes, both positive and negative, which long preceded the Holocaust, some of which we noted above. These processes established the manner of response to the Holocaust, and they also explain the manner of interpreting its significance, drawing lessons from it, and integrating its memory within the consciousness of the Jewish people.

*   *   *

We have already noted that the Spanish exiles did not bequeath to future generations a particular day and ritual to mark that event. The ninth of Av, designated as the day commemorating the destruction of the two Temples, also absorbed the memory of the Spanish exile, although some stories of the exile and its sufferings were set down in writing and some, undoubtedly, were also transmitted orally. In any event, what became part of the group memory transmitted from generation to generation was the proud lineage of those who, during their stay in Italy, North Africa, Turkey, southern France and the other countries of their dispersion, lovingly recalled their Spanish origins and their unique traditions as a noble tribe in Israel. They retained the awareness that their departure from Spain led to that country's decline, and that their arrival in the lands of their refuge brought success and prosperity to those countries. Thus, it was not the element of catastrophe that was emphasized in the memory of the exiles, but rather pride in their lineage and legacy, together with their successful integration and rehabilitation, creativity, and contributions to the lands of their new residence. This was their uniqueness, whereas the catastrophe was commemorated, together with the many destructions that preceded and followed it, as another marker in the *via dolorosa* of an exiled people moving toward its redemption.

It is clear that the memory of the Holocaust could not be incorporated into the same sense of identity of the Jewish people in the same fashion. From the beginning, it was impossible to prevent emphasis on the catastrophe, and the effort to extract its ordinary dimensions to the full extent of retentive awareness, even alongside the consoling memory of the establishment of the State of Israel. This was expressed not only in designating a special memorial day

319

for the Holocaust and giving it a character essentially different from the traditional days of commemoration, but also in the many and varied memorial projects; in the unprecedented extent of research into the subject; in the extensive literature that began to be written during the Holocaust and is still growing, out of recognition that what happened must be testified to in as much detail as possible and preserved for future generations; and in the extraordinary educational effort to transmit that memory to the general public, and particularly to children and young people.

How is one to explain the extent of the effort to expand, accurately render, illustrate, and transmit the memory of this catastrophe in detail, exactly as it happened? Today we have at our disposal means of research, representation, and communication that never existed before. Even if the exiles of Spain had wished to document and depict the memory of their destruction, they could not have done so to even a fraction of the extent of what is done today. Moreover, today's visual media, by their very quality and nature, document the event as it happened and forcefully incorporate it into conscious memory. It seems, however, that the manifest tendency to make maximum use of the capabilities of these modern tools of research and communication expresses a conscious preference based on a value decision, namely, that this is how we wish to transmit the memory. We are thus impelled to analyze both the source and the significance of such a preference, and its results. After considering the initial emotional-conceptual response initiated and effectuated mainly by the generation that experienced the Holocaust, a response that included many psychological and compulsive elements, we must at least inquire — was this response desirable? Does it teach the lesson that its initiators intended to transmit to future generations?

From the beginning, there were problems involved in the educational process of transmitting the memory of the Holocaust. Until the Eichmann trial the subject was suppressed; one could even say that it was avoided in Jewish education. The change occurred after the trial, when it was decided both in Israel and in the diaspora that the memory of the Holocaust must be a central message of Jewish education in our era. The educators then began asking themselves whether it was permissible to expose children and young people to such shocking events. Could the results be positive? How could the message be transmitted without causing psychological damage? In no way can one attribute carelessness or insensitivity to the impressive educational effort that was made. However, it appears to me that these concerned questions indicated the certainty of those who witnessed the Holocaust that it was their unequivocal obligation to transmit complete and exact testimony. The younger generation must be exposed to the events as they occurred. It had to remember them, and this memory must shape its world view, its sense of identity, its way of life as a Jew.

The goal was to transmit a certain lesson, or lessons, having historic weight; and the lessons were embodied in the inexorable, compelling weight of the events themselves, in their shocking objectivity, even though it was repeated over and over that one could not explain how such events could have occurred, and that it was impossible for normal human consciousness to absorb their full weight. This means that emphasis was placed on feeding the memory with facts of the terrible destruction, and on establishing that memory as a source for a strong sense of obligation — toward the victims, toward the Jewish people, toward the future — so that such things should never happen again.

* * *

The ideology that justified this effort ascribed great importance to historic memory as an educational message. It is still held that the importance of memory is a key element in culture, and particularly in Jewish culture. One cannot argue against such statements in general, but it seems to me that little attention has been paid to the following question: was the historic memory which endows culture, and particularly the historic memory of the Jewish people, ever intended to be this type of memory? I shall attempt to point to an essential difference in the formation of the memory of the expulsion from Spain, as well as in the traditional formation of historic memory in the consciousness of the Jewish people until our own time. Something revolutionary and pregnant with results has occurred. Even as we emphasize the extraordinary, unprecedented nature of the Holocaust, we are obliged to consider this matter fully.

First, one must note that Jewish tradition, so replete with memories of destruction and cruel persecution, never assigned such a central and decisive weight to those destructions as an experience uniting the Jewish people and fashioning its identity. Jews recalled the historic journey of their nation as a chosen people that suffered repeatedly because of its status and its special destiny; the content of their memory is mainly one of testimony about chosenness. Even at the height of destruction, this was apparent in the special documentation of deeds of *Kiddush Ha-Shem*. In the composite of events which fashioned the historic consciousness of the Jewish people, positive events were stressed in the main, deeds of redemption and deliverance that supported and delineated the people's chosenness and destiny. Memories of destructions and grief were also present, but a conscious effort was made that the latter should not overpower and darken the positive memories. It seems that this motivated the gathering together of all the destructions and confining them to one ritual commemoration — the destruction of the Temple which symbolizes the dispersion of the Jewish people.

Second, the effort to impress upon the shared national memory events which occasioned a significant turning point in the history of the Jewish people, for good or for evil, aimed at a ritual fashioning of memory in the normal psychological sense; that is, retaining the perspective of distance between the present in which one remembers, and the past whose receding image is retained in the creative memory which provides a present image through continuing interpretation. In the ritual memory inherent in the holidays and festivals such as Passover, Shavuot, Hanukkah and Purim, on the one hand, and the ninth of Av, on the other, no unnatural obsessive effort was ever made to return the one remembering to the reality of the remembered past, or to impose the past on the perception of the present. Quite the contrary, a conscious effort was made that such a thing should not happen. In the present commemoration of a holiday, festival, or day of sorrow, the retrospective memory of the past is meant to influence the present through its significance, which directs progress from the past to the future, and through the lessons to be learned from it.

Note that at Passover, every individual Jew is asked to view himself "as if he had come out of Egypt," not by a reconstruction, even if ritually, of the event as if it were taking place in the present, but, pointedly, through a ritual contemplation of the exodus from Egypt through a contemporary creative interpretation of "every generation and generation" whose uniqueness has not lapsed, through a remembrance of the past which points the way to the present. Similarly, no attempt was ever made on the ninth of Av to recreate in the memory of the mourners the events of the destruction as they occurred, but only to note that they had happened, in order to reawaken consciousness of the significance of the continuing Galut — a condition in which the Temple remains destroyed.

In order to avoid any misunderstanding, I must emphasize that this analysis does not signify agreement with those who believe that the Holocaust should be commemorated on the ninth of Av together with the memory of all the other destructions experienced by the Jewish people. On the contrary, I believe that a special Holocaust memorial day on a separate date and with its own manner of commemoration is absolutely justified. The Holocaust was an unprecedented event whose singular significance in Jewish history should not be blurred. It marked the end of a period of Jewish history, and the lessons to be learned from it should be different from those derived from previous destructions. This is not a matter of the continuation of Galut or of a destruction that underscores that condition. The Holocaust destroyed the Galut itself; it was the destruction of the exiled people. My criticism relates only to the question of how this special memory should be fashioned; and, further, whether the approach we have followed until now, to a great extent due to a spontaneous impulse expressing the compelling pressure of the extraordinary events which occurred only yesterday, is the proper approach.

We must recognize that the way the memory of the Holocaust has been fixed in the consciousness of the young generation of our time differs in essence from the manner in which the tradition of our people fashioned historic memories. How did this happen? First of all, because the Holocaust is a shared memory of a people whose component groups do not speak in the language of its tradition and religion. Therefore, in order to fashion a shared memory for all the people, it was necessary to deviate from the ritual patterns of commemoration and expressions of mourning. It is clear that without the ritual and traditional-religious story which assimilates testimony and fashions it through its symbols and interpretations, only the historic facts remain, the story told through the verifying authority of academic research — records and documents, photographs, victims' belongings, the places where the events occurred with their remaining bits of testimony, and the monuments which mark the events *in situ*, as if they had fossilized at the moment of their occurrence and remained forever fixed in time.

The pedagogic approach of schools make a not inconsiderable contribution to presenting the Holocaust in this fashion, but we must emphasize that the purpose is not one of purely historic study. It is true that very detailed teaching, which aims at the most objective and graphic presentation of facts, generally distances the pupil from the studied event by the critical element within it — study of documents, clarification of what occurred and how, verification of data. This type of study generally does not create identification; it requires educators who can deal with the implementation of an objective, academic approach that insulates the student from the material studied.

In teaching the Holocaust, we must be aware of several special factors: 1) Because of the shocking abnormality of the testimony, the urge to present an objective picture which is beyond imagination may create the opposite effect, namely, the stunning and frightening realization that those surrealistic events did indeed occur, that is to say, can occur again. 2) Academic study of the Holocaust embodies by its very presentation, and by the magnitude and weight of the data studied, a very directed purpose — to utilize the knowledge that these events occurred and thus can occur again, to develop consciousness of those to whom this threat was directed and perhaps is still directed, and thus to recognize the need to respond accordingly. Moreover, to convey this shocking message, additional tangible elements are emphasized in teaching, such as visits to Yad Vashem and memorial sites, and participation in commemorative ceremonies whose role parallels that of the traditional ritual, but at a different level and with different means. The cumulative result assumes a consciously religious image. It presents the Holocaust in it stunning and depressing reality as an event which forms Jewish consciousness, and which assumes timeless status.

Again, it is Emil Fackenheim who gave the sharpest and clearest expression to this. He characterized the Holocaust as an event similar in its authoritative and binding force to the Sinaitic Revelation. One commandment emerges from Auschwitz and reembodies the covenant that unites the Jewish people — "never again." The condition for its obedience is that the events from whose depths the commandment emerges will never cease to be imprinted in our consciousness, and will remain forever present in all its existential force. Conferring a metahistoric status on a historic memory is possible in one manner alone — by establishing the facts themselves as a memory which is not relegated to the past, but always remains at the level of existential immediacy.

Close to the end of World War II, the Hebrew poet Avraham Shlonsky wrote a powerful poem, which is frequently read on the Memorial Day for the Holocaust and Heroism, and is engraved on the wall of Yad Vashem in Jerusalem:

Pledge

By leave of my eyes that watched the bereaving
Add cry after cry to my crushed heart's burden,
By leave of my trust that taught me forgiving
Till the pall of days that seared beyond pardon,
I have sworn an oath: to remember each grieving
To remember, never to harden.

Nothing, till ten generations give way,
Till soothed is the rankling, annulled each pain,
Till the rods that punished are purged away.
I vow that the dark wrath pass not in vain.
I vow that at dawn I never more stray.
Lest now I learn nothing, again.

> Translated by Francis Landy; from *Voices Within the Ark*, edited by Howard Schwartz and Anthony Rudolf (New York: Avon Books, 1980)

It seems to me that this poem expresses in the most impressive emotional manner, but also in the most accurate conceptual formulation, the kind of memory that most Jewish educational frameworks seek to bequeath to the younger generation — if indeed one can still define such a fixing of an event in one's consciousness as a memory. For "to remember" and "never more stray" is no longer a form of memory, but is the imposition of the past with all its substantive presence on the present.

Shlonsky's response, which spoke for very many others who, like him, witnessed the Holocaust in person or from afar, was natural, perhaps inevitable. When the witnesses confronted the events, and recognized the heavy burden of moral obligation toward

325

the victims and, as a result, for the future of the Jewish people, it was impossible to even consider a return to normalcy. But at that very same moment, the inevitable return to normalcy began. From the point of view of Shlonsky and of his generation, at that moment the "vow" not to rest, nor be silent, nor forget anything, was the only way it was possible to begin the return to normalcy, without being a traitor to the moral obligation that cried out from the events which had just then come to an end.

This is not true when one imposes permanency on that vow and continues to teach it as a response to be transmitted from generation to generation, and when most of the educators are now members of a generation that was not a witness to the Holocaust. It is no longer an ambivalent way of returning to normalcy. (In any event, it has already been returned to!) There is now a tendentious and conscious attempt to regain consciousness of Jewish identity among young Jews, on the basis of the imposed factuality of the catastrophe. Through the retrospective experience of the trauma, Jewish educators seek to make a case that the Jew cannot escape his singular identity, and thus has an obligation to himself and to his children to fortify his existence in his state. And this is an entirely different matter!

Once again, this is not intended to detract from the importance of proclaiming the possibility of another Holocaust against the Jews or any other persecuted people. It is certainly not meant to undermine the Zionist lesson derived from the Holocaust, that the Jewish people has reached the fateful crossroads between the return to its land and state, and the danger of its absolute disappearance. I believe that this is essentially correct, and that it must be discussed and studied as one of the important lessons of the Holocaust. Nonetheless, beyond the discussion and debate about transmitting this lesson, we must ask an important question: do we seek to base the identity of the Jewish people as a nation, and the identity of its individual members as Jews responsible for the continued existence, independence, and character of their people, upon the most terrible of the catastrophes that it experienced, and fixing it as a permanent element in Jewish consciousness? Do we want to force Jews to retain their Judaism because of the trauma of their fate? Do we want the Jewish people to define itself in the future as the people which survived the Holocaust, and see this as the reason and significance of its struggle for continued existence?

* * *

If the answers to these questions are positive, we must continue to pursue the present way of transmitting "the legacy of the Holocaust." Nevertheless, even then we should consider how much one can succeed in fixing that memory beyond the emotion-laden ceremonials which make it real. It is also worth considering what the psychological cost of such educational efforts are, particularly the long-range message conveyed by imposing upon young people an identity based upon a trauma. Undoubtedly, the immediate "success" is sweeping. But are we certain that in the long run it will not lead to an opposite reaction — to an escape from the constraining fear of identity anchored in catastrophe? And do we truly believe that it is impossible to free oneself from such an identity or to deny it?

Indeed, do even those committed to this educational message give an absolute and unequivocal positive answer to this question? Have all the options been considered? I believe that they have not. Our task in comparing the response of the Jewish people to the Holocaust with that of the Spanish exiles to their tragedy, is to raise this question. Above all, we must bring to the awareness of educators the significance of the message projected by making the Holocaust central to Jewish education and, as a high point, recreating that shocking experience through a visit to Poland and the sites of destruction, in order to imprint into memory an unforgettable fiery brand as a sign of a covenant. We must make it clear that this is a message that places identification with the Jewish people and with Judaism outside the continuity of Jewish tradition, and anchors it in a past tragedy and in the fear of tragedies that may occur in the future.

It is true that the negative message of the Holocaust and of the vow "never again" is accompanied by the positive message of Zionism, of citizenship in the Jewish state and, for diaspora Jews, of the renewal of Jewish life in Israel and in the countries of the free world. Nevertheless, we must reiterate what was said previously: the renewal of the political independence and physical strength of the Jewish people does not necessarily signify "renewal of our days as of old" in the sense of the relationship to the Jewish legacy and sources, to the spiritual content of the Jewish national identity. On the contrary, that transformation is generally understood as a revolutionary change, even as a break with the nurturing traditional sources; the new national culture will have a national-political, linguistic basis and will draw from modern Western sources.

Let us consider the matter carefully — *post facto,* we are using the memory of the Holocaust to create consciousness of a shared identity, for the very reason that the Jewish legacy no longer is a unifying factor. A quick and effective substitute is being sought to preserve the identity of the Jewish people, without preserving its substance. If this is so, what will nourish the new culture of the Jewish people which has returned to its land, enabling it to sustain a spiritual life through its own creativity? What will identify that culture as Jewish, if all that remains of Judaism within it is only the most terrible trauma in the history of the Jewish people? And, finally, why should one want to continue bearing the burden of this depressing identity?

There is a motivation and significance in continuing the struggle to exist as a Jewish people, provided that it remains loyal to its heritage and seeks to renew, develop and expand it, and to transmit it from generation to generation, out of love and spiritual conviction. There is significance in the establishment of the State of Israel after the Holocaust, provided that it exists in order to ensure the conditions necessary for the creative renewal of the rich legacy of the Jewish people. However, it is doubtful that one whose loyalty and love for that heritage have waned and evaporated, will have any interest in remembering the Holocaust as an event in the history of the Jewish people, nor that there is any way to force him to deal with it as such. For him, the source of interest in the Holocaust and in the lessons to be learned from it is its significance as a chapter in the history of Europe. On the other hand, for one who is still devoted to the Jewish heritage which motivates his identity, the manner of conveying the memory of the Holocaust should be changed. Without doubt it is important to point to its extraordinary dimensions, to study them, and to derive the necessary lessons. But in terms of a message which will fashion consciousness of identity, the emphasis should be not on conveying the shattering nature of the catastrophe, but on memorialization of the people who were murdered, of that part of the Jewish people which was destroyed, to mourn their loss, and particularly to learn about the substance and values of the great spiritual world against which the Nazis carried out their war of annihilation.

The tremendous difference between the exile from Spain and the Holocaust makes a parallel response impossible. Even if we would wish to "renew our days as of old" by a fresh confrontation with the sources, the matter would be impossibly difficult and problematic. However, today we are obliged to learn not only the lesson of the Holocaust, but also the lesson of the response given by the first generation of witnesses, and try to draw as close as possible to the traditional pattern of Jewish response. The motivation for Jewish identity should not be one of traumatic destruction and loss. The message we should strive to transmit is one of renewal of the exceptional spiritual heritage of that part of the Jewish people which perished in the Holocaust. That will provide the motivation for our identity, and the source of our will to continue living and creating as Jews.

Chapter 8

THE HOLOCAUST AS A CHALLENGE TO JEWISH RELIGIOUS THINKING IN OUR AGE

Is the Problem of Theodicy Raised by the Holocaust Unique?

The ancient problem of theodicy was one of the first philosophical problems related to the Holocaust which Jewish religious thinkers felt obliged to confront even during the evolving events. In spite of a strong emotional difficulty to apply "cold," detached philosophical methods to such an intimate painful problem during the terrible trial and in its aftermath, it was too urgent to be avoided. Believers needed so desperately the support and consolation of faith, seemingly the only possible source of support and consolation against such events which, however, refuted so radically the deepest existential foundations of faith. One had at least to protest or pray his question, as a final act of faith, expecting an answer from the depth of his soul, if not in a methodical-philosophical manner, at least in a prophetic intuition.

Indeed, the emotional facticity which served as a necessary empirical foundation even for later philosophical reflections on this ultimate question, made itself manifest in a paradoxical tension between two "measurable" anthropological phenomena — in the majority of studied individual cases of survivors (Brenner, 1980) the Holocaust did not affect extreme changes of basic attitudes towards faith in God, both on the part of believers and of nonbelievers. Namely, the majority of those who were believers before the Holocaust remained so after the Holocaust, and the same is true of nonbelievers. Even those few whose belief was shocked and destroyed during the Holocaust, generally recovered their former position after the end of the war, while both believers and nonbelievers became only more radical in their stances after the events. On the other hand, believers, not less than nonbelievers, admitted in their immediate responses to the events (especially in diaries, prayers and homilies) their feeling that they cannot find any adequate religious

331

justification. The belief in Divine providence had acquired such dimensions of absurdity in the darkness of the Holocaust that not even one of the old known arguments of justification could hold its claim. Or let us put it in another more accurate way — in the immediate response of believers to the attacks of Radical Evil in the Holocaust one intuits an emotional rejection of most traditional arguments of justification. They refuse to accept them as if there is in such arguments, dwarfed to sheer superficiality by the extraordinarily unique reality, an unsufferable insult, or a desecration of their belief in a God of mercy and justice, making their spiritual agony even more painful. This means that even for those who remained true to their belief and faith, the gap between religious expectation and reality remained unbridged, and their protested question remained unanswered, indeed as an inner deep dimension of their tortured faith. They believed in spite of and from within their conviction that there can be no satisfying answer in this world to their shocked religiosity.

The first published responses of religious writers, poets and thinkers who survived the Holocaust were generally based on this paradox — they expressed a traumatized belief which, standing the trial of the Holocaust, was too profound to be pacified by any of the ready-made theological "solutions." One may even put it this way — the mere idea of a possible solution was anathema to their feeling of absolutely justified amazement. Precisely because they did believe in spite of what they had lived through, there could be no answer to their unjustifiable suffering, unless God Himself could be described as a victim of Radical Evil together with His chosen people. Thus, they experienced their protest as an inner necessary dimension of belief after the Holocaust. This feeling, it seems, was the source of the varieties of "Protest Theologies" or "Revolt Theologies" which occupied the greatest part of Jewish theological literature published in the aftermath of the Holocaust (Susman, 1946; Wiesel, 1960; Greenberg, 1977; Rubenstein, 1966; Fackenheim, 1982; Maybaum, 1965; Cohen, 1981). But besides these main responses there were some contradictory responses of ultra-Orthodox and modern Orthodox theologians. These religious movements, of course, could not accept such attitudes of protest as an adequate basis for their religious education. Striving to protect the foundations of their religious world views they could not admit the extraordinary uniqueness of the Holocaust in this sense; therefore, they were looking back to the traditional argumentation in spite of the felt difficulties (Wolpin, 1986; Teitlebaum, 1959; Schwartz and Goldstein, 1987). At first, the expressions were indeed reluctant, preferring a silent avoidance of direct discussion of theological topics, and proposing instead the immersion in a devoted study of the Torah and fulfillment of its commandments. But, during the last decade, the publication of traditional Orthodox responses has been multiplied and become more articulated and more assertive. They entered overtly the public theological arena and have challenged a full reflective response.

Let us state even in the start of our discussion that we should not be too easily tempted to characterize ultra-Orthodox and Orthodox responses to the Holocaust as a simple reconstruction of traditional theological argumentations, and in the following discussion we would try to demonstrate the essential differences. Still, at a first glance, and at least on the level of surface understanding, we have here a conscious reaffirmation of some old theological views. Already in the Holocaust itself the responses were oscillating between an amazed silence of passive compliance to the nonunderstandable Divine verdict, or an active readiness to sanctify the Holy Name in public, again without asking any questions or offering any explanations, on the part of the majority of Orthodox Jews, and, on the part of an ultra-Orthodox minority. There was a certain kind of fanatic ideological justification of the Holocaust as a due Divine punishment for the sins of atheism, assimilationism and defiance of the Torah and its commandments by post-emancipationist modernist Jewish movements, especially secular Zionism, Jewish materialistic socialism and reform. Even those who remained piously faithful must suffer now, this ideology explains, because the majority of the Jewish people sinned. But the righteous will, of course, be fully compensated in their life to come in heaven and in the glory of the messianic era which surely will soon arrive. On the other hand, this fundamentalist religious ideology emphasized the argument that Nazism, that diabolic Radical Evil, is the unavoidable result of atheism and revolt against God and His Law. This means that atheism had been exposed in its utter degradation and wickedness, and thus had been unrecoverably refuted. There remained only one escape from disaster, and hope of redemption for humanity — repentance and return to God and His Law.

This is a quite obvious continuation of traditional theological stances, and they were based, indeed, directly on the ancient sources, trying even to demonstrate a claim that what had happened in the Holocaust had been already foreseen and minutely proclaimed by the biblical prophets, especially by Moses. Yet, what is most important in this Orthodox response is the stubborn refusal to admit that the Holocaust was unique among the many destructions and hardships which are replete in Jewish history. It may have been bigger in quantity of murders and much more cruel, but it is not qualitatively, or essentially, different. Therefore, we should relate to it in the same ways and through the same *halakhic* norms which our people used in the past. In fact, this claim had its *halakhic* normative expression in the refusal of the institution of a special day for the commemoration of the Holocaust and its sacred victims, because accepting an established unique day in the traditional Jewish calendar means admittance of an extraordinary unique event which challenges the traditional religious thinking. No, we should add the memory of the Holocaust to the old list of destructions, and bewail it together with all other calamities of Jewish history, in one of the already institutionalized days of mourning.

The refusal to admit the uniqueness of the Holocaust is then the main characteristic of the Orthodox theological argumentation. In the past it was most clearly and definitely exclaimed by the ultra-Orthodox or modern Orthodox varieties of theological thinking. Contesting the daring theologies of revolt and protest of the "Death of God," Orthodox theologians propose some reconstituted versions of traditional theodicy. They, indeed, excluded the most fundamentalist biblical justification of catastrophes as Divine punishments, but they satisfy their intellectual and emotional burden with the more sophisticated theodicy based on the book of Job and some of its philosophical or mystical interpretations in the teachings of talmudic sages and medieval theologians. This way the field of Jewish theology in our days is mainly divided between two basic attitudes — the one which assumes the "unprecedented," extraordinarily unique, character of the Holocaust, and strives for the extremist theological conclusions; the other which emphatically denies this assumption, and strives for reconstitution of traditional theology. Every religious thinker who finds himself driven to deal with the challenge of theodicy after the Holocaust must, therefore, first decide his position to this preliminary question — is the Holocaust unique and unprecedented from the theological point of view? Did the Holocaust raise entirely new obstacles for faith in Divine providence or are we facing only an aggravated form of the same old obstacles?

Intermediate Approach of E. Berkovitz

In order to properly pose our problem we must now expand in more detail the sophisticated argumentation of modern Orthodox thinkers. The most serious effort in this field has been made by Rabbi Eliezer Berkovitz (1973, 1979), who attempted an "intermediative" approach. From the start, he sympathized with those who claim that the Holocaust has raised an unprecedented difficulty, and that it is almost impossible to find a pacifying, convincing solution. But though retaining to the end of his discussion a feeling of amazement, he succeed in leading his arguments back to the traditional sources. The first step, which is, of course, the decisive and most characteristic of a modern Orthodox approach, is the position of an uncontested testimony of direct religious experience as a truth which may balance the natural feeling that what had happened in the Holocaust definitely refutes the belief in Divine providence. It is an attested fact that hundreds and thousands of simple believers remained faithful to God until their death. They strictly adhered, as far as it was possible in those terrible conditions, to *halakhic* norms, and accepted their death with the conviction that in doing so they sanctified the Holy Name. These believing Jews evidently had an experience of Divine presence. In their utmost suffering they knew that God was with them. They did not know why they suffered and died, but their belief in a God of mercy and justice did not fail. If we still consider the problem of theodicy as a relevant problem for theological discussion after the Holocaust, so Berkovitz develops his argument, it is because we do have, even now, a firm existential foundation for faith in a personal providential God, knowing that by raising the problem of theodicy, even as an unresolvable problem, we assume belief. As said before, it is only due to the testimony of those who sanctified the Holy Name that we can reaffirm our belief, and raise the problem as relevant for theological discussion. Let us emphasize here the fact that as a theologian Berkovitz does not rely on his own formative religious experience. On the contrary, he points to a formative, publicly attested experience of other Jews, who did not need the support of theology, in order to develop a theology which will take him back to the sources, those very sources which directly sustained the victim's belief. It is he and his disciples who, lacking a direct experience, are in need of a theology, and the victims became, therefore, their supporting witnesses.

It is definitely clear that reliance on such testimonies as a first assumption excludes for Berkovitz the validity of the ultra-Orthodox response. The idea that the Holocaust was a due punishment for "sins" is for him an absolute impossibility. Far more than that, it is a desecration of the Holy Name. The signification of the belief of the faithful, if it really signified any truth beyond its facticity, is the overwhelming evidence of the victims' righteousness and purity of heart. It is impossible to assume that they suffered for their sins. Even if we take into account the gravest sins of other Jews, there is no sin that Jews could have done which would deserve such diabolical punishment. Therefore, says Berkovitz, when we explain the Holocaust as a result of Divine decision we factually describe God in diabolical terms. It is a terrible desecration. There remains only one possibility to explain the motivating causes of the Holocaust — it is the expression of utter human depravity. The Nazis and their helpers, and they alone, were responsible for their abominable deeds, which means that from the theological point of view the Holocaust can be explained only as a clear case of a "hiding of His Countenance." God refrained from intervention. He let the Nazis and their helpers accomplish their diabolical plan, and that in spite of the fact that this plan was not only a contradiction to Divine goodness and truth, it was the most daring, obnoxious case of hereticism, a brutal denial of Divine existence.

The theological problem from an Orthodox point of view is, therefore, how can we explain the "hiding of His Countenance" in such conditions? Why did God refrain from intervention? Berkovitz's answer to this query, in the third phase of his argumentation, is given by readapting a second traditional idea — human freedom of choice. God created man and endowed him with the capacity to choose between good and bad. If God really intended to let humanity actualize its freedom, He is bound by His own logic to let man actually choose, behave practically according to his decision, and take responsibility, even if the choice happens to be the most wicked contradiction of Divine intention in creating man. God suffered, then, with His victimized people, the anguish of the most terrible betrayal of man against Him and His commandment, but He was prevented by His own logic of creation from intervening.

This, then, is the heart of the explanation. It seems that Berkovitz would not have been satisfied unless he could point to the fact that, in spite of the mass extermination, the diabolical plan of a "Final Solution" had not been completely accomplished. It failed finally. The Jewish people, as a people, survived; it is very much alive. Moreover, as against the "hiding of His Countenance" in the Holocaust, we can point to the establishment of the State of Israel after the Holocaust as a "revealing of His Countenance." It was not an overt miracle, still a miracle it was, namely, an evident, though indirect, Divine intervention in the historical process. Witnessing in our own lifetime not only the Holocaust but also the establishment of a Jewish state, we may take it for granted that God did not forsake his chosen people. He is still our guide and redeemer.

Jacobovits' Attempts to "Normalize" the Problem

As formerly claimed, Berkovitz's argumentation is a dialectical retreat from admitting the unprecedented character of the Holocaust to a traditional theological solution. Rabbi Immanuel Jacobovits' (1986, 1988) solution is different from this point of view, though he relies on the same evidence of Holocaust victims' testimony. Jacobovits' approach, one may claim, is an attempt to "normalize" the whole problem, and comprise it completely in a traditional frame. This was, after all, according to his understanding, the full and exact message of the victims' testimony. They, themselves, did not consider their trial as unprecedented, or extraordinarily unique. They accepted it as their fathers and forefathers did, and they did not consider it a refutation of traditional simple faith. If we are going to rely on them and accept their guidance, let us be faithful to its full signification. Jacobovits' argumentation may be summarized in the following paragraphs.

The atrocities against the Jews in the Holocaust were, indeed, exceptionally cruel and exceptionally wide. It may well be that they were an unprecedented manifestation of diabolical wickedness in humanity. However, from the point of view of Divine providence, the differentiation between a great and a small atrocity is not valid. If sufferings and murders of innocent people disprove the religious idea of Divine providence and Divine justice, then we may not discriminate between a mass murder and one single case, because Divine justice must be absolutely perfect. The murder of one innocent child will raise, in principle, the same difficulty as the murder of six million. By the same logic, a theological explanation, which will be found sufficiently convincing in the case of the murder of one innocent child, should be regarded as sufficiently convincing even in the case of the widest mass murder. We will have to accept the fact that generally, in cases which represent explicitly human responsibilities, God does not intervene, and He should not be blamed for such deeds. Of course, those who committed them will be duly punished, whether in this world or in the world to come, while the suffering victims will be duly recompensated here or in the hereafter. Therefore, Jacobovits sums up, the theological problem of theodicy, which we face after the Holocaust, is not any different from that faced by our people in former destructions, and the theological responses of old are still valid. On the other hand, there is a valid differentiation between big and small crimes, from the point of view of human responsibility. A mass murder of six million innocent human beings, just because they happen to be born Jews, is surely a far greater crime than a murder of a few innocent people. We, therefore, have sufficient reasons to inquire about the motivation behind such human depravity. If we will expose, by our study, the obvious connection between the exceptional diabolical qualities of the Holocaust, directed precisely and mainly against the Jewish people, and the Nazi ideology which is based on radical heresy against God and His Law, and on an idolatrous apotheosis of a human leader and the state, we will be right to conclude that the Holocaust, far from being a shattering argument against religious belief, is indeed a shattering argument against theism as such. The Holocaust should be regarded as an alarming signal against the dangers of moral depravity and human deterioration, which are incorporated in atheism, while the heroism and morality of the faithful Jewish victims may teach us again the profound truth of belief and faith.

It is obvious from what had been already said above that Rabbi Jacobovits rejects the ultra-Orthodox understanding of the Holocaust as a punishment for certain sins. He puts all the burden of blame on the Nazis and their helpers. From the theological point of view the Holocaust signifies a "hiding of His Countenance." Obviously he adopts also Berkovitz's assumption of human freedom of choice. Yet, he is closer to the traditional theology in refraining from the explanation of God's "hiding of His Countenance" as a necessary result of human freedom of choice. God Almighty can intervene and save, as he did in several singular cases in Jewish history. This does not contradict the concreteness of human responsibility; even a failed attempt at murder is still a crime resulting from full human freedom of choice. Jacobovits' answer is the most basic simple act of faith; we should accept Divine decrees to intervene or refrain from intervention, in different historical cases, in good faith as they are, as we cannot know His ways nor judge His considerations. Such queries are beyond our human capacity. We should not raise them at all.

However, we should be thankful to God for the fact that, in spite of Jewish powerlessness and overwhelming Nazi power, the Jewish people has survived, it has overcome the terrible calamity, and come back to full creative life. This means that, in spite of the "hiding of His Countenance," Divine providence is not an empty word. Finally, the will of God is and will be fulfilled in the future even in the works of man.

Protest Revolt Theologies: Revelation Event with a Claim of Eternal Presence Beyond History

We showed that the modern Orthodox intellectual response, though based on the testimony of the faithful in the Holocaust itself, has been crystallized as a theological argumentation only recently and, it seems, not as a direct response to the Holocaust itself but as a response to the variety of "Protest Theologies," or the "Theologies of the Death of God" which may threaten religious education today. This is a significant fact which should be emphasized and explained.

The aforementioned variety of protest theologies incorporates in itself the full burden of pain and shock suffered in the Holocaust. Survivors who experienced these trials memorized them even later, and through their inner reflection on them, as an absolute pain which cannot and should not be "pacified" or eased. One cannot, and one should not suffer them to be considered concrete historical possibilities. It is an absolute uncomprising protest against something which *ab initio* should be impossible either from a human or from a Divine point of view. Such a response is consummated in a demand not to allow an existential distance from the events. Simple commemoration is not enough. It should not be a memory of past events, reexperienced from the growing biographical and historical distance. Rather, it should be a memory which makes the past present in its full unique intensity, because only in this way can one empathize existentially with what it really meant. It is formulated by some such thinkers as a moral categorical imperative, at least as long as we cannot be sure that such events were definitely drawn beyond the threshold of historical possibility. Until then, commemoration is the only frail dam against recurrence.

It seems that the last sentences incorporate the key for full understanding of the mentality which created the protest theologies, and then kept on its recreation from the distance of a later generation. It is a moral demand of actual commemoration for the sake of one absolute commandment, "Never again!" It is also an expression of the absolute sense of duty towards the victims of the Holocaust and towards the Jewish people. The Nazis aimed at a complete annihilation. In trying to murder every single Jew they tried to murder also all the forthcoming generations. It means that from the Holocaust onward, every Jew, even those who are not yet born, should be considered a survivor, and bear responsibility for the memory of those who were murdered, because this is the only way to let them have a continuing presence with their people. It is these emotions and these meta-ethical considerations which explain the profound source of refusal to admit any legitimate comparison of the Holocaust to any other event in Jewish or human history, or the source of the powerful reaffirmation that the Holocaust is unprecedented, or extraordinarily unique. Let us reemphasize the fact that by comparing and generalizing we necessarily create an existential distance. By failing to empathize the absolute uniqueness we are drawing the memory back into its past. Then, of course, our protest weakens, because a new, different present demands our full attention. If we allow it, then, it will be the point where we start our way to forgetfulness and acquiescence. A theology of revolt based on the assumption that a certain evil event demands absolute attention as an always-present event is, therefore, a theology of ongoing, unrelenting protest. It seems to be almost the foundation of a new religion, taking the Holocaust as its revelatory originative source.

Be that as it may, there is an element of fixation in the theology of protest and revolt, while modern Orthodox responses aim definitely to reject it. We formerly observed the fact that the modern Orthodox are relying, as much as their revolting rivals, on the testimony of believing victims of the Holocaust. However, it is clear that their intentions are contradictory. For the modern Orthodox try to legitimize, by their reliance on that testimony, the inclusion of the Holocaust in the wide continuity of Jewish historical memory. It rejects the stubborn refusal to existential distance and historical perspective. It rejects the stubborn claim of extraordinary uniqueness which shapes the Holocaust in the image of a religious revelatory event, which has a claim of eternal presence beyond history. Including even the Holocaust in a certain category of recurrent historical events, the modern Orthodox approach demands, on the contrary, a partial forgetfulness, for the sake of continuation of Jewish history as from the days of old. It is that people which was redeemed from slavery in Egypt, received God's Law near Sinai, has continued and will continue its long messianic way until the end of days.

The facticity of this observation is manifest in the denial of the special theological significance of the Holocaust. Let us now add a second observation. The growing emotional and intellectual readiness to include the Holocaust in the continuity of past events reflects also the historical experience of the Orthodox and the modern Orthodox community since the Holocaust to our own days. It seems that only the impressive success of the Jewish people in returning to full creative life immediately after the Holocaust, not only in the State of Israel but also in the main centers of the diaspora in the democratic countries, could justify the comparison of the Holocaust to former persecutions in Jewish history. For only because of the facticity of the recent redemption can we be reassured, as in former cases, that the Jewish people, and mainly its core of faithful believers, stood their trial in the period of the "hiding of His Countenance," that even now the old Divine promise, affirmed by the Covenant between God and Israel, has been fulfilled. Their enemies will not be able to destroy and uproot this chosen people. They may try as powerfully as they can, but they will not succeed, because by the hidden help of God this people will survive, come back to life, and continue faithfully in the fulfillment of its destiny.

341

Differentiation between the Modern Orthodox and the Revolt Theologies Responses

We should now clarify our differentiation between the modern Orthodox and the revolt theologies responses, because the last, as well as the first, rely on the redemptive character of the establishment of a Jewish state after the Holocaust (Fackenheim, 1982; Greenberg, 1977). There is, however, an essential difference between them in the meaning attached to the event, and in the applied consequences — for the revolt theologies, the establishment of Israel on the basis of a secular Zionist ideology is the outcome of the practical revolution of the Jewish people after two thousand years of passive messianic expectation for Divine miraculous intervention. The Jewish people has at last taken upon itself the full active responsibility for its survival, for its independence and security as a nation. This is a protesting recognition of the newly acquired truth after the Holocaust — the Jewish people should not trust any more in Divine providence, it should become the sole master of its destiny. This is the pragmatic turning point between the traditional and the "post-Holocaust" theologies.

According to both Fackenheim and Greenberg, the Holocaust marks a revolutionary turn in the history of the Jewish people. In their terms, it marks the recognition of the necessity of "reentering into history," namely the acceptance of full responsibility for survival as a nation, and as a consequence, the articulation of survival as a religious commandment, perhaps even the first one in its actual importance. Thus, the Holocaust opens a new era in the history of the Jewish people and engenders radical changes of belief and of *halakhic* norms.

While modern Orthodox theologians, even the Zionists amongst them (like Eliezer Berkovitz), may allow certain significant diversions from former ways of Jewish national behavior, in their eyes it is far from being a revolution. The revival of a Jewish state signifies for some of them, as said before, a "hidden miracle" of Divine intervention, and side by side with the establishment of a state and the beginning of the "ingathering of the exiles," they attach much significance also to the miraculous revival of Jewish life in the diaspora. In this context we should mind especially the impact of the most impressive success of the ultra-Orthodox and the Orthodox communities in reconstructing themselves, precisely after the destruction of their main East European centers in the Holocaust. New centers of Jewish Orthodoxy flourish both in Israel and in the diaspora. Much more than that, Orthodox Judaism seems now to prove, at least to its own community, the efficiency of its social, educational and ideological frames from the point of view of securing a full Jewish identity in the widely open and powerfully assimilative post-modernist Western society and culture. From this point of view, the variety of Orthodox movements claim distinct superiority over all the other Jewish movements of modernity, comprising secular Zionism. This means that the empirical evidence of precisely post-Holocaust Jewish history enabled Orthodox theologians to include the Holocaust in the "regular" continuity of Jewish history, and to interpret it in terms of traditional theologies. Precisely after the Holocaust it "happened" that Orthodoxy could discover a consoling truth sufficiently significant for it to balance the trauma of the Holocaust, and to reestablish its faith in the validity of tradition's shocked foundations.

We may conclude, then, that practically, the theological controversy on the problem of the Holocaust's "unprecedented" character reflects a much wider and longer controversy which began with Emancipation, and became much more crucial in the beginning of the post-Emancipation period in the twentieth century — what is and what should be the image of the Jewish people in the future? Must the secularist revolution drastically change the image of the Jewish people, or is there a possibility of mere readaptation through relatively small "outward" changes, keeping the main core of traditional beliefs and lifestyle of the Jewish people unchanged? Against this background we should now begin to analyze the theological argumentations themselves.

Theological Argumentations

The hypothesis which we will examine and try to prove through this analysis is that though the challenge of the Holocaust was not completely incomparable to former challenges, and though it did not utterly uproot Jewish theological thinking from its traditional sources, neither did it completely refute all the traditional argumentations of theodicy (of course from a believer's point of view), as revolt theologians claim. Nevertheless, an essential change did occur. In

343

fact, though, one may be right in claiming that such essential changes should not be considered an "absolute" novelty in the history of Jewish religious thinking, because such changes had already occurred several times in the past. Yet, the Holocaust with its background of secularism and modernity threatened an essentially deeper and more radical change. Therefore, even some of the most sophisticated arguments of traditional theodicies must be significantly reinterpreted, a fact which must affect further changes in other contents of the Jewish religious world view, and eventually also in the *halakhic* way of life.

We must now generate awareness of a fact which post-Holocaust theodicies tend to ignore due to their obsessive concentration on the traumatic experiences of the "Final Solution." In the examination of the consequences and conclusions of the Holocaust we must take into account the whole cultural-historical context. The Holocaust is not a separate "planet." It cannot be understood properly as a single event. This claim is valid also for theological consideration. The spiritual problems raised by the Holocaust are rooted not only in the life experiences of the death camps and the ghettos, but also in the compound social, political and cultural processes, relevant to problems of ethics and faith, which began much before the Holocaust, and continued in their full impact after the Holocaust. These processes obviously shaped the background of the Holocaust and of Jewish responses to the Holocaust. Furthermore, these processes created the spiritual movements and shaped the conceptual frameworks through which Jews interpreted their experiences in the evolving events, and afterwards. From this point of view, we must take into account the possibility that the essential uniqueness which most Jews tend to attach to the Holocaust in comparison to former traumatic events in Jewish history, is derived not only from the "unprecedented" qualities of the event itself, but also from its entire background; namely, from the fact that an event of such unprecedented qualities happened precisely in modern Western civilization and as an effect of some specific qualities which differentiate modernity from former traditional phases in Western history, and as a result of the newly shaped fate of the Jewish people specifically in this era. In fact, this appears directly in the aforementioned differences between the revolt and the Orthodox theodicies, though the disputants tend to cover it as much as they can; the basic difference between Orthodox and non-Orthodox theodicies is, *ab initio,* rooted in different ways of responding to the whole impact of modernity, and this difference was established much before the Holocaust, and proceeded in its development after it.

Continuing our discussion, we assume that the uniqueness of the problem of theodicy raised by the Holocaust, and the inadequacy of former traditional solutions, will appear through a precise analysis of Orthodox argumentations which claim to apply traditional solutions. Were they successful in their efforts according to their own criteria? Could they really avoid significant changes in the concrete process of argumentation? Or were they only pretending to continue the old lines of argumentation, incorporating in their discussion some profound, though unrecognized as such, changes?

Let us start with the most extreme stance, that of the fanatic anti-Zionist fundamentalist theodicy which explained the Holocaust as a direct act of providence, namely a Divine punishment for very grave sins. One must admit an obvious advantage of such fundamentalist argumentation. It is based on a aprioristic stance of absolute faith and, therefore, it is irrefutable by philosophical arguments. Whoever is able to believe, not only in a God Almighty who knows and cares for every detail in His kingdom, but also in the dogmatic absolute separation between Divine "ways" and human ethical values, defining the authentic religious stance as an absolute rejection of any kind of human pretense to understand or criticize God's ways and His decrees, and, of course, whoever is capable of feeling such utter fanatic hatred for fellow Jews who rejected God and His commandments, will be immune to refutation. First and foremost, he will not be ready to admit any claim of an existing imbalance between the so-called "sins" and their punishment, and relating the diabolical wickedness of the Nazi deeds to Divine intention will not shake his faith nor damage the "God conception" which he managed to develop according to the way he was educated in traditional sources, especially if, besides his firm belief in Divine punishment, he staunchly believes also in a Divine compensation for the righteous in life after death.

We, therefore, admit that the fundamentalist contention will appear as a religious absurdity only to a religious thinker whose concept of Divinity, developed from the traditional sources, is essentially different, and for whom the ethical criteria of revealed Torah itself, as well as the ethical judgment of Divinely inspired humanity, which was created in the image of God, are in full validity

345

even when we face deeds which are related directly to Divine decree. We may infer this, for example, from our ancestor Abraham's protesting question, "Shall not the judge of all the earth do justly?" (Genesis 18:25). However, even on the basis of what has already been said, we can raise at least the question whether this fundamentalist stance is really, as claimed by ultra-Orthodoxy, the "authentic" biblical theodicy? Or may we claim that it does incorporate a significant, though covered up, diversion which may be considered a direct impact of something unique experienced in the Holocaust, something which did make the original biblical theology insufficient precisely for a modern fundamentalist?

"The gates of interpretation are never closed up," said Maimonides, and obviously in our fundamentalists' case they are widely open. It is quite easy to develop, on the basis of certain selection of biblical and talmudic quotations, a theology of Divine relentless punishment which comes as a cruel revenge, even as a threat of an absolute annihilation precisely against His unfaithful chosen people. The fundamentalists' choice of references is, indeed, most convincing because in the two passages of extremely violent "curses" included in both Leviticus and Deuteronomy (Leviticus 26:14-25; Deuteronomy 28:15-69) one has only to accept a simplistic literal meaning of the Mosaic text in order to get an almost accurate description of cruel sufferings, mass murders and dehumanization (Deuteronomy 28:53-57) initiated by God and executed through the instrumentality of a fierce, merciless enemy (Deuteronomy 28:63).

Yet, if the basis of a thorough traditional theology demands, according to its own fundamental criteria, a comprehensive view of the biblical and the talmudic source materials, and an accurate account of every passage in its context, then one becomes immediately aware of the intended simplicity and stubborn one-dimensionalism which characterize these seemingly literal interpretations of the Mosaic text. In the first place, we should mind the fact that the above-mentioned portions of "curse" in the Pentateuch are not intended as prophecies, nor as exact descriptions of forthcoming historical events. Rather, they are intended as conditional and gradually evolving threats, in cases of a stubborn refusal on the part of a sinful people to repent after some more lenient admonitions had been heard and fulfilled with good results. Second, the curses are directly described as educational means to prevent the sin and save the people from unnecessary sufferings, rather than as acts of revenge which must come in order to "satisfy" an insulted deity. The threat is a dam against overpowering sinfulness, in order to avoid the need of punishment and purification, and in order to save the people from the bitter inner results of moral deterioration and depravity which necessarily result from idolatry. Thus, if there is an element of prophecy in these curses, it comprises not only the probability that the Jewish people will sin and be punished, but also and mainly, that the people will at last repent, cry out to God and then be redeemed forever. And a last and conclusive observation — there is implicitly in the "curses" which are attributed to Moses and in the biblical narrative about Moses' leadership, and explicitly in the prophecies of the last biblical prophets, a clear differentiation between the attitude to threats of a terrible catastrophe which might come in case of refusal to repent, and the attitude to catastrophes when they really come true, or even when there is a felt danger that they will come true; the self-same events which were first described as due punishments for sins in a far undefined future, while there still was time enough to repent, were mourned and morally condemned by the prophets when they became at last an historical reality.

The ethico-theological problem with which the prophets were wrestling in this context of theodicy was of dual character: 1) Can the real act of Divine punishment be equally justified like the threat of a forthcoming punishment, the aim of which is to prevent the sin or awake repentance? 2) Can the fulfilled threat of Divine punishment achieve at last the educational goal of the formerly failed threat, namely to awaken feelings of repentance? The answers which we find quite overtly in the Pentateuch and the prophets seem to be a clear and definite "no" on both questions. This is, for example, the implicit literal message of the narrative about Moses' response to God's threat to annihilate the whole sinful people after the sin of the golden calf, or after the sin of the spies (Exodus 32:7-14; Numbers 14:11-25). This is the explicit message of Jeremiah's laments and protests when the prophecies and admonitions that he himself proclaimed came true (Lamentations 3:42). This is the quintessence of the fully developed and sophisticated theology of the book of Jonah which deals specifically with the problem of the aim of Divine threats of punishment and the legitimacy of its fulfillment (cf. Deuteronomy 28:63; Jonah 4:10-11).

If we return after this short digression on the theodicy of punishment in the prophetic sources to the post-Holocaust fundamentalist theodicy, the novelty which is incorporated in this harsh ultra-Orthodox theodicy becomes quite evident. It interprets the threats, admonitions and curses as prophecies of forthcoming events, clearly described in its minutist details. It justifies this punishment *ex post factum* as due Divine revenge, though it was obviously ineffective, because it did not, and definitely could not, effect any repentance, because those Jewish "sinners" who survived the calamity could get from these events only the final affirmation for their "heretic" views. Therefore, even if at last, after the Holocaust, a redemptive event did occur, the fundamentalists could not accept it as such, because obviously, instead of being the result of repentance, it came as the culmination of the formerly "punished sin," being the fulfillment of the secular Zionist enterprise and not a result of repentance. Yet, in spite of all this, the fundamentalists, in an extreme contradiction to the biblical prophetic tradition, accept the interpretation of the Holocaust as a Divine punishment or even as a source of religious satisfaction.

One cannot avoid the conclusion that these differences between the biblical sources and their late simplistic interpretations are indications of a deep emotional and intellectual frustration of ultra-Orthodoxy in its confrontation with the whole syndrome of modernity, culminating in the Holocaust. It is precisely the dimension of complexity and profundity in the biblical theodicy of punishment which could not suit the ultra-Orthodox theology. Only through a radical simplification, insensitive to the point of brutality, could it use the idea of Divine punishment as a solution to the fundamentalist's spiritual anguish. It is, of course, not our aim nor our duty to evaluate or criticize this solution and its implications on the level of religious ethics and spirituality. In the context of our study it is sufficient to state that the most radical claim of a direct application of ideas derived from the ancient religious sources was proved by a thorough examination to be an obvious novelty which resulted from the insufficiency of a certain old solution to confront adequately the modern critical challenge.

Critical Challenge

There is no comparison between the dogmatic simplicism of the ultra-Orthodox solution and Eliezer Berkovitz's profound and compound response. Yet, even his attempt to return to the traditional fold, after an admission of the unique severity of the problem, seems to be only pretended. As formerly suggested, the main traditional theological assumption on which Berkovitz put the whole weight of his attempted solution is human ethical free choice between good and bad. God, who created man in His own image as a free agent, in order to do good by his own free will, is prevented by the logic of His own intention in creation to intervene even when man decides to deny Him and His commandments. Indeed, there can be no debate on the place of the assumption of human free choice in the biblical and post-biblical philosophy of Judaism. Still, one may raise the question whether the claim that human free choice is the cause which necessitates God's "hiding of His Countenance" is also implicit in this traditional theology. The answer is definitely — no. There is no hint of such understanding in the Bible nor in the talmudic oral tradition. We have, indeed, many discussions of the fact that God tolerates the sins of the wicked, allowing them a fair, or maybe even a more than fair, opportunity to repent.

In medieval Jewish theologies we have also many debates on the problem of how to assess both the recognition of human freedom of choice and the belief in Divine eternal knowledge of every thing existent and every act done upon the created earth. However, precisely these debates assume a necessary full admittance of both the belief in human freedom of choice and Divine freedom of direct intervention and guidance in human history. There is nothing further from the frame of these traditional theologies than the idea that human freedom of choice must prevent Divine intervention. On the contrary, it is precisely human freedom of choice, comprising his possible decision to act against God's will, which makes Divine intervention in human history unavoidable. In fact, already in the way which Berkovitz chooses to define the problem of relation between human freedom and Divine providence, there is an essential diversion from the traditional way of thinking. In no traditional theological discussions can we find any hint of a possible "logical" contradiction between the capacity of man to choose, decide and act according to his decision, and Divine ability to intervene and save an

349

innocent victim from the hands of the wicked murderer. On the contrary, we may definitely state that whoever claims that the freedom of choice allotted to evildoers contradicts the legitimacy of Divine intervention in human history, denies factually the very foundations of biblical theology, which after all is originally based on the story of the exodus. Indeed, we find in Jewish traditional sources many debates and even protests against the fact that God, too, patiently tolerates the aggressivity of the wicked, and, therefore, is so late in His redeeming intervention. However, we really cannot remember even one case of a traditionally inspired claim that for the sake of human freedom of choice, conferred also to the wicked, must God allow them to complete their evil intentions. Again we have no intention of proposing a thorough criticism of the validity of Berkovitz's argumentation. Our interest is focused on the obvious fact that we face here an ingenious novelty, which bears witness to the unique emotional and intellectual burden of the problem of theodicy raised by the Holocaust. The traditional argumentation could not have been really sufficient for him if he found it necessary to expand thus far the implications of human freedom of choice on the legitimacy of Divine intervention. It is, of course, not difficult to understand why such a daring expansion of the traditional argument seemed to him both necessary and convincing — this was for him the unavoidable conclusion of his recent historical experiences. Intellectual honesty demanded of him the admittance of the fact that we witnessed no direct Divine intervention in a most extreme case, which more than justified such intervention.

Factually, the Nazis were allowed to pursue their wicked intentions to the furthest point of their physical capacity. They stopped only when they could do no more, namely, when they were militarily overpowered. One may conclude by saying that Berkovitz was only mirroring in his theodicy the bare historical facts, summarizing the life experience and the general perception of the majority of Western humanity in the modern era — modern Westerners do not experience a direct preventive ethical will which interferes from above for good or evil in the execution of their plans. Whatever they consider technically, economically and politically possible, though demanding many intellectual and physical efforts, they attempt to achieve. There are, of course, some limits to human capacity, but they may be gradually overcome, giving organized humanity an overwhelming sense of power. But, factually, this overwhelming sense of power is not enhanced nor limited by ethical considerations. Thus, Western humanity does not confront either in nature or beyond it the intervention of a superior ethical will. We face here, indeed, a most impressive, daring expression of intellectual honesty on the part of an Orthodox theologian, but it seems that in order to justify these upsetting facts from an Orthodox religious point of view, based on a fundamental belief in a personal God and in Divine providence, he had to hide his problem in the depth of his proposed solution. This he achieved through expanding the weight of the traditional principle of human freedom of choice at the expense of the second traditional principle of Divine intervention. In fact, he almost completely denied this principle, narrowing its validity to the realm of pure ethical and religious commandments. We know what God directly commanded us to do through the revelation of the Torah, all the rest remains to be achieved by an interplay between human choice and objective natural conditions. This, we claim, may not be recognized as a continual development of traditional religious thinking. A daring break has suggestively been implied.

There are two more alternative traditional theodicies — that of the innocent, simple fear of God, which gives up any aspiration on the part of man to understand or criticize Divine decrees, demanding of man to accept willingly the bad as the good, to be ready to sanctify the Holy Name and to trust God that He guides whatever is done in His world for a supreme good; and that of the most sophisticated Maimonidean religious philosophy, which identifies Divine providence with natural teleological causation, and generally denies a Divine intervention beyond natural causation, thus identifying the idea of punishment and reward with the implicit goodness or badness of the human deeds and their direct effects on the life of the agent.

We must first note that both of these argumentations are far from simplistic. Factually, they are very complicated and assume much more than they overtly claim. They can convince only an already profoundly believing man whose faith in God has been established, emotionally or intellectually, in an absolute manner which cannot be refuted either by evil experiences or by philosophical refutations. Let us stress the fact that we mean here not only a firm belief in the existence of a personal God, but also the evident experience of actual relations between man and God; such relations as bear in themselves a spiritual sustenance which is experienced as the highest good, and therefore establish a criterion for measuring any other sorts of good in human life. Only a man of this stature will be able to accept such solutions as firmly convincing even in situations of ultimate suffering. We should, therefore, examine the validity of these argumentations in the trial of the Holocaust, taking into account the deep foundations of innocent belief and faith, on one side, and philosophical belief and faith, on the other side.

We claim that innocent belief and faith in a personal God, who is both king almighty and a loving, merciful father, who is far above man yet intimately close to him, hears the prayers of every single man and helps in times of hardship. Such innocent belief and faith is a result of a process of education which wakes, sustains and strengthens it from childhood by the maintenance of a religious lifestyle in family and in congregation, by study, but mainly by an ongoing, daily repeated, religious experience, enhanced by prayer, ritual and fully intended fulfillment of a religious commandment. Those who are innerly open to these messages of religious lifestyle will intuit in these experiences the direct presence of God, His love and His guidance.

It is not always and not in every person that the goal of religious education is achieved, yet when it is achieved it is manifested in an emotional and intellectual conviction founded on a high degree of what is generally recognized as absolute and ultimately subjective evidence. Again we must emphasize that such experiences naturally crystallize in a certain orientation, shaping a basic wholistic attitude to life experience and a whole world view which conceptualizes and interprets it. Therefore, when a man of such attitude confronts, in his adult life, the unavoidable gaps between his expectations as a believer and his personal or national fate, his belief and faith will not collapse as long as he is able to consider these gaps as trials, by which God offers him the opportunity to prove his faith, religion's ultimate value, and to be fully rewarded for it. But this must also be emphasized — though such subjective convictions are experienced qualitatively as absolute, they can stand up only to a certain measure of suffering, and therefore, they tend to collapse beyond a certain subjective limit. In fact, the whole conception of religious trial, very typically exemplified in the book of Job, is based on this subjective empirical fact — the greater the believer, the higher the threshold of his aptitude to be broken by suffering. Yet, the existence of a certain threshold, peculiar to every individual believer, is an established fact. When sufferings rise above this individual threshold the first original conviction might collapse, and the believer will find himself forced to change his whole life-orientation. Such a change admittedly forms a very difficult experience, especially for adult people whose faith shaped not only their ideology or philosophy, but also the very inner construction of their personalities, their sense of destiny, meaning and their ethical relation to society. In such cases a change or orientation means a drastic change of the whole personality. The fear of a total change, which borders on the fear of death, becomes an obstacle in its own right, and generally it may raise up the threshold of sufferance and even shape an antagonistic moral position towards change as a self-betrayal. Last but not least, the society in which man participates may also present many more hindrances. Still, those apparently subjective absolute positions, qua subjective, always face the threat of being broken down under an overpowering weight of suffering.

We deem these psychological observations relevant to our discussion because they expose the fact that we deal here with a certain balance of contradictory subjective experiences, and that beyond a certain subjective breaking point there always lurks the option of a personal conversion, which may revolutionize the whole personal identity of a former believer. This means that the logical exercise according to which there should not be any difference between a small or a great wrong done to an innocent victim, from the point of view of belief in Divine justice, though formally fairly convincing, is existentially shallow and, therefore, irrelevant when dealing with a problem which is essentially existential. On the contrary, there is a significant difference between the possible emotional-ethical impact of such experiences, both in their intensity and in their quality. By intensity we mean the relative weight of suffering against the weight of the original religious experience which had convinced the suffering believer to identify himself as such. By quality we mean the difference between compound experiences which may include both contradictory and reassuring elements from the point of view of belief and faith, and therefore a believer can confront them successfully, justifying the vicious elements by the weight of the morally reassuring ones, as against one-dimensional experiences, in which one cannot find any sort of a positive religious message.

In conclusion, we claim first that there is, for a believing man, a meaningful difference between slight and severe trials of faith from an individual subjective point of view, and secondly, that there is a real difference between slight and severe experiences from an essential objective point of view, which refers to the combination of positive and negative elements in the sources and causes of suffering. Not in every trial can a believer discover a certain positive message which may reassure him in his suffering. Not in every suffering can he find a grain of hope that his pain may be instrumental for a great good in the future. Therefore, at least theoretically, there may be sufficient ground to a claim that an event which is exposed as Radical Evil, an event which one cannot justify as punishment, not explain as instrumental for any possible good beyond it, will be considered above the threshold of sufferance for all, or at least for the majority of the believers, even those whose faith had been established by the evidence of a prophetic experience. Indeed, there is a solid ground for the claim that the Holocaust was an experience of such stature, and that, therefore, it put the innocent belief and faith in a God of justice and mercy before an extraordinarily unique trial, never experienced before, and therefore challenging even the defenses of "absolute" innocence.

One may state that empirical facts deny this argument. Only non-believers argue that the Holocaust is, in their eyes, a final evidence for atheism, while the great majority of believers, in fact, remained faithful. Their belief did not fail. They were not broken. On the contrary, many clung to their innocent belief and were prepared to sanctify the Holy Name in public. This is, as said before, the first and most convincing argument for Berkovitz's and Jacobovits' theodicies, in their attempt to prove that, in spite of the unique suffering in the Holocaust, it did not pose a qualitatively unique challenge of faith in God. How should we interpret these subjective testimonies of spiritual immunity? It seems that here Berkovitz's profound exploration into the depth of these testimonies is very helpful (Berkovitz, 1979, pp. 49-61) — the Holocaust was also, in the eyes of innocent believers, an unprecedented trial. Most of them did feel that they were left alone, forsaken, having no outward consolation in their agony and no objective justifying explanation. But, side by side with this feeling of a shattering spiritual crisis, at least some of them were able to discover, in the depths of their own souls, an unexpected source of strength. It was an ultimate experience which saved their inner freedom, their dignity as human beings and Jews. On the threshold of their death they experienced, like Job, an inner presence of a merciful God suffering with them, thus redeeming them with meaning and hope in the depth of their agony (Shapiro, 1969). This experience did not prevent cries of pain and protest, yet even for that bitter consolation of protest, before "someone" who may hear and respond, indeed be He their only remaining witness, one had to keep faith. Even a final revolting protest had thus been transformed into an ultimate confession of faith.

How is it possible to solve the paradox of renewal of faith out of that very experience which denied it? Should we propose a psychological explanation, claiming that for people educated as believers the ultimate need to believe, strengthened precisely in such conditions, overpowered the crushing sense of disappointment? Should we infer that precisely in conditions of ultimate suffering man may discover within him unexpected spiritual powers which save and console him, or maybe deliver him to another level of existence, even without any "outward" justification for his utterly cruel fate? Or shall we accept it innocently as a testimony of a mystical revelation?

Again, it is not our task here to prefer any one of these possible explanations. From our point of view, what is decisively important is the evidence of the fact that the belief and faith of innocent believers in the Holocaust was not sustained by any kind of theodicy, either traditional or innovative. They did not understand better than the non-believers why God was "hiding His Countenance" in the face of Radical Evil, or what sort of good can be achieved through the instrumentality of such darkness. It was belief in spite of and from within a dark recognition that there cannot be a justifying explanation for the silence of God in those moments. Therefore, it is also evidently clear that this response of faith was not a mere consummation of resources gathered through former educational and regular life experiences, though the continuity seems to be elementary and unconditionally assumed. Rather, it was a discovery of completely unexpected spiritual powers which were challenged by the trial itself. The Holocaust, which threatened to destroy the very foundations of innocent belief, paradoxically reconstituted, in those who were spiritually strong enough to confront it as a trial, an ultimate will to believe that overcame despair. And let us add here that parallel to such manifestations of faith in testimonies of innocent religious believers, there were similar expressions of ultimate faith in the Jewish people or in humanity, in testimonies of humanists, Socialists, Zionists who were, religiously speaking, professed non-believers. Belief, to put it radically, radiated from the depth of spiritually powerful human souls rather than from an outwardly intervening Divine presence.

If this description is faithful to reality, we can understand and even empathize with the way innocent believers stood the trial of the Holocaust completely unaided by theodicy. However, it is a different question whether we can assume the facticity of faith in the Holocaust in spite of having no theological solution, as an adequate basis for a theological solution which is demanded not by those who lived through the trial, but by their children and grandchildren whose unanswered questions may obstruct the effort to educate them as Orthodox believing Jews. Will it be possible to develop convincing answers on such questions lacking any new theological insights, conceptions and philosophical deliberations, which would help us in shaping adequate philosophical understanding of the sources, implications and meaning of those very experiences of faith which believers had had in the Holocaust? Can we assume that the traditional stock of arguments will suffice?

Daring New Conceptualization of the Divine Presence

On the basis of the former analysis we tend to conclude that the Holocaust did challenge even innocent belief in a uniquely severe way. In order to overcome the challenge of Divine silence in the midst of Radical Evil, innocent believers needed the support of an ultimate direct experience drawn out of unexpected inner spiritual resources, beyond their former traditional experiences, and beyond their former personal or historical expectations. This means that a systematic theological account of such experiences, for the sake of the religious reorientation of those who did not experience such inner resources but must rely upon them, will necessarily need some daring new conceptualizations of the Divine presence to man, of the meaning of providence, and of the presence of man before God. Such systematic accounts may reinterpret much of the message of traditional sources, yet besides such reinterpretations it will demand an articulation of new religious intuitions and new theological conceptualizations. The contribution of believing men, and their innerly guided activities for the evidence of Divine presence and guidance on earth, will probably demand a daring new definition, far beyond the borders of traditional conceptualizations, even those of modern Orthodoxy.

In the last sentences we have already begun our discussion of the traditional philosophical solution. This solution had been created on the background of a widening gap between belief and faith based on biblical traditions, and the acquired empirical knowledge in many realms of human experience, guided by the sciences and consummated by philosophy. Philosophical theology was burdened with the task of solving the contradiction between two complete world views which were developed each in its own ways of research and study, and validated each on its own peculiar evidence either of religious experience or of logic. Those solutions which took their point of departure from the basis of the sciences and philosophy necessarily deviated from what was considered at that time traditionally acceptable. Even those philosophers who developed and proposed such solutions were aware of their dangerous problematic character. Both Judah Halevi, from the traditional side, and Maimonides, from the philosophical side of the debate, exposed very clearly the contradiction between the philosophical idea of a metaphysical Deity and the traditional image of "the God of our ancestors." The God of the philosophers is a metaphysical entity and not a personal God, a first "unmoved mover" and not a creator, a first cause of natural order and not a commanding, judging, leading God, not a God who hears man's prayers, atones for his sins, or redeems him from his hardships. The only way to approach this metaphysical God was the intellectual way of perfect knowledge which elevates man beyond his earthly existence, and the only way for "success" in this world is to comply with the positive natural order and to adapt human freedom of choice to what was believed to be the natural destiny of man.

However, philosophers like Maimonides could bridge the gap between their philosophy and biblical faith by emphasizing a general similarity, or a parallel of general orientation, which still existed between these two contradictory world views, and could therefore serve as a common denomination. Even according to the varieties of philosophical systems current in the Middle Ages (mainly Aristotelianism, Platonism, and neo-Platonism), the cosmos had been conceived as an organic unity incorporating a hierarchical-teleological order of existents; even according to this philosophical understanding, man occupies the highest sphere of existence on earth and serves as a mediator between the corporeal and the spiritual spheres. Even

357

according to this philosophical understanding the natural order qua teleological order is ethically orientated — the striving for perfect existence as the highest good is implicit in nature and serves as its originative motivating power; and according to this philosophical view, God, as the first cause of existence, is the source and the ideal perfection of good and truth.

In sum, even according to this philosophical conception, our world is, in Leibnitz's words, "the best of all possible worlds." There is a basic harmony in the natural world, and this harmony could be identified with an ethical order originated by God. This way it was quite convincingly possible to fill up the biblical concepts of creation, revelation, prophecy, Divine commandment, providence, and Divine guidance with philosophical contents. It was also quite convincingly possible to replace the idea of Divine punishment and reward with the philosophical contention that doing good is inherently good, and therefore, it is its own highest reward, and in the same way doing bad is inherently harmful, and therefore, it is its own worst punishment. Interpreted this way as a law inscribed in the natural order of things, which serves as an absolute guarantee that the good deed must achieve its goal while bad deeds must fail, it could really be understood as "providential," or representing the inner true meaning of biblical "images" like Divine judgment, or Divine miraculous intervention, which are necessary for the education of children and simple persons.

How can we explain, then, the existence of bad and evil? According to the basic ancient philosophical understanding, the "bad" should not be grasped as existent. Rather it is a "negation," or an "absence." Natural, material existence, through its essential difference from spiritual existence, cannot but "contain" such negation, flaws, absences. It is naturally unavoidable, and therefore it is fully justified, because it is a necessary condition of existence, which is in itself good. The fact that the righteous may outwardly or physically suffer, while the wicked may have their temporal outward successes, does not pose any difficulty in such a philosophical context — it is only natural, and the suffering righteous must be consoled by the fact that their suffering is only an outward and not an inward facticity. A truly perfect person is always innerly in the state of devotion to spiritual perfection, and therefore, he is always innerly truly happy. Yet, let us not forget that beside this inner subjective consolation the ancient philosophical understanding of the teleological order of nature served as an absolute objective guarantee that there is a decisive preference of good over bad in nature, that the good will always be superior and always victorious, that wickedness will destroy itself while righteousness and truthfulness will achieve eternity.

A modern philosopher like Leibnitz could still found his theodicy on this sort of philosophical argumentation. But it was soon attacked and refuted by modern scientific study and the variety of philosophies based on modern non-teleological sciences. The conception of a teleological, quasi-ethical, order of nature was indeed the first to be withdrawn. Still, the idea of an ethical motivation which is implicit in nature and actually shapes its development could partially be defended by the humanistic-idealistic type of modern philosophies. These philosophies had only to accomplish a strategic retreat from the kingdom of nature to the kingdom of man, and define the place for teleological-ethical progressive order in the realm of human society and civilization as a law of history. In idealistic expositions of religious philosophy it has been articulated by the identification of the idea of Divine providence with the ethico-teleological law of progress in human history. Thus, it was also possible to contend that the source of evil in the social, political and cultural realms, for which man is responsible, is the necessary tension between human reason which defines the unique essence of man, created in the image of God, and his natural corporeal drives, which are part of an amoral earthly nature, and that the final or the gradually accumulative victory of reason over nature in the realm of man is guaranteed by the necessary advance of social and political order in history.

One may have his doubts, as Leo Strauss did, whether such philosophical theologies, either of the medieval Maimonidean version or the twentieth century version of Hermann Cohen, are authentically attuned to the biblical belief in the personal God of our fathers, the creator, the lawgiver and redeemer of Israel (Strauss, 1935). However, such theologies were able to keep a certain affinity to the ancient sources, to save a certain core of religious revelatory authority, or at least to mirror the religious contents of the sources in their intellectual concepts and apply these contents to the realms of ethics, learning and ritual. The question raised after the Holocaust is whether such philosophical solutions can still hold their relative educational effectiveness.

We should first admit the fact that distrust of the idealistic
version of religious philosophy preceded the Holocaust. Such criticism had been articulated by existentialist philosophers like M.
Buber, F. Rosenzweig, M. Wiener, A.J. Heschel, etc. Already some
social, political and cultural processes and events before World War
I, and certainly the traumatic events of the war itself, the Communist
revolution in Russia and what had followed it in Europe between the
two World Wars, were sufficient to refute the rationalistic optimism
both of idealistic humanism and "scientific" materialism. The advances in anthropological and psychological research also contributed their share of suspicion of the optimistic belief in the ethical-
rational essence of humanity, or of the understanding of ethical
failure and wickedness as the result of the struggle between rationality and natural drives. The fact that wickedness can become a
complete and developed world view, an ideal and a way of life, had
already cast its shades on European civilization before World War
II. However, the occurrences of World War II, and specifically the
Holocaust, concretized the crisis of idealistic humanism in a way
which prevents, at least for the direct victims of the Holocaust, the
aptitude to hide, divert or cover it by illusions, and again we face
here the fact that there is a real, essential difference between "a
murder of one innocent child" and the dehumanization and mass
murder of millions. The phenomenon of the death camps and the
ghettos poses before the religious-humanist thinker a unique problem.

Until World War I, and even during the war itself, there were still
some humanist theologians and religious philosophers, Jews not
excluded, who could find a theological justification for the cruel
ways between nations and classes in society in a way which did not
disturb their optimistic belief in the progressive messianic development of history. They tried to show that these wars, cruel, irrational
and destructive as they appear, may be instrumental for the ethical
progress of mankind, if not directly, then at least in a hidden,
disguised way, using indeed Kant's "sober" remark on "the crafti-
ness of history." Such philosophers of history made an effort to
convince themselves and their readers that there is a certain hidden
ethical wisdom behind the evergrowing social and political calamities of the twentieth century, because they push humanity, even in
spite of its own conscious motivations, towards a higher level of
internationalism, universalism and social justice. If, after World

War II, no serious thinker would dare state such claims, because it would be immediately dismantled as dangerous nonsense, this is the evident impact of the war's calamities and of the Holocaust as their consummation. It is now absolutely clear that wars could not in the past and cannot in the present advance a solution to any problem, either national or social, that they cannot be instrumental for ethical progress. On the contrary, they make use of the really great achievements of humanity in the sciences and technology for purposes of destruction, and thus, they indeed push humanity to the fulfillment of the "End of Days" — that of total self-annihilation. Until World War I, and even during the War itself, philosophers of history, ethics and politics could assume that mass murders, tortures, cruelty for its own sake, and dehumanization are pathological exceptions perpetrated by marginal individuals or groups in society and operating against firm and established law. In any case, it was considered definitely impossible to assume that such deeds may be adopted by a sovereign state as its official policy, or even as its established juridical norm. After World War II and the Holocaust, we know that the pathology may extend from the margins of society to its center and that mass murder for the sake of genocide may be officially planned and executed by sovereign governments as their policy, and not only in war against enemies, but also against populations which live under their rule.

Until World War I, and even during the war itself, the various monotheistic religions were considered, despite the rivalry and enmity between them, as basically oriented towards ethical goals, using their spiritual authority for the enhancement of moral education, lovingkindness and peace. In World War II and in the Holocaust the sharing by Christians, not only in the demoniacal hatred of the Jews, but also the participation of Christians in the execution of the "Final Solution," and the passive attitude of the Churches towards it, became obvious. In addition to the problem of theodicy, genuinely sensitive believers face, after the Holocaust, the unique problem of religiodicy, namely, the need to justify not only God's "hiding of His Countenance," but also the prevailing religion's hiding of its countenance in a crucial moment of trial (Schweid, 1988).

In all these reports the Holocaust has undermined the basic historical ground of the philosophical solution, not only in its medieval Maimonidean version, but also in its modern humanist one. It seems that the way of substituting for the biblical personal God a philosophical idea of God had arrived at a dead end. Truly, after the war and the Holocaust, religion seems to have recovered its influence on Western society. There are many who felt that religious faith is a necessary support without which modern Western society will not be able to solve its ethical and spiritual crises. They are searching for moral authority and spiritual leadership; they long for ultimate meaning and a consoling hope of a kind which only religion can supply. But precisely here we sense the hard edge of the problem, because those who are looking for a commanding authority, transcendental meaning, and redeeming hope are not looking for the God of the philosophers. Rather, they need the message which is emitted through the religious language of the old sources. It seems, therefore, that even religious philosophy will be unable to hide itself from the weaknesses of philosophical religiousness. Thus, the task of creating a new religious philosophy, able to respond adequately to religious yearnings yet not denying or giving up the totality of knowledge, experience, power and skill which Western civilization had acquired, whether for its benefit or for its damage, seems to lie beyond the historical heritage of religious philosophy, ancient and modern. The simple belief of the innocent, though in itself problematic, seems now to be much more appealing and convincing than philosophical religiosity.

Conclusion

We tried to show that after World War II and the Holocaust the whole variety of traditional theodicies, by and large, lost their validity or their convincing weight. We do not and cannot claim that they were simply refuted, or disproved, but they appear actually to be insufficient. So much so, because even those who deny the uniqueness of the theological problem raised by the Holocaust, and pretend to return to former Orthodox arguments, actually misused or significantly changed the traditional argumentations, and thus contained, or incorporated, the unique challenge of the Holocaust in their argumentation without being able either to face its full impact or to solve it as it really is. On the other hand, we tried to show that during the war and the Holocaust, and within the experience of a spiritual crisis which was effected by the war and the Holocaust, and by the whole syndrome of modernity, there has been awakened a new need, a new demand, even a new will for return to religious belief and faith, and precisely to its fundamental existential core. The great paradox seems to be that, at one and the same time, the originative sources of religious belief and faith had lost the reliability of their empirical testimony yet were recharged with existential meaning, for which people desperately long. Moreover, we claim that the demand contained in the theologies of revolt and protest to confront the Holocaust as an absolutely unique event which keeps its actuality permanently, as if beyond and above history, has no moral justification and actually cannot be fulfilled. From this point of view, the modern Orthodox thinkers are right — we should examine the Holocaust by taking into account both the short perspective of the period that passed since the end of the war and the long perspective of Jewish history before the Holocaust, and looking for religious sustenance from all the sources which incorporate Jewish religious wisdom. The uniqueness of the crisis should be recognized, but historical continuity should persist.

But the main conclusion of this discussion seems to be the clear recognition of the fact that the crisis must remain a fixed central component of religious experience and, therefore, also of religious thought. We have no ground to hope for smooth and well-rounded systematic solutions, as in traditional and post-traditional religious philosophies of the past. Relying on the accumulated wisdom of religious experience and religious thought in our long history, we may follow, phase by phase and step by step, the story of an evergrowing enigma which confronts a believing man, and a believing Jew the more so. He must take upon himself an ever-growing share of responsibility for the evidence of his own ground for faith, namely, the evidence of Divine presence in the world. His is the task of testifying by his own way of life, while only very rarely he may have the reassuring experience of achievement and response. The difficulties which this state of affairs raises on the believers' way of life, and especially on the way of religious education, is quite obvious. It seems, indeed, that these difficulties explain, and may even excuse, the desperate efforts of responsible modern Orthodox theologians like Eliezer Berkovitz and Immanuel Jacobovits to overcome the crisis and offer a full and coherent intellectual solution. But this seems to be also the main source of their failure — they incorporated the crisis in their argumentation without an admitted recognition of the fact, thus claiming the achievement of what they did not really achieve. This failure must be overcome by a full philosophical recognition. When the believer must take upon himself, in full awareness, the greatest share of responsibility for his and his communities' religious orientation, the enigma of faith, and beyond it the enigma of the Jewish believer's loneliness before a hiding God, must remain a permanent challenge.

Bibliography

Berkovitz, E., *Faith after the Holocaust* (New York: Hebrew Publishing Company, 1973).

——, *With God in Hell* (New York: Sanhedrin Press, 1979).

Brenner, R.R., *The Faith and Doubts of Holocaust Survivors* (New York: Free Press, 1980).

Cohen, A.A., *The Tremendum* (New York: Crossroad, 1980).

Fackenheim, E., *To Mend the World* (New York: Schocken Books, 1982).

Greenberg, I., "Cloud of Smoke, Pillar of Fire," *Auschwitz, the Beginning of a New Era?*, ed. E. Fleischner (New York: Ktav, 1977), pp. 7-57.

Jacobovits, I., "Religious Responses to the Holocaust: Retrospect and Prospect," *L'Eylah*, 25 (April 1986): 2-7.

——, "Some Personal, Theological and Religious Responses to the Holocaust," *Holocaust and Genocide Studies*, 3 (1988): 371-381.

Maybaum, I. *The Face of God after Auschwitz* (Amsterdam: Polak & Van Gennep, 1965).

Neher, A., *The Exile of the Word* (Philadelphia: Jewish Publication Society, 1981).

Rubenstein, R., *After Auschwitz* (Indianapolis: Bobbs-Merrill Co., 1966).

Schwartz, Y. and Y. Goldstein, *Hashoa* (Hebrew) (Jerusalem: D'var Yerushalayim, 1987).

Schweid, E., "The Meaning of the Holocaust in the History of the Jewish People" (Hebrew), *Eth Laasoth,* 1 (1988a): 18-31.

——, "The Justification of Religion in the Crisis of the Holocaust," *Holocaust and Genocide Studies,* 3 (1988b): 395-412.

Shapiro, K.K., *Esh Kodesh* (Hebrew) (Jerusalem: Yad Vashem, 1969).

Susmann, M., *Philosophie und Gesetz* (Berlin: Schocken Verlag, 1935).

Teitlebaum, Y., *Vayoel Moshe* (Hebrew) (New York: D'fuss S. Deutch, 1959).

Wiesel, E., *Night* (New York: Bantam Books, 1960).

Wolpin, R.N., ed., *A Path Through the Ashes* (New York: Mesorah Publications, 1986).

ABOUT THE AUTHOR

Professor Eliezer Schweid was born in Jerusalem in 1929. He served in the Palmach during Israel's War of Independence and joined Kibbutz Zorea after the war. Attending Hebrew University, he specialized in Jewish history and philosophy, receiving his Ph.D. in 1962. He has been teaching at Hebrew University and other Israeli universities since 1963, and became a full Professor in 1982. Professor Schweid is a Fellow and Vice President of the Jerusalem Center for Public Affairs. He is married and has three children.

Professor Schweid has been involved in a number of Jewish education projects in Israel and has published many papers on medieval and modern Jewish philosophy, Hebrew literature, and Zionism, as well as contributing to Israeli journals on current affairs. He is the author of a number of books on Jewish philosophy and literature. His most recent book in English is *Jewish Thought in the Twentieth Century — An Introduction* (Atlanta: U.S.F. Studies in the History of Judaism. The Scholars Press, 1992).